Literary Strategy
in the Epistle of Jude

Literary Strategy in the Epistle of Jude

J. Daryl Charles

Scranton: University of Scranton Press
London and Toronto: Associated University Presses

Associated University Presses
440 Forsgate Drive
Cranbury, NJ 08512

Associated University Presses
25 Sicilian Avenue
London WC1A 2QH, England

Associated University Presses
P.O. Box 39, Clarkson Pstl. Stn.
Mississauga, Ontario,
L5J 3X9 Canada

The paper used in this publication meets the requirements of the American National Standard for Permanence of Paper for Printed Library Materials Z39.48-1984.

Library of Congress Cataloging-in-Publication Data

Charles, J. Daryl, 1950–
    Literary strategy in the Epistle of Jude / J. Daryl Charles.
        p.   cm.
    Includes bibliographical references and index.
    ISBN 0-940866-16-1 (alk. paper)
    1. Bible.   N.T. Jude—Criticism, interpretation, etc.   I. Title.
BS2815.2.C45   1993
227'.97066—dc20   91-66129
                                                            CIP

PRINTED IN THE UNITED STATES OF AMERICA

to Rosi

Contents

Abbreviations

AnBib	Analecta biblica
ANF	*The Ante-Nicene Fathers*
APOT	*The Apocrypha and Pseudepigrapha of the Old Testament*
ATR	*Anglican Theological Review*
AusBR	*Australian Biblical Review*
BA	*Biblical Archaeologist*
BAGD	W. Bauer, W. F. Arndt, F. W. Gingrich, and F. W. Danker, *Greek-English Lexicon of the New Testament*
BBB	Bonner biblische Beiträge
BETL	Bibliotheca ephemeridum theologicarum lovaniensium
Bib	*Biblica*
BibSac	*Bibliotheca Sacra*
BJRL	*Bulletin of the John Rylands University Library of Manchester*
BRKGA	Beiträge zum kirchlich- und religionsgeschichtlichen Altertum
BuL	*Bibel und Leben*
BZ	*Biblische Zeitschrift*
BZAW	Beiheft zur Zeitschrift für die alttestamentliche Wissenschaft
BZNW	Beiheft zur Zeitschrift für die neutestamentliche Wissenschaft
BibS	Biblische Studien
CBA	Catholic Biblical Association
CBQ	*Catholic Biblical Quarterly*
CBQMS	Catholic Biblical Quarterly Monograph Series
CDios	*Ciudad de Dios*
CJ	*Corpus inscriptionum judaicarum*
CNT	Commentaire du Nouveau Testament
ConB	Coniectanea biblica
CP	*Classical Philology*
CPJ	*Corpus Papyrorum Judaicarum*
CTJ	*Calvin Theological Journal*

CUA	Catholic University of America
DBSup	*Dictionnaire de la Bible, Supplément*
EAC	Études d'archaéologie classique
EncJud	*Encyclopaedia Judaica*
EstBib	*Estudios bíblicos*
Expos	*Expositor*
ExpTim	*Expository Times*
FRLANT	*Forschungen zur Religion und Literatur des Alten und Neuen Testaments*
GBS	Guides to Biblical Scholarship
GCS	*Die Griechischen christlichen Schriftsteller*
HAW	Handbuch zur Altertumswissenschaft
HNT	Handbuch zum Neuen Testament
HSCP	*Harvard Studies in Classical Philology*
HTR	*Harvard Theological Review*
HUCA	*Hebrew Union College Annual*
ICC	International Critical Commentary
IBT	Interpreting Biblical Texts
JAC	*Jahrbuch für Antike und Christentum*
JAOS	*Journal of the American Oriental Society*
JBL	*Journal of Biblical Literature*
JETS	*Journal of the Evangelical Theological Society*
JHS	*Journal of Hellenic Studies*
JJS	*Journal of Jewish Studies*
JNES	*Journal of Near Eastern Studies*
JP	*Journal of Philology*
JQR	*Jewish Quarterly Review*
JSJ	*Journal for the Study of Judaism*
JSNT	*Journal for the Study of the New Testament*
JSOTSS	Journal for the Study of the Old Testament Supplement Series
JTS	*Journal of Theological Studies*
KBW	Katholisches Bibelwerk
LCL	Loeb Classical Library
LingBib	*Linguistica Biblica*
LThK	*Lexikon für Theologie und Kirche*
MeyerK	H.A.W. Meyer, Kritisch-exegetischer Kommentar über das Neue Testament
MSGVK	*Mitteilungen der schlesischen Gesellschaft für Volkskunde*
n.p.	no publisher
NCB	New Century Bible
NIV	New International Version

NedTT	*Nederlands theologische tijdschrift*
Neot	*Neotestamentica*
NovT	*Novum Testamentum*
NovTSup	Novum Testamentum, Supplement
NT	New Testament
NTD	Das Neue Testament Deutsch
NTM	New Testament Message
NTS	*New Testament Studies*
ÖBS	Österreichische Bibelstudien
ÖKB	Österreichisches Katholisches Bibelwerk
OT	Old Testament
OTL	Old Testament Library
OTP	*Old Testament Pseudepigrapha*, J. H. Charlesworth (ed.)
PG	*Patrologia Graeca*, J. Migne (ed.)
PH	Palaea Historica
PL	*Patrologia Latina*, J. Migne (ed.)
QJS	*Quarterly Journal of Speech*
QL	Qumran literature
1QM	War Scroll
1QpHab	Pesher on Habakkuk from Qumran Cave I
11QMelch	Melchizedek text from Qumran Cave II
RAC	*Reallexikon für Antike und Christentum*
RB	*Revue biblique*
RGG	*Religion in Geschichte und Gegenwart*
RHPR	*Revue d'histoire et de philosophie religieuses*
RHR	*Revue de l'histoire des religions*
RNT	Regensburger Neues Testament
RQ	*Revue de Qumran*
RSR	*Recherches de science religieuse*
RSV	Revised Standard Version
SBL	Society of Biblical Literature
SBLDS	SBL Dissertation Series
SBLMS	SBL Monograph Series
SBLSCS	SBL Septuagint and Cognate Studies
ScripHier	*Scripta Hierosolymitana*
Sem	*Semitica*
SHR	Studies in the History of Religions
SMU	Southern Methodist University
SNTSMS	Society for New Testament Studies Monograph Series
SUNT	Studien zur Umwelt des Neuen Testaments
TAPA	*Transactions of the American Philological Association*

TDNT	*Theological Dictionary of the New Testament*
THNT	Theologischer Handkommentar zum Neuen Testament
TNTC	Tyndale New Testament Commentary
TRu	*Theologische Rundschau*
TS	*Theologische Studien*
TUGAL	Texte und Untersuchungen zur Geschichte altchristlichen Literatur
TWNT	*Theologisches Wörterbuch des Neuen Testaments*
TZ	*Theologische Zeitschrift*
UBS	United Bible Society
UNM	University of New Mexico
UUÅ	Uppsala universitetsårsskrift
VT	*Vetus Testamentum*
VTSup	Vetus Testamentum, Supplement
WB	Weimarer Beiträge
WBC	Word Biblical Commentary
WBT	Wiener Beiheft zur Theologie
WMANT	Wissenschaftliche Monographien zum Alten und Neuen Testament
WTJ	*Westminister Theological Journal*
WUNT	Wissenschaftliche Untersuchungen zum Neuen Testament
ZAW	*Zeitshcrift für die alttestamentliche Wissenschaft*
ZDMG	*Zeitschrift der deutschen morgenländischen Gesellschaft*
ZKG	*Zeitschrift für Kirchengeschichte*
ZNW	*Zeitschrift für die neutestamentliche Wissenschaft*
ZTK	*Zeitschrift für Theologie und Kirche*
ZWTh	*Zeitschrift für wissenschaftliche Theologie*

1

Introduction

In the third century the letter of Jude was described by Origen as "a short epistle, yet filled with flowing words of heavenly grace."[1] This is high praise coming from a theologian and writer who embodied the literary-philosophical spirit of Alexandria, the center of learning of the Hellenistic world.

Yet it is unfortunate that despite the uniqueness of this New Testament letter the message and world of Jude remain strangely unfamiliar to the modern reader. With good reason Jude has been called "the most neglected book in the New Testament."[2] Most readers of the Bible, puzzled by cryptic references to Enoch, Michael the archangel, the devil, and a slate of Old Testament characters, are acquainted at best with the letter's doxology. General ignorance of Jude reflects at the very least a lack of understanding as to the historical situation behind the epistle.

However, comprehensive neglect of Jude is not limited to the average reader. NT scholarship has for the most part bypassed a thorough treatment of the letter. Where it is studied, Jude is normally examined side-by-side with the other "catholic" epistles or subsumed under the study of 2 Peter. Here the assumption typically follows that Jude and 2 Peter reflect near identical historical situations, with the later writing (normally considered to be 2 Peter) presumably exhibiting either a woeful lack of literary originality and integrity or the need to "smooth out" particular features in Jude.

Even more conspicuous than the lack of commentaries[3] on Jude is the paucity of monographs[4] given to historical, exegetical, or theological problems posed by the epistle. R. J. Bauckham writes:

> The tradition of scholarly contempt (this is scarcely too strong a word) for Jude has led to scholarly neglect of Jude and hence to ignorance of Jude. The usual scholarly judgments about Jude are little more than cliches which have simply been repeated for a century or more without examination.[5]

Traditionally, most discussion concerning Jude has centered around its relation to 2 Peter. The present investigation, however, rather than treating the question of literary dependence, is an attempt to focus on the issue of literary strategy—and that of *Jude* in particular. On the importance of the literary aspect in studying the biblical text, J. Muilenburg[6] has commented:

> . . . the circumspect scholar will not fail to supplement his . . . analysis with a careful inspection of the literary unit in its precise and unique formulations . . . ; his task will not be completed until he has taken full account of the features which lie beyond the spectrum of the genre. . . . For the more deeply one penetrates the formulations . . . , the more sensitive he is to the roles which words and motifs play in a composition; the more he concentrates on the ways in which thought has been woven into linguistic patterns, the better able he is to think the thoughts of the biblical writer.

It is with the literary impulse that the present study concerns itself. Literature has been said to be incarnational in character; that is, it enacts and does not merely state. Rather than simply offering abstract propositions, the literary work combines example with precept, incorporating the whole realm of imagination.[7] Herein the epistle of Jude shows itself to be unique. With remarkable brevity and apocalyptic force, the writer exploits literary conventions and motifs which are strategic to his purpose and significant for his audience. For this reason, his literary creativity and style, as well as selection and arrangement of source-material, demand closer attention.

Any attempt to recover the literary art of the Bible is bound to meet with certain obstacles. Modern readers have been accustomed to approaching the biblical text with particular governing theological, philological, or historical assumptions. Under scrutiny, the biblical text is viewed as composite and fragmentary. Analytic scholarship has forged persuasive arguments to the effect that when we are reading the Bible, in reality what we have is the stitching together of texts drawn from divergent literary (or oral) traditions with the addition of, at times, substantial interpolated material. The dominant methodology in biblical scholarship has been to dissect the text and uncover divergent strata in the development of the text from its "primitive" to final literary form. Inconsistencies, repetition, and discontinuity are assumed. In short, what we are left with, it is proposed, is a text which is not the work of a single hand or of a single moment in time.

Unity of a literary work is by no means tangential to the question of artistry. "No principle of literary study is more important than that of grasping clearly a literary work as a single whole" wrote R. G. Moulton[8] almost a century ago. One wonders, along with L. Ryken,[9] what might otherwise have been the development of biblical commentary in this century had Moulton's advice been heeded. For the "patch-work" approach stands in contradistinction to a literary analysis of biblical literature which opts to view a piece of literature as a complex yet meaningful whole rather than a mere sum of many parts. To view a literary piece as the compilation of many scarcely definable parts is to undermine the possibility of appreciating a work as an artistic creation, since unity, coherence, and authenticity are largely questioned.

Properties by which we measure an entity as "literary" include the writer's own technique, style, structure, and craftmanship in sculpting his work. A work of literature does more than simply impart information to the reader. It embodies meaning with the aim of recreating in sufficient detail a situation or scenario in such a way as to allow the reader to *experience* it. The good writers of literary pieces, just as readers of literature, exploit imagination and the sensory dimensions of discourse.[10] Nonetheless, it has been the inclination of biblical scholars to assume an absence of (conscious) literary artistry on the part of NT writers.[11] Thus, we must reexamine reigning presuppositions of biblical scholarship when seeking to analyze biblical literature.

When assessed by such literary criteria as artistic form, organic unity, balance of symmetry, contrast or repetition, design and diversity, the writings of the NT demonstrate in their own right a level of literary craftmanship. Inasmuch as the NT is comprised of three primary literary genres[12]—narrative, epistle, and apocalypse—it may be judged according to literary criteria. The NT exploits the resources of language as does other literature. Nonliteral devices—symbolism, metaphor and simile, hyperbole, parable and proverb, irony, pun and personification to name a few—combine with rhetorical devices—parallelism, patterns of arrangement, poetic diction, word- and sound-play, sarcasm, questions, the use of paradigms, unusual conciseness or brevity—to affect the reader in a striking way. To be sure, some books of the NT employ these devices more fully than others. Yet until the NT writings are examined for their stylistic or rhetorical features, these are inclined to go relatively unnoticed. W. O. Sypherd[13] has observed:

> The prose of the New Testament is often of a very high order. A good deal of it approaches the rhythm of poetry in its parallelisms of

thought and structure, in its cadences, and in its accents. Strength of conviction, intensity of belief, fervour of feeling are revealed in prose of great power and beauty. Simplicity, clarity, conciseness, harmony, rhythmic flow, homely figurative expression, sincerity and earnestness, and a great fundamental theme are the characteristics which elevate much of these writings above the plane of simple narrative or doctrinal exposition to the height of perfect style of its kind into the realm of literature of universal significance.

In defense of the NT writers' literary skill as well as their authority, Augustine[14] was forced to concede:

. . . there is a kind of eloquence that is more becoming in youth, and a kind that is more becoming in old age, and nothing can be called eloquence if it be not suitable to the person of the speaker, so there is a kind of eloquence that is becoming to men who justly claim the highest authority, and who are evidently inspired of God. With this eloquence they spoke; no other would have been suitable for them.

An underlying thesis of the present investigation is that form is as valuable as content, for it constitutes the *vehicle* of content. This is perhaps a genuine contribution that literary criticism brings to the sphere of biblical studies. *How* a message is expressed is indivisible from the *what* of its contents.

Such a literary approach is not all that needs to be done with the New Testament. But it is a necessary first step in understanding what the New Testament says, and it has the additional advantage of enhancing our enjoyment of the New Testament. Historical and theological approaches to the New Testament are also incomplete by themselves, and it is no discredit to the literary approach that it leaves much unsaid . . . in any kind of written discourse, meaning is communicated *through* form. . . . Without form (beginning, of course, with language itself), no meaning is conveyed. . . . The literary critic's preoccupation with the "how" of New Testament writing is not frivolous. It is evidence of an aesthetic delight in artistic form, but it is more than that. It is also evidence of a desire to understand what is said in the New Testament, in keeping with the tendency of the New Testament writers to incarnate their content in literary forms that demand careful scrutiny.[15]

The style of Jude is brief, energetic, and vivid and reflects a high degree of moral tension inherent to the historical setting behind the epistle. The writer has a force and pungency which convey the impression to the reader of character and theological conviction. The moral tenor is that of a prophet more than a pamphleteer. His few words are felt with intensity, having the inflection of authority. Allusions not only to historical lessons but to apostolic, received teaching haggadically and authoritatively enforce moral truth which is consistent with God's eternal revelation.

The means by which Jude communicates his urgent message is consistent with the message itself. The Christian community is in need of a reminder—a reminder of God's ability to keep those who *desire* to be kept. Using an arsenal consisting of elocutionary, structural, and inventive subtleties, the writer aims via positive as well as negative reminders to underscore graphically yet succinctly this profound theological truth.

2
Literary-Rhetorical Analysis of the Epistle of Jude

Earlier this century A. Deissmann[1] demonstrated that nonliterary memorials of the Hellenistic era opened our eyes to the true linguistic character of the NT. The NT was proven to be, as a whole, a monument of late colloquial Greek, and the great majority of its component parts were seen to be popular colloquial language. And yet it has not been sufficiently recognized that the Jews were the most literary of all Mediterranean peoples—they gave literary expression to their history, their poetry, their religion. They were par excellence people of "the books." It could as well be argued that no other nation demonstrated as ready an assimilation of Hellenistic culture as they. Considering the Jewish matrix of the early Christian community, this has significant bearing for a study of the literature of the NT.

THE FORM OF JUDE'S POLEMIC

Literary Form

A majority of the epistles found in the NT, unlike private conversations, were means by which the writer could publicly address a congregation without being physically present. If the possibility of a personal visit was precluded, the epistle was in essence the apostle's preaching. Thus, it is possible to note both the epistolary as well as homiletical character that Jude possesses. The body of Jude (vv. 5–23) is strongly hortatory, as if prepared as a sermon. Furthermore, the doxological conclusion would appear to be more fitting in a sermon. Yet with a formal opening and specific audience addressed, Jude conforms to the ancient epistolary genre.

Whether intended for a public or private audience, a piece of literature belongs to the epistolary genre if it occurs within the "epistolary situation,"[2] that is, the writer reflects a clear intent to communicate to an addressee geographically removed. Letter form distinguishes itself in literature in general by its presence of the combination of sender, addressee, greetings, and reflected purpose (explicit or implicit). Although Jude does not conform to the fairly consistent structure recognized in the Pauline epistles— opening (including sender, addressee, and salutation), thanksgiving, body, and closing (normally a benediction and concluding greeting)—it reflects nonetheless the "epistolary situation."[3]

The ancient letter, an important means of communication among Greeks, became even more commonplace among the Romans.[4] The significance of the letter is accurately reflected in the NT. With twenty of twenty-seven books purported to be epistles, and two of the remaining seven—Acts and Hebrews—containing some epistolary material, the epistle dominates as *the* literary form of the NT. The epistolary genre indeed mirrors a genuine relationship between the writer and the reader.

Factors influencing the literary forms found in the NT are apologetic as well as sociological. They arose out of intercourse with a surrounding pagan society. While the secular world offered a form, the Christian community bestowed the content.[5] A. Malherbe[6] asserts the need for NT students to become better acquainted with ancient letter writing due to its role in ancient rhetoric. Malherbe's contention is certainly valid in light of the long tradition in which first-century literary culture stood, a tradition extending back to the fifth century B.C.[7] To be sure, a public career required training in public speech.[8] According to Aristotle, speeches were forensic *(dikanikōn)*, political or deliberative *(symbouleutikōn)* or public *(epideiktikōn)* in nature.[9] By the time of Cicero (first century B.C.), Greek grammar and rhetoric seem to have already left their imprint on the Roman Empire; the Greek private letter[10] had acquired a standard form and was thus useful in the hands of rhetoricians.[11] The traditionally held view of Greco-Roman education is that it progressed along three stages: primary, secondary, and rhetorical training. Reading and writing comprised the core of the former, while secondary or "grammar" school was given primarily to language and literary instruction.[12] In secondary schools, boys, ages twelve to fifteen, were instructed in seven liberal arts with emphasis on the language arts.[13] The concept of *paideia* is no longer merely the training of a child to become an adult, but a signification for "culture," a "mind fully developed."[14] Among the disciplines belonging to higher education in Hellenistic culture, rhetoric was viewed as the "queen of subjects."[15]

Unlike some of the more modernist schools of literary criticism where formal literary devices are often separated from and opposed to content, the form-content dichotomy is not observable among the ancients. In order to appreciate more fully particular aspects of letter writing,[16] and hence, Jude's competence as a practitioner of the epistolary genre, consider several ancient definitions of what *epistolē*[17] was thought to represent:

> A letter is one half of a dialogue or a surrogate for an actual dialogue. (Demetrius)[18]

> The letter is, in effect, speech in written medium. (Cicero)[19]

> A letter reflects the personality of its writer. (Cicero)[20]

> It may be said that everybody reveals his own soul in his letters. (Demetrius).[21]

as well as characteristics of effective epistolary style: plainness and clarity,[22] conciseness,[23] deliberation (in contrast to dialogue),[24] picturesque language,[25] poetic diction,[26] rhythm,[27] grace of style in the arrangement of material,[28] suitability for the occasion, circumstance or mood of the audience,[29] skill and artistry,[30] the use of repetition to enhance vividness,[31] euphony,[32] harshness of sound when appropriate for effect,[33] the use of metaphor to produce animatism,[34] sarcasm when appropriate,[35] suitable embellishment when possible,[36] and brevity for maximum force.[37]

Although further studies are needed in the area of the general epistles in light of their forensic nature,[38] Pauline literature has produced a number of scholarly attempts to show how the apostle utilized contrast as a current rhetorical device.[39] C. Forbes[40] contends that Paul was extremely subtle and skilled in his rhetorical skills. Cited as evidence are two factors: (1) the apostle's frequent traveling and subsequent need to preach and debate as well as (2) possible formal rhetorical training in which many of Gamaliel's pupils were engaged. Many are quick to assume that a Palestinian writer such as Jude would have lacked sufficient education and training for the purpose of literary and rhetorical skill. However, this simplistic assumption necessitates reexamination. In his 1968 Society of Biblical Literature address, J. Muilenburg, considered by most rhetorical-critical practitioners to have laid the groundwork for applying a literary-rhetorical method to biblical studies,[41] made a call for appreciating the *literary* character of ancient texts. Specifically, Muilenburg offered this maxim for appreciating the literary character of *biblical* texts:

> In the Scriptures we have a literary deposit of those who were confronted by the ultimate questions of life and destiny, of God and man, and of the past out of which the historical people has come and of the future into which it is moving, a speech which seeks to be commensurate with man's ultimate concerns, a raid on the ultimate, if you will.[42]

Muilenburg continues:

> Persistent and painstaking attention to the modes of Hebrew literary composition will reveal that the pericopes exhibit linguistic patterns, word formations ordered or arranged in particular ways, verbal sequences which move in fixed structures from beginning to end. It is clear that they have been skillfully wrought in many different ways, often with consummate skill and artistry. It is also apparent that they have been influenced by conventional rhetorical practices. This inevitably poses a question for which I have no answer. From whom did the poets and prophets of Israel acquire their styles and literary habits?[43]

What Muilenburg applies to the OT prophets can also be said of Jude, whose elocution follows in the OT prophetic tradition. On the influence of Hellenism in Palestine as a cultural force, Martin Hengel has offered this assessment: "There was no stopping the penetration of the Greek language even in Jewish Palestine, and the young Jew who wanted to rise a stage above the mass of the simple people had to learn it."[44] Further, in Jude's favor, any amateur rhetorician, as Forbes has observed, would have followed textbook rules in the use of rhetorical skills.[45]

Indeed it would appear that to some extent Greek rhetoric provides the background for the epistolary "word of exhortation," a categorical heading under which the letter of Jude would fit (*anagkēn eschon*[46] *grapsai hymin parakalōn epagōnizesthai*, v 3). The "word of exhortation" as a classification is predicated on a homiletical pattern observable in Hellenistic Jewish and early Christian works.[47] The setting of Acts 13, in which Paul, present in the synagogue at Pisidian Antioch, is invited by the rulers to offer a *logos paraklēseōs* (v 15), affords an illustration of this type of discourse. Standing and addressing his Jewish brothers, Paul preaches in a format which contains several conspicuous parts: he recounts Israel's past (vv 16b–31), utilizes OT quotations with a corresponding interpretation (vv 32–37), and then draws a conclusion (vv 38–41). The epistle to the Hebrews (note the writer's clarification of purpose in 13:22 by his own designation: *logos tēs paraklēseōs*) is a similar illustration.[48] The "word of exhortation" might also be applied to 1 and 2 Peter.[49]

Consider the basic structure of Jude.[50] The writer's (1) greeting (vv 1–2), (2) occasion and purpose for writing (vv 3–4), (3) use of illustrative paradigms from the past plus a citation (vv 5–16), (4) authoritative reminder and exhortation (vv 17–23), and (5) concluding doxology (vv 24–25) combine to reflect the "word of exhortation" character through the discernible paradigm-citation-interpretation-exhortation pattern.[51] As with Paul's speech in Acts 13, Galatians, Hebrews, and perhaps even the Petrine epistles, one notes in Jude the presence of a decidedly rhetorical tone and pattern of speech in the writer's attempt to counter a disturbing trend within the believing community.

Following the letter's opening in which the sender, audience, and intention of the writer are clarified, a major transition in the epistle occurs in v 5 where the writer moves from his opening to the body proper. Here the shift is marked by "reminder" terminology, not unlike that often employed by Paul.[52] In this section of the epistle are featured types of ungodliness from the past which are used as supporting evidence for the "negative" aspect of the writer's thesis. These appear in an exhortation-paradigm-exhortation pattern and comprise the main body of the letter.

Verses 20–23 strengthen the "positive" component to Jude's thesis and affirm the admonition given in v 3. Jude's exhortation, which indeed may reflect his own indebtedness to a common paraenetic tradition of early Christianity,[53] consists of several injunctions that stand in antithesis to the actions of the ungodly.

Following the historical paradigms (vv 5–19) and paraenetic section (vv 20–23), the epistle concludes with the "proclaiming of glory," i.e., doxology (*legein tēn doxan*). Three basic patterns of speech to God are to be found in the OT: petition, praise, and thanksgiving.[54] Hymnic material could take the form of either of these. The origin of doxology is owing to a Jewish matrix. Although Palestinian Judaism knew certain stages in the development of the doxology, its arrangement did not become liturgically rigid.[55] The early Christian doxology, in style and content, resembled that of the Jewish synagogue. It was not uncommon for it to be accompanied by an eschatological deliverance-call.[56] The doxology functioned to proclaim God's praise, normally in the third person, as in Jude 25 (*tǭ dynamenǭ phylaxai . . .*), and to affirm His eternality (*. . . eis pantas tous aiōnas*).[57]

Normally positioned at the conclusion of kerygmatic or hymnic material, the doxology consisted of three parts:[58] (1) the person named (usually in the dative, e.g., *tǭ dynamenǭ*),[59] (2) an expression of praise often comprised of two or more elements with the term *doxa* included (e.g., *doxa megalōsynē kratos kai exousia*), and (3) a formula for time (e.g., *pro pantos tou aiōnos kai nyn kai eis pantas tous aiōnas*). The doxology typically concluded with the affirmation *amēn*.[60] Equally common to the OT as well as rabbinic milieu, *amēn* reinforces that declarations, confessions, or oaths are valid.[61] At times ending a prayer,[62] and frequently a Psalm,[62] *amēn* can also be doubled in the OT for emphasis.[64] In extracanonical apocalyptic literature, *amēn* is used with eschatological statements (e.g., 1 Enoch 98:1,4,6; 103:1; 104:1; 2 Enoch 49:1; Asc. Isa. 1:8; 3:18; and Apoc. Mos. 18).[65] In the synagogue it constituted the most common benediction pronounced by the rabbis.[66] It is only natural then for the expression to have found its way into the liturgy of the early church.[67]

Having briefly observed the undeniable homiletical character of the Jude, we have noted that it reflects the "epistolary situation" and thus qualifies as a representative of the epistolary genre. Its contents are highly stylized, didactic, liturgical, and rhetorical in mode. These elements of form deserve a more thorough examination. As with any type of written discourse, meaning is communicated through *form*. This encompasses any aspect which measures *how* a writer expresses his message. Understanding literary form is, thus, tantamount to understanding the content which is expressed.

Jude as a Rhetorician

The modern notion of a rhetorician holds him to be, in the words of G. Kennedy,[68] an "unscrupulous trickster with words." Yet among the ancients,[69] the art of rhetoric was essential in order to discuss topics which were not scientifically demonstrable.[70] To persuade was to illustrate the existence of two contradictory moral sides to a question and to demonstrate the probability of truth, for truth marshals a convincing argument. Rhetoric[71] was viewed as "discourse that aims to influence men."[72] Persuasion is the province of rhetoric. It is the "employment of all available means of convincing an individual or an audience of a particular point of view."[73]

Three kinds of speeches are to be found in Greco-Roman rhetoric: (1) forensic (normally accusatory or defensive and hence judicial in tenor), (2) deliberative (often political in nature, used in public gatherings with a view of admonition), and (3) epideictic (emotive and stylistic in character).[74] The genre of argumentation persuades and dissuades. Incompatible notions are brought into open conflict. Thesis and antithesis are presented in rigid opposition. More important, however, was the *verbal articulation* of this argumentation. To the Greeks, reading was to be done aloud, i.e., it was to be *heard*. G.M.A. Grube[75] has noted that silent reading was almost unknown even as late as the fourth century A.D. Because *sound* represented the writer's mind, stylistic features such as rhythm, alliteration, precision, accent, and brevity were decisive in the argumentation.[76] In reading Jude, one receives the impression that the writer, on every count, was careful to exploit every possible device for maximum effect with his audience.

Two fundamentally different strategies were employed in rhetoric:[77] one for legal purposes and another for stylistics.[78] The latter is particularly relevant for the study of Jude, since it seeks through the manipulation of speech to elicit a desired effect, and hence, a response. It was the view of Cicero, expressed in 55 B.C. in his *De oratore partitione oratoriae*,[79] that "the listener will never be set on fire unless there is fire in the words that reach him."

One finds in the logical argumentation of Aristotle frequent use of *parabolē, eikōn* and *paradeigma*.[80] The first two are essential as a means of comparison. The latter, the historical example, establishes a point of contact with the hearers' experience. Paradigmatic language is important to Jude and explicit in v 7: *prokeintai deigma pyros aiōniou dikēn hypechousai*.[81] The abundance of historical types in Jude serves the function of marshalling evidence from the context of similar relationships and moves the thesis from the unknown to the known.[82]

The "Sitz im Leben" of the *rhētōr* is one of public discourse. Thus, his particular art is that of addressing an audience. A public discourse differs from the private chat. The speaker waxes more artistic than when merely engaged in everyday language. He chooses words with precision; he is quite logical and orderly. Rhetoric therefore entails the whole dynamic which is operative between speaker/writer and audience. How proficiently does he communicate? How skillfully can he argue? How artful is he in the marshalling of comparisons, paradigms, and sources? When considering the Greeks' devotion and sacrifice to the goddess Persuasion in Athens, it is not difficult to understand their love for persuasive speech, disputation, eloquence, and intellectual prowess (and, hence, the significance of certain sarcastic statements by Paul found in 1 Cor. 1:18–2:16).[83] In truth, these represented a virtually divine capacity. Thus, we gain understanding in the response of the crowd in Lystra to Paul and Barnabas: " 'The gods have come down to us in human form!' Barnabas they called Zeus, and Paul, Hermes, because *autos ēn ho hēgoumenos tou logou*" (Acts 14:11–12).

In broad terms, the usefulness of rhetoric in understanding Jude is manifold. First, as noted by G. Kennedy,[84] words create and reflect their culture, and to read them outside that culture environment is to invite a basic level of misunderstanding. Much the same applies to rhetorical conventions. There is need for some knowledge of ancient rhetorical practice when reading the NT.

> Rhetorical analysis thus might be compared to the process of translating the Scriptures for modern readers, a task necessitated every generation or two by the continual change in ways of hearing words. As a result of such efforts of scholarship the religious truths of the Bible can be made more easily available to the general reader, and its powerful impact on Christians can be better understood.[85]

Second, the usefulness of rhetoric is that it offers insight into the writer's goal. His appeal is to the whole man; he engages the reason, the emotions, and the will in his persuading and dissuading.[86] His aim is to *win* the audience over. Third, by virtue of their discipline in keeping the prospective audience in mind, classical rhetoricians were logical and consistent in their argumentation. Hence, we begin to recognize the key role that *form* plays in the address. This is certainly true with regard to Jude. The audience/reader becomes attentive to the importance of the arrangement of material—introduction, main points, recapitulation, conclusion—all of which are not simply arbitrary in their connection. This extends as well to the selection and employment of particular sources. Fourth, the matter of style or elocution receives greater consideration. *How* the content is expressed is indivisible from *what* is being expressed.[87]

Three "species" of rhetoric were formulated by Aristotle which are applicable to all discourse. There can be more than one species identified in discourse, however, one dominant species is the rule.[88] Observing the ascendant type will aid in determining the writer's purpose. D. F. Watson classifies the letter of Jude as deliberative rhetoric due to the writer's strong attempts to exhort, dissuade, and warn.[90] Indeed Jude would seem to reflect a controlling deliberative or "political" character. The epistle is epideictic as well in that the writer's aim is *strongly* emotive. He is attempting to incite his audience—to action and reaction. And one can observe the judicial or forensic element in Jude, for the epistle concerns itself with accusation, woe, and sentence. The *houtoi*, mentioned eight times in twenty-five verses,[91] are subject to irresistible *krima*. A spate of eight historical or apocalyptic paradigms is served up to reinforce the certainty of their fate.[92] Jude's motive is to declare in no uncertain terms what is righteous and what is wicked.

The emotion with which Jude writes has contributed to a foremost "negative" reading of the letter. The epistle, however, does not consist *solely* of denunciations. The writer is also positive—indeed quite positive—in his exhortation and in keeping with the character of the predominant deliberative discourse. Divine *agapē* and *eleos*, which hold the faithful securely, are mentioned a total of eleven times throughout the brief epistle.[93]

The basic divisions in the rhetorical arrangement *(taxis)* of the material are as follows: (1) an introduction *(prooimion)*[94] which functions to secure audience interest, (2) a narration *(diegēsis)*[95] which informs the audience as to the nature of the argument being set forth, (3) the proof(s) *(pistis)*,[96] i.e., a development of the main proposition by the marshalling of supporting evidence or paradigms, and (4) the conclusion *(epilogos)*,[97] often a recapitulation of the main points and an emotional appeal to the audience. Following this scheme, the material in Jude could be arranged accordingly:

prooimion: vv 1–2 (greeting: Jude . . . to those loved, kept and called, mercy, peace and love)

diegēsis: vv 3–4 (purpose/thesis: contend for the faith; certain ungodly, condemned to judgment, have wormed their way in, perverting grace and denying the Lord)

pistis: vv 5–16 (historical and apocalyptic paradigms as supporting and persuasive evidence: unbelieving Israel, the rebellious angels, Sodom and Gomorrah, Michael and the devil, Cain, Balaam, Korah, Enoch)

epilogos: vv 17–23 (conclusion, recapitulation, final appeal: apostolic reminder, the contrast of the faithful to the ungodly, closing exhortations)[98]

As formally taught in the handbooks of the ancient rhetorical schools, five aspects of rhetoric were brought into view when preparing any discourse—invention (planning of the discourse with arguments to be used), arrangement (composition into an effective whole), style (the choice of words and composition of words into sentences for literary effect), memory (preparation for delivery), and delivery.[99] The three parts relating to written discourse—invention, arrangement, and style—constitute a grid through which the literary character of any book of the NT can be evaluated. These three will be the focus of our examination of Jude.

Invention

According to ancient rhetorical theory, the percept[100] of *inventio*[101] represents the creative ability and resources employed by a writer. Specifically, it relates to the devising of material to persuade and the marshalling of proofs to support a case.[102] These may take the form of external *(atechnos)* proofs which make use of witnesses, historical paradigms, citations, documents, etc., as well as eternal or artistic *(entechnos)* proofs such as maxims, ethical arguments, probability, or reasoning.

The epistle of Jude, in spite of its brevity, is replete with examples of both types. Instances of external proof being utilized by the writer include unbelieving Israel (v 5), the rebellious angels (v 6), Sodom and Gomorrah (v 7), allusion to the tradition ascribed to the Assumption of Moses (v 9), a citation from the Book of (1) Enoch (vv 14–15), the triad of Cain, Balaam, and Korah, and the words of the apostles (vv 17–18). Internal proofs being employed in Jude include the allusion to divine foreknowledge and fate (v 4), a judgment as to the opponents' deficient character and moral state (vv 4, 16, 19), presenting the opponents' moral inferiority against the moral superiority of Michael (vv 8–10), graphic metaphorical depiction of the opponents (vv 12–13), the contrast of the faithful rescuing the unfaithful (vv 22–23), and the promise of divine keeping to the extent of being presented morally blameless (v 24).

The artistic mode of the writer, as taught by ancient theorists, might be logical, whereby persuasion is sought via inductive reasoning or deductive argumentation; it might be ethical, whereby the writer seeks to demonstrate the moral high ground against his opponents; or it might be pathetic, i.e., the writer attempts to stir the emotions of his audience by playing on their feelings.[103] Jude would appear to incorporate all three modes into his polemic. He seeks to prove the superiority to his *ēthos*, embodied in faithfulness, in sharp contrast to the *houtoi* who have perverted divine grace. His use of vivid imagery and articulating of the fate of both the faithful and the apostate are designed to arouse the *pathos* of his audience, evoking sympathy for his position and an abhorrence for the wicked. Further, Jude's use of *logos*, primarily effective through *inductive* reasoning based on the parallels between the historical paradigms and the *houtoi*, is aimed at eliciting agreement on the part of his audience. After all the evidence is gathered and presented, the recipients of the letter should be fully persuaded of Jude's thesis: God is able at once to keep the wicked for irresistible judgment while preserving the faithful for divine glory.

Arrangement

Having noted earlier the role of Greco-Roman rhetoric in understanding the background to the *logos tēs paraklēseōs*, we turn to the question of composition. Our concern is to determine the structure (*taxis, collocutio*) of a rhetorically effective literary work. How does a writer mold the component parts of discourse into a unified literary structure?[104]

In considering the structure of Jude,[105] one is struck by the writer's repeated use of particular catchwords. Words which are recurring are not the result of haphazard or arbitrary construction, rather they are rhetorically significant. Moreover, the frequency of these catchwords which link material together is, in light of the epistle's brevity, astounding. In the mere twenty-five verses, *nine* terms occur *five or more* times with five of these appearing *seven or more* times. Consider the following examples: *asebeis/asebeia* (vv 4, 15 [3x], 18), *hymeis/hymas/hymin* (vv 3 [3x],5 [2x], 12, 17, 18,20 [2x],24), *terein* (vv 1,6 [2x],13, 21,24 [*phylassein*], *houtoi* (vv [*tines*],8,10,11 [*autois*],12,14,16,19), *kyrios* (vv 4,5,9,14,17,21,25), *hagios* (vv 3,14,20 [2x], 24 [*amōmos*]), *sarx* (vv 7,23), *epithymia* (vv 16,18), *agapē/agapētoi* (vv 1,2,3,12, 17,20,21), *eleos/eleein* (vv 2,21,22,23), *krisis/krima* (vv 4,6,9,15), *planē* (vv 11,13 [*planētai*]), *pas/pan/panta* (vv 3,5,15 [4x],25 [2x]), *doxa* (vv 8,24,25),and *spilas/spiloun* (vv 12 [?], 23).

A conspicuous use not only of catchwords but conjunctions as well reflects conscious deliberation on the part of the writer in the structuring of his material. Logical argumentation is set forth in Jude, a feature one might expect to find particularly in the general epistles due to their frequently polemical tenor.[106] The function of the conjunction is to give prominence to the modal character of a clause or sentence as well as expressing the interrelation of the same.[107] Note the progression of Jude's argumentation within sections of material as well as between them:

vv 1–2, greeting	
vv 3–4, occasion/purpose	. . . [for] certain individuals have slipped in . . .
vv 5–16, illustrative paradigms	[Now] I wish to remind you . . .
	[for] the Lord destroyed . . .
	[and] the angels who did not keep . . .
	[rather] abandoned . . .
	[just as] Sodom and Gomorrah . . . gave themselves over . . .
	[Yet] in the very same manner these dreamers also defile . . .
	[But] Michael . . . did not dare . . .
	[rather] he said . . .
	[yet] these blaspheme . . .
	[and] . . . are ruined . . .
	[for] they walk . . .
	[Indeed] Enoch, the seventh from Adam, prophesied . . .
vv 17–19, reminder	[But] you, beloved, remember . . .
	[for] they said . . .
	[that] . . . there will be . . .
vv 20–23, exhortation	[But] you, beloved, build . . .
	[and] . . . be merciful . . .
	[and] save . . .
	[and] show mercy . . .
vv 24–25, closing	[Now] to the One Who is able . . .

One can observe through the structure, as delineated above, a thoughtfulness in the design of the epistle. As regards this design, D. J. Rowston[108] comments: "Lest a cataloguing of quotations, allusions, reminiscences and catchwords should leave a false impression of the author of Jude as a scissors-and-paste expert, one must note the employment of his own catchwords and the grouping of his traditions."

Making a similar observation, E. E. Ellis[109] uses the term "midrash" to describe the material in Jude 5–19, whereby the illustrative paradigms are linked to an interpretation via particular catchwords not unlike the Qumran pesharim. Pesher interpretation related prophetic oracles of the past to circumstances of the present.[110] R. J. Bauckham[111] expands this line of thinking, applying "midrash" in a broader structural sense (as opposed to a stricter rabbinic sense). Bauckham, perhaps more so than Ellis, distinguishes between Jude's hermeneutic and the Qumran pesharim, noting that Qumran literature really exhibits no typology in the strict sense.[112]

It would be misleading to assume that there exists among scholars full agreement on what precisely constitutes midrash. W. H. Brownlee[113] uses the term in a somewhat restricted sense, classifying a work as midrashic only if it exhibits a specific rabbinic[114] mode of exegesis. R. Bloch,[115] on the other hand, views it as reflection on a text which has as its aim a reinterpretation or actualization of that text for present circumstances. J. Doeve[116] extends the basic idea of Bloch, viewing the Gospels themselves as Christian midrashim. Speaking of the postexilic phenomenon, which he called *style anthologique,* A. Robert[117] considers this the earliest form of midrash. Yet, regardless of how restrictive or inclusive one's definition of midrash is, its purpose is to make a text relevant by means of "creative historiography" and "creative philology."[118]

Indeed Jude's "midrashic" method deserves some comparison with contemporary Jewish exegesis. In spite of the wide range of opinion as to the exact nature of the exegesis employed in QL, the underlying principle that governed rabbinic exegesis might also apply to that of Qumran. All knowledge necessary for a proper interpretation of the past, present, and future is contained within the Torah. Simple expressions in the Torah are often thought to hide latent meaning, since it is not bound by spatial or temporal limitations (thus, *pĕshāt* is often subservient to *dĕrāsh*). The interpreter therefore utilizes certain hermeneutical devices to expose these eternal truths in the text.

One specific rule of exegesis in QL is worthy of note: the *Gezerah Shawah.*[119] By this principle of interpretation, two biblical passages are linked together by means of an identical word or phrase found in both. This ultimately may aid the commentator in identifying some of his characters. Several examples of usage may suffice. An association between two "houses" mentioned in Exod. 15 : 17 and 2 Sam. 7 : 10 can be drawn based on the root *nt'* found in both. Psalm 1 is conceived by the Qumran community as a hymn of praise to the *community,* since the "sons of righteousness" did not enter the "counsel of the wicked." The pesher of Hab. 1 : 13 in 1QpHab 5 : 8−11 identifies the enemies of the "Righteous

Teacher" with the house of Absalom on the basis of the root *ḥrs* found in both.

In the text of 11QMelch, we encounter a midrashic development of a particular theme—the Jubilee year (Lev. 25), a year of "release" or "deliverance." Thus the figure of Melchizedek, in this "eschatological midrash,"[120] is linked to the year of Jubilee, the Day of Atonement and *divine deliverance*. This midrashic treatment of Melchizedek may well have influenced the writer in Hebrews 7, where the superiority of Christ over the levitical priesthood is developed.

"Midrash" may be viewed as a kind of activity, a process of interpretation. The central issue behind this interpretive "activity" is the need to deal with *present* realities of cultural and religious tension. New problems and situations must be addressed. Midrash comes into play to address, resolve, and affirm the religious community by utilizing traditions from the past. In linking OT traditions with the present, the midrashist might also help fill in those gaps which have been teasingly left out. Why did Cain kill Abel? What motivated Balaam? Why did the angels rebel? What happened at Moses' burial?

The usefulness of the observations of Ellis and Bauckham for the exegetical task should not be overlooked. Rather than having in Jude an opaque, obscure, and incoherent volley of passionate denunciations (assumed by many commentators), we learn to appreciate Jude's concise, calculated and pungent style and use of sources along with their application for his opponents. Certain ungodly (*houtoi*) are being contradistinguished from the faithful (*hymeis*). Juxtaposed to these faithful, who are depicted as *hagios* and *amōmos,* the *asebeis* are linked to ungodly types of the past, which speak prophetically in the present, and, thus, are ripe for judgment. While the faithful are to be built up, praying, preserved, and anticipating—God in Christ is eternally committed to their preservation—the ungodly are being "kept" for sure and irreversible judgment. Ultimately, the godly are "kept" from falling, preserved for the purpose of glorious presentation.[121]

Having already examined the exhortation-paradigm-exhortation pattern which reflects a very deliberate structuring of material by the writer, and thus identifying the framework on which the whole epistle of Jude is constructed, we might propose to arrange the text poetically in the following manner:

(v 1)   *Ioudas*
       Iēsou Christou doulos,   *adelphos de Iakōbou,*

tois en theǭ patri ēgapēmenois   kai Iēsou Christǭ tetērēmenois
                                      klētois.
eleos hymin kai eirēnē   kai agapē plēthyntheiē.

*****

(v 3)   Agapētoi,
        pasan spoudēn poioumenos   peri tēs koinēs hymōn sōtērias
            graphein hymin
        anagkēn eschon grapsai   parakalōn epagōnizesthai
            hymin
        tǟ hapax paradotheisǟ   tois hagiois pistei.
        pareisedysan gar tines   hoi palai progegrammenoi eis
            anthrōpoi,   touto to krima, asebeis.
        tēn tou theou hēmōn charita   metatithentes eis aselgeian
        kai ton monon despotēn kai   Iēsoun Christon arnoumenoi.
            kyrion hēmōn

*****

(v 5)   Hypomnēsai de hymas   eidotas hapax panta
            boulomai,
        hoti ho kyrios laon   ek gēs Aigyptou sōsas
        to deuteron tous mē   apōlesen.
            pisteusantas
        aggelous te tous mē tērēsantas tēn heautōn archēn
        alla apolipontas   to idion oikētērion
        eis krisin megalēs hēmeras   desmois aidiois
                                       hypo zophon tetērēken.

        hōs Sodoma kai Gomorra   kai hai peri autas poleis
        ton homoion tropon toutois   kai apelthousai opisō sarkos
            ekporneusasai   heteras,
        prokeintai deigma   pyros aiōnious
                                       dikēn hypechousai.

        Homoiōs mentoi kai houtoi   enypiazomenoi
        sarka men miainousin,   kyriotēta de athetousin
                                       doxas de blasphēmousin.

        ho de Michaēl ho   hote tǭ diabolǭ diakrinomenos
            archaggelos,   dielegeto peri tou Mōÿseōs
                                           sōmatos,
        ouk etolmēsen   krisin epenegkein blasphēmias
        alla eipen,   Epitimēsai soi kyrios.
        houtoi de hosa men ouk   blasphēmousin,
            oidasin
        hosa de physikōs   hōs ta aloga zǭa epistantai,

en toutois phtheirontai.

ouai autois,

hoti tę̄ hodǭ tou Kain
   eporeuthēsan

kai tę̄ planę̄ tou Balaam
kai tē antilogiạ tou Kore
houtoi eisin hoi en tais
   agapais hymōn

misthou exechythēsan
apōlonto.
spilades syneuōchoumenoi,
aphobōs, heautous
   poimainontes,

nephelai anydroi

hypo anemōn
   parapheromenai,

dendra phthinopōrina
  akarpa
kymata agria thalassēs

dis apothanonta ekrizōthenta,

epaphrizonta tas heautōn
   aischynas,

asteres planētai

hois ho zophos tou skotous
eis aiōna tetērētai.

Proephēteusen de kai toutois

hebdomos apo Adam Henōch
   legōn,

Idou ēlthen kyrios
poiēsai krisin kata pantōn
peri pantōn tōn ergōn
  asebeias autōn
kai peri pantōn tōn sklērōn

en hagiais myriasin autou
kai elegxai pasan psychēn
hōn ēsebēsan

hōn elalēsan kat' autou
   hamartōloi asebeis.

Houtoi eisin goggystai
  mempsimoiroi
kai to stoma autōn lalei
  hyperogka,

kata tas epithymias heautōn
   poreuomenoi,
thaumazontes prosōpa
ōphelias charin.

*****

(v 17) Hymeis de, agapētoi,

mnēsthēte tōn rhēmatōn
tōn proeirēmenōn

hypo tōn apostolōn

tou kyriou hēmōn Iēsou
   Christou

hoti elegon hymin

hoti Ep' eschatou tou chronou
esontai empaiktai

kata tas heautōn epithymias
  poreuomenoi
Houtoi eisin hoi
  apodiorizontes,

tōn asebeiōn

psychikoi,

pneuma mē echontes.

hymeis de, agapētoi,

epoikodomountes heautous
tę̄ hagiōtatę̄ hymōn pistei,

en pneumati hagiǭ   *heautous en agapę̄ theou*
  proseuchomenoi,   *tērēsate*
prosdechomenoi to eleos tou   *Iēsou Christou*
  kyriou hēmōn   *eis zōēn aiōnion.*
kai hous men eleate   *hous de sǭzete ek pyros*
  diakrinomenous,   *harpazontes,*
hous de eleate en phobǭ   *misountes kai ton apo tēs*
                   sarkos espilōmenon
                   chitōna.

*****

(v 24) *Tǭ de dynamenǭ phylaxai*   *kai stēsai katenōpion tēs doxēs*
    hymas aptaistous   *autou*
                   amōmous en agalliasei,
    monǭ theǭ sōtēri hēmōn   *dia Iēsou Christou tou kyriou*
                   hēmōn
    doxa megalōsynē   *kratos kai exousia*
    pro pantos tou aiönos   *kai nyn*
    kai eis pantas tous aiōnas,   *amēn.*[122]

Style

Two foci of a writer's style *(lexis, elocutio)* were in the purview of Greco-Roman rhetoric as taught from the textbook, that is, diction and composition.[123] The level of style for the ancient writer was commensurate with the occasion and needs of the audience. Cicero[124] describes three levels or degrees of style: grand, middle, and plain. Each is practiced according to the amount of ornamentation and force demanded by the rhetorical situation.

It is unfortunate that much in the past has contributed to the notion that the Greek of the NT writers was the language of the street and that their rhetoric is largely representative of the illiterate. To the contrary, NT Greek, wrote W. G. Ballantine,[125] was no careless colloquial. It was rich in thought as well as expression and exact in syntax. In the main, opinion of the present century no longer views NT language as a backwater from the mainstream of Greek literature.[126] N. Turner[127] has noted that with regard to refinement of diction, Luke-Acts, Hebrews, 2 Peter, and Jude[128] approach the Atticists in comparison.

With an understanding of rhetorical skill, A. Augustine[129] expressed his own estimation of the NT writers, offering the following appraisal:

. . . (one) will learn that these divinely-inspired men are not defective
in any of those points which he has been taught in the schools of the
grammarians and rhetoricians to consider of importance. And he will
find in them many kinds of speech of great beauty—beautiful even in
our language, but especially beautiful in the original.

A writer's style can clothe and transform his message with
beauty and spiritual force. The NT might be viewed as a blend of
poetry and history. It has been said that it "reads like a work of art
and yet we are simultaneously aware that actuality is so stamped
on it that there can be no fiction."[130] The epistle of Jude exhibits
an impressive display of diction, vocabulary, and compository
skill. Figures of speech, symbolism, ornamentation, and unusual
brevity combine to strengthen the writer's polemic. Poetic force is
marshalled for the urgency of the historical occasion. D. F. Watson[131] has classified Jude as having a "middle" style. If, according
to Watson, the "middle" lacks intellectual appeal or force of the
"grand,"[132] how does one account for the aforementioned skill in
vocabulary, poetic diction, art of composition, uses of figures
(especially metaphor and hyperbole), and high degree of graphic
symbolism, not to mention the writer's *passion*? If Jude does not
belong to the "grand," he certainly deserves very high ground in
the "middle," particularly if Jude, along with Hebrews, has been
placed in a category approaching Atticism.

Let us then consider several areas in which we may observe
stylistic features peculiar to Jude.

1. GRAMMATICAL-LEXICAL DISTINCTIVES. Jude shows a normal
use of the Greek idiom with bits of artistic flare. He uses the article
skillfully with participles, and his free use of participles—all told,
participial forms occur thirty-four times in the short twenty-five
verses—would indicate a command of the Greek. With regard to
word order, Jude, in good Greek fashion, has the article and noun
separated by a prepositional phrase three times (vv 1,12,23). Thir-
teen times (vv 3[2x],4 [2x],6 [2x],7 [2x],9,10,11,18,20) he places
an adjective, adverb, or participle between the article and noun.
And once he uses the repeated article (v 17), a Semitic feature.
Semitisms, apart from the lone occurrence of the repeated article,
the expression *tē hodō Kain poreuesthai* (v 11), and the woe-cry (v
11), are not abundant. Of the twenty-seven sentences in the epistle, Jude uses the connecting particle seventeen times, employing
de eight times, *kai* four times, *hoti* four times, *hōs* twice, *alla* twice,
and *homoiōs, mentoi*[133] *te*, and *gar* once each.[134] The remaining

cases of asyndeton are most notably lists of descriptions given to the *houtoi* (e.g., vv 12,16,19).

Jude's fluid use of Christian "technical" terms such as *klētoi* (v 1), *pistis* (vv 3,20), *pneuma* (v 19), *psychikos* (v 19), and *hagios* (v 20) is not unlike that of Paul. Twice in the short letter he employs an adverbial accusative—*to deuteron* (v 5) and *ton homoion tropon* (v 7)—and the use of the superlative *hagiōtes* (v 20), common to both secular and ecclesiastic usage, is a mark of the writer's skill.[135]

Commentators are quick to acknowledge in Jude the use of a very good literary Greek, whether in writing flare or vocabulary. In light of the epistle's brevity, the richness of vocabulary and abundance of *hapax legomena* found in the letter are noteworthy. E. Fuchs and P. Reymond[136] have called attention to at least twenty-two rare terms found in the epistle. This diversity over against the letter's length—a mere twenty-five verses—magnifies the originality of the writer. Of the fourteen *hapax*, six (*epagōnizesthai* [v 3], *pareisdyein* [v 4], *ekporneuein* [v 7], *hypechein* [v 7], *epaphrizein* [v 13], and *apodiorizein* [v 19]) are verbs; four (*deigma* [v 7], *spilas* [v 12], *planētēs* [v 13], *goggystēs*[137] [v 16]) are substantives; three (*phthinopōrinos* [v 12], *mempsimoiros* [v 16], and *aptaistos* [v 24]) are adjectives; and one (*physikōs* [v 10]) is an adverb.[138] Three additional words (*syneuōcheisthai* [v 12], *hyperogka* [v 16], and *empaiktēs* [v 18]) are used in 2 Peter (2:13,18; 3:3) but occur nowhere else in the New Testament.[139] What most impresses the reader, however, apart from these statistics, is the economy with which Jude writes. Originality and diversity are all the more remarkable when seen within such brevity.

2. PARALLELISM. The utilization of particular catchwords in the epistle, noted earlier, serves several functions. It lends stylistic effect, aids in clarifying the epistle's structure, and reveals a strategy in the author's use of sources. The writer leaves indelibly imprinted on the audience's mind desired images and stereotypes for the purpose of eliciting from them a clear response. A similar effect is accomplished stylistically by means of repetition or synonymous parallelism and contrast or antithetical parallelism, both of which are exploited in Jude. Examples of the former include: *spoudēn poioumenos* and *anagkēn eschon* (v 3); *despotēs* and *kyrios* (v 4); *hypomnēsai* and *eidotas* (v 5); *archē* and *oikētērion* (v 6); *krisis* and *zophos* (v 6); *ekporneusasai* and *apelthousai opisō sarkos heteras* (v 7); *prokeimai* and *hypechein* (v 7); *pyr* and *dikē* (v 7); *miainein, athetein* and *blasphēmein* (v 8); *kyriotēs* and *doxa* (v 8); *diakrinein* and *dialogizomai* (v 9); *krisin epipherein* and *blasphēmia* (v 9); *hosa ouk oidasin* and *aloga* (v 10); *oida* and *epistamai* (v 10); *akarpa* and

apothanonta (v 12); *astēr* and *planētes* (v 13); *zophos* and *skotos* (v 13); *prophēteuein* and *legein* (v 14); *poiēsai krisin* and *elegxai* (v 15); *goggystēs* and *mempsimoiros* and *to stoma lalein hyperogka* (v 16); *psychikos* and *apodiorizontes* (v 19); *hagiōtatos* and *hagios* (v 20); *agapē* and *eleos* (v 21); *sǭzein* and *harpazein* (v 23).

Antithesis, essential to argumentation, also finds full expression in the epistle. Incompatible notions are brought into open conflict. Thesis and antithesis are presented in rigid opposition. In Jude contrast is exploited to the maximum: *doulos* (v 1) versus *kyrios* (vv 4,5,9,14,17,21,25) and *despotēs* (v 4); *houtoi* (vv 4,8,10,11,12,16,19) versus *hymeis* (vv 3,5,12,17,18, 20,24); *asebeis* (vv 4,15,18) versus *hagios* (vv 3,14, 20,24); *eleos* (vv 2,21,22,23) versus *krisis* (vv 6,9,15) and *krima* (v 4); *pyr* (vv 7,23) versus *doxa* (vv 24,25); *houtoi* (vv 8,10) versus *Michaēl* (v 9); *oida* and *epistamai* versus *alogos* (v 10); *aphobōs* (v 12) versus *en phobǭ* (v 23); *sarx* and *epithymia* (vv 7,16,18,23) versus *amōmos* and *misountes ton apo tēs sarkos espilōmenon chitōna* (vv 23,24); *charis* versus *aselgeia* (v 4); *kyrios hapax . . . sōsas* versus *to deuteron . . . apōlesen* (v 5); *skotos* and *zophos* (vv 6,13) versus *doxa* (vv 24–25); *to stoma autōn* (v 16) versus *rhēma hypo tōn apostolōn* (v 17); *apodiorizein* (v 19) versus *epoikodomein* (v 20); *eleein* versus *diakrinein* (v 22).

Yet another type of parallelism found in Jude, which seeks to add rhetorical force through sound resemblances for the sake of literary effect, is paronomasia. Although paronomasia may be defined differently according to connotation—e.g., recurrence of the same word or word-stem, recurrence of like-sounding words, or simply a play on words—in its widest connotation the term includes all cases where resemblance in sound is exploited for literary effect.[140] This broader definition would include alliteration, assonance, homoioteleuton, rhyme, and word- or name-play. Technically speaking, imaginative or impassioned literary works would call for a more varied literary style than did narrative, since the aim of the work was to persuade and convict.[141] Jude's short but lively polemic is not lacking in colorful "sound-structure" which achieves a notable literary effect:

v 3:   *Agapētoi, pasan, spoudēn, poioumenos, peri, grapsai, parakalōn, epagōnizesthai, hapax, paradotheisę̄, pistei*

   7:    *ekporneusasai . . . apelthousai . . . prokeintai . . . hypechousai*

   8:    *mentoi . . . houtoi . . . enypniazomenoi*

   8:    *miainousin . . . athetousin . . . blasphēmousin*

   9:    *hote tǭ diabolǭ diakrinomenos dielegeto*

10:	*oidasin, blasphēmousin*
10:	*epistantai, phtheirontai*
11:	*eporeuthēsan, exechythēsan*
12–13:	*dendra phthinopōrina akarpa dis apothanonta ekrizōthenta kymata agria thalassēs epaphrizonta*
15:	*pasan psychēn peri pantōn tōn ergōn asebeias autōn hōn ēsebēsan kai peri pantōn tōn sklērōn hōn elalēsan*
16:	*Houtoi eisin goggystai mempsimoiroi kata tas epithymias heautōn poreuomenoi*
19:	*Houtoi, hoi, psychikoi*
19:	*apodiorizontes, mē echontes*
20–21:	*epoikodomountes heautous . . . en . . . heautous en*
20–21:	*en pneumati hagiō proseuchomenoi heautous en agapē theou tērēsate prosdechomenoi*
22–23:	*hous . . . hous . . . hous*
22–23:	*eleate . . . sōzete . . . eleate*[142]

The varieties of parallelism amply demonstrated in Jude deepen, strengthen and enrich the writer's fundamental thesis: namely, his admonition by means of contrast between the ungodly, the *houtoi,* and the faithful. Often such parallels accommodate fresh nuances. In its function, parallelism does not merely repeat, rather it amplifies. Repetition, symmetry and contrast give the writer a literary advantage. These devices are exploited in Jude for optimal effect. This stands in stark contrast to the assertion of E. Norden[143] that Christian literature was lacking in *Formenschönheit,* i.e., that it possessed no stylistic technique. This is certainly not true of the NT, and particularly of Jude. In this epistle we are witnesses to a literary-rhetorical artist at work.

3. TRIADIC ILLUSTRATION. One cannot help but be struck by the abundance of triple descriptions in Jude. Not one or two illustrations suffice, but three. The writer, whether by use of prophetic types or in his explanation of these types, exploits the method of a threefold "witness"[144] to condemn the opponents while exhorting the faithful. The validity of testimony in the OT was affirmed by the mouth of two or three witnesses (Deut. 17:6 and 19:15). The same principle is applied in the NT as well (Matt. 18:16; John 5:31–33; 8:17–18; 2 Cor. 13:1; 1 Tim. 5:19; Heb. 10:28). In essence, the three represent one: a threefold concurrence yields completeness.

Repetition is one of the most fundamental tools of the literary artist, whether oral or written. A matter, a thesis, or a description is repeated in order to *fix the teaching* in the mind of the hearer/

reader. All told in Jude, twenty sets of triplets appear within the letter's mere twenty-five verses. A like phenomenon, demonstrating such a high degree of density, is unparalleled anywhere else in Scripture.

v	1:	the writer's self-designations: *Ioudas, doulos, adelphos*
	1:	attributes ascribed to audience: *ēgapēmenois, tetērēmenois, klētois*
	2:	elements in the greeting: *eleos, eirēnē, agapē*
	4:	participles modifying the main verb: *progegrammenoi, metatithentes, arnoumenoi*
	5–7:	paradigms of judgment: *ho laos [Israēl], hoi aggeloi, Sodoma kai Gomorra*
	8:	indicative actions of opponents: *miainein, athetein, blasphēmein*
	9:	indicative actions of Michael: *dielegeto, ouk etolmēsen, eipen*
	11:	examples of woe: *Kain, Balaam, Kore*
	11:	escalation of rebellious action: *poreuomai, ekchein, apollymi*
	12:	traits of those at the love-feasts: *spilades, syneuōchoumenoi, aphobōs*
	12:	characteristics of the trees: *phthinopōrina, akarpa, dis apothanonta ekrizōthenta*
	13:	characteristics of the waves: *agria, thalassēs epaphrizonta, aischynē*
	14–15:	actions of the Lord: *ēlthen, poiēsai krisin, elegxai pasan psychēn*
	16:	traits of the opponents: *goggystai, mempsimoiroi, kata tas epithymias heautōn poreuomai*
	19:	further traits of the opponents: *apodiorizontes, psychikoi, mē pneuma echontes*
	20–21:	participles relating to the imperative: *epoikodomountes, proseuchomenoi, prosdechomenoi*
	20–21:	presence of the Trinity: *en pneuma hagiǭ, en agapǭ theou, to eleos tou Iēsou Christou*
	22–23:	imperatives for the faithful: *eleate, sǭzete, eleate*[145]
	25:	divine designations: *theos, sōtēr, kyrios*
	25:	view of time: *pro pantos tou aiōnos kai nyn kai eis pantas tous aiōnas*

4. FIGURES OF SPEECH. To increase the force of expression, new linguistic forms developed. To the Greeks, these were known as *schēmata;* to the Latins, *figura*. Simply stated, a "figure of speech" is

a word or sentence thrown into a peculiar form, different from its original or simplest meaning or use.[146] The modern English designation "figure of speech" is somewhat misleading in that we tend to view this as a *weakening* of a word; but in fact, it *increases* the force.[147] The following are examples of figurative language in Jude: (1) metonymy in v 3 ("the faith" = the saving Gospel message); (2) metaphor in v 3 ("fighting" for the faith); (3) adjunction in v 6 ("angels . . . he kept"); (4) irony in v 6 (the angels who did not "keep" are now being "kept"); (5) reflexio in v 6 ("keep"); (6) hysteresis in v 9 (a syntactical "following after" regarding Michael's action); (7) simile in v 10 ("as unreasoning beasts"); (8) metaphor in v 11 ("walk . . . abandon . . . perish"); (9) antimerism in v 11 (a series of ungodly types—Cain, Balaam, and Korah—are enumerated instead of the use of a collective statement);[148] (10) a string of graphic metaphors in vv 12–13 to depict the *houtoi;* (11) pleonasm in v 15;[149] (12) metaphor in v 20 ("building yourselves"); (13) two instances of hyperbole in v 23 (by force "snatching out of the fire" and "hating even the garment stained by the flesh"); (14) antonomasia in v 24 ("his glory" = God's name); and (15) metaphor in v 24 ("keeping you from falling").[150]

Through the stylistic effects of a distinctive vocabulary, marked poetic diction, synonymous and antithetical parallelism, rampant use of triplets, vivid imagery, and figures of speech, the writer clothes his message with elegance and force. Past paradigms of apostasy are graphically called forth to serve as a warning— negatively to those who presently threaten the Christian community, and positively to the faithful themselves, that they might learn from God's dealings in the past and remain firmly established in the love and mercy of God.

The Apocalyptic Mode in Jude

The Babylonian exile marked a significant turn in Jewish perspective. It also brought about a whole gamut of permutations which would fall under the rubric of "Judaism." Although pre- and postexilic OT writings mirror bits of an "apocalyptic"[151] perspective, the "classical" apocalyptic perspective is essentially postexilic.[152] From this point on, the burning question for the Jew was whether the Lord had forsaken His people.[153]

The rise of apocalyptic literature has been accounted for by G. E. Ladd[154] on the basis of three historical developments: (1) the emergence of the Hasidim, the "righteous remnant," (2) the failure of a restored kingdom of Israel to be manifest, set within a context of political, cultural, and social upheaval, and (3) the cessation of prophecy. In light of these factors, a goal of apocalyptic writers was to give literary expression to the sentiments of their day. Borrowing from Hebrew notions of the past, they transmuted traditionally received material into new conceptions. Attempting to make sense of the future in light of the present, they envisaged eschatological intervention by God. Their writings, considered a type of "crisis literature,"[155] reflect a deep concern for the relationship between events in heaven and events in the world, and hence, preoccupation with theophany, vindication, mysteries, angels and demons, and the supramundane.

In the attempt to translate history (which was not bringing salvation), several obstacles confronted the Jewish mind: interpreting the Lord's punitive will (Babylon) as well as the prolonged Gentile domination (Persia, Greece, then Syria). Thus, by the second century B.C., history was being preempted.[156] Earlier, we observe the Chronicler's view of history—a distinctly Hebrew perception. Now a shift has taken place toward a more Hellenistic point of view through the Maccabeans. Whereas a younger Israel had written faith-inducing historiography (in contrast to the mythological representation of history of surrounding pagan cultures), a change was occurring. To admit that the Lord's purpose was being fulfilled while Persian and Greek rule were creeping by with agonizing slowness was to concede that the Lord was uninterested in His chosen covenant people. One means of solving this dilemma of perspective was a transferral of locus to angelic beings. Angels, not God, became the cause of the present disorder. Hence, for example, we note the prominence of the "Watchers" in 1 Enoch, the Testaments of the Twelve Patriarchs, and Jubilees. The root of evil, based on a model such as the "prince of Persia" or the "prince of Greece" in the book of Daniel, was celestial. Therefore, God could not intervene until things had run their course, based on a heavenly timetable.

For the Jewish apocalypticist[157] the veil which prevented one from understanding was the Flood. Those living prior to this catastrophic event, Enoch as an example, had greater access to divine secrets. Whereas, to the prophets, the exodus from Egypt marked a crucial turning point in Israel's history, to the apocalypticist, the Flood was pivotal. The apocalypticist's view of history differs from that of the prophets in its justification of the mundane events of the present. Whereas the prophets portrayed Yahweh as working *through* the kingdoms of the earth (Assyria, Babylon, etc.) to bring about His purpose, the later apocalypticist[158] viewed deliverance and the fulfillment of the divine purpose as *suprahistorical*, necessitating divine intervention.

1 Enoch 6–11 furnishes a paradigm to illustrate the importance of apocalyptic for the study of the NT and Jude in particular. This material is an extrapolation of the brief allusion in Gen. 6:1–4 to the *běnē hā'elōhîm* and the statement in Gen. 5:24 that Enoch walked with *'elōhîm*.[159] From a Jewish standpoint, apocalyptic furnishes imagery necessary to articulate any situation where affairs seem out of control and sin is rampant.[160] The story of the "Watchers" supplies a mythic paradigm to illustrate a type of situation which might reoccur at various times. Evil may be rampant on the earth, however we can be assured of the place of *judgment* and ultimate vindication that have been prepared in heaven.

The underlying value of the apocalyptic mode[161]—one that early Christianity inherited from its Jewish forbears[162]—is its mirroring of the transcendent perspective in its wrestling with the problem of theodicy. Apocalyptic is rooted in the conviction that the present world is passing away. Yet, whereas the epistle of Jude utilizes apocalyptic themes and imagery, the writer's perspective is clarified in his prophetic statement in the letter's doxology, *pro pantos tou aiōnos kai nyn kai eis pantas tous aiōnas*. Aligning himself with the OT prophetic view of history, he sees the past, the present, and the future as all working toward the consummation of the divine purpose, unlike the perspective of apocalyptic. The present situation as well as the future purpose work for the glory of the transcendent Lord.

In addition to the characteristic presence and prominence in Jewish apocalyptic of angels and the revering of mediatory antediluvian patriarchs, one also encounters in this literature recurrent allusions to the cosmic order and solar phenomena—phenomena which, as P. Minear[163] has observed, are not fully appreciated by the modern reader and have prompted not a few scholars to go outside the OT for explanation.[164] While the derivation of the apocalyptic genre is considered to be owing to a combination of two factors—a Jewish matrix and Hellenistic influence—one need not go outside a Hebrew milieu. L. Morris[165] writes: "Nobody seems to have disposed of the stubborn fact that apocalyptic is a Jewish and Christian phenomenon." Minear agrees, maintaining that our measuring-stick for apocalyptic language in the NT should be the OT.[166]

Several recurrent phenomena of apocalyptic depiction of the cosmos are cited by Minear: (1) the God of Israel has created the solar entities—the sun, moon, and stars; (2) God, as Creator, retains power over these; (3) any worship of these bodies becomes idolatry; (4) due to the divine Source of light, judgment on evil takes the form, symbolically, of falling stars; and (5) a clear distinction between light and darkness in the Genesis account is made. The NT writer, as argued by Minear, is a legitimate successor to the OT prophet in utilizing the lessons of the cosmos. Rebellion in heaven and warfare, assumed in the background of Jude's epistle, are cosmic in scope. The association between divine judgment and cosmic changes among the solar phenomena, crucial to Jewish apocalyptic[167] and assumed in the polemic of Jude, is by no means foreign to the NT. Indeed these alterations, epitomizing sudden and total catastrophe, occur in the Synoptic Gospels,[168] Acts,[169] the Epistle to the Hebrews,[170] and the Revelation.[171]

Rather than stepping outside of a Hebrew milieu, one can observe that thinking in terms of solar bodies is very much part of the OT. In fact, solar bodies have a distinctly theological significance.[172] The heavens declare the glory of God (Ps. 19:1–16). God has established the orbits of the luminaries so that succession of days and seasons is ascribed to Him (Ps. 74:16; 104:19). The regularity of sunrise and sunset are reminders of God's steadfast love (Ps. 136:7–9; Jer. 31:35). As Creator, God possesses the authority to alter aspects of the solar phenomena. For example, He can alter the shadow on the sundial (Isa. 38:8), or He can command the sun not to rise, sealing off light from the stars (Job 9:7).[173] God Himself is viewed in the OT as the true sun (Ps. 84:11; Isa. 60:19–20). Therefore, light is blessing (Ps. 84:11; Isa. 30:26; 60:1–2, 19–20) while darkness is typical of woe and curse (Isa. 13:10; 45:7; Jer. 15:8–9; Ezek. 32:7; Joel 2:2, 10, 31; Amos 8:9; Mic. 3:6; Zeph. 1:15). The division of light and dark is almost immediate in the Genesis creation account. Given the testimony in the scriptures as to the cosmos, it should not come as a surprise that the worship of solar phenomena in the OT is idolatry and expressly forbidden (2 Kings 23:5,11; Jer. 8:1–3; Ezek. 8:16).

Two examples of material from the prophetic corpus are further evidence that OT "theology determines cosmology."[174] Solar imagery is used to depict the effects of divine judgment which is to fall. The first is an oracle delivered against Babylon found in Isa. 13. YHWH Ṣĕbāʾôt, the divine warrior (v 4), is assembling an army and weapons of wrath against the exalted Babylonians (vv 4–5) in a way that will cause men's hearts to melt (v 7). So great will be the terror and cruelty of His anger against sinners (vv 8–9), it will affect the very sun, moon, and stars of the heavens (v 10). The heavens themselves will be shaken due to God's wrath (v 13). The glory of Babylon's pride will be utterly destroyed, to be no more just as Sodom and Gomorrah (v 19).

The oracle of Joel 2 contains both elements of judgment and redemption. On the one hand, the Day of the Lord spells gloom and dread (vv 2,11), "a day of darkness and gloom, . . . clouds and blackness" (v 2). As judgment approaches, "the earth shakes, the sky trembles, the sun and moon are darkened, and the stars no longer shine" (v 10). The prophet on the other hand declares the redemptive side of the Day of the Lord, in which time God would pour out His Spirit on all people. The accompanying imagery is similar: "I will show wonders in the heavens and on the earth. . . . The sun will be turned to darkness and the moon to blood before the coming of the great and dreadful day of the Lord." As depicted in Joel 2, Israel stands in the valley of decision (3:14). The cosmic imagery serves to help illustrate the choice lying before her: "The sun and moon will be darkened, and the stars no longer shine. The Lord will roar from Zion and thunder from Jerusalem; the earth and sky will tremble. Nevertheless, the Lord will be a refuge for His people, a stronghold for the people of Israel" (vv 15–16).[175]

Yet another feature specific to Jewish apocalyptic and deserving of mention, which occurs in Jude as well, is the notion of cosmic rebellion. This is closely related to the aforementioned solar phenomena. In Jude, the angels who rebel and lose their heavenly abode are cast as *asteres planētai*, "wandering stars" (v 13), an allusion which would trigger immediate association with 1 Enoch.[176] Chapters 6–11 of 1 Enoch revive and aggrandize an ancient notion regarding the polarity of good and evil and would appear to be a midrash[177] on Gen. 6:1–4, drawing perhaps from mythological parallels in Ugaritic, Babylonian, Hittite, and Hurrian materials. P. D. Hanson[178] has noted the proliferation of such myths in the second century B.C. and attributes this occurrence to two factors: the loss of nationhood (with its resultant pessimism over the historical process) and the power of oriental myth. Within apocalyptic mythology, a frequent pattern tends to emerge: (1) war erupts in heaven, often depicted in astral terms, followed by (2) a spilling over of this foment to the earth, then culminating in (3) ultimate vindication and punishment by the king of heaven. This scenario is assumed by Jude in his polemic.

In noting an early but brief veneration of apocalyptic

pseudepigrapha in the first and second centuries, J. T. Milik[179] suggested that early Christians had ascribed to an Essene canon of writings. However, a more suitable explanation for the use of apocalyptic genre in early Christianity would be that Christians quite naturally followed in the literary tradition of their Jewish forerunners.

> The penumbre of the Christian prophetic movement, therefore, would be almost bound to include certain people (whether originally Essenes, Pharisees, or of some more mixed or obscure allegiance) . . . who could think of no better service to the new faith than to adapt existing apocalypses to make them support Christianity.[180]

The themes of theophany and judgment, as well as the antithesis of the ungodly and the faithful, constitute a thread running throughout Jewish apocalyptic literature. For the writer of Jude, the borrowing of these motifs serves a useful function. They remind the audience of the divine ability to "preserve": God is committed to keep the faithful in His love and mercy while at the same time reserving the ungodly for certain judgment.

In sum, we have attempted to gain understanding into the apocalyptic mindset. Traces of apocalyptic are detected in the oracles of the OT prophets, however they come to fuller expression in the "classical" apocalyptic of the intertestamental period. Salvation for the Jew of the Hellenistic era had not yet come to Israel; through his writings, the apocalypticist was seeking to provide explanation for continuing Gentile domination over Palestine. Among the features of this apocalyptic genre which we have noted in particular are its elaborate angelology, allusion to antediluvian patriarchs, an abundance of cosmic-solar imagery, and the notion of cosmic rebellion. While much of the influence which helped shape apocalyptic can be attributed to Israel's contact with Hellenistic culture, many of the apocalyptic motifs have their roots in a distinctly Hebrew way of thinking and are amply borne out in the OT.[181] Although Jude is not necessarily endorsing the breadth of Jewish apocalyptic theology, his mode is distinctly apocalyptic. This method is designed to counter the effects of his opponents as well as have a strategic impact on his audience for reasons not expressly stated in the epistle. We may grant the possibility that Jude's readers—or perhaps even some of the adversaries themselves—were in some way devoted to apocalyptic literature and therefore open to persuasion by the use of familiar literary conventions in the epistle.

Summary: Literary-Rhetorical Artifice in Jude

The epistle of Jude mirrors a sharp and calculated polemic against certain opponents *(houtoi)* who are posing a threat to the faithful *(hymeis)*. By means of unusual verbal economy, apocalyptic force, strategic use of catchwords and word-play, synonymous as well as antithetical parallelism and rhyme, triadic illustration, and rhetorical skill, the writer associates past paradigms of ungodliness with his opponents of the present. There exists throughout the short epistle a fundamental tension between the ungodly and the faithful. Both poles of this contrast are being "reserved" for their appointed end—the *houtoi* for divine retribution and the *hymeis* for divine inheritance.

Attending to the notable literary features in Jude provides the reader with an important basis on which to proceed with the letter's interpretation. The writer's method indeed is indivisible from his message. With passion, force, and eloquence, he engages his audience. We become witnesses to a literary-rhetorical artist at work.

THE POLEMIC OF JUDE: A THEOLOGICAL ANALYSIS

Jude's Opponents

A general consensus prevailing among commentators of this century is that the adversaries of Jude are gnostic or protognostic in nature.[182] The view of W. Grundmann, expressed in his commentary on Jude and 2 Peter, is representative: "In the ancient church up through modern exegesis, there have not been enough attempts to correlate the false teachers of the Jude epistle with a particular gnostic system. . . . It is with precursors (to the later sophisticated gnostic systems) that we have to do in the letter of Jude, yet the fundamental nature of this conflict is already apparent."[183] The assumption of a "gnostic" scheme, which permeates scholarly approaches to Jude, might serve as a prime example of how the letter has suffered from its association to 2 Peter.[184] One need only examine the letter of 1 Corinthians to see many of the supposed "gnostic"/"protognostic" features cited traditionally in Jude (and 2 Peter)—features that are already prevalent in A.D. 55, scarcely twenty years after the birth of the church. Some of the excesses that Paul is obligated to address include: sexual license (5:1–13; 6:9–20; 10:8); division (1:10–17); arrogance due to a distorted view of gnosis, sophia, and spiritual mysteries (2:1–16; 5:2; 8:1–13; 12:1–14:49); a disdain for the bodily or material (6:9–20; 7:4–6,34; 15:1–58); abuse of personal freedom (7:20–24; 8:1–13; 10:15–33; 11:2–34; 14:1–40); and a questioning of his apostolic authority (4:1–21; 9:1–27). W. Schmithals[185] has argued persuasively for the appearance—in the midfirst century—of protognostic tendencies among Corinthian believers. Whether or not one accepts Schmithal's basic thesis, we need not look any later than A.D. 55 to see evidence of fertile soil in which later heretical features may have germinated. The assumption that Jude reflects early or mid second-century (i.e., gnostic) phenomena is made virtually without challenge.

In contrast to the bulk of commentators who see in Jude only denunciation and invective, we are quick to point out that the epistle was written with a view of exhorting the faithful to press on, and not merely excoriating those who rebel. A further clarification of Jude's aim would be to determine whether his opponents are lapsed believers. And if he views apostasy as possible, what antidotes are offered?

From the epistle we may gather a portrait of the opponents. They are foremost antinomian in spirit, denying the basis for all moral authority (v 4). They pervert the faith, having crept in from the side (v 4) under false pretenses.[186] They participate in the love-feasts (v 12), which evidently were not yet separated from the Eucharist.[187] Morally degenerate (vv 4, 8, 16, 18, 19 and implied in 7), they are rebellious, arrogant, and blasphemous (vv 8, 9, 15, 16, 18), speaking slanderous and harsh words against God with their mouths (v 16).[188] They presumptuously scoff at angels, failing to discern the realities of authority in the created order. Divisive (v 19) and worldly (v 19), they are void of the Spirit (v 19), a pronouncement probably intended to strike at a false sense of spirituality engendered by estatic experience (v 8).[189] It should be noted that the paradigms of vv 5, 6, 7, and 11 are examples of recession and apostasy; each in its own way left a normative status and was disenfranchised. Israel, after salvation from Egypt, fell away. The angels, occupying an exalted habitation, chose to rebel and were consequently dispossessed. Sodom and Gomorrah, giving themselves to utter corruption, became no more. Cain, made in the image of God, destroyed the image of God and thus perished. A bona fide prophet,[190] Balaam hired himself out for selfish gain. And Korah, having stirred up many of Israel's leaders, convincing them to join in deserting Moses, was immediately destroyed. Hence, the paradigms are meant to warn not only

Jude's opponents but the faithful as well. This would imply that the *houtoi* may well have been those who deserted the faith.[191]

There remain several other pieces of evidence in Jude which would suggest that these were former believers. The *hapax . . . deuteron* construction of v 5 is a matter of interest. The proper understanding of v 5 is that Israel, no less than the very people of God, was delivered *"once for all"* from Egypt. They were delivered once, *not to be delivered again*, i.e., a second time. The reason for this was that Israel "knew all things," and therefore incurred a sure judgment. This is what links the readers to Israel in the mind of Jude. He can thus write: *Hypomnēsai de hymas boulomai, eidotas [hymas] panta.* (The abiding maxim is that to whom much has been given, much is required.) The tendency of most commentators has been to examine the *panta* of v 5 as if it would relate to apostolic tradition, orthodox doctrine, and a general "early Catholic" scenario. However, the issue of v 5 is not the *doctrine* having been given once for all, rather the *people of God* having been delivered once for all. Here one encounters the dilemma when an "early Catholic reading" is automatically applied to the text, yielding a quite different result than what the text is seeming to say. If it is assumed that the epistle is mirroring second-century phenomena,[192] then faithfulness to the past apostolic tradition, as opposed to a warning against apostasy, is "read out" of v 5.

However, apostasy need not be viewed as a singularly second-century occurrence. It is rather a proclivity which runs parallel to the growth of the Christian community and which was manifest almost from the beginning. Most heresiologists consider Simon of Acts 8 as a precursor to the deviations from the Christian faith which burgeoned in the second and third centuries. One can assume from Paul's exhortation in Rom. 16:17 that heretical teaching was already in the early 50's[193] a potential threat.[194] In both the Colossian and Ephesian epistles the apostle implies that false teaching is indicative of those who have lost their connection to the head of the church.[195] In the midfirst century, Paul could warn the Corinthians: "If anyone does not love the Lord, let him be anathema" (1 Cor. 16:22).[196]

Another indication that the opponents of Jude were former believers is the contrast between "these" and "those" running throughout the letter. *Hymeis* with cognate forms and *houtoi* are important catchwords in Jude. They occur eleven and eight times respectively and form the link between Jude's use of OT types and the interpretation of these types. Past paradigms of certain judgment speak prophetically to the present danger. While the *houtoi* are being "reserved" *(tērein)* for judgment, the faithful are being "reserved" *(tērein, phylassein)*[197] by God for glory.

Yet a third hint at the nature of those threatening the faithful in Jude is the metaphor employed in v 12: "fruitless trees in late autumn, twice dead and uprooted" *(dendra phthinopōrina akarpa dis apothanonta ekrizōthenta)*. It is not clear in what sense the trees are "twice dead." J. B. Mayor[198] notes that the primary characteristic denoted by words containing the *phthino-* prefix is not a sudden destruction, rather a perishing due to inner decay, not unlike the sense of *phthora*, "rottenness."[199] Moreover, "late autumn," at least in some parts of the world, would not be the supposed fruit-bearing season; it would be well past with winter approaching. Bauckham's suggestion that "twice dead" would correlate with the "second death" after the last judgment[200] does not fit. The two verbs Jude uses in v 12 are Aorist, implying that the opponents are already "twice dead." However, one possibility is that these have sadly returned to the death that characterized their *former life*. Although it is difficult to be conclusive in identifying those in v 12, the suggestion that they have departed from the faith cannot be dismissed.[201] What is clear about this metaphor is that it (1) calls to mind the imagery of 1 Enoch 2–5:

> Examine and observe everything—and the trees, how all their leaves appear as if they wither and had fallen, except . . . trees whose leaves do not fall but the old foliage remains for about two to three years until the new leaves come.[202]

> Observe how the verdant trees are covered with leaves and they bear fruit.[203]

and (2) is a picture of the ungodly, paralleling the previous image: clouds unable to offer any rain. In both cases, the outward form is present, yet neither has the inherent capacity to produce.

Thus far we have attempted to set forth an understanding of the opponents in Jude. We have argued that these are not the second-century gnostic variety based on an "early Catholic" understanding of Jude, but that they are quite possibly those roughly contemporary with the apostolic era who have departed the faith, and, hence, who pose a serious threat to the faithful due to their stealth (v 4). In spite of Jude's passionate cry, forceful denunciations, expressions of woe, and fervent admonitions, his view of falling away is one of willful deliberation. Israel of old should have known—and hence, chosen—better. The angels deliberated and chose disenfranchisement. Sodom and Gomorrah sank to the lowest level of depravity. Cain had every opportunity, as Abel, to please God. Balaam, though receiving mixed reviews in the OT, acquiesced to the very selling of *himself* (demonstrated by the extent to which God went in seeking to speak to him: via a jackass). Korah was not content to resist Moses alone; he brought with him as many Israelite leaders as he could muster. Therefore, seeing that the human will is actively and *fully* involved in the decision to hold fast to the faith, Jude's audience need not be shaken by the sobering paradigms of judgment if they indeed desire to be established. Once again, we see the tactical and rhetorical value of Jude's catchwords—e.g., the word-play using *tērein* and *phylassein*, the greeting (the believers are *ēgapēmenoi, tetērēmenoi* and *klētoi*), the frequent use of *agapē*,[204] the building imagery in v 20, and the anticipating of mercy (v 21).

If there is any doubt left on the part of the readers, Jude concludes with a doxology: "Now to Him Who is able to keep *(phylassein)* you from stumbling and present you faultless before His presence with great joy." Persevering requires action; the faithful are to struggle, indeed "agonize" (*epagōnizesthai*, v 3), for their faith. Yet, they can rest in God's ability to keep them. At work, then, is a paradox—a marvelous but mysterious tension. Though stated, it is not comprehended. It is a state "whose limits may be charted, but whose depths cannot be plumbed."[205]

In sum, once the gnostic grid normally imposed upon Jude is set aside, the opponents at hand may simply be viewed as bold libertines[206]—perhaps those who have deserted the faith—who are, due to their stealth, posing a threat to the faithful.[207] By reading second-century phenomena into Jude, we miss much of what might help to illuminate the scenario in which the first-century Christian communities found themselves. At this point, it is necessary to examine at some length what has traditionally been a controlling assumption of scholarship in approaching the epistle of Jude. It has become customary to view Jude as a specimen of what would be labeled as "early Catholicism."

Jude's Theology

It has already been suggested that Jude has suffered under the shadow of 2 Peter. This outcome, which has significant implications for the letter's historical setting, literary style, and theology, is owing at least in part to the influence of Ernst Käsemann, who concluded in 1952 that "the Second Epistle of Peter is from beginning to end a document expressing an early catholic viewpoint and is perhaps the most dubious writing in the canon."[208] Käsemann encountered two different views of church organization, tradition, and concept of the Spirit in the NT—one root reaching back into Jewish Christianity and another distinguished from primitive Christianity.[209] For Käsemann, "early Catholicism" meant "that transition from earliest Christianity to the so-called ancient Church, which is completed with the disappearance of the imminent expectation."[210]

Käsemann's thesis, firmly entrenched for almost four decades among students of the New Testament, remains for the most part unchallenged. Most attempts to analyze Jude, with few exceptions, have subsumed the epistle under the "early Catholic" rubric. R. J. Bauckham is one of the few to offer a dissenting opinion. Writes Bauckham:

> In reality, it is only because it is first assumed that Jude is "early Catholic" that it is read in an "early Catholic" sense. The "early Catholic" reading of Jude is a reading between-the-lines which the text of Jude itself does not require. It has blinded scholars to the evidence that Jude really belongs to a quite different theological milieu: that of Palestinian apocalyptic Christianity. . . . To suppose that such an approach to the problem of false teaching could not have occurred in the earliest period of the church is historical romanticism.[211]

Bauckham's remarks are quite useful in demonstrating that much of what falls under the umbrella of "early Catholicism" in Jude is built upon a mistaken notion concerning the writer's polemical approach. Given the "early Catholic" bias as a starting point, the reader is quite naturally inclined to (1) fail to appreciate that Jude's style of argumentation is at home in apocalyptic Jewish-Christian circles, (2) neglect the positive argument of the letter (e.g., vv 3,17,20–23) while focusing on the writer's denunciations, and (3) ignore the pastoral concern the writer exhibits for his readers, even with respect to the more hardened among his adversaries (*eleate . . . sōzete . . . eleate . . .*, vv. 22–23)![212]

The "early Catholic" epistles are purported to reflect the institutionalization of the church several generations removed from the apostles. In this literature, one is said to encounter the codification of beliefs into creedal confessions, a normative "rule of faith," a fading of the Parousia hope, and a general pervading post-apostolic mentality.[213] K. H. Schelke[214] sees numerous evidences in Jude which reflect a second-century setting:

- v 3—the "faith once delivered" as pertaining to apostolic teaching several generations removed
- v 4—reference to the ungodly who were "formerly recorded for judgment" as pertaining to statements made earlier by the apostles
- v 12—allusion to the love-feasts as a reflection of a later defilement of the sacraments
- v 17—remembrance of the words of the apostles as pertaining to an earlier era[215]
- vv 4,8,12,18,22–23—indications that a full-fledged heresy is growing

Schelke's verdict is unequivocal: "The letters (2 Peter and Jude) say themselves that the generations of the church are past. . . . The apostolic era is closed and lies behind."[216] E. M. Sidebottom[217] similarly concludes that Jude emits definite traces of second-century influence. He cites as evidence (1) the name of "Jude," which, as the brother of Jesus, would have carried considerable weight as a counter-blast against the gnostics, (2) an allusion to Jude found in the Gospel of Thomas, and (3) v 17, in which the writer purportedly shows himself to be disassociated from the apostles. For H. Windisch[218] the epistle of Jude is "catholic" inasmuch as the opponents of Jude are threatening the *whole* church, a decidedly second-century development.

The postapostolic classification of Jude continues to hold sway among scholars. In attempting to locate the confrontation between Jude and his opponents and thereby distinguish between first-century distortions and second-century gnosticism, D. J. Rowston[219] claims that the epistle "cannot be confined to early Palestinian Christianity," rather it must be consigned to an atmosphere in which antinomianism and gnosticism are at home, preferably at the turn of the century. The letter of Jude, concludes Rowston, represents an attempt "to be apostolic in the postapostolic age."[220] More recently, F. Hahn,[221] noting the strong emphasis of "tradition" in Jude 3,17, and 20, consigns the epistle as well to the postapostolic era. He writes:

. . . es liegt die vielleicht in ihren Konzequenzen noch nicht immer klar gesehene, aber praktisch doch schon gewonnene Erkenntnis vor, dass die "apostolische" Zeit definitiv abgeschlossen ist und dass auch die unmittelbar "nachapostolische" Periode schon bald zu Ende geht, so dass jetzt das vorhandene Traditionsgut in seiner fundamentalen Bedeutung festgehalten und in seinem Bestand gesichert werden muss.

[Even though the implications might not yet be clearly seen, there is a practical awareness that the apostolic era is surely closed and that the immediate postapostolic period is soon ending. Hence, now the present tradition-material must be preserved in its basic meaning and form.]

The main anchor for a second-century dating, according to Hahn, is that heresy *requires* a "fixed confession of faith."[222]

The extent to which the "early Catholic" designation has been a controlling assumption in New Testament studies is perhaps illustrated best by a statement of D. J. Harrington. He writes: "It was the genius of the second-century church to combine the various solutions presented in Luke-Acts, the Pastorals, Ephesians, Jude and 2 Peter in a truly 'catholic' way."[223] The pervasiveness of the "early Catholic" bias has led one scholar to counter: "The whole concept of early Catholicism as New Testament scholars have used it to illuminate the history of first-century Christianity is ripe for radical reexamination. It has undoubtedly promoted too simple a picture of the development of Christianity. . . . Even if the usual theory of early Catholicism is accepted, Jude's right to be included in the category must be seriously questioned."[224]

On what basis, then, given the scholarly consensus of placing Jude, at the very earliest, at the turn of the century or, preferably, in the second century, should we attempt to locate Jude's opponents and hence his theology? Is an "early Catholic" reading of the epistle a reading "between the lines," or does the text indeed support such a notion? If an alternative view is tenable, several factors require examination: (1) the writer's christology, (2) the writer's use of "the faith," (3) the presence or absence of institutionalization in the letter, (4) the presence of any "fading Parousia hope," and (5) the epistle's Jewish character.

Not unlike the epistle of James, Jude is rarely cited for its christology. Yet the epistle exhibits a definite christology—one which, at first glance, might evade the reader.[225] *Kyrios* occurs within Jude's mere twenty-five verses five times (vv 4,5,14,21,25), i.e., once every five verses, and is used of Jesus four times. Moreover, the Jesus-as-Lord portrayal is strengthened by three additional elements: the *kyrios-doulos* analogy implicit in v 1, the "only God as Savior" epithet of v 25, and the description of Jesus in v 4 as both *kyrios* and *despotēs*,[226] conveying the notions of "legitimate authority" as well as arbitrariness.[227] Third, as J. Fossum[228] has argued, the text of v 5[229] can support the notion that *kyrios*-Jesus is the one *laon ek gēs Aigyptou sōsas*.[230] A similar example is 1 Cor. 10:1–5, where Jesus is also associated with Israel in a context of disobedience.[231] One consequence of ascribing to Jesus the *kyrios*-title is that the NT writers can apply to Him OT passages which speak of Yahweh (note, e.g., John 1:1; 1 Cor. 8:6; Col. 1:16 and Heb. 1:18).[232]

J. A. Fitzmyer[233] has pointed to evidence that among Jews of the first century B.C., *YHWH* was being called "Lord," something unthinkable historically to any Jew. Hence, the use of *kyrios* in the NT of Jesus is all the more significant. It underscores His kingly and transcendent status. In the final analysis, the strong *kyrios*-christology[234] found in Jude can well fit a mid first-century milieu and certainly agrees with that of Paul. It bespeaks foremost *sovereignty* and exaltation (cf. Acts 2:36; Rom. 10:9; and Phil. 2:9), not *lateness*. Jude's concluding doxology of praise accentuates this notion: *monǭ theǭ sōtēri hēmōn dia Iēsou Christou tou kyriou hēmōn doxa megalōsynē kratos kai exousia* (v 25). Majesty is suggestive of sovereignty, authority, and rule; dominion is the express realm of that rule extended, a royal "province," so to speak; power relates to one's ability to exercise that rule. All the honors that accompany the title of *theos* and *kyrios* are transferred to Jesus. The confession of Jesus as Lord (cf. 1 Cor. 12:3)[235] is a decidedly *first-century* feature of the church, indeed, an early development.

It is customary for commentators to treat *hē pistis* of vv 3 and 20 as a reflection of "early Catholic" crystallization of apostolic teaching into creedal confessions.[236]

Agapētoi, pasan spoudēn poioumenos graphein hymin peri tēs koinēs hēmōn sōtērias anagkēn eschon grapsai hymin parakalōn epagōnizesthai tę̄ hapax paradotheisę̄ tois hagiois pistei. (v 3).

hymeis de, agapētoi, epoikodomountes heautous tē hagiōtatę̄ hymōn pistei, en pneumati hagiǭ proseuchomenoi (v 20)

The common assumption is that while *hē pistis* in Pauline literature refers to "the Gospel," i.e., the message that demands faith, in Jude it represents a normative "deposit" of tradition, an "assent to the dogmas of orthodoxy."[237] Is the reference to *hē pistis* in Jude 3 and 20 the creedal form of the second century? Based on the text itself, what is the evidence for our interpretation? There is no argument based on the text of Jude which *requires* that *pistis* be different in meaning than that of the other NT writers.[238] The imperative of Jude to "remember the words already spoken by the apostles" (v 17) need not be interpreted as a statement of *distance* between the writer and the apostles, rather it fits naturally as an exhortation by a brother of Jesus and James who was not one of the twelve apostles—indeed one who was not a believer (John 7:5; note the absence of Jesus' brothers in Acts 1:14), yet who in humility considers himself a *doulos* (v 1) of Jesus. *Mnēsthēte*, a catchword of both Jude and 2 Peter, does not place sixty to one hundred years between the audience and the apostles. To the contrary, *elegon hymin* [*hoti*] in v 18 requires that the apostles had ministered *personally* to those in Jude's audience. A responsible reading of vv 17–18 disallows us from placing a distance of several generations between the apostles and the readers. The implication of the text is that the readers themselves were taught by the apostles. The *hapax paradotheisē tois hagiois* faith[293] of v 3 is the teaching which was delivered "once for all," not "once upon a time." The link between vv 3 and 5 is one of *permanence,* not "pastness." The foundation need not—indeed *cannot*—be laid again. Thus v 3 is consistent with the *hapax ek gēs Aigyptou sōsas* in v 5. An "early Catholic" reading of these verses simply rides roughshod over their plain sense.

The imperative *mnēsthēte* points to the inherent *danger* in *forgetting,* not a particular *time-lapse.* The call to remember (*mnēmoneuein*) appears uniformly throughout the New Testament, whether in the Gospels, Acts, the Epistles, or the Apocalypse.[240] It should be noted that within the Pauline corpus we find numerous formulations which take on the form of a creedal confession. These include 1 Cor. 8:6, 15:3–4, Rom. 1:3–4, Eph. 4:5, 1 Tim. 3:16 and 2 Tim. 2:11–13.[241] Such formulations of "faith" were used in the *early* church as well, from the very beginning.[242]

Based on a cursory reading of the epistle, one notices a total *absence* of any hint at institutionalization of the church. No reference is made to bishops, ecclesial authority, or governing. To the contrary, the writer makes a direct appeal to his *readers.* It is Jude's *audience* which is to deal with the danger of the heretics. *They* are to remember, *they* are to consider the examples of old, *they* are to discern and respond accordingly (note the emphasis on *hymeis-hymas-hymōn* in the letter: eleven times in twenty-five verses). Governing terminology surfaces only once—in v 12—in the verb *poimainein;* however, it is used of the opponents themselves, not the spiritual authorities. In contrast to Jude, the Epistles of Ignatius (early second century) offer a glimpse into a different type of church administration—one in which the role of the "bishop" has begun to emerge in the guarding of orthodoxy:

spoudasōmen oun mē antitassesthai tō episkopō, hina ōmen theou hypo-tassomenoi.[243]

[We are zealous not to resist the bishop in order that we submit to God.]

pantes tō episkopō akoloutheite, hōs Iēsous Christos tō patri, kai tō presbyteriō hōs tois apostolois.[244]

[You must all follow the bishop, as Jesus Christ followed the Father; and follow the presbytery as you would the apostles.]

Jude, it should be noted, does not appeal to the *episkopos,* nor to the *presbyterion.* Rather his appeal, already observed, reaches directly to his hearers. Moreover, Jude calls *directly* upon the apostles, unlike Ignatius, whose claim for authority is more indirect: *hōs tois apostolois.* If the letter is reflecting a second-century setting, the chief weapon in the writer's arsenal would most likely be the *office* with its vested authority. Yet the focus in Jude is not *ho episkopos* but *hē hapax paradotheisē tois hagiois pistis.*

The "fading Parousia hope," traditionally viewed as a hallmark of 2 Peter,[245] is considered a notable feature of the "early Catholic" era.

To the anger of the writer, the rejection of the primitive Christian hope has sunk to the level of derision . . . those fathers of the first Christian generation who still fervently expected the Parousia are dead, and the world goes on in the same way. . . . The whole community is embarrassed and disturbed by the fact of the delay of the Parousia.[246]

According to Käsemann there are no opponents to the imminent Parousia expectation until the postapostolic era, since all early Christians held to the Parousia hope. Hence Jude and 2 Peter cannot mirror a first-century church.

This concern for the delay in the Parousia, is absent from the apostolic fathers. The polemic of Jude, on the other hand, presumes an impending Parousia. The tone of the writer is one of *imminence.* The judge is standing at the door. *Theophany* is a necessary counter to the opponents of Jude.

Although the Jewish character of the Jude epistle has been observed by some,[247] it has not been sufficiently appreciated in locating the epistle within a possible Jewish-Christian Palestinian milieu, and hence, within an earlier dating than most critics are willing to concede. Jude's use of OT types and Jewish pseudepigraphal source-material, the apocalyptic mode, and the likeness to the epistle of James all underscore the marked Jewishness of the letter.

D. J. Rowston[248] has offered an interesting hypothesis as to the use of apocalypticism in Jude, holding that the author, writing in the second century, was attempting to revive an apocalypticism found in Paul (cf., e.g., 1 Cor. 15:20–28, 51–58; 1 Thess. 4:14–18; 2 Thess. 2:3–12). According to Rowston, by employing apocalyptic material, the writer is seeking to "turn back the clock."[249] Rowston is actually building upon R. M. Grant's thesis that prophecy evolved into apocalyptic after the Maccabean War, with apocalypticism leading to gnosticism following the Jewish War.[250] Grant also traces a movement toward gnosticism in Paul.[251]

R. J. Bauckham's response to Rowston's proposal is worth noting. Bauckham points out that Jude is not *asserting* apocalyptic eschatology; rather, he merely takes it for granted, assuming his readers will do the same.[252] It is possible that Jude is using this device because it was important to his readers.[253]

Commentary on Jude, with a few exceptions, has not deviated much in the last one hundred years. To illustrate, Jude's use of 1 Enoch is normally explained from the standpoint of the *writer's* supposed esteem for the work. However, one must question whether his virtual verbatim citation from 1 Enoch (1 Enoch 1:9 = Jude 14–15) is evidence of *his* high regard for Enochic literature, or whether it is possible that Jude is borrowing source-material because some of his audience were devoted to this literature.[254] While fuller treatment of Jude's use of extrabiblical source-material is reserved for later discussion,[255] the subject should be introduced at this point, since we might expect to find a relationship—indeed a crucial one—between Jude's use of sources, which are integral to his literary strategy, and his theology.

The oldest of three pseudepigraphal writings attributed to the antediluvian patriarch whose transposition gave cause for considerable speculation, the Ethiopic Book of Enoch (= 1 Enoch) portrays Enoch, the son of Jared, as the recipient of cosmic secrets. He is granted understanding into the future of the world which is predestined by the Lord who judges the righteous and the wicked. Although a full analysis of the theology of 1 Enoch remains outside the scope of the task at hand, a survey of the five books comprising 1 Enoch is in order. Book 1, the Book of Watchers (chaps. 1–36), begins with theophany from Mount Sinai, describes final judgment which is to befall both the righteous and the wicked, and then leads into a quite lengthy narrative concerning the fallen angels and the strategies they employed in order to corrupt men dwelling on earth. Book 2, the Similitudes (chaps. 37–71), portrays once again the judgment which is to come, the Messiah (= "Elect One") in His role as Judge, ultimate punishment of the fallen angels, and the role of the Flood[256] in the judgment scenario. In the third part, the Book of Astronomical Writings (chaps. 72–82), Enoch is confronted with a divine timetable, regulated according to the sun, moon, and stars. Section 4, the Book of Dream Visions (chaps. 83–90), reveals to Enoch history from two particular perspectives: a view of the world running its course toward the judgment culminating in the Flood, and a history of Israel from Adam to the time of the Maccabeans. The last major section, the Epistle of Enoch (chaps. 91–105), is designed to exhort the faithful. Hope for the righteous is contrasted with woe for the wicked; comfort awaits the faithful while terror is pending for the ungodly.

Viewing 1 Enoch as a composite work, whose contents are dated as early as pre-Maccabean and as late as late first century A.D.,[257] and yet not seeking to discern five different "theologies" in the work, we would benefit from a sketch of Enochic ideas and motifs as they reflect a particular theological vantage point. Concerns for the writer are (1) the disenfranchised angels, (2) theophany (which, interestingly, introduces the apocalypse), (3) the constant antithesis between good and evil, (4) the certainty of final judgment (spelling woe and punishment for the wicked and vindication for the righteous), (5) a heavenly Messiah who sits on his throne for the purpose of judgment, (6) cosmic disorder which is linked to spiritual causes, and (7) closing admonitions to the faithful.[258]

In sum, we encounter all seven aspects listed above—to a greater or lesser extent—in the epistle of Jude. Though not necessarily incorporating the fanciful Enochic angelology, Jude nonetheless assumes this as background to v 6, taking for granted that his readers are familiar with this tradition. It is from chap. 1 of 1 Enoch, i.e., the introduction to the apocalypse, that Jude borrows a citation; his interest too is theophany. An important theme running throughout Jude is that of certain judgment; God preserves the righteous while certain woe is reserved for the wicked. Although the Jewish apocalyptic notion of Messiah cannot be compared to the christology found in the NT, the context for "the Elect One" in 1 Enoch and *kyrios* Jesus in Jude is similar: He comes to *judge*. In both, we also observe cosmic imagery which has its basis and out-workings in the spiritual realm. Throughout 1 Enoch and Jude, the reader is suspended between two poles: he observes on the one hand the sure punishment of the wicked while the righteous on the other hand are comforted by the expectation of mercy. And, finally, both works close with an admonition to the faithful. The effect of both writings is to cultivate faithfulness among the true believers who are surrounded by sinners and apostasy. If those in Jude's audience (or among his opponents) are familiar with, or perhaps devoted to, Enochic literature, his use of sources and theological motifs, reflecting manifest similarities to 1 Enoch, would naturally inform, and for the modern reader, help explain, his literary strategy in dealing with the urgent need at hand.[259]

Summary: The Polemic of Jude

In considering the basis for the long-standing view that Jude mirrors second-century phenomena, we have called attention to the nature of the adversaries being countered in the epistle. The character of the opponents is largely antinomian. Based on this characterization coupled with the selection of historical paradigms employed by the writer as a counterpolemic, we may take these to be apostate former believers, roughly contemporary with the apostolic era, who have departed the faith and thus pose a threat to the faithful. The text of Jude does not require that the opponents are a gnostic second-century variety. It has been noted that the seeds of heresy are already sufficiently present in the midfirst-century Christian community (e.g., in Corinth in A.D. 55).

In analyzing the portrait of the adversaries in Jude, we have sought to demonstrate the need for a thorough reexamination of the "early Catholic" thesis. An "early Catholic" reading of Jude has prevented most commentators from recognizing the Palestinian Jewish-Christian character of the epistle and thereby engendered a misunderstanding as to the letter's proper literary-cultural milieu. The writer is at home in Jewish-Christian apocalyptic circles and emanates genuine pastoral concern for and intimacy with his audience, an aspect virtually ignored in most commentary on the epistle. Contrary to the "early Catholic" view, Jude reflects not a trace of ecclesial institutionalization or codification of beliefs into creedal formulas. The authority of the Spirit rests with the individual believers, not an office of the church. Jude's appeal is directed to his readers; *they* are to respond accordingly. Moreover, the epistle presumes an imminency in the Lord's coming. Eschatology and ethics are closely associated in Jude. Specific weapons in the writer's theological arsenal include the authoritative apostolic tradition, a strong *kyrios*-christology, theophany, dualism (good versus evil), and the finality of judgment which is cosmic in proportion.

A further effect of the "early Catholic" reading of Jude was noted to be the neglect of the positive and pastoral side of the writer. His exhortation to his readers is initially positive as they are to contend earnestly for the faith. Following the paradigms of negative, faithless behavior from the past, the writer concludes with several positive admonitions which should set his readers apart from the opponents. Overriding themes in Jude include the love and mercy of God which are available to those who desire to be "kept."

CONCLUSION

In departure from the broadly accepted approach toward Jude which has traditionally subsumed the study of Jude under that of 2 Peter, we have sought to examine the literary rhetorical character of the epistle. This character is reflected in the writer's unique style, technique, structuring of material, and persuasive force. With regard to literary skill, the epistle of Jude exhibits a level of diction which draws comparison to the Attic dialect as well as an elevated use (by ancient standards) of rhetorical invention, composition, and style.

The literary form of Jude was noted to be epistolary, in spite of its strongly homiletic tone and structure, satisfying the requirements for the "epistolary situation" according to ancient canons of letter-form. More specifically, Jude can be subsumed under the heading of "word of exhortation" discourse, based on a discernible paradigm-citation/interpretation-exhortation pattern that can be traced in other Hellenistic Jewish and early Christian literature.

The contents of Jude strike the reader as highly stylized, didactic, liturgical, and rhetorical in character. The epistle, due to its manifest attempt to persuade and dissuade, belongs to the rhetorical category of deliberative discourse, although strong elements of epideictic and forensic argumentation are present. The writer employs both external and internal proofs to support his polemic against the opponents while exhorting the faithful. Examples of external proofs in Jude are the use of historical paradigms, documents, and a citation. Internal proofs include logical, ethical, and pathetic arguments to convince his audience.

The writer's syntax and vocabulary reflect a conscious rhetorical structure in the epistle. Jude's composite use of other texts is broadly "midrashic" in character, aimed at drawing parallels between ancient examples of ungodliness who incurred divine judgment and those who are presently perverting divine grace.

The elevated style of the epistle was observed to approximate the "rhetorical situation." Parallelism, antithesis, figures of speech, repetition, ornamentation, vivid symbolism, word- and sound-play abound in this very short work. Jude exploits particular apocalyptic conventions in characterizing the ungodly and their fate. Allusion to the angelic world, an antediluvian patriarch, cosmic phenomena, theophany, vindication of the faithful, and judgment of the wicked are to be found in the letter.

After having examined the form of Jude's polemic, we have sought to analyze its content. Contrary to the prevailing scholarly consensus, we observed the historical situation mirrored in Jude to be a first-century and not a second-century "gnostic" scenario. Here we noted that only decades after the resurrection the NT gives evidence of an embryonic emergence of heretical tendencies which would carry the potential of germinating into full-scale heresy. The paradigms, interpretations, and exhortations in Jude bespeak apostasy—a first-century variety—into which certain former believers had receded. An issue central to the interpretation of the epistle is not that *doctrine* has been once-and-for-all delivered, but rather that the *people of God* have been once-and-for-all delivered. A thorough reexamination of the "early Catholic" thesis, which imposes a second-century phenomenological grid upon the text of the epistle, is argued for. A date for Jude, which is roughly contemporary with the apostolic era, is maintained.

Evidence cited in favor of a first-century setting includes the writer's *kyrios*-christology, his allusion to "the faith" as parallel to Pauline usage (noting that Jude's relationship to "the apostles" is not intended to speak of *distance* to the twelve as much as it is a natural formulation from one who was not one of the *original* twelve), the absence of any hint of institutionalization in the epistle (in marked contrast with his *direct* appeal to his audience), the imminent tone of the writer as he depicts the coming of the Lord, and incorporation of Enochic theology (a phenomenon more likely to hold sway with a first-century audience). Vitriolic denunciations as well as pastoral concern are both found in the epistle. God is equally able to reserve the faithful for presentation before the divine Presence and to reserve the ungodly for certain and final judgment.

3

The Epistle of Jude in Its Palestinian Milieu

In the preceding chapter we analyzed the polemic of Jude, focusing initially on the literary impulse of the writer, then proceeding to an analysis of the content of the epistle itself. With regard to matters of style, structure, and use of source-material, the writer was observed to be best understood against the backdrop of current Hellenistic literary and rhetorical conventions. While it has been the proclivity of biblical scholarship to assume an absence of conscious literary skill on the part of NT writers, we have sought to demonstrate a level of literary craftmanship in Jude which, judged by conventional literary criteria, is of a very high order.

Having sufficiently noted the aspect of form in the polemic of Jude, we have attempted a reexamination of the traditionally held view of Jude that situates the epistle in the second century. The "early Catholic" approach to Jude was found to be fraught with presuppositions that are not required by the actual text of the epistle. Not peripheral to the matter of locating Jude in the first or second century is the question of the relationship of Christianity to Judaism—discontinuity and continuity. The history of Christianity, particularly in the first century, is in large measure the account of the early church's attempts to explain herself as the fulfillment and continuity of Israel.

Jewish-Christians, certainly by no means a homogenous group, were not conscious of a decisive rupture with their Jewish past. To the contrary, the apostolic preaching found in the book of Acts takes great pains to establish this link with the OT community of faith.[1] In the NT are several documents which often have been singled out as notably "Jewish" in character, e.g., James, Hebrews, and the Apocalypse. To this list can be added yet another: Jude. But to designate these books in such a way is to invite several questions. First, what is a reasonably satisfying definition of "Jewish Christianity" (a matter in which there is to be found little agreement)?[2] Second, what is the precise nature of first-century Judaism itself? Scholarship over the last forty years has become increasingly aware of the variety of sectarian divisions, all of which fit under the "Jewish" rubric.

With regard to the first question, it should be observed that nice neat distinctions as to what constitutes "Christian" and "Jewish" may not be so clear-cut. The very fact that evidence of a schism between Judaism and Christianity is mirrored in so much of the NT is itself a testimony to the *intimate relationship* of the two traditions, and both lay claim to birthright privileges. The thoroughly Jewish matrix of Christian origins is observed by one church historian:

> According to tradition, only one of the writers of the New Testament, Luke, was not a Jew. As far as we know, none of the church fathers was a Jew, although both Hermas and Hegesippus, for example, may have been; Justin Martyr was born in Samaria but was a Gentile. The transition represented by this contrast had the most far-reaching of consequences for the entire development of Christian doctrine.[3]

An illustration of how difficult the second question becomes is to survey the running theological discussions as to the origins of the Fourth Gospel. Scholarship has ranged from categorizing John as eminently Jewish to the most Hellenistic of the Gospel narratives. Is it possible that a Palestinian Jew might have had access to or contact with religio-philosophical schools of his day and that he may have been disposed to employ current literary-rhetorical conventions as a form for his theological treatise? Martin Hengel's exhaustive work of two decades ago, *Judaism and Hellenism*,[4] certainly was aimed at the clear distinction which was assumed by biblical scholarship. He writes: "This . . . distinction does, of course, pass too lightly over the fact that by the time of Jesus, Palestine had already been under 'Hellenistic' rule and its resultant cultural influence for some 360 years. Thus, even in Jewish Palestine, in the New Testament period Hellenistic civilization had a long and eventful history behind it."[5] In the same vein, S. Sandmel[6] comments on the extent of Hellenization of Palestine:

> Jews inherited from the third, second, and first pre-Christian centuries aspects of Hellenized Judaism which by the first Christian century they took to be normal Judaism. . . . If only we knew more about the kind of communication that went on between Dispersion Jews and the religious leadership in Judea, we would be able to see more clearly to what extent there was a substantial difference in the acuteness and extent of Hellenization in Judea and the Dispersion. . . . We should . . . avoid some of the modern anachronistic

preconceptions which would dictate that Jewish Palestine rejected every kind of Hellenization and that Diaspora Judaism accepted it only in externals.

The implications of studies done by the likes of Hengel and Sandmel are far-reaching and strike at traditionally held presuppositions of NT scholarship. In general terms, one cannot assume that the prevading influence of Hellenistic culture is removed from Palestinian Judaism and Christianity. Rather, its presence should be presumed. It reminds us that the Christian community *at its origins* was shaped by the Greek language.[7] It should remind us as well that Palestinian Jews and Christians would have necessarily been strongly influenced by Hellenistic educational practice and cultural norms—a premise which is salient to the present study of Jude.

It has been said that for Gentile Christians, the question of continuity between Judaism and Christianity was the question of their relation to their mother-in-law; for Jewish Christians, it was the question of their relation to their mother.[8]

A thorough study of the Jewish matrix of the New Testament . . . is of importance for New Testament interpretation not primarily as providing sources for particular passages, but rather as making clear the rich, complex human reality out of which Christianity, which eventually defined itself in opposition to a newly restricted Judaism, emerged.[9]

It is to the aforementioned aspects—the influence of Hellenistic education in Palestine and the relationship of Jewish Christians to their Jewish matrix—that we now wish to turn. Specifically, the relationship of two epistles of the NT—James and Jude—to their "mother" deserves further attention.

THE INFLUENCE OF HELLENISM IN FIRST-CENTURY PALESTINE

The epistle of Jude exhibits a strong Jewish flavor (a quality to be expected of a first-century Palestinian[10] Christian community) combined with the rhetorical influences of Hellenistic culture which permeated Jewish Palestine even well before the first century A.D. As early as the third century B.C., Greek schools—not only the traditional Jewish wisdom types—existed in Jerusalem.[11] During the first century B.C., Roman education began the transition of formally assimilating Hellenism.[12] After completing grammar school, Roman youths who aspired to a public career would enter rhetorical schools for a furthering of their education. The trained orator, writes W. A. Smith,[13] became synonymous with an educated man: "Palestine has always been a country of transit, which has never ceased to absorb the cultural influences of the neighboring lands and to adapt them, successfully or otherwise, to its own original culture. . . . Hellenization encompassed Palestine on every side."[14]

In formal Hebrew education, by contrast, we find an emphasis in the postexilic period on the training of "specialists," e.g., scribes, priests and Levites, court and temple chroniclers, and accountants. In their own right they required a formal education and training.[15] Secondary schools were established in Palestine after the Maccabean period in the early first century B.C.[16] As to the content of the education, Hebrew, Aramaic, and often Greek were the norm.[17]

Greek culture increasingly affected Palestinian Jews since prior to Alexander. Under Herod the Greek in particular, Hellenization sped forward. V. Tcherikover[18] cites some thirty cities and towns which were transformed during Herodian rule.[19] J. A. Fitzmyer[20] points to the frequency of Greek inscriptions on grave sites throughout Palestine. The vast majority of epitaphs seem to have been written in Greek.

Numerous Jewish authors wrote in Greek.[21] We learn of Josephus's own facility in the language in *Ant.* 20.262–65.[22] He adds that many, even slaves, acquired a measure of linguistic facility. His tone leaves the reader with the distinct impression that many a Jew in Palestine spoke Greek fluently. As to the question of exactly how widespread Greek in Palestine was, one is left to conjecture. Yet, it is most probable that the *Hellenistoi* of Acts 6:1 and 9:29 were Jews or Jewish-Christians from Jerusalem whose everyday language was Greek.[23] It would stand to reason that Jewish Christians of the first century were just as eager as Josephus to spread their message in a Greek-speaking world. Philo writes as if Greek was spoken in the *synagōgoi* all around the Mediterranean region. Evidence best supports the view that Jesus was triglossal.[24] He probably spoke Greek to Pilate (Matt. 27:11–14; John 18:33–38), to the centurion (Matt. 8:5–13), and to the Canaanite woman (Matt. 15:22–28). The inscription posted atop the cross (John 19:20) was in Hebrew, Greek, and Latin. It is generally agreed that "Galilee of the Gentiles" (Matt. 4:15) was in proximity to Grecophone districts such as Decapolis and that it was more Hellenized than Judea.[25] G. A. Williamson[26] notes that Galilee, which bordered on very Hellenized regions and which had a mixed population, would have offered as much or greater opportunity for fluency in Greek than Judea. After the martyrdom of Stephen, the Hellenists were scattered over Palestine in missionary activity. Note the good Greek names in Acts 6:5. One rabbi best described the linguistic situation of Palestine: "There are four languages most suited for use in the world: Greek for singing (poetry), Latin for warfare, Aramaic for elegy and Hebrew for speech."[27]

The term *hellēnizein* meant firstly "to speak Greek correctly," and only second, as J. N. Sevenster[28] has noted, "to adopt a Greek lifestyle." Indeed, the dissemination of *koinē* was the most *permanent* fruit of Alexander's relatively brief career. According to the well-known legend of Aristeas (mid second century B.C.), six men representing each of Israel's twelve tribes were chosen to translate the Torah into Greek. These seventy-two, accordingly, were distinguished by their *paideia*[29] in addition to their thorough knowledge of the Greek language (Ps. Arist. 121). Though consigned to the realm of legend, this account of the LXX translation nonetheless reflects the significance of such a literary feat. The continuing task of translating and editing the LXX advanced in Palestine during the first two centuries A.D. through the work of Theodotion and Aquila.[30]

All told, the realities of Diaspora, writings such as the books of the Maccabees,[31] the work of Herod, the infiltration of Greek loanwords and names, and Greek inscriptions are all evidence of the pervasiveness of the Greek language in Palestine.[32] Even the Essenes, arch-zealots who resisted the spirit of Hellenism, could not avoid the language; Greek papyrus fragments were found in Qumran. Thus, what the fourth-century B.C. orator Isocrates could state of "Hellenization" continued to be valid even up to the time of the Christian advent: "The designation Hellene seems no longer to be a matter of descent but of disposition, and those who share in our education have more right to be called Hellenes than those who have a common descent with us."[33]

The influence of Greek culture in Palestine took linguistic, literary, political, and cultural expression. One illustration of the extent of this diffusion is the *agōn-motif* found in Jude 3 and in numerable Jewish[34] and Christian[35] writings. Although employed most commonly in the realm of athletics with its physical exercise and variety of sports competition, the term *agōn*[36] was used in every type of competitive context known to the Greeks—war, athletics, and civilian life.[37] At the heart of the *agōn* is the goal of supremacy, a quality inherent to the Greek mind. This notion even reaches back to the Homeric era. For example, in his *Theogony,* Hesiod depicts the contest for power between Zeus and Prometheus in the forum of an *agōn.*[38] It was only natural then that the Games of Greece would be associated with the gods. The "gymnasium," found in cities as well as in larger villages,[39] became a center of "agonistic" ideals of Greek life throughout the Empire,[40] offering the Jew access to Greek education and way of life—whether it was grammar, music, military training, or athletic competition.[41]

The writings of Philo teem with the *agōn* concept.[42] To the writer of 4 Maccabees,[43] the *agōn* means suffering.[44] In 4 Ezra and the Testaments of the Twelve Patriarchs, the *agōn* represents the struggle against temptation, deception, and Satan.[45] The sparring athlete who endures pain and wins the crown is the metaphor used in the Testament of Job to depict Job's patient endurance of the afflictions of Satan.[46]

On a linguistic plane, the influence of *koinē* went far beyond that of Aramaic.[47] Greek was required for commerce, laws, treaties, and art. It was the language of diplomacy and letters. Of the abundant Jewish literature published in Greek in Palestine, Alexandrian Jews tended toward writing philosophy whereas Palestinian Jews tended toward historiography (a prime example being the Maccabean books, written in a tradition similar to Kings-Chronicles). Martin Hengel[48] attributes this Palestinian inclination primarily to the need of arguing for Jewish purity. Even in Jewish apocalyptic writings one finds a leaning toward history, an "encoded history,"[49] based on the model of Daniel and mirrored in the likes of 1 Enoch 85–90 or the Assumption of Moses. Although the crisis resulting from the rule of Antiochus IV dramatically altered the religious face of Palestinian Judaism (accentuating the notion of Jewish piety that characterizes the NT era), this did not affect the role of Hellenistic culture in Palestine. Rather, the Greek language with its forms of rhetoric became *the vehicle* to polemicize concerning the essentials of Jewish piety, and later, the Christian ethic. The epistle of Jude is a perfect specimen of this development.

In sum, all of Judaism from the third century B.C. must be designated, to some degree, as "Hellenistic Judaism," even that of Palestine. Following the lead of W. L. Knox,[50] M. Hengel has argued persuasively that it is wrong to make a strict distinction between "Palestinian Judaism" and "Hellenistic Judaism," as if there was a great cleavage between the two. Even the remotest parts of Galilee as well as the secluded life of the Dead Sea community had contact with Greek influence. R. Gamaliel[51] states that in his father's house there were five hundred men learning Jewish wisdom and five hundred learning that of the Greeks. Whether or not one accepts the account's accuracy, it reflects the mixture of Jewish-Hellenistic culture existing in the first century. Paul is a fitting illustration. Educated under Gamaliel in Jerusalem, it is in Palestine that the "apostle to the Gentiles" would have acquired, at least in part, his knowledge of Greek thought, literature, and rhetorical skills. One must assume that individuals growing up in Jewish Palestine were bilingual and lived with one foot in each culture. This is true not only of Jerusalem but of Galilee as well, which leads us to suppose that the inner core of Jesus' disciples were themselves bilingual. Several of the twelve had Greek names.[52] Further, the apostolic ministry of Peter would take him westward away from Palestine, where only Greek would be spoken.

In this light, particular reigning assumptions of biblical scholarship with regard to the NT writers are in need of reassessment. W. G. Kümmel[53] reflects this long-standing scholarly bias with respect to "Galilean peasants." For Kümmel, just as the possibility that the Gospel of Matthew may have originated from Greek-speaking Jewish-Christian circles is to be rejected, so too the "pure Greek" of Jude "fits poorly a Galilean."

We have considered the influence of Hellenistic culture in Palestine, noting in particular its effects on education and literary works of Jewish writers. Aside from Jude, one other literary sample from the NT, the epistle of James, serves as a noteworthy representative of Palestinian Jewish-Christian circles. In both is to be seen the application of Hellenistic literary and rhetorical training, and both illustrate the richness of the Jewish matrix out of which the Christian community emerged.

JAMES AND JUDE: EARLY CHRISTIANITY AND THE JEWISH MATRIX

Early Christianity and the Jewish Matrix

The epistle of James is usually regarded today as either a general epistle or a sermon. Indeed, both designations are accurate. In form and style it shares many literary features of the epistle to the Hebrews and the book of Proverbs.[54] Perhaps the primary contribution of Martin Dibelius's commentary on James was the recognition that the letter is best understood by Hellenistic literary-rhetorical conventions.[55] Dibelius argued that James is paraenetic or hortatory literature. Paraenesis, a method which presents moral teaching[56] by means of loosely connected units, paragraphs, or maxims, flourished in the first centuries B.C. and A.D. and is to be found in both Jewish and Hellenistic pre-Christian literature.

Recognizing paraenesis in James, while prohibiting a precise restoration of the setting behind the epistle, does allow us, based on the writer's assumed familiarity on the part of his audience with doctrine, source-material, and exhortation, to view James in a clearer, more coherent fashion. It frequently is characterized by single asyndeton exhortations which are sometimes linked together by a theme or catchword.[57] Paraenesis consists in the use of material which is traditional and not original. It offers precepts which are applicable in a *wide* variety of life situations. Not only does it presume the audience's familiarity with these traditions, but it makes use of paradigms understood to be proverbial examples of moral virtue being presented. The exhorter with his audience is reminiscent of the relationship between a father and his son or a master and his pupil, as is the custom of wisdom literature.[58]

The paraenetic text also affords a window into the soul of the audience.[59] Picking up on F. Mussner's recognition of James's eschatological perspective, R. W. Wall[60] analyzes the apocalyptic character of James's ideas, vocabulary, and thought patterns, suggesting that the writer and his audience may well have belonged to the apocalyptic tradition.[61] Hence, the message of James can be understood as an eschatological ethic which calls for James's audience to persist since the present age is nearing its end.[62]

Three aspects of "apocalyptic paraenesis,"[63] according to Wall, are to be noted in James: an apocalyptic worldview, theological motifs which approximate apocalyptic preaching, and the fluidity of literary genre which embodies the apocalyptic tradition.[64] Note the viewpoint of the eschatological community, for example, in the opening of the letter: *Iakōbos . . . tais dōdeka phylais tais en tę̄ diaspora chairein* (1:1). This perspective shares an affinity with the social world of apocalyptic; it indicates a community which is in some measure disinherited. Wall reiterates J.A.T. Robinson's[65] linking of the pilgrim community reflected in James's audience with the Jewish Church of Acts 1–8,[66] i.e., the community of believers living in the generation following Jesus' death and resurrection.

Wall[67] calls our attention to three trajectories in apocalyptic preaching which find correlative material in James: (1) a deterministic view of history,[68] (2) the good-evil dualism of human existence,[69] and (3) a futuristic view of divine salvation embodied in the imminent Day of the Lord.[70] The writer concludes by returning to his opening exhortation toward endurance, reminding his audience of the eschatological perspective: "Be patient, therefore, brothers, until the Lord's coming . . . the Lord's coming is near. . . . Behold, the Judge is standing at the door!" (5 : 7–9).

There remains yet a very significant aspect in the relationship of James to the Jewish matrix which demands our attention—an aspect treated at some length in the previous chapter. Certain NT passages have traditionally posed formal, stylistic, or structural difficulties due to statements or teaching based on OT sources for which explicit reference has been omitted, a phenomenon that one scholar has aptly described as "invisible midrashim."[71] As noted in the previous chapter, the midrashic method carries implications for a work's structural coherence.[72] Where midrashic activity is more manifest, with explicit reference and commentary, interpretation is not so problematic. Where, however, the form of midrash is more covert or paraphrastic, the task of interpretation by a reader removed from the *Sitz im Evangelium* can be a bit more perplexing.

How then is the midrashic method of a NT writer to be identified? By knowing the text upon which the midrash is being built, identifying the particular meaning of the text, and recognizing the hermeneutical technique by which to arrive at this interpretation. Perhaps even more so than Jude, James provides an example of this sort of covert or "invisible" midrashic activity.[73] M. Gertner[74] views the aim of James as working with the doctrinal essence of a midrashic "Vorlage" rather than compiling a commentary on the OT passages related to the Abraham-, Rahab-, Job-, and Elijah-traditions being employed. In this way the threads of biblical verses are omitted which otherwise might explicitly bind the units of material together. This produces for the modern reader the effect of veiling or paraphrasing the related OT passages. Yet the discovery that James is a midrashic composition alleviates many problems which might initially appear baffling.

Perhaps more than any NT writer, James shows a familiarity

with the Jewish haggadic tradition. In his relatively short epistle, four traditions based on OT narrative—Abraham,[75] Rahab,[76] Job,[77] and Elijah[78]—are cited. These traditions exhibit an embellishment and reinterpretation and seem to have been known to his audience.[79] James takes great liberty in the synthesis of OT and extracanonical traditions that may be assumed to have been recognized by his readers.

This tradition-material is cited because of its particular usefulness for the present situation. In the hands of the haggadist it serves to illustrate or explain a point of emphasis. James's method of exegesis is not unlike that employed in Jude. Upon closer inspection, James and Jude contain numerous points of contact which point back to the Jewish matrix common to both. Several of these features—the apocalyptic mode, the midrashic reworking of OT narrative, and the use of historic paradigms—have been identified. In addition, similarities in style, vocabulary, and theology are worthy of our consideration.

James and Jude: New Testament Paradigms of Jewish-Christian Literary Form

On the distinctly Jewish character found in James, Jude, and 2 Peter, S. Segert[80] writes: "They go back to Jewish traditions; nevertheless the tools of Hellenistic rhetorics, known in Palestinian Judaism long before, were effectively used for conveying a non-Hellenistic message." Aside from the epistle to the Hebrews and arguably the Apocalypse, James and Jude are the most "Jewish" among the writings of the NT. The similarities of the two books are not merely superficial however. Both are attributed to the brothers of Jesus and hence challenged with regard to their authenticity.[81] Both are "servants."[82] Neither is viewed as the possible literary product of a Palestinian hailing from Nazareth.[83] Both encountered difficulty in achieving broad canonical recognition in the early Church.[84] Both lack evidence of a specific or local audience being addressed, in contrast to the majority of the NT epistles. Both are characterized by an elevated and "polished" literary style. Both reflect a high esteem for the OT.[85] Both incorporate midrashic exegesis in support of their theological premise, making use of extracanonical tradition-material, and both have a fondness for graphic imagery and historical paradigms as proofs for argumentation. Further, both focus on ethical concerns while assuming that a doctrinal foundation has already

been laid with the audience,[86] and both are characterized by a
strongly hortatory tenor as well as the use of rhetorical devices.[87]

Among the objections to the authenticity of James and Jude,
perhaps the primary argument marshalled by traditional scholarship has been the literary argument. In light of the elegant and
fluent higher Koine demonstrated in these two letters, it is asked
with considerable skepticism whether Galilean Jews could have
indeed written such works. G. H. Rendall[88] wrote this response:
"It is time surely to discard the figment of Galilean illiteracy. . . .
Philodemus the philosopher, Meleager the epigrammatist and
anthologist, Theodorus the rhetorician, and one may almost add
Josephus the historian, were all of Galilee." The comment of J. N.
Sevenster[89] echoes the same expressed sentiment: "It is no longer
possible to refute such a possibility by recalling that these were
usually people of modest origins."

Three specific areas of similarity between James and Jude deserve further attention. The first two are literary, involving matters of style and verbal parallel. The third sphere relates to
theology. The illustrations being cited for their correspondence
are viewed essentially in light of the discussion of invention,
arrangement, and style presented in the previous chapter.

An appreciation of the poetic and hortatory structure in James
and Jude suggests that they belong to a similar literary school.
Consider the affinity of the two letters along the following lines.
Each:

(1) has a general address (Ja 1:1 ‖ Ju 1–2)
(2) has a hortatory conclusion (5:20 ‖ 22–23)
(3) contains a sizable presentation of demonstrative proofs
    (2:1–4:12 ‖ 5–11)
(4) follows with a series of admonitions (4:13–5:18 ‖ 12–23)
    which are grouped into two pairs, the first being aimed
    at the writer's opponents (4:13–17 and 5:1–6 ‖ 12–13,
    14–15) with the second aimed at the believers (5:7–12,
    13–18 ‖ 17–19, 20–23)
(5) has an introduction which hints at the problem (1:2–8 ‖
    3–4)
(6) contains an inversion of order which addresses an issue
    twice (2:1–3:14 and 3:15–4:8a ‖ 5–6 and 7–10)
(7) contains concatenatio (3:6; 4:7–11a ‖ 12–13, 22–23) and
    inclusio (1:2 and 12; 2:14 and 16; 2:17 and 26; 4:13
    and 5:1; 5:9 and 12 ‖ vv 6 and 13; 22 and 23)

(8) employs strategic and frequent use of catchwords
(9) includes hymnic material (3:13–18 ‖ vv 24–25)
(10) closes the body of exhortation with the admonition to turn
     a sinner from his way (5:20 ‖ 23)[90]

Much in the way of rhetorical-structural design in James and Jude
is illuminated when the homiletical character of the two epistles is
appreciated.[91]

With regard to style, James, much like Jude, exhibits a skillful
use of literary Koine. This finds confirmation in the writer's use of
participial constructions and word order. Although the tone of
the writer is thoroughly Jewish, the number of Hebraisms is
relatively few,[92] and the Greek with which he writes is smooth.
Asyndeton is conspicuous in James; exhortations are frequent
(seventy-nine sentences begin without a conjunction). The writer's
vocabulary is impressive. The rate of *hapax legomena,* as with Jude,
is quite high. All told, seventy-three *hapax* occur in the epistle.[93]
The writer's choice of words also exhibits creative expression. In
James one encounters bountiful figurative language: metaphor,[94]
simile,[95] personification,[96] hyperbole,[97] anthropomorphism,[98]
hendiadys,[99] incongruity,[100] amplification,[101] epanadiplosis,[102]
ellipse,[103] and climax.[104]

One is also struck by the element of "sound structure" which
characterizes the style of James. The writer is extremely paronomastic; sound-play abounds.[105] Of the numerous instances,
several examples are worthy of note: 1:1, 2 *(chairein . . . charan);*
1:2 (Pasan . . . peirasmois peripesēte poikilois); 1:13–14 (peirazomenos
. . . peirazomai . . . apeirastos . . . peirazei . . . peirazetai); 1:17 (dosis
. . . dōrēma); 2:18 (erei . . . echeis . . . erga echō); 1:21 (ton emphyton
logon ton dynamenon); 1:24 (apelēlythen . . . epelatheto); 2:3 (hypo to
hypopodion); 2:20 (ergōn argē); 3:5 (hēlikon . . . hēlikēn hylēn); 2:22–
23 (eteleiōthē . . . eplērōthē hē graphē); 3:7 (thērion . . . peteinōn . . .
erpetōn . . . enaliōn); 3:7–8 (damazetai . . . dedamastai . . . damasai
dynatai); 3:8 (akatastaton kakon); 3:17 (epeita eirēnikē, epieikēs, eu-
peithēs; and adiakritos, anypokritos); 4:2–3 (epithymeite . . . echete . . .
phoneuete . . . zēloute . . . dynasthe . . . machesthe . . . polemeite . . .
echete . . . aiteite . . . lambanete . . . aitesthe . . . dapanēsēte);* 4:7–11a
*(hypotagēte . . . antistēte . . . eggisate . . . katharisate . . . agnisate . . .
talaipōrēsate . . . penthēsate . . . klausate . . . tapeinōthēte . . . ka-
talaleite); 4:14 (phainomenē . . . aphanizomenē); 5:5 (etryphēsate . . .
espatalēsate . . . ethrepsate . . . katedikasate . . . ephoneusate);* and 5:17
(proseuchē prosēyxato; and brexai . . . ebrexen . . . hex).

A third point of affinity between James and Jude is the striking array and frequency of verbal parallels. Aside from Jude–2 Peter and Colossians–Ephesians comparisons, the verbal correspondence in James and Jude, considering the brevity of the latter, is unmatched anywhere else in the NT.[106] All told, ninety-three cases of verbal agreement occur in the two letters, with twenty-seven terms occurring two or more times in both.[107] Astonishingly, *each* of the twenty-five verses of Jude averages approximately four words found in the epistle of James—an extraordinary rate of verbal correspondence:[108]

1. Greeting (vv 1–2). V 1: *patēr* (= James 1:27; 3:9); the writer as *doulos* (= 1:1); *Iēsous Christos* (also 25 = 1:1; 2:1); *theos* (also 25 = 1:1,5,13,27; 2:5, 19,23; 3:9; 4:4,6,7,8); *adelphos* (= 1:2,9,16,19; 2:1,5,14,15; 3:1,10,12; 4:11; 5:7,9,10,12,19); *Iakōbos* (= 1:1); *kalein* (= 2:5,7,23); *agapē/agapētoi/agapan* (also 2,3,12,17,20,21 = 1:12,16,19; 2:5, 8); *tērein* (also 6,13,21,24 = 1:27; 2:10); v 2: *eleos/eleein* (also 21,22,23 = 2:13; 3:17); *eirēnē* (= 3:17,18); *agapē* (cf. v 1); *plēthynein/plēthos* (= 5:20).

2. Occasion/Purpose (vv 3–4). V 3: *eirēnē* (cf. v 2); *pas/pan/panta* (also 5,15,25 = 1:2; 2:10; 5:12); *pistis* (also 20 = 1:3,6; 2:1,5,14–26; 5:15); v 4: *anthrōpos* (= 5:20); *graphē/prographein* (= 2:8, 23); *kyrios* (also 5,9,14,17,21,25 = 1:1; 2:1; 4:10,15; 5:4,7,10,11,14, 15); *charis/charein* (also 16 = 1:1; 4:6); *krima* (= 3:1).

3. Historical Proofs (vv 5–16). V 5: *bouleuomai* (= 1:18); *sōzein* (also 23 = 2:14; 4:12; 5:15,20); *kyrios* (cf. v 4); *apollymi* (also 11 = 1:11; 4:12); *ginōskein/oida* (v 10 = 1:3; 2:20; 4:17,20); *pisteuein* (= 2:19); *hoti* (also 11,18 = 1:3,7, 10,12,13,23; 2:19, 20,22,24; 3:1; 4:4,5; 5:8,11,20); v 6: *aggelos* (= 2:25); *idios* (= 1:14); *krisis/krinein* (also 9,15 = 2:12,13; 4:11,12; 5:12); *apollymi* (= 4:12); *leipein/apoleipein* (= 1:4,5; 2:15); *megas* (= 3:1,5; 4:6); *hēmera* (= 5:3); *tērein* (cf. v 1); *alla* (also 9 = 2:18; 3:15); v 7: *houtos* (also 8, 10,11,12,14,16,19 = 1:23,25; 3:2); *polis* (= 4:13); *sarx* (also 16,23 = 5:3); *heteros* (= 2:25); *aperchomai* (= 1:24); *deiknyein/deigma/hypodeigma* (= 2:18; 3:13; 5:10); *pyr* (also 23 = 3:5, 6; 5:3); v 8: *homoiōs/homoioun* (= 2:25; 3:9); *mentoi* (= 2:8); *houtos/houtoi* (also 10,11,12,14,16,19 = 1:23,25; 3:2); *blasphēmein/blasphēmia* (also 9 = 2:7); *doxa* (also 24,25 = 2:1); v 9: *diabolos* (= 4:7); *diakrinein* (also 22 = 1:6; 2:4); *sōma* (= 2:16,26; 3:2,3,6); *blasphēmia* (cf. v 8); *kyrios* (cf. v 4); v 10: *epistamai* (= 4:14); *blasphēmein* (cf. v 8); *thēriōn/zōē* (= 3:7); *physikōs/physis* (= 3:7); v 11: *hodos* (= 1:8; 2:25; 5:20); *poreuomai* (also 16,18 = 4:13); *planan/planē/planētēs* (also 13 = 1:16; 5:19,20); *misthos* (= 5:4); v 12: *agapē* (cf. v 1); *hydōr/anydros* (= 3:2); *anemos* (= 3:4); *thanatos/apothanoumai*

(=2:15); *karpos/akarpos* (=3:17; 5:7,18); v 13: *thalassa* (1:6); *planētēs* (cf. v 11); *tērein* (cf. v 1); v 14: *prophētēs/prophēteuein* (=5:10); *legein/logos* (also 18=1:13,18,21,22,23; 2:14,23; 3:2 4:5,6,13,15); *idou* (=3:3, 4,5; 5:4,7,9,11); *kyrios* (cf. v 4); v 15: *krisis* (cf. v 6); *poiēin* (=3:18; 4:17); *elegchein* (=2:9); *psychē* (=1:21; 5:20); *ergōn* (=1:4,25; 2:14,17,18,20,21,22,24,25; 3:13); *sklēros* (=3:4); *lalein* (also 16=1:19; 2:12; 5:10); *hamar- tōlos* (=4:8; 5:20); v 16: *epithymia* (also 18=1:14,15; 4:2); *por- euomai* (cf. v 11); *stoma* (=3:3,10); *lalein* (cf. v 15); *prosōpon/ prosōpolēmptein/prosōpolēmpsia* (=1:11,23; 2:1,9); *ophelos/ōpheleia* (=2:14,16); *charis* (cf. v 4).

4. Reminder and exhortation (vv 17–23). V 17: *agapētoi* (cf. v 1); *kyrios* (cf. v 4); v 18: *eschatos* (=5:3); *epithymia* (cf. v 16); v 19: *psychikos* (=3:15); *pneuma* (= 4:5); v 20: *agapētoi* (cf. v 1); *pistis* (cf. v 3); *pneuma* (cf. v 19); *proseuchomai* (=5:13,14,16,18); v 21: *agapē* (cf. v 1); *tērein* (cf. v 1); *prosdechomai/dechomai* (=1:21); *eleos* (cf. v 2); *kyrios* (cf. v 4); *zōē* (=1:12; 4:14); v 22: *diakrinein* (cf. v 9); *eleein* (cf. v 2); v 23: *sōzein* (cf. v 5); *pyr* (cf. v 7); *sarx* (cf. v 7); *spiloun/ aspilos/[spiloi(?)]*[109] (=1:27; 3:6).

5. Closing (vv 24–25). V 24: *dynamai* (=1:21; 2:14; 4:12); *monos* (=1:22; 2:24); *ptaiein/aptaistos* (=2:10; 3:2); *histēmi* (=2:3; 5:9); *doxa* (cf. v 8); *nyn* (=4:16).

In addition to the aforementioned cases of specific verbal agreement, numerous general and thematic similarities between James and Jude surface upon examination: (1) a richness of imag- ery (Jude 6,10,12,13,23 and James 1:6,10,11,17,18; 2:2, 3, 6; 3:3–12; 4:1,2,4,7,12; 5:1–6, 7–9, 19,20); (2) examples drawn from nature (vv 12–13 and 1:6,18,23,24; 3:3–12; 4:14; 5:3,7); (3) ethical teaching built upon an assumed doctrinal foundation already laid; (4) antinomian counterargumentation (vv 4,6,7,8– 11,15,16,18,19); (5) a *kyrios*-christology and Jesus' activity in the OT (vv 4,5,14,17,21,25 and 1:1; 5:7–8); (6) cosmic or solar phenomena (v 13 and 1:17); (7) an ethic motivated by eschatology (vv 5–7, 14–15,21,24–25 and 2:12–13; 4:12; 5:4, 7–9); (8) the juxtaposing of judgment and mercy (vv 5,6,23 and 2:12–13; 5:19–20); (9) erring from the truth/being led astray (vv 11,13 and 5:20); (10) fundamental dualism of good versus evil (vv 3–4; 8– 10; 18–21 and 1:13,17,20–21; 2:10–11,19,26; 3:5,6,8,9–12,15– 18; 4:4,6,7; 5:6); (11) exhortation to recall what has been learned (vv 5,17 and 2:22–25); (12) being saved from death (v 23 and 5:20); (13) remaining unspotted (v 23 and 1:21,27; 4:8); (14) the devil and demons (vv 6,9 and 2:19; 3:15; 4:7); (15) stumbling (v

24 and 3:2); (16) prophets or prophesying (v 14 and 5:10; (17) the unbridled mouth (vv 8–10,16 and 3:1–12); (18) gloom or Gehenna (vv 6,13 and 3:6); and (19) the last days (vv 6,17 and 5:3).

While both James and Jude are strongly motivated by ethical concerns, each assumes a doctrinal foundation already laid with the readers.[110] One particular theological touch-point shared by both epistles, in connection with their eschatological perspective, is the lordship-christology,[111] a distinct earmark of first-century Christian writings. For James, the coming of the Lord draws near (5:7–8). The Judge, *YHWH Ṣĕbāʾôt*, stands before the door (5:9). Those who are patient, obedient, and established have the Lord's compassion and mercy to anticipate (5:8–11). In Jude the Lord comes to execute judgment upon all the ungodly. Those who are established, praying, and kept in the love of God can anticipate mercy.

An intriguing feature of the christology already alluded to is the equation of Jesus with God *(kyrios),* and hence, a transfer of the honor and qualities ascribed to *YHWH* in the OT. This can be observed in James 5:7–11, where *kyrios* appears five times. Three of these occurrences have to do with "the *parousia* of the Lord" and prayer "in the name of the Lord" (in 1:1, Jesus Christ is designated *kyrios*). Thus, OT theophany and NT christology merge in the view of the writer. *Kyrios-Iēsous* spans both testaments in His involvement with the people of God. A similar case is found in Jude 5, where the paradigm of Israel being delivered from Egypt is employed. Jude 5 is instructive in that it helps to trace early Christian interpretive patterns of God's dealings with Israel in the OT. As has been noted earlier,[112] the text of Jude 5 can support a *Iēsous* reading, a reading favored by E. E. Kellett,[113] F. F. Bruce,[114] A. T. Hanson, [115] R. G. Hamerton-Kelly,[116] and J. Fossum.[117] Apart from vv 5 and 14, *kyrios* is used four times in Jude expressly of Jesus Christ, i.e., it is Jesus who is associated with Israel's deliverance. If the *Iēsous* reading is correct, we can assume that the writer viewed Jesus as *Kyrios-YHWH*, and therefore, responsible for the acts attributed in the OT to the Angel of the Lord.[118]

The proclamation of Jesus as Lord, as we have noted, is distinctive of the preaching of the first-century church. Both the epistles of James and Jude, Jewish to the core and displaying a lordship-christology, are legitimate attestations to and worthy specimens of this period.

Conclusion

In this chapter we have observed the Jewish matrix out of which the early church emerged. Jewish-Christians were not conscious of a rupture with their Jewish heritage, as demonstrated by the movement of the book of Acts. Two fundamental difficulties, it must be noted, arise in the attempt to discuss the "Jewishness" of NT writings: laying hold of a satisfactory definition of "Jewish Christianity" and coming to terms with the precise nature of first-century Judaism in light of its diversified character. The Fourth Gospel illustrates the problems associated with seeking to draw a clear distinction between what might be considered "Palestinian" and "Hellenistic." Already by the Christian advent, Palestine had been "Hellenistic" for roughly three-and-a-half centuries, and thus, the early Jewish-Christian community, at its origin, was shaped by Hellenistic culture.

This influence is most notable in the spheres of language and formal education, as evidenced by the abundance and fluency of Palestinian Jews writing in Greek. A border region such as Galilee would be particularly susceptible to Hellenistic cultural influence; thus, out of *necessity,* one is obligated to reappraise the traditional scholarly consensus concerning "Galilean illiteracy," a premise for which support is conspicuously lacking.

Two specimens of Palestinian Jewish-Christian literature may serve as case illustrations. The epistles of James and Jude mirror the richness of their Jewish matrix. Both demonstrate literary skill of a high order; both employ a literary technique, style and theological perspective which suggest they belong to a similar literary "school" as well as cultural and theological milieu. Both letters exhibit a sharply hortatory character. As paraenesis, James sets forth moral teaching consisting of loosely knit units, paragraphs or exhortations; paraenetic literature is a prominent literary type of the first century B.C. and A.D. Jude, falling in the category of "word of exhortation," in similar fashion seeks through persuasion and dissuasion, by means of the use of historical proofs, to exhort the audience toward a moral-ethical decision. Both reflect a distinctly homiletical character while qualifying as epistolary genre.

Additionally, James and Jude each employ an apocalyptic mode. This is apparent not only by the use of symbolic and literary conventions but in their worldview. A deterministic view of history, human existential dualism, and eschatological motivation as applied to ethical concerns all point to this subculture of primitive

Christianity. A noticeable lordship-christology characterizes both epistles. The imminence of the Lord's coming is central to each. Set against the backdrop of the Day of the Lord motif, paraenetic instruction and exhortations are perceived with greater force.

A significant feature of both James and Jude was noted to be midrashic reworking of tradition-material based on OT narrative. Reinterpreted and applied to the present situation and based on audience familiarity, these traditions serve the writers' purpose in addressing particular needs in the Christian community. The use of midrash in the two epistles has a didactic and edifying effect and should not be construed as a homiletical commentary per se on OT passages.

With regard to theology, attention was given to the lordship-christology of both epistles in which we find the equation of Jesus as *kyrios*. Of particular significance is the merging of OT theophany with NT christology in both, shedding light on how the early Christian community interpreted God's dealings with Israel in the OT. The attributes of YHWH are thus seen to be transferred to Jesus in the preaching of the first-century church.

In sum, a considerable degree of similarity is to be noted between the epistles of James and Jude. This comparison has been executed along literary-rhetorical, stylistic, structural, and theological lines. As two closely related representatives of Palestinian Jewish-Christian circles, James and Jude demonstrate a rich debt to the Jewish matrix while wrapping their message in the garb of current Hellenistic literary-rhetorical conventions.

In the preceding two chapters, we have touched from time to time on Jude's use of Jewish tradition material. This will require further examination. In the following chapter, we hope to elucidate one crucial aspect of Jude's hermeneutic—his dependence on and use of material found in the OT.

APPENDIX: THE CATHOLIC EPISTLES AND THE QUESTION OF PSEUDONYMITY

It is assumed by virtually all commentators that Jude is pseudonymous. With regard to this prevailing view, various explanations of and justifications for a pseudonymity theory are offered. Ancient writers, it is maintained, were not burdened by the modern "copyright" mentality. M. Rist writes: "The early Christians, orthodox and heretical, used pseudepigraphy frequently and . . . unashamedly in order to promote their . . . doctrines"

("Pseudepigraphy and the Early Christians," *Studies in New Testament and Early Christian Literature. Festschrift A.P. Wikgren*, 75). H. H. Rowley views pseudonymity as an essentially "transparent" literary device, not meant to deceive anyone (*The Relevance of Apocalyptic. A Study of Jewish and Christian Apocalypses*). To the other extreme, N. Brox holds ancient pseudepigraphy as a technique that advanced deception, manipulation, and conscious distortion (*Falsche Verfasserangaben. Zur Erklärung der frühchristlichen Pseudepigraphie*, 12). Some would seek to interpret it "religiopsychologically" (e.g., D. S. Russell, *The Method and Message of Jewish Apocalyptic 200* B.C.–A.D. *100*). Others focus on its "ecstatic" identification (e.g., J. A. Sint, *Pseudonymität im Altertum. Ihre Formen und ihre Gründe;* W. Speyer, *Die literarische Fälschung im Altertum;* idem, "Fälschung, pseudepigraphische frei Erfindung und 'echte religiöse Pseudepigraphie,'" *Pseudepigrapha 1,* 195–263; and F. Torm, *Die Psychologie der Pseudonymität im Hinblick auf die Literatur des Urchristentums*). Yet others see NT writings as literary products of a school of disciples: a Johannine, a Petrine, a Matthean, etc. (see, e.g., K. Stendahl, *The School of St. Matthew and Its Use of the Old Testament* and H. Conzelmann, *The Theology of St. Luke*).

While each of these theories may stress an area which has traditionally been lacking, they all fail to note the distinction between first-century *Christian* writings and other literature of the period.[119] K. Aland's thesis, that A.D. 50–150 was an era of anonymity and pseudonymity, with the writers functioning merely as well-intentioned "tools" of the Holy Spirit ("The Problem of Anonymity and Pseudonymity in Christian Literature of the First Two Centuries," *The Authorship and Integrity of the New Testament,* 1–13), though intended essentially to be a response to many of these views, is not a great improvement. People have wrongly lumped together anonymity with pseudepigraphy in the same way that forgery, ascription, interpolation, textual alteration, and literary convention are frequently lumped together indiscriminately. Given the reigning assumptions of NT pseudonymity with their implications for individual books, one is virtually left then to agree with K. M. Fischer, who views no book of the NT, apart from several "genuine" Pauline epistles, as having been written by the designated author ("Anmerkungen zur Pseudepigraphie im Neuen Testament," *NTS* 23: 76–81). We may identify then the general underlying suppositions for NT pseudonymity which have influenced NT interpretation through the last century: (1) a conflict with gnosticism of the second century, (2) a full break with Judaism, (3) a delay in the Parousia, (4) the need, in light of the distance of the apostles, to continue the apostolic tradition authoritatively, and (5) the observation that pseudepigraphy was a "normal" literary convention.

While the phenomenon of copyright is a relatively modern notion, Jerome, to use an example from among the fathers, acknowledged two types of pseudepigrapha: forgeries and false attributions. K. K. Hulley ("Principles of Textual Criticism Known to St. Jerome," *HSCP* 55: 104–9) has identified in Jerome a set of criteria for the distinguishing of spurious works. In general, the Reformers were more critical than their counterparts of the medieval period, but their views on pseudonymity are not very helpful. Luther virtually created a deutero-canon of Hebrews, James, Jude, and Revelation—books in which he did not find Christ present. His complaint, however, was not *authorship*. On 2 Peter, Calvin held the view that if it was canonical, it came from Peter, even if his disciples wrote it. Grotius, perhaps in some respects a forerunner to the Tubingen school, tended toward a speculative resolution. To him, 2 Peter was a letter written by Simon, the successor to James the Bishop of Jerusalem; Jude, correspondingly, was a bishop in Hadrian's time. Yet, the notion of canonical pseudepigraphy does not develop until the nineteenth century. We find in Schleiermacher, the aesthetic and the critic, doubts concerning 1 Timothy. Eichhorn followed suit, contending that all three Pastorals were spurious. De Wette maintained that the Pastorals as well as 2 Peter were nonapostolic and therefore pseudonymous. He also had doubts with regard to Ephesians and 1 Peter. The line of thinking advanced by F. C. Baur was that the presence of one canonical pseudepigraphon in the NT logically leads to others. This included Colossians, Ephesians, Philippians, and Philemon. With the turn of the century, one can see Baur's influence exerted on scholars such as Holtzmann, Jülicher, Moffatt, Dibelius, Goodspeed, and Cadbury.

Dissenting voices emerged from time to time. In 1891, J. S. Candlish challenged English scholars who had assumed the pseudonymity theory ("On the Moral Character of Pseudonymous Books," *Expos* 4: 91–107, 262–79). His contention was that no one had evidence of ancient pseudepigrapha being received in good faith. Normally a work was received either as authentic or as an imposture. Content for Candlish had priority over literary considerations. R. D. Shaw's thesis ("Pseudonymity and Interpretation," *The Pauline Epistles*, 477–86) proceeded essentially along the lines of that of Candlish. G. Wohlenberg (*Der erste und zweite Petrusbrief und der Judasbrief*, 316–20) doubted that the church would recognize a work that was not authentic. For J. I. Packer (*"Fundamentalism" and the Word of God,* 184), "pseudonymity and canonicity are mutually exclusive," since to have one's product equated with that of someone else is fraudulent, even when perpetrated by the noblest of motives. D. Guthrie (*New Testament Introduction. Hebrews to Revelation,* 142) submits that there is no evidence from any part of the church that 2 Peter or Jude were ever rejected as spurious (see also his essay "The Development of the Idea of Canonical Pseudepigrapha in New Testament Criticism," *Vox Evangelica* 1, 14–39, as well as T. D. Lea, "The Early Christian View of Pseudepigraphic Writings," *JETS* 27 65–75). C. Pinnock (*Biblical Revelation—The Foundation of Christian Theology,* 191) also ponders the ethical consideration. He writes: "The ethical question is unavoidable. The view that a disciple of Peter's may have reworked his master's notes is less objectionable, but wholly speculative. But if we believe pseudonymity is involved, we have no right to consider the book inspired and canonical."

In a more recent monograph, D. G. Meade, in *Pseudonymity and Canonicity. An Investigation into the Relationship of Authorship and Authority in Jewish and Earliest Christian Tradition,* surveys the landscape of the various pseudonymity theories propounded by biblical scholarship while undertaking the lofty goal of addressing the "fundamental lack in the history of the investigations of NT pseudonymity."[120] Meade examines positions to the far right and far left of the theological spectrum. The former, notes Meade, rejects the notion of biblical pseudonymity on dogmatic theological grounds and leaves no room for literary-critical concerns.[121] The latter, on the other hand, is characterized by an absence of theological concern, though it acknowledges the need for the use of literary-critical tools.[122] For Meade, it is "fortunate" that "the vast majority of scholars belong [*sic*] to the second major perspective."[123] The task then, if the "left" side of the theological spectrum in Meade's eyes is to be validated, is to demonstrate that pseudonymity and canonicity are *not* mutually exclusive. The aim is to show how pseudonymity could be a "legitimate part of the early Christian's . . . moral conscience."[124]

Meade correctly notes a weakness inherent to most modern critical attempts at dealing with the question of NT pseudonymity: treating NT literature in the same light as literature of late antiquity.[125] He attempts to identify a "pattern" of anonymity/pseudonymity through the OT and intertestamental literature, observing how the notions of revelation and tradition relate to the concepts of authorship and authority. This "pattern" is then traced by Meade through the NT. What we find in his basic approach to the NT, however, is not much different from that of past critical scholarship from which Meade seemingly has tried to distance himself "objectively." The gaping hole in the history of pseudo-nymity study is evidently not so large after all: "The problem arises when we turn to the gospel record. The question is whether (and how much) the material we have recorded has its source in prophetic 'words of the Risen Christ,' as opposed to the words (or voices) of the historical Jesus."[126]

In essence, Meade has continued the pre- and post-Easter dichotomy with which NT scholarship has grown so familiar:

> Certainly the manifold evidence of interpretive redactional activity shows that the expansion of the Jesus tradition cannot be solely (and probably not even primarily) attributed to the oracular activity of Christian prophets, but must also be seen as part of the early Church's (charismatic) teaching activity.[127]

Sure evidence of what Meade views as "the expansion of the Jesus tradition" through "the early Church's (charismatic) teaching ministry" are 2 Peter and Jude.[128] For Meade, the evidence for pseudonymity in 2 Peter is so "thorough" and the arguments so "overwhelming" and "preponderate" that one need hardly attempt to consider another viewpoint, in spite of the "heroic (and ingenious) tenacity" of a lonely few on the hermeneutical horizon.[129] To Meade's way of thinking, any attempt to employ a *theological* criterion for judging what is canonical falls short of accepted (and therefore) authoritative historical-critical standards. The theological component, states Meade, is not a "relevant criterion" for the question of authorship.[130] This leap, by which authorship (and therefore integrity) are no longer "relevant" concerns for the interpreter, allows him to view *Symeōn Petros*, at best, as a source of "canon-consciousness," a type of "community-creating identity."[131]

In truth, what Meade assumes for the *Sitz im Leben* of 2 Peter and Jude is no different than the position that NT scholarship has assumed for the last one hundred years. These epistles mirror a later, "gnostic" (i.e., second-century) libertinism.[132] It is because of Meade's presupposed "fundamental distinction between the era of the NT and the later church"[133] that pseudonymity is required of the NT documents. Removed from the first century, these writings necessitate pseudonymous authorship inasmuch as the church struggles to lay hold of an "authoritative tradition" with which to deal with the encroaching nature of heresy. By means of *Vergegenwärtigung* (i.e., a present application or new realization), the writers harken back to apostolic traditions in order to deal with the pressing needs of the Christian communities, displaying various levels of "canon-consciousness."[134] Meade writes:

> The pseudonymous epistles, then, are simply different members of the same family that we found in the 'anonymous' gospels and various literary genres of the prophetic, wisdom, and apocalyptic traditions. In other words by now quite familiar, attribution in the pseudonymous . . . epistles must be regarded as an assertion of authoritative tradition, not of literary origins.[135]

One can thank Meade for his service rendered in relating his main thesis to the issue of canon. Nevertheless a discussion of canon will necessarily lead to a discussion of theological commitments—implicit or explicit. Theology is perhaps more "relevant" than Meade might concede.[136] With regard to any book of the Bible, historical, literary, *and* theological components are inseparably interwoven. In reality, historical and theological questions *cannot* be divorced from one another—or considered less "relevant." Since the biblical books are historical documents, theology and history condition one another.

In seeking to establish normative criteria by which canonicity can be established, R. B. Gaffin, Jr.[137] notes the inability of the church historically to demonstrate a uniform set of criteria. In discussing the most frequently proposed criterion, apostolicity, Gaffin notes the difficulties with Mark, Luke-Acts, Hebrews, or Jude when one's definition of "apostle" is expanded to others who were *associated* with an apostle. And what if the writer of Hebrews was not an apostle? Did the church make the right decision for the wrong reason (assuming non-Pauline authorship)?[138] Can we be sure the church in fact made the right decision? What of the other materials circulating in the early Christian era?[139] Should the criterion of "inspiration" hold sway in measuring canon, what of the countless writings of the first century which are not extant? And Paul's previous letter to the Corinthians (cf. 1 Cor. 5 : 9), was it not sufficiently "apostolic," "authoritative," or "inspired"? Who or what is to serve as our guide?

Although Meade's stated purpose was to address the "fundamental lack in the history of the investigations of NT pseudonymity," Meade is unable to deliver as he stands squarely in the mainstream of historical-critical investigation of NT pseudonymity. The overriding premise of traditional historical-critical scholarship has been that the church's historic conception of the canon is outdated and unenlightened.[140] Meade affirms this view:

> it is the *prophetic* model that has dominated theories of inspiration in the church almost from the very beginning. While the validity of the prophetic mode of inspiration has never been called into question, the discovery of modern criticism as to how the Bible actually came about has made this model inappropriate for the inspiration of the Bible as a whole.[141]

The translation of Meade's reflection is as follows. Until the advent of modern criticism, the "prophetic mode" of inspiration served a purpose in the history of the church—until which time enlightened man did not need to recognize any longer the *divine* character and origin of Scripture.

In effect, then, divine "inspiration" is no longer *theopneustos;* it becomes "canon-consciousness." The church, writes Meade, has been guilty, until "the discovery of modern criticism," of overdependence on the model of prophetic inspiration.[142] With the arrival of scholarly consensus on a "canon within a canon," which posits that only a smaller nucleus of NT documents are authentic, we are left with two levels of "authoritative tradition": the *truly* authoritative documents (i.e., those verifiably Pauline) and the remaining (i.e., results of "canon-consciousness," nostalgic extensions of what the apostles would have taught).

Aside from Meade's basic operating assumption that Jude and 2 Peter are "early Catholic," a subject fully dealt with in the previous chapter, a second assumption carries significant implications. The assumption, accurate in and of itself, is that a need for control of doctrine arises.[143] Meade observes that this need for control led to the role of the magisterium, the closure of the canon, and stress on apostolic literary attribution.[144] Absent from Meade's thesis, as is the case with much of "enlightened" historical-critical inquiry, is the role that the Holy Spirit plays with regard to canon. Not *God Himself,* rather the magisterium, the church's hierarchy, it is argued, must sanction what is canonical. But here an important distinction must be made. That the church *recognizes* canon does not mean that the church *produces* canon. The activity of the church does not constitute canon, rather the activity of the *Sovereign Lord* of history, Who "in many and various ways in the past spoke by the prophets, but in these last days has spoken by His Son."[145]

The proposed need for control, interestingly, was expressed by Paul already in the mid first century:

> Keep watch over yourselves and all the flock of which the Holy Spirit has made you overseers. Be shepherds of the church of God, which he bought with his own blood. I know that after I leave, savage wolves will come in among you and will not spare the flock. Even from your own number men will arise and distort the truth in order to draw away disciples after them. So be on guard! Remember that for three years I never stopped warning each of you night and day with tears.[146]

Note the *origin* of "overseeing" *(episkopein)*: not an institution, not an office, rather the person of the Holy Spirit. It is the *Spirit* who produces, guards, and affirms what is canonical. The divine will is merely *recognized* by the church, which belongs to *God*. Seen as such, Jude's awareness of the need for control approximates that of Paul and rests as well with the *effective working of the Spirit*. In the context of Jude's exhortation, it is the responsibility of Jude's readers to recognize the *will* of the Spirit (vv 19, 20).

Crucial to our understanding of canonical "authority" is the unique function and place in the early church of the apostle, the authoritative ambassador of Christ, sent in the sense of Jesus, the Apostle of God (Heb. 3:1–2). Although the NT seems to imply other "apostles" besides the twelve (cf. Rom. 16:7), the character of the "apostles and prophets" (Eph. 2:20) is redemptive-historical. That is to say, their function in the "building" is unique:

> laying a foundation of a building is a one-time activity; the ensuing construction is on the superstructure, not the constant, repeated re-laying of the foundation. This temporal limitation ties in with the fact . . . that the foundation involves the work of Christ in its once-for-all historicity.[147]

What we must glean from this redemptive-historical aspect to apostolicity is the revelatory dimension of the apostle as a witness-bearer. Paul reminds the Corinthians that basic to the Christian *paradosis* received is that Jesus appeared to the apostles, even to him, the "least of the apostles."[148] This testimony borne by the apostles is crucial when seen in the light of the promise of the Spirit-Paraklete:[149]

> Apostolic witness . . . is not merely personal testimony. Instead, it is infallibly authoritative, legally binding deposition, the kind that stands up in a court of law. Accordingly, that witness embodies a canonical

principle; it provides the matrix for a new canon, the emergence of a new body of revelation to stand alongside the covenantal revelation of the Old Testament.[150]

The role of the apostles, then, is not tangential to the question of pseudonymity and canon. It is indeed the *apostles* themselves, not the Petrine, Johannine, or Matthean "schools," who were entrusted[151] with saving truth, a truth upon which the whole of the Christian faith stands.[152] The *apostolic* word was God's word (1 Thess. 2:13). For this reason, "canon" should not be viewed as a second-century invention of the church. It was, to be sure, inherited from the Jewish and early Christian view of the OT and, as an underlying premise, was present from the beginning. It was only natural then to view the apostolic writings of the first century as *theopneustos* (2 Tim. 3:16) and *hypo pneumatos hagiou pheromenoi elalēsan apo theou* (2 Pet. 1:21).

Thus, in light of (1) the *hapax* redemptive-historical character of the apostle, the divinely commissioned witness-bearer of truth and representative of Christ, and (2) the divine origin of the concept of "canon," to consider Jude, 2 Peter, or any books of the NT as pseudonymous is to acknowledge that they possess *less than fully divine authority.* To attempt to secure the weight of apostolic authority, even with the most noble of motives, is to *fall short* of genuine apostolic authority and, therefore, of the measure of canonicity. Thus, our criteria are eminently theological *and* historical and meet the standard set forth at the outset.[153]

In considering the attitude of NT scholarship to Jude, it will become clear that a circular reasoning, along literary as well as historical-critical and theological lines, has restricted Jude from being viewed outside of the second century. Related arguments have been adequately treated in the previous chapter. Since it is generally agreed that 2 Peter is literarily dependent on Jude, and Jude is subapostolic, neither could be authentic. Both clearly reflect a second-century gnostic scenario, not first-century Christianity. Moreover, the literary-rhetorical character of Jude does not fit the standard modern perception of a "Galilean peasant." In addition, an inadequate (by modern standards) external attestation would seem to exist regarding apostolic authorship.

What indeed typically does show up as *inadequate* in many discussions of NT pseudonymity is the amount of existing *external evidence* for pseudonymity. Had the church in the second and third centuries in fact been inclined to receive into the canon of the NT pseudonymous writings, the argument against authenticity of particular books would warrant some consideration. Noting evidence from the NT itself,[154] one is struck by the "canon" of *truthfulness* (=integrity) which undergirds all of its teaching. NT injunctions to think, speak, and act the truth would render the practice of pseudonymity, at best, inconsistent with the standards of the OT, Jesus, and the apostles.[155] This is particularly significant for 2 Peter, where we find several explicit attempts by the writer, if indeed the letter is pseudepigraphic, to deceive the readership in his identifying with Petrine *experience:* 1:1, 1:14; 1:16–18; 3:15. It is one thing to continue a Petrine tradition. It is *quite another,* being generations removed, to claim eyewitness experience with Christ—at best an unethical practice based on the teaching of Jesus. The writer, in spite of any sense of "canon-consciousness," can hardly bear what Meade would call "authority" if he is seeking *to this extent* to identify with the apostle Peter. While no scholarly agreement exists as to how to perceive the ethical element of pseudonymity, T. D. Lea[156] is correct in stating that those who dismiss the ethical question as irrelevant have not succeeded in explaining how a church concerned with truth could have condoned the deceit of false literary attribution.

Having observed then that there exists no evidence from the history of the church suggesting that canonical pseudepigraphy was accepted, the claim of NT pseudonymity fails to be convincing for lack of support—on historical and theological as well as ethical grounds.

4

The Use of the Old Testament in Jude

The Jude epistle manifests a high regard for the OT; use of OT source-material is pervasive. It has been commonly assumed that Jude's knowledge and use of the OT were dependent on the LXX,[1] due in part to his employment of vocabulary found in the LXX. If, however, Jude is quoting apocryphal works representative of Palestinian Judaism and hence dealing with Semitic texts, it cannot be taken for granted that he was dependent on a Greek version of the OT. While the fluidity of Jude's Greek has already been established, it should be noted nonetheless that his overall knowledge of the OT is more significant in and of itself than whether he was dependent on the LXX or a Hebrew version.

In general terms, Jude feels at home with material from the Torah, the prophets, or the wisdom corpus. In addition to the cosmic/solar phenomena already brought under consideration,[2] OT concepts surface in the use of election, theophany, the great day of the Lord, judgment by fire, rebellion in heaven, angelic administration, apostasy, divine foreknowledge and predestination, divine justice and mercy, deliverance, and divine kingship/sovereignty. The writer's method is apocalyptic, paraenetic, didactic or catechetical, liturgical, and as argued earlier, rhetorical. Devices incorporated into his strategy include contrast, typology, midrash, a woe-cry and a hymn, in addition to the stylistic features already noted.

Consideration has already been given to the "midrashic" working of material in Jude.[3] In vv 5–16, historical paradigms are set forth by the writer to furnish proof of his argument. These historical types are linked by particular catchwords and applied to Jude's opponents. The structure of type, interpretation, type, interpretation, etc., becomes a form of midrash on the fate of the ungodly.[4] Jude is skillful in his reworking of OT material, i.e., in his bringing the text to the readers.[5] Not unlike the practice of Jewish apocalyptic writers, Jude makes frequent allusion to the OT without formal citations. Although such allusions are selective in character and not prophetic citations or "prophecies" in the strict sense, they owe nonetheless to scriptural tradition. This approach to the OT differs notably from the more explicit and tedious midrashic activity of the rabbis. The relating of the OT tradition prophetically to the situation at hand, a modifying of the text to suit the present need, and the use of catchwords to form links in the polemic all give reason to compare, in a broad sense, Jude's hermeneutic with the technique employed in Qumran.[6] A prime feature of QL is that it abounds in allusions to the OT without utilizing explicit quotations—what might appear to be verbal echoes or reminiscences.[7]

JUDE'S DEPENDENCE ON OLD TESTAMENT MOTIFS

The last two centuries B.C. and the first century A.D. were crucial to the formation of Judaism as well as the Christian faith, whose birth is owing to its Jewish matrix. While the literature of Judaism during this period derived its inspiration from the Hebrew scriptures, it took on a variety of faces. It may be characterized on the one hand by reverence for the temple, the Torah, and Jewish tradition, or it may reflect on the other hand a devotion to monastic community or a focusing on the coming of the new age, i.e., a terminating of the present one. At the root of much of Jewish thinking lies the belief in God's justice—the conviction that the righteous will be vindicated while the ungodly incur judgment. Hence, the coming of God means vindication, a release of the ungodly-faithful tension.

What follows is an examination of several motifs figuring prominently in the OT which are employed by Jude in his marshalling of evidence for addressing the urgent need in the Christian community. Past paradigms speak forcefully in the present setting.

The Ungodly Faithful Antithesis

1. TYPES OF UNGODLINESS IN JUDE. On center stage in the epistle are the opponents of Jude, *hoi asebeis,* who sever any ethical link to fellowship and pursue license. Apart from the epistle of Romans, the term *asebeia* or cognate forms occur only in the Pastorals, 1 and 2 Peter, and Jude. Of the total of sixteen NT occurrences, five are in Jude.[8] At the root of *asebeia* is the despising of order or authority, and hence for Jews and Christians alike, divine commandments.[9] Therefore, the burning issue in Jude is the rela-

tionship between eschatology and ethics. It is here that the boundaries of *asebeia* become visible.

Two sets of triplets (vv 5–7 and 11) are employed by the writer as paradigms for ungodliness. In 5–7, unbelieving Israel, the rebellious angels, and Sodom and Gomorrah all serve to illustrate a crucial point. Each departed from a normal condition, hence undergoing judgment and subsequent disenfranchisement. Unbelieving Israel, after having been delivered *once for all (hapax)* from Egypt, was destroyed "the second time" *(to deuteron)*. The angels who had not "kept" their rule have been henceforth "kept" (note the perfect *tetērēken,* placing stress on the continuing effects of the divine action of the past) for "the judgment of the great day." And Sodom and Gomorrah, whose judgment in v 7 is linked correspondingly to that of the angels in v 6, presently serves as an abiding example *(prokeintai deigma)* of divine judgment.

A particular relationship exists between vv 6 and 7, demonstrated by the uniting particle *hōs.* It is specifically the element of judgment, i.e., the *effects* of sin, and not the particular *kind* of sin, which is in the view of the writer. A misunderstanding of this small but crucial point by virtually all commentators past and present causes us to miss the true sense of the polemic in Jude. His purpose is *not* to link the fall of the angels with elaborate late Judaistic construals of sexual sin between the angels and "the daughters of men" (cf. Gen. 6 : 1–4), such as one finds in 1 Enoch. Rather, the emphasis of the text is willful *departing* from the truth.

A second triad of ungodly types appears in v 11. Cain, Balaam, and Korah are united by means of a woe-cry. Moreover, each of the three is signified by a formula—"the way of Cain," "the error of Balaam," "the rebellion of Korah"—which would give the appearance of a standardization of type that had already been formulated in Judaistic circles. The three verbs of v 11—*poreuomai* ("walk"), *ekcheein* ("abandon"), and *apollymi* ("perish")—describe the course of *hoi asebeis* in three levels of ascending gravity. The *houtoi* at first walk, next they abandon, and finally they perish.[10]

2. THE ESSENTIAL NATURE OF ANTITHESIS IN JUDE. Two sides to *asebeia* are to be seen in the epistle. There is manifest a distortion in behavior, a perverting of grace to the point of sexual license (*tēn tou theou hēmōn charita metatithentes eis aselgeian,* v 4c) as well as a denial of divine lordship (*ton monon despotēn kai kyrion hēmōn Iēsoun Christon arnoumenoi,* v 4d). The inherent character of any heresy is that it is both doctrinal and ethical. It entails beliefs and conduct.[11] In ascribing to Jesus both *kyrios* and *despotēs,* the writer seeks to counter his opponents with the oneness and *absolute*

sovereignty of the Lord. Apostates tend toward libertinism, and because their proclivity is to lead others astray, they are marked for certain judgment, as the letter of Jude stresses.

The fundamental dichotomy expressed in the epistle is the tension between the ungodly and the faithful. The *houtoi* (vv 8,10,11 [*autois*],12,14,16,19) and *hymeis* (vv 3,5,12,17,18,20,24) represent antipodal characters. The former are depicted in terms of *asebeia* (vv 4,15,18), *aselgeia* (v 4), and *epithymia* (vv 16,18). Both in doctrine and conduct they deny the only Sovereign and Lord Himself (v 4). The faithful, on the other hand, are portrayed in Jude as *hagios* (vv 14,20), *misountes kai ton apo tēs sarkos espilōmenon chitōna* (v 23), and *amōmos* (v 24). This fondness for juxtaposition is a notable feature of OT wisdom literature, and particularly, the book of Proverbs, where the righteous and the foolish stand as irreconcilable opposites. As noted earlier, innumerable contrasts or contradictions appear throughout the letter. The writer is a true interpreter of Israel's wisdom of old.

Theophany and Judgment

Perhaps one of the most central themes to the OT is that of *YHWH's* "coming." What is striking concerning *YHWH's* appearance, however, is not so much the description given to His *form* as the *manner* in which He manifests Himself—through fire, a flood, a storm, etc.[12] Theophany in the OT entails two aspects: a description of God's advent and an ensuing upheaval in nature.[13] OT theophany statements tend to exhibit a particular pattern. This would include (1) a prophetic introduction formula, often *kî hinneh* or *hinneh* (e.g., Isa. 26:21 [LXX: *idou gar*]; 35:4: *hinneh* [*idou*]; 40:10 [*idou*]; Mic. 1:3 [*dioti idou*]; 66:15: *kî hinneh* [*idou gar*]); (2) the declaration that the Lord comes, often in the prophetic perfect (e.g., Deut. 33:2: *bāʾ* [LXX: *hēkei*]; Isa. 35:4: *yābôʾ* [*hēxei*]; 40:10: *yābôʾ* [*erchetai*]; 66:15: *yābôʾ* [*hēxei*]; Mic. 1:3: *yōṣēʾ* [*ekporeuetai*]; Hab. 3:3: *yābôʾ* [*hēxei*]); (3) the accompaniment of myriads of His holy ones (e.g., Deut. 33:2: *mēribebōt gōdeš* [LXX: *syn myriasin Kadēs;* 33:3: *hoi hagiasmenoi*]; Ps. 68:18: *baqqōdeš* [*en tō hagiō*]; Zech. 14:5: *kāl-gĕdōsîm immāk* [*pantes hoi hagioi met' autou*]); (4) the execution of judgment upon all (e.g., Isa. 26:21: *lipqōd ʿaôn yōsēb-hāʾāreṣ ʾālāw* [LXX: *epagei tēn orgēn epi tous enoikountas epi tēs gēs*]; 35:4: *nāqām . . . ʾelōhîm* [*krisin antapodidōsin kai antapodōsei*]; 66:16: *kî bāʾēš . . . nišpāṭ wûbĕḥarbô et-kāl-bāśār* [*en tō pyri . . . krithēsetai pasa hē gē kai en tē rhomphaiᾳ autou pasa sarx*]; Nah. 1:2: *nōqēn . . . lĕzārāw wĕnôṭēr . . . lĕʾōyĕbāw* [*ekdikōn . . . meta thymou ekdikōn . . . tous hypenantious autou, kai exairōn . . . tous ech-throus autou*]; Jer. 25:31: *nišpāṭ . . . lĕkālbāśār*); (5) the godless perish (e.g., Isa. 66:16: *wĕrabbû ḥalĕlē YHWH* [LXX: *polloi trau-matiai esontai hypo kyriou*]; Jer. 25:31: *hārĕshāʾîm nĕtānām laḥereb*); and (6) ensuing upheaval in the earth (e.g., Isa. 26:21: *wĕgillĕtāh hāʾāreṣ etdāmehā* [LXX: *anakalypsei hē gē to haima autēs*]; Mic. 1:4: *wĕnāmassû hehārîm taḥtāw wehāʿamāqîm yitbaqāuʿ*[LXX: *saleuthēsetai ta orē hypokatōthen autou, kai hia koilades takēsontai*]; Nah. 1:5: *hārîm rāʿašû mimmennû wehagbāʿôt hitmōgāgû wattiśśāʾ hāʾāreṣ mippānāw* [*ta orē eseisthēsan ap' autou, kai hoi bounoi esaleuthēsan kai anestalē hē gē apo prosōpou autou*]; Zech. 14:6: *lōʾ yihyeh ʾôr yĕgārôt yĕqipāʾôn* [*ouk estai phōs kai psychos kai pagos*]).[14] The theophany statement in Jude, it should be noted, conforms to the pattern of theophany as employed in the OT.

In his examination of apocalyptic literature, L. Hartman[15] has noted the extent to which the OT has furnished the source of theology, language, and details for these works. The theophany statement found in 1 Enoch 1:4–9, from which Jude 14–15 is taken, is explicitly derived from the Sinai theophany and blessing of Moses in Deut. 33:11ff:[16]

> The Lord came from Sinai
>   And dawned over them from Seir;
>   He shone forth from Mount Paran.
> He came with myriads of holy ones
>   From the south, from his mountain slopes.
> Surely it is you who love the people,
>   All the holy ones are in your hand.
>   (Deut. 33:2–3)

The actual text of Jude 14–15 (and 1 Enoch 1:9), upon closer analysis, not only draws heavily from theophany statements as already highlighted, but is immersed in the language and imagery of the OT in general:

Idou ēlthen kyrios . . .	Deut. 32:2; Judg. 5:4; Pss. 18:9; 68:18; Isa. 19:1; 26:21; 31:4, 27; 40:10; Dan. 7:10; Amos 1:2; Mic. 1:3; Hab. 3:3; Zeph. 1:7; Zech. 9:14; 14:1, 3; Mal. 3:1–3.
en hagiais[17] *myriasin autou* . . .	Deut. 33:2; Ps. 68:17; Isa. 40:10; 66:15; Dan. 7:10
poiēsai krisin peri pantōn . . .	Deut. 10:18; Pss. 76:9; 96:13;

| | Isa. 33:5; Jer. 25:31; Dan. 7:10, 13, 26; Joel 3:2; Zeph. 3:8; Hab. 1:12; Mal. 2:17; 3:5 |
| *elegxai pasan psychēn* . . . | Isa. 66:15–24; Jer. 25:31; Zeph. 1:8–9, 12; Mal. 3:3–5 |

More recently, C. D. Osburn[18] and L. Hartman[19] have examined the theophanic motif common to Jude and 1 Enoch. In both Jude and 1 Enoch the Lord appears for the purpose of judgment (*poiēsai krisin kata pantōn*). The text of 1 Enoch reads *hoti erchetai*;[20] Jude reads *Idou ēlthen* and adds *kyrios* in his christological reshaping of the tradition.[21] Most significant, however, is the catchword *asebeia*, appearing three times in v 15, which links both sources. As with the majority of the preexilic prophetic judgment speeches, theophany frequently occurs within the context of denouncing both the wickedness of the nations and that of Israel. The sins of *YHWH*'s people are not relegated to being a private matter; they affect the whole of the covenant community. Thus, the prophets sought to awake a corporate sense of national guilt, for "the soil was not infertile for the prophetic proclamation of God's judgment on Israel."[22]

The possibility of a covenant relationship predicated on unmerited favor, yet conditioned by certain non-negotiable stipulations, already implies the possibility of punitive intervention and abrogation:

> Just as it is impossible in the case of a covenant between human beings to dismiss the thought of the *ᵓālāh*, the covenant curse on the breaker of the contract, so in the case of the *bĕrît* at Sinai such a curse is found. . . . The force and earnestness with which it was impressed on the people of Israel that these stipulations must never be broken, and that Yahweh would watch jealously to see that they were not, effectively inhibited any complacent feeling of possessing in the covenant a relationship with God that would hold good automatically and as a matter of course.[23]

The "divine reversal," in which the anticipated doom hanging over the nations was with unambiguity applied to *Israel*, was preached with intensity by the Hebrew prophets. As far as Amos is concerned, the day of the Lord is darkness, not light, and is designated for the faithless among Israel, i.e., those who have become apostate. The prophet forcefully points to this unexpected reversal:

Do not rejoice, O Israel;
  Do not be jubilant like other nations.
For you have been unfaithful to your God;
  You love the wages of a prostitute
  At every threshing floor.

(Amos 9:1)

To the degree that divine favor has been poured out, divine judgment is meted out. The prophet grimly promises not one sinner will escape (Amos 9:1).

Jude refers to the divine reversal as *hē krisis megalēs hēmeras* (v 6) and includes angels in this event. The angels who chose to rebel, just as Israel, which, after having been *hapax* saved, was destroyed *to deuteron* (v 5), have been reserved in chains of darkness. Darkness (*zophos:* vv 6, 13; *skotos:* v 13) is the prominent mode depicting the day of the Lord in the OT. Darkness, doom, and gloom depict the nature of *YHWH*'s visitation.[24]

With absolute abandon, the prophets decried covenant breaking, for this perversion of the faith was as a cancer that would corrupt the whole nation, causing the people of God to turn away from *YHWH*. Righteousness could only be restored when the ungodly, the apostate, had perished (e.g., Pss. 12:1–5; 58:6–11; 75; 82; Hab. 3:2,13). The prophets await this restoration in the form of theophany. The statement from 1 Enoch, then, rooted in antecedent pronouncements from the OT, rings prophetically true with regard to Jude's opponents. Theophany and judgment merge in the writer's response to the distortions of the *houtoi*. In line with the OT theophany tradition, the Lord "comes" to judge His enemy (be it the faithless outside of the people of God or *within*). He comes from His holy dwelling, and this coming is attended by His holy ones as well as upheaval in the natural phenomena. Manifested simultaneously as salvation for the upright, this visitation spells punishment and divine wrath for the ungodly. With the potential of corrupting the believing community through the cancer of their unbelief, the apostates are consigned in Jude to judgment in the most forbidding terms.

Jude's hermeneutic is here facilitating two goals: he is faithful to the OT tradition of theophany statements—"Behold, the Lord comes"—and in the use of 1 Enoch he exploits a literary source of sectarian Judaism to which possibly his audience, or the apostates themselves, were devoted. Theophany in Jude is strategic. The focal point is the *fate* of the ungodly; hereby the past is linked to the present. Jude's opponents must acknowledge this: behold, the

Lord comes, to execute judgment upon the ungodly, and this with awesome fury.

Judgment by Fire

As befits the symbolism and language of judgment, the Jude epistle alludes to the fiery judgment which beset Sodom and Gomorrah. The cities of the plain serve as an ongoing illustration of divine vengeance upon the wicked (prokeintai deigma pyros aiōniou dikēn hypechousai, v 7). Occurring seventy-three times in the NT,[25] "fire" also appears in all but four books of the OT. The mention of fire in the OT falls primarily within two contexts: Israel's cultic activity and YHWH's judging. All of the prophets speak of YHWH's acts in terms of fire. It is the chief prophetic metaphor used to depict divine judgment, whether directed toward Israel or the nations. Fire throughout the history of Israel's religion is only meaningful when its theological significance is understood.[26] Whether seen in the cult or through the prophetic eye to depict judgment, the nature of fire is one of mystery, unpredictability, unapproachableness, immutability, fluidity, and absolute consumption. In its essence, it is inseparable from the concept of YHWH's holiness. Hence, it can be accurately described as a symbol for divine holiness, representing God's nature, His very manifestation. He is a "consuming fire."[27]

Offerings within a cultic context are fully burnt and begin with Noah's sacrifice (Gen. 8:20). They continue up to the constant burning of the fire on the altar in the Holy Place, as prescribed according to Mosaic law (Lev. 6:9,12,13). The fire itself was lit by God (Lev. 9:24), in the same way that fire came down from heaven and consumed David's and Solomon's offerings (1 Chron. 21:26; 2 Chron. 7:1) as well as the sacrifice of Elijah in the presence of the Baal prophets (1 Kings 18:38). All other fire for cultic use was unauthorized, attested to by the death sentence on Aaron's sons Nadab and Abihu (Lev. 10:1–3; Num. 3:4; 26:61): "Among those who approach me I will show myself holy" (Lev. 10:3).[28] The sin offering was to be burned outside the camp (Exod. 29:14; Lev. 4:12,21,25,30; 16:27; Heb. 13:11). On the day the Nazirite ended his vow, he was required to make several offerings, among them a sin- and burnt-offering, to the Lord (Num. 6:13–15) in addition to having his hair shorn, which was then to be burned in conjunction with the fellowship offering (6:18). Even spoils which were accrued from Israel's military conquests were to be cleansed by fire (Num. 31:21–23).

Marking cases of greater severity, particular instances of wickedness were to be met with punishment by burning with fire—for example, a man marrying both a woman and her daughter (Lev. 20:14), the daughter of a priest becoming a prostitute (Lev. 21:9), Achan's hoarding of spoils from the battle at Ai (Josh. 7:15,24),[29] and rebellion against the leadership of Moses (Num. 16:35).

Insofar as it symbolizes God's transcendent nature and inherent holiness, fire becomes the instrument through which He manifests Himself. Fire in the OT is foremost theophanic. The appearance of *YHWH*'s presence and glory is most closely akin to fire, awesome and purifying in its very essence. Men could not bear sight of Him. A flame of fire burst forth from the bush (Exod. 3:2). As Israel moved into the wilderness after deliverance from Egypt, *YHWH* led them by means of a cloud by day and a pillar of fire by night (Exod. 13:21,22; 14:24; Num. 9:16; 14:14; Deut. 1:33). Upon Mount Sinai, *YHWH* descended as fire (Exod. 19:18; Deut. 4:11; 5:4,22,23–26); during Moses' forty days and nights on the mountain, the divine glory was as a devouring fire (Exod. 24:17). Ten times throughout the book of Deuteronomy the statement "And *YHWH* spoke to you from the midst of the fire" occurs.[30]

Appropriately, fire is also a primary vehicle of divine judgment. When Israel complained in the wilderness, *YHWH*'s anger was stirred so that He sent fire to consume parts of the camp (Num. 11:1–3). Pertinent to our study of Jude, the two hundred fifty men among Israel's leaders who sided with Korah in his rebellion against Moses' leadership (Num. 16:2,35; 26:10) were consumed by fire from heaven, a fire which was subsequently to consecrate the rest of Israel (16:36–50). Judgment by fire, not surprisingly, is a theme found in every book of the OT prophetic corpus with the exception of Jonah. Alone in Isaiah, Jeremiah, and Ezekiel, ʾēš occurs 115 times.[31] The Hebrew prophets in general depict Yahweh's visitation as a roaring, consuming fire that burns with incomprehensible fury. They all declare Him to be foremost the Sovereign Judge. More often than not, the prophetic indictments are aimed at the people of God.[32]

In line with the Hebrew prophets of old, Jude reinforces for his readers the fate of the ungodly. Judgment by fire was manifest in past history and serves as a reminder to his audience in the present. Eschatology is a strong motivation for ethics.

Divine Foreknowledge and "Keeping"

The language of foreknowledge and predestination—a fundamentally Jewish concept—is woven into the epistle of Jude. Three words with the prefix *pro*—*prographein* (v 4),[33] *prophēteuein* (v 14), and *prolegein* (v 17)—accentuate the theme of sovereign and eternal purpose hinted at already in the greeting of the letter, where the readers are addressed with election terminology *(klētoi*, v 1).[34] In addition to the vehement denunciations contained in the letter, the writer is using the language of *strong affirmation* with a view of exhorting his audience. The faithful have been *destined* for God's love and mercy. The inheritance of the Christian is the future as well. The believer has been appointed to a privileged status in the total divine plan. Here the emphasis is on *God*. We are chosen to live by faith for *His* purpose. That privilege is not to be squandered or taken lightly.

A feature not uncommon to the OT and apocalyptic literature in particular is the notion of names written in heavenly books (e.g., Exod. 32:32–33; Pss. 40:4; 56:8; 69:28; 139:16; implied in 90:12; Isa. 4:3; Jer. 22:30; Dan. 7:10; 12:1; Mal. 3:16; 1 Enoch 81:1–2; 89:62; 90:14,17,20,22; 104:7; 108:3,7; Jub. 5:13; 6:31; 16:9; 23:32; 28:6; 30:9; 32:21; T.Ass. 7:5; 2 Apoc. Bar. 24:1; Rev. 3:5; 5:1–5,7,8; 10:8–11; 20:12).[35] These "heavenly books" reflect a religious self-understanding fundamental to Jewish thought, namely that the divine purpose, though hidden from the view of man, is predetermined and revealed in history. The "scroll" of Revelation 5, to illustrate, is a view of history from the divine perspective. The heavenly books point to the divine foreknowledge by which "the chosen" of Israel were called to be Yahweh's own possession and, hence, instruments (note, e.g., Ps. 139:16 and Jer. 1:5).

Reminiscent of Ps. 69(68):29 ("May they be blotted out of the book of life and not be listed with the righteous"), Jude 4 refers to the ungodly as *hoi palai progegrammenoi eis touto to krima* ("those whose judgment was written down long ago"). The essence of the verb *prographein,* which occurs four times in the NT,[36] is juridical and proscriptive. It carries a specific penal sense, viz., that of a public accusation against criminals.[37] In their use of the term, Josephus (*hē progegrammenē hēmera: Ant.* 2.283) and the writer of 1 Maccabees (*prographētōsan tōn Ioudaiōn eis tas dynameis,* 10:36) reflect the inherent OT concept: appointment or predetermination. Jer. 22:30, Mal. 3:16–18, and Dan. 7:10 capture the sense of divine destiny associated with the heavenly scroll:

> This is what the Lord says:
> Record this man as if childless,
> A man who will not prosper in his lifetime,

For none of his offspring will prosper,
    None will sit on the throne of David
Or rule anymore in Judah.

Then those who feared the Lord talked with each other, and the Lord listened and heard. A scroll of remembrance was written in his presence concerning those who had feared the Lord and honored his name. "They will be mine," says the Lord Almighty, "in the day when I make up my treasured possession. I will spare them, just as in compassion a man spares his son who serves him. And you will again see the distinction between the righteous and the wicked, between those who serve God and those who do not."

A river of fire was flowing,
    Coming out before him.
Thousands upon thousands attended him;
    Ten thousand times ten thousand stood before him.
The court was seated,
    And the books were opened.[38]

Some disagreement exists as to the precise rendering of *hoi palai progegrammenoi eis touto to krima* in Jude 4. Four alternatives are normally suggested. Verse 4 could be interpreted as (1) a particular OT prophecy which has found its fulfillment (the approximate sense of Heb. 1:1, for example); (2) fulfillment of an apostolic prophecy regarding apostasy;[39] (3) the recalling of the prophecy of doom appearing in 2 Pet. 2:1–3;[40] or (4) the Jewish apocalyptic notion of heavenly tablets. In that apocalyptic writings are roughly contemporary with the NT and these works, as we have sought to demonstrate, build upon OT motifs, we would favor the latter view as being most plausible. *Progegrammenoi* need not be restricted to a temporal or contemporary sense,[41] since *prographein* stands in conjunction with two other *pro*-words in the letter.[42] Together these terms intensify the predestination motif which is central to OT and apocalyptic writings.

Casting his opponents as ungodly antitypes for which judgment, long since prescribed, has already been established on "the great day,"[43] Jude views judgment as fulfilled in the *houtoi* of the present. A tension exists in Jude between divine sovereignty and human freedom. The readers are secure as those *ēgapēmenoi* and *tetērēmenoi* by God; these are *klētoi* (v 1). Furthermore, they are "kept" (*phylassein*) most securely in God (v 24), yet they must choose to be established (*histēmi*, v 24). They are to be terrified at the *possibility* of falling away from the Lord, a fate as devastating as the prophets of old had declared.

The Divine Glory

One of the most central of biblical concepts[44] appears thrice in Jude: *doxa* (vv 8,24, and 25). The NT use of *doxa* distinguishes itself markedly from customary secular usage, in which the term frequently denotes "opinion" or human "honor."[45] It is the equivalent of the *kābôd YHWH* in the OT and signifies foremost the grandeur, majesty, and brilliance of God which proceeds from His presence (e.g., Exod. 24:16ff; Lev. 9:6; Num. 14:10; Deut. 5:24; 1 Kings 8:11; 2 Chron. 5:14; Pss. 29:9; 72:19; Isa. 6:3; Ezek. 1:28). God's power is an expression of His nature, and the divine *doxa* reveals His nature in creation. In strong contrast to the "darkness" *(skotos)* and "gloom" *(zophos)* awaiting the apostate, be it men or angels (vv 6 and 13), the faithful in Jude have the "glory" *(doxa)* of divine presence to anticipate (vv 24,25).

The divine "glory" is experienced by the people of God in the OT in several notable contexts: the giving of the Law (Exod. 19:16ff), sanctification of the Mosaic tabernacle (Exod. 29:43; 40:34), and the Temple (1 Kings 8:10ff; 2 Chron. 7:1ff). Nevertheless, this same glory may not be seen by mortal men (Exod. 33:20); the *kābôd YHWH* is always veiled—on Mount Sinai (Exod. 24:15ff) or in the tent of the meeting (Exod. 16:10; 29:43; 40:34; Lev. 9:6,23; Num. 14:10; 17:7; 20:6). It passes by Moses (Exod. 33:19–23; 34:6) and Elijah (1 Kings 19:11). Notably, it is Moses and Elijah who appear on the mountain with Jesus in His transfiguration (Matt. 17:1ff = Mark 9:2ff = Luke 9:28ff). In the NT, the Son is the brilliance of the *doxa* and "exact representation" *(charaktēr)* of God's being, the sustainer of all things (Heb. 1:3). All of the attributes ascribed to God in the OT are transferred to *Kyrios*-Jesus.

Although the reference in Jude 8 to "glories" *(doxai)* is apocalyptic in mode (T.Jud. 25:2: *hai dynameis tēs doxēs;* T.Lev. 18:5: *hoi aggeloi tēs doxēs;* cf. also 2 Enoch 21:1,3; 1QH 10:8; Rev. 18:1; and Philo [*De specialibus legibus* 1.45]),[46] the notion is rooted in the OT, where the cherub is the bearer of the divine *kābôd* (Ezek. 9:3; 10:4,18,22; cf. also Sir. 49:8). As vehicles for transmitting the divine glory, the angels thus became an extension of that glory; hence, they are *doxai*, "rays of glory"[47] emanating from the throne of God.[48] This would sufficiently explain why in Exod. 15:11 the LXX uses the plural dative *doxais* in translating *baqqōdeš*. The views of L. Brun,[49] J.N.D. Kelly,[50] and J. Cantinat,[51] who hold the use of *doxai* as a counter to gnostic theology and hence an abstraction for Christ's lordship or worthship, essentially miss the flavor of the allusion. By reading into v 8 a second-century scenario, one over-looks the OT and apocalyptic sense of *doxai.*

Both *doxai* and *kyriotēs* stem from an apocalyptic milieu which knows between four and nine levels of heavens. An illustration is found in the Ascension of Isaiah: "Worship neither throne *(kyriotēs)* nor angel which belongs to the six heavens—for this reason I was sent to lead you—until I tell you in the seventh heaven."[52]

The "rulers" and "glories" of v 8 are parallel to and belong with Michael, mentioned in v 9. All are bearers of *kābôd* and stand in poignant contrast to *hoi aggeloi . . . eis krisin . . . desmois aidiois hypo zophon tetērēmenoi* (v 6). Just as the *houtoi* and *hymeis* are in antag-onism, the fallen angels stand in antithesis to the *doxai* and *kyriotētes* in Jude. A further hint as to the identity of the *doxai* is the link *homoiōs* between vv 7 and 8. The attitude of Jude's opponents in v 8—*sarka miainousin,*[53] *kyriotēta athetousin, doxas blasphēmousin*—is reminiscent of Sodom's attitude toward the angelic visitors in Gen. 19. This link is also found in T.Ass. 7 : 1: "Do not become like Sodom, which did not recognize the Lord's angels and perished forever."

The contrast of doom and glory is accentuated in Jude. While the fate of the apostate is clearly delineated in the judgment of types from history, Jude's readers, in remaining established in the faith, can be assured of future glorious presentation before the Lord.

TYPOLOGICAL EXEGESIS IN JUDE—A CLOSER LOOK

Typology is integral to the question of the use of the OT in the NT. It is the characteristic method of interpretation found in the NT and probably constituted a key in the church's hermeneutic from the beginning.[54] For the first-century Jew it was entirely natural to see the past episodes in Israel's history as a shadow of the future, to view the significance of the present in terms of the past. By means of typology, the NT writer applies a deeper sense of application, often christological or "heilsgeschichtlich," to the present. A type presupposes a purpose in history which is wrought from age to age;[55] it bears out a spiritual correspon-dence and historical connection between people, events, or things.[56]

The NT portrait of salvation-history reflects a definite awareness of continuity as well as differentiation. The aspect of

continuity is established by prophecy or promise and fulfillment.[57] Constituent elements of typology include (1) a historical,
factual correspondence, (2) a distinction between type and symbol
(the latter being a token of expression of a general truth), and (3)
a distinction between type and allegory.[58]

Whereas the Greeks devoted themselves to allegory, myth, and
symbolism, the employment of typology is to be understood as a
distinctly Jewish phenomenon. Typological exegesis flowers particularly in the later Judaistic period, i.e., 150 B.C.E.–C.E. 100. It is
found to be more prevalent among Palestinian Jewish, that is
rabbinic and pseudepigraphal, writings than among Alexandrian.
This is owing to the inherent link between typology and eschatology.[59] In general terms, Palestinian exegesis proceeded
along literal-symbolic-typological lines while its Alexandrian
counterpart was primarily symbolic-allegorical.[60]

Stemming from the verb *typtein*, "to strike," "blow," or "leave a
mark," *typos* eventually came to signify a "figure" or "pattern." Of
the five substantives in the NT which denote "pattern,"[61] three—
deigma, hypodeigma, and *typos*—are applicable to the epistle of Jude
in describing the writer's use of the OT.[62] Jude 7 is the lone NT
occurrence of *deigma* ("sample," "specimen," i.e., a "particular
instance of a general pattern").[63] As is the case with Jude 7, *deigma*
often has an attached moral connotation. We can interpret Sodom
and Gomorrah as either a sample of divine retribution and
punishment of sinners (with *pyros* qualifying *dikēn*) or, less probably, an instance of a particular kind of punishment pending (in
which case *pyros* goes with *deigma*).

2 Pet. 2:6 uses *hypodeigma* to describe the destruction of Sodom
and Gomorrah; it is a "sign" or "example" of that which is coming
and appointed for the ungodly. This approximates the sense of
Jude 7. *Hypodeigma* has the sense of teaching by *suggestion* or
intimation.[64] Significantly, Israel in the wilderness serves as an
"example" of unbelief in Heb. 4:11. The readers are warned of
imitation and admonished to learn by instruction.[65] The cognate
paradeigma is used of Sodom and Gomorrah in 3 Macc. 2:5 and
involves the notion of contrast.[66] Interestingly, one of only two
occurrences in the NT of *paradeigmatizein* is found in Hebrews 6 in
a context of apostasy. The writer announces that repentance is
impossible for those having fallen away from the faith inasmuch
as they have crucified again the Son of God and made Him a show
of public disgrace (6:6).

The most frequently occurring term in NT paradigm terminology is *typos*.[67] Normally rendered "type," "pattern," or "mold,"

it conveys the idea of *resemblance*.[68] The type is a visible representation of a spiritual reality. Correspondence, it should be noted, goes beyond mere metaphor. An organic or historical relationship exists between type and antitype.[69]

The NT's use of typology facilitates the announcement that the fulfillment of redemption has arrived, comprehended in Christ.[70] Although a certain tension yet remains between present fulfillment and future, hidden consummation, one may speak of fulfillment nonetheless. The effect of NT typology is to comfort, exhort, and warn; the end, though certain, is hidden and unannounced.

One is struck by the relative density of types appearing in the epistle to the Hebrews, 2 Peter, and Jude. All three letters have a fondness for instruction using comparison to OT events or persons. Specifically, the paradigms in Jude are marshalled chiefly to warn against the cancer of apostasy. Evidence is compounded against the guilty. The writer calls up exhibit after exhibit as supporting proof of his argumentation. The past in Jude explains the present and serves as a token for the future.

Unbelieving Israel (v 5)

Jude 5[71] contains the first of a triplet of examples in unfaithfulness which seem to have belonged to popular tradition. Similar paraenetic sayings are to be found in Ben Sira,[72] Jubilees,[73] 3 Maccabees,[74] the Testaments of the Twelve Patriarchs,[75] the Damascus Document,[76] and the Mishnah,[77] all of which speak to the issue of hardheartedness, apostasy or disregard for God's commandments.[78]

Several examples from apocryphal and pseudepigraphal writings are sufficient for illustration. The writer in Sir. 16:5–15 gives a catalog of historical paradigms which includes Korah (v 6), Assyria (v 6), giants (v 7), Sodomites (v 8), Canaanites (v 9), and Israel's falling away (v 10). Catchwords occurring in Sirach 16 include *sklērokardia*, *sklērotrachelos*, *apeithein*, and *aphistēmi*. The context of 3 Macc. 2:3–7 is a prayer for Israel against a Ptolemy. It enumerates as paradigms Pharaoh, Sodomites, and giants and warns that God judges a heart in which is found a mixture and arrogance (2:3). T. Naph. 2:8–4:3, a text not unlike 1 Enoch 2:1–5:4, draws lessons from the Flood, the Watchers, Sodom, and the Gentiles. The Watchers (3:5), as the Gentiles (3:3) and the men of Sodom (3:4; 4:1), departed from nature's order. Yet the sun, moon, and stars do not alter their course. At work, explains the writer, is a spirit of deception (*planē*, 3:3) which seeks to evoke lawlessness and a falling away (4:1–2).

While allusion to ancient models of unfaithfulness is not unique to Jude (or 2 Peter)—particular models which appear in most of the extrabiblical sources include Sodom and Gomorrah, the fallen angels or "Watchers," giants, the Flood, and unbelieving Israel[79]— Jude's use of these is his own unique work. These examples are linked prophetically in the epistle to those who have apostatized yet who seek to exercise influence among the faithful (*pareisedysan*[80] *tines anthrōpoi*, v 4; *houtoi eisin hoi syneuōchoumenoi*, v 12; *houtoi eisin hoi apodiorizontes*, v 19). Verses 5, 6, and 7 represent evidence—exhibits A, B and C—compounded against the guilty, the *houtoi* (vv 8, 10, 11, 12, 14, 16 and 19).

Jude's interest in the initial case illustration is Israel, *hoi klētoi*, God's *chosen*.[81] Allusion to Israel would suggest that the apostate are former "orthodox," i.e., they had formerly experienced divine redemption. Note the emphatic reminder terminology in v 5. The readers already know *all things* (i.e., not just a minimum of traditions, rather all that they need to live accordingly),[82] therefore Jude wishes to recall to their mind the Israel of old (*hypomnēsai de hymas boulomai, eidotas [hymas] panta*). Accounts of Israel's unbelief in the wilderness, after the incredibility of miraculous deliverance from Egypt, are found in Numbers 11, 14, 26 and 32 (cf. 1 Cor. 10:1–5 and Heb. 3:7–4:10). Throughout the OT, there is a constant calling back prophetically to Egypt and that for which it stood in Israel's past. Egypt is mentioned eleven times in Leviticus, twenty-eight and forty-six times in Numbers and Deuteronomy, seventeen times in Joshua, and fifty times in Samuel-Kings. Isaiah, Jeremiah, and Ezekiel allude to Egypt over thirty times each. The latter prophets, with the exception of Obadiah, Zephaniah, and Malachi, each make reference to Egyptian bondage.[83] Having seen the might of Yahweh's hand in deliverance and then forgetting or ignoring it was a colossal grievance to the prophetic spirit. There was no excuse for *mē pisteusantas*. God delivered Israel once-for-all (*hapax*) in the OT; the second time (*to deuteron*) God did not deliver, rather He judged.

> The Lord said to Moses, "How long will these people treat me with contempt? How long will they refuse to belief me in spite of all the miraculous signs I have performed among them?" . . . Nevertheless, as surely as I live and as surely as the glory of the Lord fills the whole earth, not one of the men who saw my glory and the miraculous signs I performed in Egypt and in the desert but who disobeyed me and tested me ten times, not one of them will ever see the land I promised

on oath to their forefathers. No one who has treated me with contempt will ever see it. (Num. 14:11, 22–23)

The adverb *hapax* emphasizes a *definite number,* carrying the connotation of perpetual validity that precludes the possibility of or need for repetition.[84] It is used in this sense seven times in the Epistle to the Hebrews, of which four instances relate to Christ's salvific work:

Now only the high priest entered the inner room, and that only *hapax* a year, and never without blood, which he offered for himself and for the sins the people had committed in ignorance. (9–7)

Then Christ would have to suffer many times since the creation of the world. But now he has appeared *hapax* at the end of the ages to do away with sin by the sacrifice of himself. Just as man is destined to die *hapax,* and after that to face judgment, so Christ was sacrificed *hapax* to take away the sins of many people; and he will appear *ek deuterou,* not to bear sin, but to bring salvation to those who are waiting for him. (9:26–28)[85]

Two instances parallel the theme of apostasy in Jude:

It is impossible for those who have *hapax* been enlightened, who have tasted the heavenly gift, who have become sharers in the Holy Spirit, and who have tasted the goodness of the word of God and the powers of the coming age, if they fall away, to be brought back to repentance, because to their loss they are crucifying the Son of God all over again and subjecting him to public disgrace. (6:4)

For the worshipers would have been cleansed *hapax* and would no longer have felt guilty for their sins. But those sacrifices are an annual reminder of sins, because it is impossible for the blood of bulls and goats to take away sins. (10:2–3)

By implication, Jude is saying the same applies of *Kyrios-Iēsous* to the *houtoi.* Because the effects of Jesus' redemptive work have perpetual validity and His saving act precludes the possibility of or need for repetition, those who have formerly experienced redemption and are fallen away will be judged at Jesus' coming the second time. Having chosen to disregard *YHWH*'s work on their behalf, Israel denied the Lord (cf. Jude 4). The contrast which is before the readers concerns two divine acts—one of mercy and a second of judgment. The present need calls for a prophetic reminder: *eidotas [hymas] panta.*[86]

The Rebellious Angels (v 6)

A further case illustration of the gravity of relapse in Jude is the fall of the angels. Perhaps sensing great interest in angels among his readers, Jude strategically chooses a second paradigm—a heavenly one—to complement his didactive use of Israel. The issue is clearly the utterly incomprehensible nature of falling away. The angels "deserted" (note the *apo-* prefix in the Aorist participle *apolipontas,* a strengthened form of *leipein*) their heavenly home: *apolipontas to idion oikētērion.* They fell from a domain of divine liberty and light *(archē)* to imprisonment and darkness *(desmoi aidioi hypo zophon).*

"There were angels in Jewish beliefs before there were demons" wrote C. Guignebert[87] concerning the world of the unseen. In the OT, angels are depicted foremost as the servants of the Most High. In orthodox Judaism, they remain God's ministers. Aside from "the Angel of the Lord," angels in general receive less prominence in the OT before the Exile. Following the exile experience, they acquire increasing importance and a more clearly defined function (e.g., Ezek. 9:2ff; 40:3ff; 43:6ff; Dan. 3:28; 4:13; 6:22; 7:16; 8:13; 10:5ff; 12:1ff; Zech. 1:8ff; 2:1ff; 3:1ff; 4:1ff; 5:1ff; 6:1ff).

Several features differentiate the angelology of the intertestamental period from that of the OT. In the former, their depiction becomes far more systematic,[88] while a particular number have their names and functions expressly stated. Jewish apocalyptic literature knows between four and nine echelons of angelic authorities. Four levels of hierarchy are found in 1 Enoch 40:2; T.Levi 3:2–7; Jub. 1:27,29; 2:1,3; seven levels are stated in 1 Enoch 81:5; 90:21; T.Levi 8:2; Tob. 12:15; and nine are listed in the Testament of Adam 4. In 1 Enoch, the chief angels in heaven's multitiered hierarchy develop strategies (chaps. 6–9), superintend nations (20:5),[89] reveal secrets (chaps. 41–43; 46:2; 71:3), and filter prayers of the righteous (14:4). In T.Dan 6:2, Michael intercedes for the saints on earth, and in 1 Enoch 40:6, the archangel[90] is "supplicating in the name of the Lord of the Spirits."

Michael is presented in Dan. 10:13 and 12:1 as "one of the chief rulers" (*ʾaḥad haśśārîm hāriʾšōnîm;* LXX: *heis tōn archontōn tōn prōtōn*) and "the great angel" (*haśśar haggādôl;* LXX: *ho aggelos ho megas*).[91] In late Judaism, he achieves an incomparable stature. He mediates the prayers of the saints, offers the souls of the righteous (hence, for example, Jude 9), and accompanies them into paradise.[92] Further, and with particular regard to Jude 6, the intertestamental period exhibits a proliferation in speculative explanations as to Gen. 6:1–4 and "the sons of God." By the time of the Christian advent, most of Judaism—mainstream and sectarian—had embraced the notion that the *běnē* hā *ʾĕlōhîm* in Genesis 6 were angels who had introduced sexual promiscuity among "the daughters of men."

Virtually all commentary, past and present, has related Gen. 6:1–4 in some way to Jude 6 and 2 Pet. 2:4, following the lead of Clement of Alexandria (*Paedagogus* 3.2).[93] This is largely due to two reasons: (1) a mistaken linking of the angels in v 6 with Sodom and Gomorrah in v 7[94] and (2) the association of demons with Gen. 6:1–4 which began to emerge in the second century B.C.[95] The thread in Jude that links Israel (v 5), the angels (v 6), and Sodom (v 7), however, is not sexual sin, rather *dispossession, falling from their allotted place*. This is supported grammatically as well as contextually.[96]

The explicit association of sexual promiscuity with the angels' fall is to be found in Jewish literature from the second century B.C. on. This understanding encompassed mainstream as well as sectarian Judaism.[97] The elaborate midrash[98] in 1 Enoch[99] which is attached to Genesis 6,[100] though somewhat more expanded than its counterparts, is representative. Following are several examples of this linking, excluding material from 1 Enoch:

And some of them came down and mingled themselves with women. At that time they who acted like this were tormented in chains. But the rest of the multitude of angels, who have no number, restrained themselves. And those living on earth perished together through the waters of the flood. (2 Apoc. Bar. 56:12–15)

Accordingly, my children, flee from sexual promiscuity, and order your wives and daughters not to adorn their heads and appearances so as to deceive men's sound minds. For it was thus that they charmed the Watchers, who were before the Flood. As they continued looking at the women, they were filled with desire for them and perpetrated the act in their minds. Then they were transformed into human males, and while the women were cohabiting with their husbands they appeared to them. Since the women's minds were filled with lust for these apparitions, they gave birth to giants. For the Watchers were disclosed to them being as high as the heavens. (T.Reub. 5:5–6)

For many angels of God cohabited with women and gave birth to insolent children who despised all that was good on account of what they did in their own strength. For according to the tradition these dared to do acts which resembled those of whom the Greeks call giants. (*Ant.* 1.3.1)

It should be noted, however, that in Jude the fall of the angels is one from *authority, domain,* and *position (tērēsantas tēn heautōn archēn alla apolipontas).* The picture is one of *contrast* (note the emphatic particle *alla*). As with unbelieving Israel of v 5, the issue at hand is one of *privilege.*[101] Having deserted their position, the angels were cast down.

Several important observations need to be made at this point. On the one hand Jude freely draws from Enochic language and imagery. Consider, for example, the verbal parallels in v 6 alone: 1 Enoch 10:4 ("binding" and "darkness"); 10:6 ("the great day"); 10:12 ("bind them . . . until the day"); 12:4 ("the Watchers of heaven . . . abandoned the high heaven"); 15:3 ("you abandoned the high, holy . . . heaven"); 22:11 ("until the great day of judgment . . . they will bind you"); 24:4 ("the Watchers of heaven who have abandoned"); 54:5 ("imprisonment" and "chains").[102] On the other hand, the reader should take care to note what Jude emphasizes and what he omits. The presentation of the angels in v 6 is abrupt. This can mean one of several things. It may well reflect the assumption that the audience is familiar with the traditions, needing no introduction or explanation. It may also indicate that Jude is borrowing from Jewish apocalyptic imagery without necessarily endorsing its theological content, employing the imagery for his own purpose. To illustrate, Jude is *not* asserting, or even intimating, that two hundred angels bound themselves to a curse, descended upon Mount Hermon, and took wives for themselves (1 Enoch 6:4–7:1). He is not suggesting that these angels did in fact teach magic and incantations, or that the women, having been impregnated, brought forth giants three hundred cubits (roughly five hundred feet?!) in height (1 Enoch 7:1–2).[103] Furthermore, the "Watchers" of Dan. 4:13,17 and 23 are holy and servants of God, whereas in 1 Enoch, the Testaments of the Twelve Patriarchs, and Jubilees they are fallen.[104]

The sin of the angels, though veiled to humans, was very real. The point of Jude's witness, however, is not to focus on the *nature* of their sin. Rather, the angels of v 6, mentioned parenthetically, share something in common with Israel of v 5 and Sodom and Gomorrah of v 7: *punitive intervention.* Inasmuch as he exploits apocalyptic imagery, Jude should not be naively interpreted as advancing wholesale Jewish apocalyptic theology.[105] For the writers of the NT, Christ is the center of time and the historical process. With the death and resurrection of Christ, Christian history is the "end of time." All things, hence, whether "life or death, angels or demons, the present or the future, or any powers,"[106] are measured according to Christ. For the writers of the NT, all of history finds its eschatological fulfillment in Christ. Christian theology is radically divergent from its apocalyptic Jewish counterpart.[107]

We have been careful to call attention to what Jude, in his borrowing of apocalyptic motifs, stresses and what he omits. Contrary to what most commentators would interpret in v 6, there is no trace of sexual sin. F. Dexinger[108] has correctly noted that

> für die Engeldeutung von Gen 6,2ff ist nämlich durch den Judasbrief wirklich nichts gesagt; die Auffassung im Judasbrief ist vielmehr bloss ein Zeugnis für das kontinuierliche Bestehen der Engeldeutung von der Entstehung des Henochbuches.

> [there is nothing concerning angels from Gen. 6:2ff that is mentioned in the epistle of Jude; rather, the conceptualization of angels is simply evidence of a continuation of that which emerged from the Book of Enoch.]

The center point of Jude's illustration involving the angels is the fact that they were dispossessed, not how or why they were dispossessed. Hence our focus is concerned with *Jude's use of 1 Enoch*, not *1 Enoch's use of Genesis 6*. To speculate as to how much of Enochic theology Jude might have endorsed remains inconclusive.[109] We are left only with the combined writings of the NT to act as our guide in assessing the theology of its individual writers. M. E. Stone[110] argues that material from 1 Enoch should not be construed as commentaries on *Genesis,* but rather as distinctly *new* articulations which are *divorced* from Genesis. As demonstrated by Jude's vocabulary and syntax, his concern is apostasy, *not* fornication:[111]

v 5—I want to remind you, though you already know it all, that the Lord, after having delivered His people from Egypt once and for all, destroyed those who afterward did not believe . . . *(hapax . . . sōsas to deuteron . . . apōlesen)*

v 6—. . . and the angels, who did not keep their position but who deserted their own dwelling-place, He has kept in everlasting chains of darkness for the great day of judgment . . . *(aggelous . . . mē tērēsantas . . . alla apolipontas . . . tetērēken)*

v 7—. . . just as Sodom and Gomorrah . . . are set forth as a paradigm of those who are undergoing a judgment of eternal fire. (*hōs Sodoma kai Gomorra . . . prokeintai deigma pyros aiōniou dikēn hypechousai*)

Verses 5–7 of Jude, taken together as they are meant to be syntactically, stress the *loss* or *disenfranchisement* of the three subjects. Apart from mention of Israel's disbelief in v 5, no attention is given in v 6 to the specific nature of the angels' sin—only that they abandoned their heavenly position. Nor is the *primary* focus of v 7 the specific nature of the sin of Sodom and Gomorrah; the writer wishes foremost to remind his audience that the cities of the plain are an *enduring* reminder of those reserved by God for eternal judgment.

In one sense or another, all three of these paradigms from the OT have lost their *allotted place*. This, then, is the writer's focus. The lesson for Jude's readers is simple yet profound: apostasy has its reward—a sobering one, at that. Any speculation as to the particular nature of the sins associated with Israel, the angels, or Sodom and Gomorrah, intriguing as it may be, is of secondary importance according to the text of the epistle.

It is furthermore significant that Jude does not associate the fall of the angels with the Flood as in 2 Pet. 2:4–5. In that he is using source-material from 1 Enoch (vv 14–15 = 1 Enoch 1:9), it is possible, indeed we would maintain probable, that Jude is deliberately distinguishing between the tradition of the fall of rebellious angels—otherwise not delineated in the OT—and apocalyptic (specifically, Enochic) theology of the fall, which is an intertestamental expansion of Gen. 6:1–4.[112] This is crucial, particularly due to the prominence in the OT pseudepigraphal and apocryphal books of the Flood event and Noah as a paradigm of righteousness.[113] With Jude's borrowing of a theophany statement from 1 Enoch (vv 14:15–1:9), any allusion to Noah and the flood would automatically sanction in the minds of his readers Enochic theology, due primarily to the link in 1 Enoch between the fallen angels and the flood as a means of their punishment (cf. especially chaps. 54–67).[114] In apocalyptic literature, several views of the Flood and Noah emerge, none of which shows interest in the Deluge as an isolated event. In 1 Enoch 65–69 and 106–7, the Flood is included in the past as an apocalyptic survey of history. Jubilees 7:20–39 and 10:1–15 treat the Flood apocalyptically, yet are a bit more midrashic. The Genesis Apocryphon devotes a sizeable amount of material to Noah.[115] The Sibylline Oracles[116] were attributed by Jewish and Christian writers to the pagan Sibyl, who was identified as the daughter[117] of Noah; Books one and seven include a Flood narrative.

Jude, then, is utilizing apocalyptic motifs without necessarily embracing Jewish apocalyptic theology. At work are two very different attitudes with regard to handling mythological material. The Jewish apocalypticist is inclined to assimilate mythology; hence, we encounter a mixture of Jewish and Greek notions. The biblical writers, on the other hand, tend toward demythologizing. One may consider the material in Gen. 6:1–4 as an example. The writer incorporated this material into the Genesis account with a view of relating it, *from the divine perspective*, to *judgment*. This can be seen in Jude as well, where the angels' rebellion is depicted as foremost against *God* (it should be noted that this is *not* the emphasis of 1 Enoch 1–36). The writer of 1 Enoch, in contrast, has unraveled an expanded midrash of Gen. 6:1–4—an embellishment which perhaps was derived from Greek Titan mythology.[118]

Thus, two different views of the world and movement of history are on display in Jude: the one to which perhaps many in Jude's audience can relate is "remythological,"[119] while Jude himself is demythological. Jude's point, consistent with the other historical types employed in the epistle, is very simple: the angels exercised free will—to their discredit.

It is worthy of note that neither the OT nor the NT makes any explicit statements as to the fall of the rebellious angels. The NT implies at most the notion that Satan, a fallen angel chief among many,[120] was cast down (cf. Luke 10:18; John 12:31; Rev. 12:4, 7, 9, 10), yet gives no clear time of the Fall. Some, as did Origen,[121] hold Jesus' words in Luke 10:18 as referring to an original fall. Others hold the statement to be a dramatic way of expressing Satan's certain ruin.[122] Still others view the fall as coinciding with Jesus' ministry on earth.[123]

Corresponding typology to the fallen angels of Jude might well be drawn from several prophetic oracles in the OT—oracles that serve as graphic illustrations of fall or ruin: (1) Isa. 14:5–23, a taunt (*māšāl*, v 4) against the king of Babylon, (2) Isa. 24:21–22, a symbolic representation of Yahweh's judgment, and (3) Ezek. 28:1–19, a prophetic funeral dirge (*gînāh*, v 12) against the king of Tyre. Both Isaiah 14 and Ezekiel 28 appear to be shaped similar to ancient Canaanite creation myths,[124] and both enunciate the same principal reason for the king's demise: pride, self-exaltation, and corruption. The object of condemnation in the Isaiah oracle is characterized by wickedness (*reša*, v 5) and oppression (vv 2,6). In light of the great rejoicing of vv 7–8, this must

have been an arch enemy. Evidence of his pompous nature are his
"I will" assertions (ʾeeleh, ʾēsēb, ʾeeleh, ʾeddammeh in vv 13–14); he
dared even to presume upon the glory of the Most High. At his
reception in Sheol, the underworld (vv 9–11), he is greeted by the
spirits (rĕphāʾîm, v 9):

> How you are fallen from heaven,
> > O morning star, son of dawn!
> You have been cast down to earth,
> > You who once laid low the nations.
> You said in your heart,
> > "I will ascend to heaven;
> I will raise my throne
> > Above the stars of God;
> I will sit enthroned
> > On the mountain of the assembly,
> > On the utmost heights of the sacred mountain.
> I will ascend above the tops of the clouds;
> > I will make myself like the Most High."
> But you are fallen to the grave,
> > To the depths of the pit.
> > > (Isa. 14:12–15)

The funeral dirge in Ezekiel 28 is directed against an arrogant
ruler (nāgîd, v 2). This figure is corrupted through his own perception of exaltedness (ʾel ʾānî, v 2; ʾĕlōhîm ʾānî, v 9).[125] Allusions to
"Eden, the garden of God" (v 13), "the anointed cherub" (vv
14,16), and fire (v 16) are reminiscent of Genesis and suggestive
of traditions familiar to the readers.

> In the pride of your heart
> > You say, "I am a god;
> I sit on the throne of a god
> > In the heart of the seas."
> . . . Your heart became proud
> > On account of your beauty
> And corrupted your wisdom
> > On account of your splendor.
> So I cast you down to the earth
> > And made a spectacle of you before kings.
> > > (Ezek. 28:2,17)

The oracles of Isaiah 14 and Ezekiel 28, as does Jude 6, reflect
the utter *fall from glory*. Several elements are common to all three

texts. The first is a conspicuously abrupt transition from an earthly to a heavenly plain. This occurs without any explanation or bridge. Second, there is a correlation between the earthly and heavenly in all three cases (the angels in v 6 of Jude being a parallel to Israel in v 5). Third, the objects of condemnation in all three texts tumble from the heavens as if stars (cf. Jude 13). A key in interpreting Isaiah 14, Ezekiel 28, and Jude 6 lies in recognizing *antecedent action*. Falling from glory—whether it is the king of Babylon, the ruler of Tyre, or the Christian community to whom Jude is writing—has an antecedent in the heavenly realm. The angelic spirits have been kept in darkness, bound for judgment on the great day.

While the idea of imprisonment of spirits in the OT is undefined, in Jewish apocalyptic literature it is pronounced (e.g., 1 Enoch 10:4, 12–14; 13:1; 18:14,16; 21:3,6,10; 67:4; 69:8; 88:1,3; 90:23; 2 Apoc. Bar. 56:13; Jub. 5:10; cf. also Rev. 18:2 and 20:7) along with the notion of a pit or "abyss" (e.g., 1 Enoch 10:4; 18:11; 21:7, 22:1–2; 54:5; 56:3; 88:1,3; 90:24,26; cf. also Rev. 20:3). Jude combines typological treatment of the OT with conventions and imagery contemporary to sectarian Judaism—conventions that would have been readily understood by his audience. The apocalyptic imagery surrounding the angels in v 6 is strengthened by v 13, where the *houtoi* of Jude's polemic are compared to "wandering stars"[126] *(asteres planētai)*, a description that would have triggered immediate association with 1 Enoch (e.g., 18:14–16; 21:6; 86:1–3; 90:24). Within apocalyptic mythology, a frequent pattern tends to emerge: (1) war erupts in heaven, often depicted in *astral* terms, followed by (2) a spilling over of this rebellion to the earth, then culminating in (3) ultimate vindication and punishment by the king of heaven.[127]

Utilizing a play on the catchword "keep" *(tērein),*[128] Jude unites typologically in v 6 the events of the fall with the theme of judgment. Without necessarily endorsing conceptions of cosmic warfare which have their roots in pagan mythology, Jude assimilates imagery current to his day and exploits it for his own purposes. The motif of "rebellion in heaven," a notion vaguely hinted at in the OT, illustrates graphically the effects of choosing to fall away. Jude's readers should be mindful of the lesson of the angels: punishment is proportionate to privilege. In heaven, the angels were exposed to great light; now they are consigned to darkest darkness. Having decided not to "keep" their unique and privileged status, they have consequently been "kept" in chains of darkness awaiting a fate—"the great day"—which should cause men to shudder. The angels are like Israel of old. Both departed their *allotted place*. Apostasy in the Christian community has both earthly and heavenly antecedents.

Sodom and Gomorrah (v 7)

Consistently throughout the OT and Jewish literature the example of the cities of the plain (Genesis 19) stands out. Sodom's overthrow is reiterated again and again (e.g., Deut. 29:33; 32:32; Isa. 1:9–10; 3:9; Jer. 23:14; 49:18; 50:40; Lam. 4:6; Ezek. 16:49–59; Amos 4:11; Hos. 11:8; Zeph. 2:9; Jub. 16:5,6,9; 20:5; 22:22; 36:10; Wis. 10:6–7; Sir. 16:8; T.Ass. 7:1; T.Naph. 3:4; 3 Macc. 2:5; Gen. Rab. 27:3; m.Sanh. 10:3; m. ʾAbot 5:10; Philo;[129] and Josephus).[130] Perhaps what is most striking about the OT depiction of Sodom is its flaunting of sin (e.g., Gen. 19:4–5, 12; Isa. 1:9; Ezek. 16:49–50) and the permanent nature of its judgment. The prophet Jeremiah enunciated that no man would henceforth live there (49:18 and 50:40). In late Judaism, Sodom remained the classic Jewish example of immorality and a paradigm of the certain and consuming nature of divine judgment.

> In the same way God will bring judgment on places where the people live by Sodom's uncleanness, in accordance with the judgment of Sodom. (Jub. 16:5)

> She [wisdom] . . . saved the righteous man,
>   Escaping the descending fire on Pentapolis,
> Of whose wickedness still exists as a testimony,
>   A wasteland that smokes . . .,
>   A pillar of salt standing as a memorial of an
>   unbelieving soul.
>   (Wis. 10:6–7)

> But you, my children, shall not be like that . . . discern the Lord who made all things, so that you do not become like Sodom, which departed from the order of nature.
>   (T.Naph. 3:4)

According to the rabbis,[131] there were seven groups which had no portion in the coming world: the generation of the flood, the generation of the diaspora, the spies who brought an evil report of the land, the generation in the wilderness, the congregation of Korah, the ten tribes, and the men of Sodom.[132]

For Jude, Sodom and Gomorrah are the type par excellence for the finality of divine judgment. Three times in Gen. 18–19 there occurs the cry of the anguished oppressed (zāʿaq, 18:20,21; 19:13), mandating divine visitation. The Genesis account with Abraham is painstaking in order to show that God is absolutely just. As *prokeintai deigma*,[133] the fate of these cities is always open to exhibit. According to the description given to the whole "plain of Jordan" in Gen. 13:10 ("well watered, like the garden of the Lord"), the region of the cities of the plain was evidently luscious and extremely fertile. Later generations are still to learn from them.[134] The emphasis of v 7, however, is not on the precise kind of sin for which Sodom and Gomorrah were proverbially known. Mention is made of the fact that their sin was sexual in nature (*ton homoion tropon toutois ekporneusasai*[135] *kai apelthousai opisō sarkos heteras*), indeed, deviantly sexual,[136] yet this aspect is secondary to the writer's main focus. Even though the sin of Sodom and the fallen angels is linked together in 3 Macc. 2:4–5 and T.Naph. 3:4–5, for example, Jude's intention is to link Sodom with the angels *and with Israel*, not just with the angels.[137]

It is customary for commentators to view the phrase *ton homoion tropon toutois* as standing in subordinate relationship to *ekporneusasai* and *apelthousai opisō sarkos hēteras*,[138] in addition to assuming that v 6 is dealing with *sexual* sin. Jude is careful, however, to attribute *asebeia* to *men*, not to angels.[139] This is true of his use of apocalyptic motifs in v 6 as well as his approach to Sodom and Gomorrah in v 7. Whereas fallen angels, i.e., unseen forces, explain to the apocalypticist the state of the world, Jude, in line with the OT prophets, focuses on the evil of the *human* heart to account for wickedness. Of the three objects to which *ton homoion tropon toutois* could possibly refer—the angels, Sodom and Gomorrah, or Jude's opponents (the *houtoi*)—the latter fits best; in the next twelve verses, *houtoi* is used six times. The particle *hōs*, normally thought to identify the *type of sin* which linked Sodom with the angels, should rather be seen as a link between two paradigms of *fate*. The "same manner as these" speaks to the same *end* met by Israel and the angels which awaits the opponents of Jude. Sodom illustrates the punitive intervention of God in history, as do the fallen angels and Israel of old. In the words of Paul, the ancient paradigm serves as *endeigma tēs dikaias kriseōs tou theou*, "proof of God's righteous judgment" (2 Thess. 1:5). Indeed, Sodom and Gomorrah and the cities of the plain as a paradigm *were* immoral. Nonetheless, the theme in Jude is *asebeia*, not *porneia*. Verse 7, then, could be translated accordingly: "just as Sodom and Gomorrah and the surrounding cities in the same manner as these (having given themselves to utter sexual immorality and perversion) are an ongoing example of those undergoing the punishment of eternal fire."[140] This rendering, we would maintain, would do justice to the context of vv 5–7, which underscores the fall from privilege; i.e., all three paradigms—unbelieving Israel, the dispossessed angels, and Sodom and Gomorrah—are for the present purpose of Jude and his audience ongoing examples (note the present tense of *prokeimai*) of divine judgment. The reason is that they *all exhibit an unnatural rebellion.*[141] The text of Jude does not support the common assumption that sexual sin of an uncommon variety is the thread uniting these paradigms. It does however unite the cities of the plain with the angels and Israel based on their sure fall and incontrovertible judgment. *Together,* the three paradigms reflect the intention of Jude: the characterization of his opponents, the *houtoi,* who have despised normal life and are perverting the good. Thus, the writer has formally bridged v 4 (*charita metatithentes*) with v 8 (*sarka miainousin, kyriotēta athetousin, doxas blasphēmousin*).

Michael and the Devil (v 9)

The OT background for Jewish traditions regarding Moses' burial is found in Deut. 34:5–6 and Num. 27:12–13. Imagery from Dan. 10:4–21, 12:1 and Zech. 3:1ff is also being incorporated. In Daniel 10, Michael the archangel[142] comes to overrule the "prince of Persia." He stands for and defends the sons of Israel in 12:1. In the visions of Zechariah, the prophet is shown Joshua the High Priest standing before the angel of the Lord with Satan standing at his right side opposing him. Twice the command "The Lord rebuke you" is pronounced on behalf of Joshua. The issue in Zechariah's vision is Joshua's unclean garments (3:3–5). A secondary motif in Zechariah 3 is the authority of the angel Satan.

While the Tg. Jon. on Deut. 34:5–6 and other rabbinic literature bring us a bit closer to the background of Jude's illustration, they do not inform us that Satan and Michael fought over Moses' body.[143] Essentially an a fortiori argument, v 9 is a forensic representation of conflict. It is set in the context of antithesis—the arrogance of the *houtoi* on the one hand and the humility of Michael on the other. If Michael, who certainly was qualified to exercise authority, did not dare to utter a word of rebuke against Satan, then how much less should the *houtoi?* The point of v 9 is blasphemy. Vindication and judgment are rooted in divine fiat. In their insolence, Jude's opponents have become totally blinded to this sobering reality.[144] The argument behind v 9 preserves the link to v 7: the men of Sodom affronted the angels sent by God.

Verse 9 is full of the language of legal disputation (diakrinein, dialogizomai, epipherein, blasphēmia, epitiman). In light of the accusation raised by the devil, Michael appeals to the Lord's judgment, not his own authority. Of course, the whole argument of v 9 implies that the devil is functioning in an accusatory role. This would indeed seem to be consistent with both OT and NT portrayal of ho diabolos. He functions foremost in the role of an accuser or prosecutor (e.g., Job 1–2; Ps. 10:6 [?]; 1 Chron 21:1; Zech. 1:1; Matt. 4:1–11; Mark 1:12, 13; Luke 4:1–13; implied in 2 Cor. 2:11 and Rev. 2:9; 12:10).

The LXX translation of the Hebrew haśśāṭān, katēgor, or diabolos[145] ("accuser," "persecutor," or "adversary"), reflects the Jewish and almost human character ascribed to the figure of "satan" by the OT. He is part of YHWH's heavenly court, acting as a type of public prosecutor. What is striking about the few allusions in the OT to a satan figure is that he seems to fall into the same category as the bĕnē hāʾĕlōhîm, one who is part of the heavenly council (e.g., Job 1:6 and 2:1). This has caused many commentators to see in haśśāṭān only another of the many members of YHWH's heavenly court which was given a particular task to carry out,[146] perhaps the result of a developing phenomenon that emerged from Persian influence.[147]

There are nonetheless several OT passages in which one can find faint traces of hostility orchestrated toward God. The serpent in the Genesis 3 narrative is endowed with a peculiar cunning. He is doing more than merely acting as one of YHWH's court lawyers. He questions the veracity of God's imperatives regarding the tree of the knowledge of good and evil. Indeed, he contradicts God's statements, causing Adam and Eve to disregard God's words altogether. Although the hostility is unexplained, a bitter enmity between the serpent and the woman's seed surfaces in 3:15. Mention has already been made of the "son of the dawn," hēlāl, fallen from heaven, in Isaiah 14, after desiring to exalt himself to heaven's throne. This oracle paralleled the dirge of Ezekiel 28, in which the reader is given a prophetic glimpse at an "anointed guardian cherub" who was expelled from the holy mountain of God. A slight variation on the 2 Samuel 24 passage is observed in 1 Chronicles 21, where David is tempted to number Israel by śāṭān (with use of the proper name). The influence of this "accuser," according to the Chronicler, is not neutral, nor is he performing action normally associated with the heavenly council. Before all is done, seventy thousand of Israel's men have died.

On certain of Satan's attributes enumerated in the NT, there is corroboration from the OT:

- temptation: Gen. 3:1–7 ‖ Matt. 4:1–11; Mark 1:12–13; Luke 4:1–13; 1 Cor. 7:5
- hostility: Gen. 3:14–16; Job 1:12–19; 2:7–8 ‖ Luke 22:31; Rom. 16:20; 1 Thess. 2:18
- deception: Gen. 3:1–7; 1 Chron. 21:1 ‖ Matt. 16:23; Mark 8:33; Acts 5:3; 2 Cor. 11:2, 14; Rev. 13:14
- accusation: Job 1:6–12; 2:1–6; Zech. 3:1 ‖ Rev. 12:9–10
- self-exaltation: Isa. 14:13–14; Ezek. 28:2, 9 ‖ 2 Cor. 4:4; 2 Thess. 2:4; Rev. 13:4–6
- being bruised: Gen. 3:15 ‖ Rom. 16:20

The motif of spiritual warfare, vaguely hinted at in the OT, is assumed by Jude in his polemic against the *houtoi*. Employing the language of the courtroom, Jude uses Jewish traditions which grew out of the OT account of Moses' death. Opposing the devil, that ancient accuser of old, Michael the archangel does not fall back on his own authority as the defense attorney, rather he makes an appeal to the highest authority in the court of heaven. The opponents of Jude, on the other hand, rail against that which they do not understand in the slightest. As brute beasts, they are corrupted and brought to ruin (v 10).

Cain, Balaam and Korah (v 11)

A second triplet of OT paradigms[148] appears in v 11, belonging to a contextual flow which began in v 8 (*houtoi* [v 8] . . . *houtoi* [v 10] . . . *ouai autois* [v 11]). Cain, Balaam, and Korah are in their own right proverbial as far as Jewish tradition is concerned. They appear together in the Tosefta as "chief sinners."[149] In Jude, they are objects of a woe-cry, i.e., a prophetic denunciation, issued by the writer. Having blasphemed (v 8), much in contrast to Michael (v 9), the opponents of Jude have brought themselves under divine curse.[150]

In a story that N. M. Sarna[151] describes as "tantalizingly incomplete," the text of Gen. 4:3 states that Cain brought as an

offering to the Lord the fruits *(peri)* of the earth. His brother
Abel, meanwhile, is said to have brought first-fruits *(běkôr,* v 4).
The Lord consequently looked upon Abel with favor, but not
Cain (v 5).[152] Two things strike the reader: the fruit/first-fruit
distinction and the fraternal relationship between Cain and Abel
(this occurs seven times in this short narrative). One is left to
conclude, as Heb. 11:4 indicates, that Abel's worship is heartfelt
and acceptable, while that of Cain represents tokenism.[153] Cain
acts in utter contrast to the divine image by *destroying the divine
image.* His sin is indeed against man, but it is foremost against *God,*
the supreme source of all morality.

A. Lapple[154] has described Cain as "a theological and psycho-
logical statement on sin's nature." In the early parts of the Genesis
narrative, he is one of several *concrete examples* of evil which are
presented in typological historiography with a definite purpose:
illustration. Adam, Cain and Abel, Noah and the Flood, and the
Tower of Babel are four paradigms arranged for the purpose of
teaching the effects of ungodliness. These are set in sharp contrast to Abraham (chaps. 12–23), the man of faith who pleased
God.

To the Jewish mind, Cain represents the epitome of wickedness,
the ungodly man par excellence (Wis. 10:3; cf. also 1 John 3:12:
Kathōs Kain ek tou ponērou ēn). In the endowment of man with
moral autonomy, he reflects the human side of moral evil and is
the first man in the Hebrew scriptures to defy God and despise
man. Hence, he is prototypical. In the Testaments of the Twelve
Patriarchs, Cain represents one of seven evils:

> The first is moral corruption, the second is destruction, the third is
> oppression, the fourth is captivity, the fifth is want, the sixth is tur-
> moil, the seventh is desolation. It is for this reason that Cain was
> handed over by God for seven punishments. . . . For he was con-
> demned on account of Abel his brother as a result of all his evil
> deeds. . . . Until eternity those who are like Cain in their moral cor-
> ruption and hatred of brother shall be punished with a similar judg-
> ment. (T.Ben. 7:2–5)

Philo sees in Cain and Abel the contrast between orthodoxy and
heresy.[155] Josephus presents Cain as a type of ungodliness and
avarice.[156] Interestingly, the rabbis, taking note of the wording of
Gen. 4:10 ("your brother's bloods [*děmē'āhîkā*] cry out"), charge
Cain with destroying a whole world, for the scriptures indicate
"both his blood and the blood of his succeeding generations."[157]
Rabbinic literature associates him with the "void" of Gen. 1:2;

Cain intended to "reduce the world to waste and voidness."[158] Thus, numerous rabbinic legends developed which characterized him as the offspring of an evil angel.[159] In Heb. 11:4, Cain is the antithesis of faith; 1 John 3:12 presents him as the antithesis of love within a greater context of comparison between the children of God and the children of the devil.

Summarizing Cain in Jewish tradition, he is "type and teacher"[160] of ungodliness. Significantly, Cain was the firstborn. Thus he had legal right to an inheritance and a privileged status— a status shared by Israel, Yahweh's firstborn (Jude 5), the angels (v 6), and the cities of the fertile Jordan plain (v 7). Cain's religious obduracy becomes clearer and clearer. As with Jude's opponents, no repentance stirs within. This is the "way of Cain."

The story of Balaam is a look at the growth of Jewish haggadah.[161] Numbers 22–24 is given to the account of Balaam, son of Beor. These three chapters offer a mixed review of the Midianite prophet. Essentially, two strains of tradition exist concerning Balaam: he is cast as a villain and as a tragic hero. In Num. 31:16, Deut. 23:4–5, Josh. 13:22, 24:9, and Neh. 13:2, Balaam is portrayed as a strictly negative memorial, having hired himself out to curse Israel.[162]

The OT gives witness to the binding power of blessing and curse. This is seen graphically in Gen. 12:3 ("I will bless those who bless you, and whoever curses you I will curse; and all peoples of the earth will be blessed through you.") and Num. 16:28–35 (Moses' prediction of the fate of Korah). The ethical-prophetic nature of the blessing and curse in the OT prohibits us from associating this phenomenon with a form of magic or incantation, rather it is inextricably woven together with the concept of covenant.[163] God is sovereign and, hence, makes covenant with man. With covenant come particular sanctions—curses and blessings. The power of the curse is derived from the effective power of prophetic speech. The blessing-cursing motif associated with the prophet Balaam, as well as Jude's resultant interpretation thereof and prophetic application of woe to his opponents, is to be understood in this light.

Traditional hostility toward Balaam in Jewish tradition would appear to be based on Num. 31:15–16. While being the paradigm of self-seeking and greed, Balaam more importantly led Israel into idolatry and immorality at Baal-Peor (cf. Num. 31:16). He was the subject of much fascination to the Jews, as reflected by Josephus's explanation: "This [Balaam] was the man to whom Moses did the high honor of recording his prophecies. And though it was possible for him [Moses] to claim the credit for them himself . . ., he has given Balaam his testimony and deigned to perpetuate his memory."[164]

In rabbinic literature, Balaam provides the antithesis to Abraham. The three qualities associated with the latter are a good eye, a lowly mind, and a humble soul. Balaam, contrarily, was characterized by an evil eye, a haughty mind, and a proud soul.[165] The "deception (*plane*)[166] of Balaam" is the deception of selfish profit.[167] Balaam typically "loved the wages of wickedness."[168] Three of Jude's catchwords—*pareisdyein* (v 4), *plane* (v 11), and *planetai* (v 13)—could be standard catchwords for Balaam. Corrupted and errant at heart, Jude's opponents have become as wandering stars, fallen from their fixed pattern in heaven.

The third component of the prophetic triad in Jude 11, Korah, is perhaps the most arresting illustration of insubordination in all the OT. It is he who challenged the authority of the man who talked with God (Numbers 16). Moreover, siding with him were some two hundred fifty men among Israel's leaders (Num. 16:17,35). The term used in Jude 11 to describe Korah's rebellion, *antilogia*, is the same term used by the LXX in Num. 20:13 (*hydor antilogia*), Deut. 32:51, 33:8, Ps. 80:8 and 105:32 (*epi tou hydatos antilogia*) and rendered "Meribah." "Meribah," then, is symbolic of the strife and contention of the wilderness. Along with the men of Sodom, Korah and his following, according to the rabbis, would find no place in the world to come.[169] In effect, Korah's fate is commensurate with his deed.

Numerous terms of expressions from Jude's vocabulary epitomize Korah: *blasphemein/blasphemia* (vv 8,9,10), *me terein ten heauton archen* (v 6), *antilogia* (v 11), *goggystai* and *mempsimoiroi* (v 16), and *apodiorizein* (v 19). The behavior of the *houtoi* is shown to resemble the shocking irreverence of the one man in the OT who dared to challenge Moses' leadership. Theirs is a similar fate which awaits.

Cain, Balaam, and Korah are united in Jude by means of a woe-oracle. The woe-cry in the OT is found in several contexts: a call for attention (e.g., Zech. 2:6), mourning for the dead (e.g., 1 Kings 13:30; Jer. 22:18), a cry of excitement (e.g., Isa. 55:1; Zech. 2:10), a cry of revenge (e.g., Isa. 1:24), and the announcement of doom (e.g., Isa. 3:9,11; Jer. 13:27; Ezek. 13:3,18; Hos. 7:13; Amos 6:1; Mic. 2:1). The vast majority of incidents fall under the latter heading. In the mind of the prophets, to whom the primary use of *hoy* was restricted, the promise of judgment was synonymous with judgment itself.[170] The woe-form proper decried deplorable deeds and appeared with or without a following threat. The OT prophets normally attach specific behavior to the woe-cry: e.g., Isa. 1:4; 5:8,11,18,20,21,22; 10:1; Jer. 22:13; Ezek. 34:2; Amos 5:18; Mic. 2:1; and Zeph. 3:1.

The prophetic woe-oracle has its origin in ancient legal practice.[171] Three passages in the OT—1 Kings 13:1–34, Jer. 22:1–30, and Jer. 34:4–7—contain the use of *hôy* expressly in a funerary context.[172] Prophetic literature provides evidence that in the eighth century B.C. this funerary setting is already present. The woe-cry came to incorporate a vengeance pattern, and hence, a "reversal" image.[173] Death demanded mourning, hence, the professional mourners with their gestures of tearing the garments and throwing dust on their heads. But the woe-cry was not complete with mourning. Those affected by the grief at hand were moved to channel their vehemence in the direction of the guilty party. At the funeral, the guilty party would be cursed.[174] It should be noted that, in the main, the OT prophets spoke woe over the *living;* i.e., they were previewing a *certain death.*

For Jude's purposes, the trio of v 11 foreshadows the fate of the *houtoi.* Having blasphemed (vv 8,10), Jude's opponents have brought themselves under divine curse. With the cry of condemnation and the threat of divine vengeance hanging over their heads, the *houtoi* await the execution of irrevocable judgment. Calamity and ruin are their portion, for in every instance where the Hebrew prophets use *hôy,* death or destruction was in view.[175] Apostasy is deadly serious.

Types and Triplets: Affirming the Old Testament Witness

The validity of testimony in the OT was affirmed by the mouth of two or three witnesses. Herein a matter was established (Num. 35:30; Deut. 17:6; 19:15). The same principle of *martyria* is borne out in the NT as well (Matt. 18:16; John 5:31–33; 8:17–18; 2 Cor. 13:1; 1 Tim. 5:19; and Heb. 10:28). Every matter should be confirmed by multiple witnesses. Ultimate testimony to the truth lies in the very triune nature of the godhead itself. In essence, the three represent one. They are diverse, yet one and the same. A threefold concurrence strengthens the validity of testimony presented; it yields completeness.

The unsurpassed use of triplets in the epistle of Jude—a phenomenon which, within the constraints of a mere twenty-five verses, defies comparison—has already been treated cursorily, specifically in the light of its *literary* function.[176] Jude's formulas are not incidental. By means of parallelism, whether synonymous, antithetical, or synthetic,[177] the writer enriches and deepens his illustration utilizing a second component. Yet a third descriptive parallel creates the notion of *fullness*. The result is a completed record, a full-orbed depiction.

In a very Jewish and calculating way, then, Jude corroborates evidence by means of the rampant use of a threefold witness. This method applies to (1) his presentation of prophetic types (vv 5–7,11), (2) the explanation of those types as they relate to the *houtoi* (vv 8–10,12–13,16,19), (3) epistolary features of his address (vv 1–2,24–25), as well as (4) the grammatical-lexical particularities of his writing style (e.g., vv 1,8,9,11,20–23). He thus creatively seeks to exhort the faithful while simultaneously condemning his opponents. His testimony is valid, securely buttressed by the cords of multiple witnesses.

Conclusion

The relationship between the epistle of Jude and the OT, as we have observed, is one of close association—both in language and logic. At work is the writer's midrashic activity, bringing people or events identified in OT narrative to the reader for present application in the Christian community. Jude's sustained use of particular catchwords lends rhetorical force to his message: the *gravity* of apostasy must be underscored. Throughout the epistle, the faithful and the ungodly are set in rigid contrast. Both, significantly, are being reserved by God for their appointed end.

Among specific OT motifs being utilized in Jude are the ungodly-faithful antithesis, theophany and judgment, the day of the Lord, judgment by fire, election and divine foreknowledge, and the divine glory. The principal witnesses to past judgment in Jude's antithesis are provided in two sets of triplets: Israel of old, the fallen angels, and Sodom and Gomorrah; and Cain, Baalam, and Korah. With regard to the Lord's "coming," a prominent theme of the OT, the *manner* of His coming—resulting in cosmic upheaval—as well as its purpose—to bring judgment upon the earth—is to be noted. The extent to which Jewish apocalyptic literature is dependent upon this OT motif is exemplified by 1 Enoch, and thus has significance for Jude. Due to covenant breach, one is witness to the "divine reversal," whereby the Lord comes in terror and dread to judge the ungodly. In the OT, fire is often associated with this judgment. Symbolizing the very essence of divine nature—unapproachableness, invincibility, immutability, and mystery—fire represents the very consumptive nature of God's manifestation, particularly with regard to man's sin.

Jude exhibits the thoroughly Jewish conceptualization of God by stressing divine foreknowledge—as it applies to the apostate but also, and more importantly, as it bears upon his audience. God's purpose is sovereign, His decrees stand written in the heavenly books, and this reality should undergird the faithful. They are destined to be presented stainless, without blemish, before the very divine presence. In vivid contrast to the ungodly, for whom only gloom and darkness are being reserved, the faithful can anticipate the promise of appearing in glory—a promise based on the divine purpose which is immutable.

In order that Jude's audience might be graphically reassured of the certainty of his claims, types from Israel's past are called forth to serve as a reminder of God's sure dealings in history. Consistent with the OT view of history, the NT writer's use of types has spiritual and historical significance. Those who treat the Lord's sovereignty lightly will give account, and this accounting will take place within history. The effect of the use of such types is to comfort and exhort as well as to warn.

Israel, the dispossessed angels, and Sodom and Gomorrah are all united in Jude's polemic by their being divinely disenfranchised. Israel was not saved a second time after having been delivered once; the angels voluntarily left their exalted domain and thus, having forfeited their privilege, are consigned to darkness; and the cities of the plain, perhaps among the most striking of OT examples for their flaunting of sin, remain a living testimony to the awesomeness and consuming nature of divine judgment. These three paradigms together mirror the intention of Jude. Having despised normal life in the faith, the *houtoi* distort divine grace, deny Christ's lordship, and scorn spiritual authority in general, while having a contaminating effect on others whom they seek to influence. It is for the purpose of illustration and contrast that the tradition surrounding Moses' burial—derived from but not based on the OT—is marshalled: the *houtoi*, in their deluded self-sufficiency and self-indulgence, are an affront to the very glory and name of God. Railing at what they do not comprehend, they stand in utter contrast to Michael, who, of all creatures in the created order, would be qualified to rail at the prince of demons. Yet even Michael humbly appeals to a higher authority in his confrontation with the accuser of all men.

The second triad of historical paradigms—Cain, Balaam, and Korah—is united in Jude by means of a woe-cry. Just as these three in Israel's history, through their rebellion, brought themselves under divine curse, so Jude's opponents stand to incur the avenging wrath of God. Their epitomizing of wickedness, self-seeking, and obstinate rebellion is reminiscent of the trio from ancient Israel. Through the "reversal" concept associated with the woe-oracle as practiced particularly by the eighth- and seventh-century B.C. prophets, the guilty party is depicted as standing under the threat of divine curse. For Jude's purposes, the trio of historical examples foreshadows the fate of the *houtoi*. Calamity and destruction await.

Jude's way of affirming his argument is consistent with OT witness: he lists, enumerates, and explains in terms of "three's." Inasmuch as every matter in the OT was to be confirmed by multiple witnesses, the assertions found in Jude yield a threefold concurrence. By means of corroborating evidence from not only a second witness but a third as well, the various aspects to his polemic achieve a notable strength and completion. His claims are *fully* buttressed. There can be no doubt in the minds of his audience God is absolutely committed to fulfilling His promises, whether on behalf of those who hold His authority in contempt or those who eagerly anticipate His coming.

5

The Use of Extrabiblical Source Material
in Jude

In his response to the general twentieth-century neglect of the
Jude epistle, D. J. Rowston[1] comments: "If the neglect of Jude
arises out of its response to its own milieu, then an appreciation of
Jude could well result from a study of the book in its original
setting." The history of the letter's interpretation since the time of
the early fathers through the Reformation period and into the
modern era is, broadly speaking, one of omission, relative ignorance, or misunderstanding. Where Jude has been studied, it has
generally lacked creative and responsible inquiry. Indeed, when
contrasted with the attention afforded the other general epistles,
for example, or even the NT Apocalypse, Jude has not fared so
well. Its place in NT study is much like that of John the Baptist in
comparison to Jesus. Untold volumes written about Jesus of
Nazareth—and fittingly so—fill the stacks of theological libraries,
while the Baptist remains in relative obscurity, even though John
furnishes the proper perspective with which to fully grasp Jesus'
messianic ministry. Similarly, one is hard-pressed, apart from a
few multiple work commentaries, to name a *single* work devoted
to the exegesis of Jude in spite of the fact that Jude, along with the
epistle of James, is an important specimen of Palestinian Jewish
Christianity and, thus, significant for the study of Christian origins.[2]

There is no disputing the fact that the lack of the letter's internal evidence as to the historical situation contributes to the widespread disregard that Rowston laments. To a greater or lesser
extent, this is the lot apportioned to the general epistles. Several
specific factors, however, might be singled out as contributory to
Jude's place, or lack thereof, historically in NT studies. It is often
thought that Jude is void of theology, that it specifically lacks a
strong christology which is so fundamentally characteristic of the
epistles of the NT. It is sufficient to reiterate that, upon examina-

tion, the letter shows itself to be remarkably rich in its christological awareness. The writer seeks to transfer to *Kyrios*-Jesus all the
attributes of glory, majesty, dominion, and power which are ascribed to Yahweh in the OT, including the deliverance of Israel
from Egypt (v 5). Jesus is both *kyrios* and *despotēs* (v 4). This status
underlines His kingly and transcendent nature. His authority is
legitimate, absolute and arbitrary. One of the key realms of divine
fiat in which this execution of authority is to be asserted is judgment. In that *Kyrios*-Jesus saves, He is qualified to judge. Hence,
theophany is important to the writer.

A second basis for the relative neglect of Jude is the very
language, symbolism, literary-rhetorical style, and tone employed
by the writer—elements that have already received considerable
attention. At a technical level, poetry and prose, whether oral or
written, are at their best when various devices of sound, economy,
arrangement, parallelism, and imagery are composed with *thrift*,
that is to say, when the writer-speaker expresses as much as is
possible in as few words as are possible.[3] It is unfortunate that the
modern reader often is unable to fully appreciate the dynamic of
Jude's thoughtful and well-conceived polemic or that his argument is as *positive* and reinforcing as it is negative and threatening.

Yet another factor that might discourage serious study of Jude,
or at the very least raise questions for which solutions are not so
clear-cut, is the writer's use of extracanonical tradition-material.
Surviving Jewish literature from the last three centuries B.C. and
first century A.D.[4] is decisive in helping to explain religious
thought, concepts, metaphors, and symbols found in the NT.
These writings bridge the chronological hiatus between OT and
NT eras.

A crucial question relating to the Pseudepigrapha and Apocrypha—one which has engendered no little discussion—is their
status in relationship to the accepted Jewish canon of the Hebrew
Bible. Sufficient evidence exists to reflect that a Jewish canon was
established by the midsecond century B.C. and that any challenge
to so-called "disputed" books emerged subsequent to their recognition.[5] If the NT writers had made only infrequent or isolated
allusion to the OT, the boundaries of the OT canon prove to be
less decisive. However, inasmuch as Jesus and the writers of the
NT considered the OT authoritative and freely quoted from it,
their statements painted against the backdrop of contemporary
Judaism—whether mainline or sectarian—indicate a body of literature which has taken on a canonical shape. That is to say, it

possesses a sacredness and authority which is assumed in the first century A.D. by the NT writers.

At work are both historical as well as theological assumptions. The use of the OT by Jesus as well as the NT writers[6] implies what the OT as a source for the early Christians was considered to be, with its acknowledged sacred boundaries.

> . . . it is not credible that the structure of the Old Testament canon and the order and number of its books would be referred to in the New Testament in relation to matters of such significance as the witness of the Old Testament to Jesus, the judgements coming upon Jesus's own generation, or God's heavenly throne, if the structure, order and number were in themselves of no significance.[7]

The writers of the NT should not be viewed merely as "children of their time." The remarkably unsuspicious attitude of many in the first century toward apocryphal or pseudepigraphal writings should not be interpreted to mean that the writers of 1 and 2 Peter and Jude viewed 1 Enoch, to illustrate, or the Assumption of Moses, as "inspired" or on a par with OT writings. What this phenomenon however *does* indicate is that they share a thought-world, reflected in their use of common theological concepts and literary conventions. The writers of the NT, particularly those molded by their Palestinian Jewish-Christian heritage, feel at home in this world of thought and ideas.

On the basis of early Christian usage, any argument for viewing apocryphal works as part of the canon fails to marshall convincing evidence. *At best,* Christian usage of apocryphal or pseudepigraphal works is a double-edged sword. Indeed, the strongest case that can be built speaks *against* this view.[8] Inferred in J. H. Charlesworth's "twofold category of canon"[9] is the idea that the canon has "fringes," i.e., that there are "inspired" works which were considered sacred by some in the church, such as 1 Enoch, yet which somehow failed to make it into the inner sanctum—works which nonetheless warrant our consideration because of their influence in the early Christian era. That such works did indeed exercise influence is granted, yet this is not the issue which must be resolved. Rather, the question of pseudo-nymity, treated at some length earlier, must be addressed in the light of the church's understanding of canon and cannot be skirted, nor can its implications be ignored. Why is it necessary to attribute a literary work to an obviously "inspired" man of God from Israel's past? Is the writer consciously aware that the spirit of prophecy has disappeared? And what, or who, determines the *sacred* and *prophetic* character of a work? To contend that the scriptures are in fact the word of God is to concede that it is God the Holy Spirit who is the source and custodian of the scriptures. To argue or suggest that canon is "twofold" in its categories is to suggest that several levels or degrees of "inspiration" exist: purely prophetic and partially prophetic. As soon, however, as we view inspiration in terms of levels of inspiredness, "canon," "inspiration," and "sacredness" are no more. Either the Spirit of God moves upon men prophetically to express the divine will in a literary fashion, or He does not.[10]

The issue being addressed is not whether an extracanonical source is "inspiring" or containing truth or historically useful or even edifying. "A dog returns to its vomit" (2 Pet. 2:22), "For in him we live and move and have our being. . . . We are his offspring" (Acts 17:28), and "Bad company corrupts good character" (1 Cor. 15:33) are all true not because they are "sacred" or *theopneustos* in origin, but because they are in accord with divinely revealed truth, i.e., the word of God. More concretely, acceptance of the notion of a canon of sacred OT literature[11] stands on two merits: whether Jesus and the NT writers evidence such[12] as well as any grounds on which it had prior recognition within contemporary Judaism.[13] As to the objection that some of the Church fathers considered certain apocryphal works as "inspired," it should be noted that the level of patristic "acceptance" of apocryphal works varied from place to place. Some fathers quoted or used apocryphal works which they themselves would not include in canonical lists. This practice would seem to be best explained by homiletical needs reflecting a specific situation.

Although the influence of 1 Enoch on the NT is undeniable,[14] indeed more so than any apocryphal or pseudepigraphical work, can it be assumed—in fact, established as likely—that Jude, in making inspired use of 1 Enoch, purposed to popularize this Jewish writing? Does he, as virtually all commentators over the last hundred years have assumed, highly esteem 1 Enoch or even view Enoch as inspired? Can it be established that Jude's attitude toward the Pseudepigrapha is in fact any different from the other writers of the NT? It is worthy of note that the writer of the Apocalypse—i.e., the one NT book which would conceivably be most prone to incorporate Enochic theology—apparently does not borrow material from 1 Enoch. Rather, he shows a most conspicuous debt to the OT—particularly the prophets Isaiah, Daniel, and Ezekiel. Even 2 Peter, although linked to Jude via near verbatim parallels, makes no *explicit* allusion to an extra-biblical source. If the hypothesis suggested earlier is valid, namely that Jude's use of extracanonical source-material is one specific device in his overall literary-rhetorical strategy for addressing particular needs in his audience, what evidence can be marshalled to support this conviction? Can it further be reasonably demonstrated that Jude's use of extrabiblical source-material is in fact a sample of Jewish haggadic exegesis, a phenomenon which can be found elsewhere in the NT? Without seeking to be overly simplistic, we might state the nature of the problem thusly: Does Jude, who is representative of the writers of the NT, view the extracanonical sources which he has employed as "inspired," or is he making "inspired use" of "inspiring" literary (or oral) traditions?

THE USE OF TRADITION-MATERIAL IN THE NEW TESTAMENT

Pauline Dependence on Tradition-Material

In a general sense, Jude's exploiting of popular literature or traditions is not unique in the NT. Paul is not averse to marshalling such sources and using them for his own strategic purposes when seeking to illustrate. Several instances from Pauline literature are worth noting.

While in Athens, Paul spent time debating with Jews and God-fearing Greeks in the synagogue as well as in the marketplace on a day-to-day basis (Acts 17:16ff). From the text of Acts 17, it becomes clear that Paul was familiar with the legend behind the altar "to the Unknown God" (17:23). His statements "in him we live and move and have our being" and "we are his offspring" are taken from Greek poets. Rather than denounce the pagan idolatry of the city's populace,[5] Paul incorporates the legend into his preaching and "makes known" the God unknown to the Athenians (vv 23–31).

The Apostle's knowledge and use of contemporary Jewish and pagan traditions surfaces elsewhere in the NT. As a former pupil of Gamaliel (Acts 22:3), he doubtless had recourse to much in the way of rabbinic traditions. This is evident in 1 Cor. 10:1–5, a midrash on "the Rock following." Instead of elaborating on the significance of the manna or the water from the rock during Israel's time in the wilderness, he builds upon Jewish legend, commonly ascribed to popular rabbinic tradition,[16] which envisaged the rock as moving with the people for the duration of their forty years in the wilderness and providing a constant source of water. Irrespective of Paul's relationship to this tradition (which is impossible to define), he utilizes the tradition—evidently familiar to many—to underline spiritual truth. Interpreting the Israelite experience of water from the rock christologically, Paul is concerned to identify the *source* of provision, i.e., Christ. In so doing, Paul stresses the typological character of Israel's experience and establishes continuity between the OT church and the Corinthians.

2 Tim. 3:1–9 represents another case of Paul using Jewish tradition for the sake of illustration. The passage presents a context in which the apostle outlines particular characteristics of the "last days." Not unlike the *tines anthrōpoi* of Jude 4, the ungodly, which are the subject of Pauline exhortation, are described in terms of stealth, blasphemy, and evil lusts. Incapable of acknowledging the truth, they are depicted in v 8 as the antitypes of two figures of Jewish midrash unknown to the OT, Jannes and Jambres,[17] who are identified with the magicians in Pharaoh's court and who are said to have opposed Moses, producing resistance even after their defeat (cf. Exodus 7). Their legend evidently derives from cumulative traditions, of which there is no known author or source. In this sense, allusion to them parallels use of the Pseudepigrapha. Whether Paul is dependent on an oral or written tradition, the names of these two rebels come to us from several sources: the Pseudepigrapha,[18] Pliny,[19] rabbinic literature,[20] Origen,[21] Eusebius,[22] and a host of pagan writers.[23] The legends surrounding Jannes and Jambres are quite varied and anachronistic, yet amid this diversity a central theme stands out: these two figures are typical of all those who resist the purposes of God. In this Palestinian haggadah, Moses and the deliverance from evil (epitomized by Egypt) serve as a type of messianic deliverance from the ungodly by the "second Moses."[24] Timothy would no doubt have been well acquainted with the legend and thus have recognized its didactic function. Paul's use of this tradition in 2 Timothy is comparable to the use of typology and the theme of ungodliness in Jude.

Even if somewhat tongue-in-cheek, Paul alludes in Titus 1 to a Greek poet by acknowledging his status among the locals as *prophētēs*. This reference is set within the context of instruction on character qualities which befit an elder (vv 5–9). The life-style of the overseer is to be above reproach. In vv 10–11, Paul explains what the elder is *not* to personify. This is underscored with good reason, since the Cretans were famed drunks, liars, and general gluttons, so much so that the ancient world spoke of three evil "C's"—the Cilicians, the Cappodocians, and the Cretans.[25] Polybius[26] confirms this portrait of the Cretans, noting the excess greed, duplicity, and wantonness for which they had become a proverb.[27] The actual citation used by Paul derives from the Greek poet Callimachus,[28] with close parallels found in the earlier poet Epimenides (who had taken on almost mythological proportions) and Hesiod's *Theogony*.[29] Whether Paul, in using *prophētēs*, has precisely in mind the Cretan false teachers who were self-styled prophets or one of the poets remains inconclusive, although evidence would seem to speak in favor of the latter. Interestingly, it was at the suggestion of the Cretan Epimenides that the Athenians are said to have built the altar *Agnostō Theō* (cf. Acts 17:23) in the early sixth century B.C. Five centuries later Cicero could speak of Epimenides as a "prophet."[30] Similar to the episode in Athens recorded in Acts 17, Paul utilizes a familiar maxim, accommodating even the secular point of view by attributing it to a poet considered on the popular level to be a "prophet" who hailed from Crete. Paul makes "inspired" use of an "uninspired" yet known tradition.

Petrine Dependence on Tradition-Material (1 Pet 3:18—22)

Before returning to Jude it is necessary to consider at some length several verses in 1 Peter 3, doubtless one of the more difficult passages in the NT[31] and a portion of scripture which in the history of interpretation has engendered no clear consensus with regard to its exegesis. Notoriously dim to the rational Western mind, this passage rivals much of Jude for obscurity and raising questions. Our interest, however, lies not in its seeming unintelligibility, but rather in its bearing upon our understanding, and thus, interpretation, of Jude. At issue is the incorporation in 1 Peter of relevant Jewish tradition-material into the overall theme. In light of its pertinence for the study of Jude, a discussion of 1 Pet. 3:18—22 and the issues raised by these verses is appropriate.

For Christ also suffered once and for all on account of our sins, the righteous for the unrighteous, in order that he might bring us to God, having been put to death in the flesh but made alive in the spirit, in which process he also went and preached to the spirits in prison which earlier had disobeyed when God's patience endured in the days of Noah as the ark was being built. In the ark only a few persons, eight in all, were saved through water. Baptism, which corresponds to this, now saves you—not a washing off of physical dirt from the body, rather a stipulation toward God involving a clear conscience, through the resurrection of Jesus Christ, who has gone into heaven and is at the right hand of God, with angels and principalities and powers having been made subject to him.[32]

A whole spate of questions is raised by the text. Is the subject Christ, Enoch (based on Jewish apocalyptic tradition), or Noah? Is the reference to Christ a reference to His preexistent, resurrected, or postexistent state? Is the author speaking of descent or ascent? Is the nature of Christ's preaching salvific or condemnatory? Are the objects of this preaching souls of deceased people or demonic spirits? What is the location of this preaching? And, on a broader plane, what is the purpose of this material as it relates to the overall thrust of the epistle?[33]

In 3:18–22 we seem to pass from Christ's suffering, a central theme of the epistle, to Christ's triumph, all of which relate to His *saving work*. In 2:8ff the author had traced the psychology of the believer's suffering for Christ in a pagan and hostile world. Here he views the effect of Christ's work in terms of complete triumph, for Jesus goes[34] into heaven and is enthroned at the right hand of God with all angelic powers subject to His authority.[35] The writer exhorts and comforts his audience with the reassurance that there is nothing in the cosmos outside of the conquest and reign of Christ. In that 4:1 resumes discussion of the prior theme ("Since, then, Christ suffered in the flesh . . ."), 3:18–22 may be viewed as a parenthesis. As judgment fell on the ancient world in Noah's day, so the judgment of God fell on Christ. All that Christ's death entails, however, does not meet the eye. Those who henceforth take refuge in Christ, the Victorious One, come through the flood of divine retribution.

In v 18 solidarity is established between Christ and Peter's audience ("For Christ also suffered . . ."). The reason for Christ's suffering follows with a *hina*-clause: "that he bring you to God," reminiscent of the cult in the OT. The substitutionary (*dikaios hyper adikōn*) death of the Righteous One opens the way to God.[36] The method of justification is stated: *thanatōtheis men sarki* and *zōopoiētheis de pneumati*. Death to the flesh brought life in the spirit. In v 18 several important assertions are contained: (1) Christ is set forth as an *example (hoti kai)*; (2) Christ's work is definitive *(hapax)*; (3) Christ's suffering is vicarious *(dikaios hyper dikōn)*; and (4) Christ's work has a goal *(hina hymas prosagagē tō theō)*.

Several crucial questions are raised in vv 19–20a—questions which have found capable exegetes at considerable variance in terms of exegetical results. The difficulties revolve around the prepositional phrase *en hǭ* which introduces v 19, the identity of *ta pneumata,* the expression *en phylakę,* the nature of the message which was "preached" *(ekēryxen),* in addition to the accompanying clause *apeithēsasin pote hote apexedecheto hē tou theou makrothymia en hēmerais Nōe kataskeuazomenēs kibōtou.* Three principal views of 3:19 characterize the history of interpretation: (1) Christ, in His preexistent state, preached in the spirit through the person Noah to Noah's contemporaries; (2) after Christ died, He preached to Noah's contemporaries to convert them; and (3) Christ preached victory and conquest over fallen, hostile angelic powers. For the sake of argumentation, we shall classify views (1) and (2) together, so that two principal historic lines of interpretation—Christ's preaching in the underworld to *human beings* against His preaching to *fallen angels*—are to be contrasted.[37]

As has been noted, the history of interpretation has known no clear consensus regarding these two positions, both of which have been represented by serious exegetes.[38] Among the arguments normally cited in support of rendering *pneumata* in 3:19 as human souls are: (1) the use of *pneumati* in v 18 and *pneumasin* in v 19; (2) *instances* in 1 Enoch (associated with the opposing line of interpretation) of *pneumata* meaning souls of the dead (e.g., 1 Enoch 9:3,10; 22:3,6,7,9, 11,12,13), i.e., in the sense of *psychai;* (3) the low probability of Peter's readers scattered throughout several provinces in Asia Minor understanding any allusion to 1 Enoch; (4) "preaching" to humans in 4:6; (5) a similar *sarx/pneuma* dualism found in 4:6; (6) reconciling the time and place of preaching to fallen angels with the clause "when God's patience endured in the days of Noah as the ark was being built"; (7) the emphasis in Genesis 6 on *human* disobedience as the cause for divine judgment; and (8) the emphasis in 1 Peter on *human,* not demonic, sources of persecution.

Without merely examining individual words and phrases in these verses, an approach taken in most commentaries, we would also propose to consider 3:18–22 in the light of the immediate and more general context. As already indicated, the reader of 1 Peter moves from Christ's sufferings, which are paradigmatic for the believers, to Christ's conquest. Those to whom Peter is writing are being confronted by pagans of Asia Minor who are antagonistic toward the Gospel. "Suffering" *(paschein:* 2:19,20,21,23; 3:14,17,18; 4:1,15,19; *pathēma:* 1:11; 4:13; 5:1,9) and "trial" *(peirasmos:* 1:6; 4:12) are being encountered by the Christians. Indeed their experience is a "fiery ordeal" *(pyrōsis,* 4:12), coming at the hands of those who "refuse to believe" (*apeithein:* 2:8; 3:1,20). Thus the believers are being tested to the limits of their faith, perhaps even facing death (*thanatoun,* 3:18).[39] However, they are not to fear the threats, blasphemy, and abuse of the pagans. Rather, they are to hold fast faithfully to Christ their hope and maintain a clear conscience, for it is better to be found *innocent* though persecuted than *guilty* and condemned to the judgment of Almighty God, as the antecedents, mentioned parenthetically in vv 19 and 20, bear out.[40]

It is therefore important for them that Christ be presented as their "captain," the one who went before them and suffered as well. For this reason, in 3:13ff the parallels between Christ and the audience are close. Yet, it is not an end in itself that Christ suffered. His suffering in the flesh was the initial and necessary step in fulfilling the divine plan of *hymas prosagein tō theō* (3:18). What resulted in the spirit due to Christ's work is mentioned, parenthetically, in 3:19–20a. These verses, it should be reiterated, contain *significant* parallels to the situation at hand. The writer is freely delineating in his teaching: Christ suffered in the flesh at the hands of unbelieving men, just as the recipients of the letter. Christ's work, however, was not *merely* sacrificial (v 18). The *kai* introducing v 19 indicates a *further activity* of Christ besides His death. It is this further activity which necessitates clarification and hence deserves further attention.

J. S. Stewart[41] has pointed to a deficiency in our understanding of the doctrine of atonement (a doctrine by no means insignificant to 1 Peter). In his opinion, it has been stripped of a vital aspect: the realization of the *cosmic* dimensions of Christ's atonement, and specifically, the *defeat of the powers of darkness.* Due to Christ's role in creation as the Preexistent One, the angelic powers[42] were created *di' autou* and *eis auton* (Col. 1:16). They should thus be subservient to the execution of *His* will. It should not shock the reader of the NT that the angels who disobeyed (2 Pet. 2:4; Jude 6) warrant the most severe condemnation. Having been bearers of divine glory, they chose to rebel nonetheless.[43] It should be noted, with regard to the discussion of 1 Pet. 3:19, that "spirits" in the NT normally designates angelic beings.[44] Christ's work as it touches the angelic world is by no means tangential to the epistle. Indeed, the holy angels curiously long (*epithymein*) to peer into the realm of redemptive experience (1:12).[45]

While the thrust of 1 Peter, correctly noted, is the suffering which is being inflicted by *pagans* living in Asia Minor, the writer's interest in the unseen angelic realm should not be underesti-

mated. He depicts angels as inquisitve of the redemptive process
(1:12). With Christ seated at the right hand of God, the epistle
represents the effects of this reign as *hypotagentōn autō aggelōn kai
exousiōn kai dynameōn* (3:22). Before concluding his letter, the
writer admonishes his audience to be sober and alert, for "your
enemy the devil" prowls around as a roaring lion, seeking someone to devour. Whether *ta pneumata* of 3:19 should be understood as demonic angels, standing contextually in association with
the "angels and principalities and powers" of 3:22 (the climax of
3:17ff), over against the souls of men, remains to be clarified.
Our exegesis will also necessarily entail identifying the relationship between 3:19 and *nekrois euēggelisthē* in 4:6 structurally.

The language being used in 1 Peter 3 is to be taken literally.
Believers are indeed suffering *real* persecution for the sake of
Christ. Upon Christ, the writer responds, was inflicted *real* suffering to the point of physical death. His being made alive, His
descent, His ascension, and His glorification in Heaven—creedal
elements in the church's confession and liturgy from the beginning[46]—were to be perceived as real and literal events,[47] though
performed by the might of the Spirit. A major flaw in the approach of many historically to 1 Pet. 3:18–22, epitomized perhaps best by the Augustinian interpretation which has endured
through the centuries, is that Christ's "going," i.e., His descent
(*poreutheis*, v 19), is often spiritualized,[48] while His ascent is viewed
literally. We do not have the liberty to spiritualize the "going" of v
19; the text says *poreutheis ekēryxen*.

This preaching—and the variance of scholarly opinion as to the
content of this preaching is as great as the identity of the "spirits"—
is best explained by the prepositional phrase *en phylakȩ̄*. *Phylakē* is
not to be understood as a place of departed souls, rather it speaks
of punishment. Its use in Rev. 18:2 *(phylakē pantos pneumatos
akathartou)* and 20:7 *(lythēsetai ho Satanas ek tēs phylakēs autou)*
would help clarify our definition.[49] Mention of an *abyssos* in Luke
8:31; Rom. 10:7; Rev. 9:1,2,11; 11:17; 17:8; and 20:1,3 would
confirm this.[50] Such usage, furthermore, agrees with that found
in standard Jewish apocalyptic depiction of the demonic realm.[51]
Imprisoned fallen angels are a favorite theme of Jewish apocalyptic writers.[52] We may therefore take *phylakē* to stand in direct
contrast to *kolpos Abraam* (Luke 16:22) and *ho paradeisos* (Luke
23:43) in the NT.[53]

As to the much debated question of whether in this text we have
to do with a "descent" or "ascent,"[54] the verb being used, *poreutheis*[55] (in both vv 19 and 22), is neutral and does not in and of

itself tell us, as compared to the verbs *katabainein* or *anabainein*.[56] Is it possible that the writer is using an expression which is *not* designed to give a precise location? In Jewish apocalyptic literature, it is difficult to locate *phylakē*. 1 Enoch is exemplary. In 1 Enoch 10:4,6, and 13, it is depicted as a hole and fire. In 13:9, it is located on earth. In 14:5, it is described as "the ends of the earth" (cf. 15:8). And in 27:2, it is called a "cursed valley," while in chapters 17 and 18 *phylakē* is "in the direction of the west" (note especially 17:5 and 18:6). In other intertestamental works, the location of *phylakē* is equally difficult to place although generally ascribed to the heavens.[57]

Regardless of the imprecision with which Christ's *poreuthesis* is associated, we may assert that the text of 3:19 is alluding not to a "descent" (in the traditionally understood sense) to the place of the dead to preach salvation, but to a going to the place of demonic "imprisonment" for the purpose of declaring utter conquest over the forces of evil. The resurrected Christ is Lord over all.[58]

The place of 3:19 in the contextual flow beginning in 3:13 should be noted. The thread uniting this material is the persecution of Christians by hardened pagans who refuse to believe. Nothing in these verses hints at positive receptivity toward the Gospel message (and, hence, a "salvation" message). In v 22, Christ is pictured as enthroned with all principalities and powers subject to Him—the language of enmity and conquest. 1 Peter, it should be reiterated, is concerned for the *endurance of the Christians, not the salvation of spirits*. The question of precise location of *phylakē* cannot be answered here with certainty.

At this point it should be noted that our discussion of these verses has necessitated reference to the work 1 Enoch. Whether or not we may assume that the Asian readers of 1 Peter were familiar with Enoch traditions will need to remain unanswered. Certainly the probability would have been less than a Palestinian audience to whom Jude was writing. That notwithstanding, the perception developed in apocalyptic literature of the fallen angels which was prevalent in the first century, coupled with the numerous points of contact with 1 Peter 3:19–20[59] and Enoch's commission to go and preach to the fallen angels (1 Enoch 12:4), make it exceedingly difficult to interpret 1 Pet. 3:19 in an alternative sense.[60] Indeed, the fallen angels are being *reserved* for *judgment* (2 Pet. 2:4; Jude 6). The text of 3:19 reads *kēryssein*,[61] not *euaggelizein*. The issue is not salvation or a "second chance,"[62] but rather the *announcement of conquest* over Satan and his minions.[63] The power of evil has been broken. Christ has disarmed the principalities and powers, making a public spectacle of and triumphing over them (Col. 2:15). 1 Peter depicts Christ as an "end-time" Enoch, who indeed proclaimed judgment over the fallen spirits.[64] What Jewish apocalyptic tradition ascribed to Enoch is transferred to Christ. That Peter only writes "he preached to the spirits in prison" would suggest, as Goppelt[65] maintains, that this was a familiar tradition.[66]

Moreover, the allusion to the days of Noah in v 20, coupled with the reference to "spirits in prison," would further indicate to the audience that the writer is drawing from Jewish apocalyptic tradition.[67] Noah receives fairly frequent mention in Palestinian Jewish writings—he is the epitome of the righteous man, a type of righteousness by faith.[68] Notably, after A.D. 100, Noah is portrayed in Palestinian literature as a preacher of righteousness to pre-Flood contemporaries.[69] In the early church there appears to have been much interest in Noah and the Flood story. Its mention in Matt. 24:37–39; Luke 17:26–27; Heb. 11:7; 1 Pet. 3:20; 2 Pet. 2:5, and 3:5–9 would suggest that it was the subject of much midrashic interpretation in the Christian community, an element doubtless inherited from the early Christians' Jewish forbears.[70] *En hēmerais Nōe* would be considered representative, since the Flood was *the* great judgment of the ancient world.

In 1 Peter 3 a parallel exists between the age of the Flood and the present, expressed by the words "God's patience endured"[71] in v 20 (cf. Gen. 6:3a). Both the fallen angels and the flood typology[72] are analogous to the situation to which 1 Peter is addressed. Both are types of final judgment.[73] Enoch was sent to preach doom to the disobedient angels who remained hostile to God; Noah's contemporaries refused to repent during the period of the construction of the ark; and those persecuting the Christians in 1 Peter refuse to believe *(apeithein):* "They are surprised that you do not join them in the same wild profligacy, and they abuse you. But they will give account to him who is ready to judge the living and the dead" (4:4).

The parallel that "a few were saved" (v 20) also has clear implications for Peter's audience. Perhaps feeling as if they were a mere "eight souls" amidst a scornful and hostile world looking on, the believers can take courage in the fact that the few righteous *were* indeed saved—by water. Hence, for them, baptism is significant. The *eperōtēma eis theon* (v 21) does not have the mere effect of outwardly removing dirt from the physical body, rather it cleanses internally, by means of one's unity with the resurrected Christ. Marking the faithful as God's chosen few, the baptismal pledge elicits utter loyalty to God and constitutes a very real and intensely relevant assurance of salvation to a persecuted minority.[74]

In contrast to 3:19, where the cosmic effects of Christ's saving and triumphant work are hinted at, with 4:1 the writer returns to the main theme which he began in 3:13—suffering unjustly. As to the question of the relationship between 3:19 and 4:6, several things are held in common: attitudes of unbelief and hostility, the assurance of judgment, and "preaching." What distinguishes 4:6, however, is worthy of note. A fundamental error, by which 3:19 and 4:6 are frequently and mistakenly linked, is the *sarx-pneuma* dichotomy from 3:18. The "dead" of 4:6 are not the "spirits" of 3:19. These are rather deceased saints. Significantly, the verb *euaggelizein* is used in 4:6. 3:19–20a, on the other hand, does not correspond; the contemporaries of Noah did *not* repent. Structurally, 3:18–20 appears to be, in fact, a digression in thought, while 4:6 relates to the overarching thesis in 1 Peter of suffering.

Of the attempts which have been made to see the structural coherence of these verses, two analyses—one recent and one not so recent—are worthy of mention, both of which seek to organize this material chiastically. The allusion to the disobedient spirits and Noah, as already noted, is parenthetical, yet it owes its existence to the main theme of the epistle and is not some alien object.[75] S. E. Johnson[76] shows in chiastic fashion the paradigm of Christ's suffering, followed by His resurrection with the effects of His preaching to the spirits, the comparison of past with present, and glorification. The literary structure[77] can be represented as follows:

A   Christ suffered and was put to death (3:18)
  B   He went and preached to the spirits in prison (3:19)
    C   who were in the past disobedient when God's patience was enduring (3:20)
      D   in the days of Noah during the building of the ark, in which a few souls were saved by water (3:20)
      D'   This pattern corresponds to baptism which now saves you (3:21)
    C'   (not a washing off of physical dirt from the body, rather a stipulation toward God involving a clear conscience) (3:21)
  B'   through the resurrection of Jesus Christ, who has gone into heaven and is at the right hand of God, with angels and principalities and powers having been made subject to Him (3:21–22)
A'   Since then Christ has suffered . . . (4:1ff).

A more recent attempt to view 1 Pet. 3:18–4:6 chiastically by A. Pinto da Silva[78] is based on the use of the terms "flesh" and "spirit" occurring in these verses:

A—flesh (3:18)
  B—spirit (3:18)
  B'—spirit (3:19–22)
  B'—flesh (4:1–6)[79]

Summing up the teaching found in 1 Peter 3, the work of Christ, done on behalf of the Christians in Asia Minor who are suffering, is depicted in terms of its *realm* and *scope*. The realm of Christ's suffering is that of death, which through the cross and resurrection was dealt a decisive defeat. Its scope is universal and absolute, reaching to the ends of the cosmos. Not only did Jesus taste death; most importantly, He conquered it. Christ's journey to heaven entailed proclamation to the demonic realm of God's vindication exhibited in Christ's enthronement. In light of this reality, Peter's audience should be encouraged, for the very nerve center of evil has been destroyed. Although conflict for the Asia Minor Christians was very real and intensely spiritual, the hostile unseen powers in relationship to Christ are now *hypotagentōn autō*.

This portrait, even when set forth in a seemingly cryptic fashion, is in full harmony with the teaching of the NT.[80] The work of Christ, as presented in the teaching of 1 Peter 3:18–22, ultimately epitomizes grace *and* judgment. Christ, the faithful witness,[81] preaches to all beings, even to those fully at enmity with God. This allusion to an extracanonical Jewish tradition in 1 Peter serves the greater purpose of paraenetic teaching on the victorious conquest over the demonic realm. The writer is not concerned about the *Sitz im Leben* of the tradition, nor about elements such as precise locale or time. What ultimately matters is the victorious work of Christ. In a modified and judicious manner, Peter makes inspired use of a tradition to illustrate the effects of Christ's redemptive activity and thereby encourage his audience in a fashion scarcely appreciated by the modern reader.[82]

Early Christian Use of Tradition-Material: An Overview

The aforementioned instances of the Pauline and Petrine utilization of tradition-material serve to illustrate a phenomenon which is not isolated in the NT. NT writers borrow popular tradition-material and exploit this for their own end. As we have seen, the Petrine example is particularly significant for the present study because of its link to 1 Enoch.

1 Peter 3 borrows from Jewish apocalyptic tradition to illustrate the cosmic scope and ramifications of the redemptive work of Christ. Conquest over evil has been wrought. There is no corner of the universe, no power or principality, which is not subject to Christ's rule. Jude, writing to an audience whose milieu is Palestinian Jewish-Christian, also draws on Jewish apocalyptic tradition—most notably material from 1 Enoch and a tradition ascribed to the Assumption of Moses. The reason for such a literary phenomenon, as we have attempted to demonstrate in 1 Peter, is to be sought chiefly in the writer's *literary strategy*, i.e., in conscious awareness of the appropriateness for the need of the situation,[83] and not so much by reason of the writer's *personal* veneration of these works. What may seem obscure to the modern reader would doubtless have been intelligible to Peter's and Jude's audience. As authors with pastoral burdens, the writers shared the Jewish-Christian thought world of their readers and required no qualification or explanation of ideas or literary conventions.

And yet, just as we do not require that Peter or the early Christians endorsed the Enochic view of the Flood tradition or the Jewish apocalyptic understanding of the "sons of God," in the same way we need not require that

> everything in those books [e.g., Jewish apocalyptic] is edifying, still less that the books have divine authority. He [Jude] is treating the incidents he selects as pieces of narrative haggadah—edifying but not necessarily historical. . . . [The] story from the Assumption of Moses is indeed a piece of narrative haggadah, which has a close parallel in the midrash Deuteronomy Rabbah,[84] and there is no real reason why Jude should not have viewed the alleged prophecy by Enoch in the same way and treated it in the same manner.[85]

Z. H. Chajes[86] has shown how that narrative haggadah often does not intend to be historical in nature. It can also be used for the purpose of exaggeration, persuasion, or edification. Inasmuch as the NT writers were Jewish-Christians, one might expect that they reflect from time to time haggadic tendencies, teaching by means of characters or events which were proverbial to their prospective audiences. This is all the more true of Jude who writes for those whose background is Palestinian Judaism.

Once the Christian message has moved out to a broader, increasingly Gentile context, the understanding of the Jewish exegetical method is lost.[87] Hence, it would be natural to find that

THE USE OF EXTRABIBLICAL SOURCE MATERIAL IN JUDE

patristic recognition of the epistle of Jude is somewhat reserved. Generally speaking, the Western church regarded apocryphal works highly; in the East, however, they were deemed less so, causing Jude to be excluded from the Syrian canon.[88] Jerome[89] explains that because Jude appealed to the Book of Enoch as an authority, it was rejected by some. In the fourth century, Didymus of Alexander[90] defended the inspiration of Jude. The epistle was included as well in the canon of Athanasius.[91] Eusebius admits that Jude's authenticity is "doubted"; however, he continues: "the fact remains that these two [James and Jude], like the others [general epistles], have been regularly used in very many churches."[92] Circa A.D. 350, Cyril the Bishop of Jerusalem makes no distinction between *ta homologoumena* and *ta antilegomena*.[93] By the late fourth century, the church had become sufficiently alerted to and reactionary against the gnostic abuse of pseudonymity in distorting Christian truth.[94] Augustine[95] and Chrysostom[96] described the two extracanonical sources found in Jude as "blasphemous" and "fabulous." However, at the same time most doubts concerning Jude had been laid to rest, and the epistle was included in most canonical lists.

Returning to the context of Palestinian Judaism, we may briefly note the potential influence of the pseudepigrapha among first-century converts to the Christian faith who would naturally bring with them the thought world of this literature. Jewish apocalyptic works such as 1 Enoch and the Assumption of Moses, which appear to contain traces of an Essene and Pharisaic, that is, Hasidic worldview[97]—e.g., the doctrines of predestination, resurrection, future judgment, the Essene solar calendar, the intense interest in angels, and the rejection of the sacrifices in the temple—would very naturally assume a place in the faith of Palestinian converts to Christianity. Indeed the epistle to the Hebrews considers certain doctrines foundational to Judaism (cf. Heb. 6:1–3) as constituitive of the young Christian's faith, yet admonishes those being addressed to move on in Christ.

The Pseudepigrapha serve then as a window into the religious thought and world of sectarian Judaism. They mirror how Jews contemporary with the early Christians interpreted and applied the OT.

JEWISH TRADITION-MATERIAL IN JUDE

Jude 6 and the Imprisoned Spirits

In the last chapter it was suggested that several OT figures who are condemned through prophetic oracles serve as possible links via typology to the notion of fallen angels. The imprisonment of spirits, though not confined to Enochic literature, is most elaborately developed in 1 Enoch, viz., chapters 6–36.[98] These demonic spirits, described variously as "fallen trees," "wandering stars," "giants," and "spirits," most frequently appear as *ēgrēgoroi*, "watchers."[99] Of note is the close association in 1 Enoch between these fallen angels and the flood—an association which, though present in 1 Pet. 3:19–20 and 2 Pet. 2:4–5, is conspicuously absent in Jude.

The angels in Jude 6 are described as being kept *eis krisin megalēs hēmeras desmois aidiois hypo zophon.*[100] Undoubtedly, the notion of the imprisonment of spirits has much in common with angelological notions current with the last two centuries B.C. and first century A.D., a period when Jewish interest in angels reaches a zenith. "In prison" *(en phylakē* or *en desmois/desmōtēriǭ)* is an apocalyptic convention and is rampant in 1 Enoch.

Jub 5:10   . . . and after this they were bound in the depths of the earth forever, until the day of the great condemnation.

1 Enoch 10:4   Bind Azazel hand and foot and throw him into the darkness.

10:12   . . . bind them . . . until the eternal judgment is concluded.

10:13   . . . in the prison they shall be locked up forever.

10:14   . . . those who collaborated with them will be bound together . . . until the end of all generations.

13:2   They will put you in bonds, and you will not have rest and supplication.

18:14   This place is the end of heaven and earth; it is the prison house for the stars and powers of heaven.

18:16   And he was wroth with them and bound them until the time of the completion of their sin in the year of mystery.

21:3   And there I saw seven stars of heaven bound together in it, like great mountains, and burning with fire. At that moment I said, "For what sin are they bound and . . . cast in here?"

21:6   These are among the stars of heaven which have transgressed the commandments of the Lord and are bound in this place.

21:10   This place is the prison house of the angels; they are detained here forever.

69:28   But those who have led the world astray shall be bound with chains, and their ruinous congregation shall be imprisoned.

88:3   . . . he bound all of them hand and foot and cast them into the pits of the earth.[101]

The "binding" of spirits, further, is often associated with the notion of a bottomless "pit" or "abyss" (*abyssos*). Upon Jesus' deliverance of the demon-possessed man as recorded in Luke 8:31, the demons who had been cast out implored Jesus not to be cast into the *abyssos*. In the Revelation of John,

> The fifth angel sounded his trumpet, and I saw a star that had fallen from the sky to the earth. The star was given the key to the shaft of the abyss. When he opened the abyss, smoke rose from it like the smoke from a gigantic furnace. The sun and the sky were darkened by the smoke from the abyss. And out of the smoke locusts came down upon the earth and were given power like that of scorpions of the earth. (9:1–3)

Not found in the OT, the "abyss" figures prominently in 1 Enoch:

10:4   . . . the Lord said . . . , "Bind Azazel . . . and throw him into the darkness!" And he made a hole in the desert . . . and cast him there.

18:11   And I saw a deep pit with heavenly fire on its pillars; I saw inside them descending pillars of fire that were immeasurable in respect to both altitude and depth. And on top of that pit I saw a place without the heavenly firmament above it or earthly foundation under it or water.

22:1–2 Then I went to another place, and he showed me . . . a great and high mountain . . . ; and it was deep and dark to look at.

54:5   And he said to me, "These are being prepared for the armies of Azazel, in order that they may take them and cast them into the abyss of complete condemnation."

56:3   And he said to me, "They are going to their elect and beloved ones in order that they may be cast into the crevices of the abyss of the valley."

88:3   . . . then he bound all of them hand and foot and cast them into the pits of the earth.

90:26   In the meantime I saw how another abyss like it, full of fire, was opened wide . . . ; and they brought those blinded sheep, all of which were . . . cast into this fiery abyss, and they were burned.

In light of the strong resemblance of imagery in 1 Pet. 3:19, 2 Pet. 2:4, and Jude 6 to that of 1 Enoch, evidence would support the linking of "spirits in prison," concealed in the OT, with the Jewish apocalyptic notion so elaborately developed in 1 Enoch. This is lent credence in Jude by the reference to the disenfranchised angels as "fallen stars" (v 13); these serve as a type of the *houtoi* which, having deserted their course, stand under condemnation. The issue in Jude, as in 1 Enoch, is deliberate disobedience:

Then the angel said to me, "This place is the end of heaven and earth; it is the prison house for the stars and the powers of heaven. And the stars which roll over upon the fire, they are the ones which have transgressed the commandments of God from the beginning of their rising." (1 Enoch 18:14–15)

These are among the stars of heaven which have transgressed the commandments of the Lord and are bound in this place . . ., according to the number of their sins. (21:6)

Again I saw a vision with my own eyes . . .; and as I looked, behold, a star fell down from heaven. . . . Once again I saw a vision, and I observed the sky and behold, I saw many stars descending and they were casting themselves down from the sky. (86:1–3)

Then his judgment took place. First among the stars, they received their judgment and were found guilty, and they went to the place of condemnation. (90:24)[102]

The designation of "watchers" which predominates in 1 Enoch

would serve to link the fallen angels with the stars; in Jewish apocalyptic literature, they "watch" the children of men.[103]

The connection between Jude 13 and 14 is worthy of note. In v 13, Jude mentions the "errant stars" (asteres planētai), for whom the gloom of darkness has been kept. This depiction of his opponents calls forth in the minds of the readers immediate association with 1 Enoch.[104] It is then followed by the promise of severe judgment which takes the form, in vv 14–15, of an explicit, near verbatim citation of 1 Enoch 1:9. Judgment, significantly, is the context in which the "stars" in 1 Enoch are presented.

The significance of the use of the fallen angels as a paradigm in Jude is not the volume of *legends* which stand behind the Enoch tradition, but rather the *role* which the angels play in the epistle. The allusion to angels in Jude 6 is paradigmatic, not merely etiological.[105] They are one of several examples of *lapse* or apostasy. In this light, they serve as a *warning*. To the *hymeis*, this warning is implicit; to the *houtoi*, it is outright.

One further consideration of note regarding the fallen angels remains. The identification of the "spirits in prison" with the "sons of God," assumed by many to be sinful angels and thus linked to the interpretation of 1 Pet. 3:19, 2 Pet. 2:4–5, and Jude 6, has already been called into question.[106] We have noted that a definitive interpretation of the *běnē hā'ĕlōhîm* of Gen. 6:1–4 has been lacking historically among exegetes. In dealing with a passage which of itself is inherently difficult, e.g., 1 Pet. 3:19 or Jude 6, one's exegesis is at best tenuous when one's interpretation rests upon the exegesis of another notoriously problematic passage, e.g., Gen. 6:1–4. It must be stated that with respect to 1 Pet. 3:19, 2 Pet. 2:4–5, and Jude 6, commentators are inclined to *assume* that the "sons of God" in Genesis 6 are angels, and therefore, inasmuch as the angels appear immediately before the Flood in the sequence of the Genesis narrative, they are *assumed* to be the fallen angels alluded to in 1 and 2 Peter and Jude.

Several comments are in order. Although both 2 Pet. 2:4 and Jude 6 allude to the punishment of rebellious angels, neither states explicitly that these angels were disobedient in the period of Noah. More importantly, the reference to these angels in 2 Pet. 2:4 and Jude 6 is found in a *sequence* of paradigms. The link which binds the angels in 2 Pet. 2:4 with Noah in 2:5, Sodom and Gomorrah in 2:6, and Lot in 2:7 must be identified, in the same way that the link between the angels of Jude 6, Israel of Jude 5, and Sodom and Gomorrah of Jude 7 must be established. This link, in both cases, is not Genesis 6, nor is the link sexual sin (at least, the author does not state or imply this).[107]

Moreover, the emphasis in the Genesis narrative, upon examination of the text, would seem to be *human* wickedness that characterized the time of Noah:

> The Lord saw how great man's wickedness on the earth had become and that every inclination of the thoughts of his heart was only evil all the time. The Lord was grieved that he had made man on the earth, and his heart was filled with pain. So the Lord said, "I will wipe mankind, whom I have created, from the face of the earth—men and animals. . . ." But Noah found favor in the eyes of the Lord. . . . God saw how corrupt the earth had become, for all the people on earth had corrupted their ways. So God said to Noah, "I am going to put an end to all people." (Gen. 6:5–8, 12–13)[108]

The text indicates that *human* sin was the reason for divine judgment. *Men* had grieved the heart of God; *men* were to be blotted out.[109]

While the "angelic" interpretation of Genesis 6 is indeed abundantly attested in Jewish literature (e.g., apart from 1 Enoch, 2 Apoc. Bar. 56:12–15; Jub. 5:1; 10:1–6; CD 2:18; Philo, *Quaestiones et solutiones in Genesim* 1.92; and Josephus, *Ant.* 1.73), it does not have the *unanimous* support of Jewish tradition (see, e.g., Tg. Onq. Gen. 6:2,4; Tg. Neof. Gen. 6:2,4; t.Soṭa 3.9a; Gen. Rab. 26.5; Num. Rab. 9.24; b. Sanh. 108a).[110] If we are to weigh the evidence of extrabiblical tradition along with that of biblical tradition, any connection between the "spirits in prison" and the "sons of God" as angels is unsubstantiated and, at best, problematic.

Jude 9 and the Assumption of Moses

The task of identifying source material in Jude 9 is not as cut and dried as in vv 6 or 14–15. What we encounter is a complex interdependence of diverse Jewish legends which surround the death of Moses. The task is further complicated by the incorporation in v 9 of imagery from Zechariah 3, a text that admits no apparent connection to the tradition of Moses' death in Deuteronomy 34. It is commonly agreed that the source for the tradition behind Jude 9 is a lost first century A.D.[111] writing, perhaps a midrash on Deuteronomy 34, or oral tradition of Palestinian provenance which is preserved only through a Latin manuscript, a work referred to as the Assumption or Testament[112] of

Moses. That we have to do here with a known tradition is evidenced by the quotation ascribed to Michael the archangel and the narrative structure in which a dispute between Michael and the devil over the body of Moses is documented. What can be said with relative certainty is that the Assumption[113] of Moses was not widely known in the early church and therefore reflects a Palestinian Jewish-Christian milieu.[114]

Since the time of the Exodus, Israel's national identity was rooted in Yahweh's having delivered the people from Egypt. Thus, it was only natural that in times of crisis Israel's memory of Moses would be recurring.[115] Moreover, Moses was a prophet and worked miracles, hence, "a prophet like Moses" (Deut. 18:15,18) was integral to any Jewish messianic expectation. Moses' death occupied apocalyptic and midrashic writers unceasingly. In that the biblical account is shrouded with mystery, the tradition was already a problem in biblical times. Two types of difficulties arise in the mind of a Jew. Moses was required to die outside the promised land (cf. Num. 20:12; 27:12–14; Deut. 3:21–29; 32:48–52), yet he above all others was worthy of entering. Thus, one is confronted with the problem of God's justice. The second difficulty inherent to Moses' death is that his burial is attended to by God alone. Generally speaking, Jewish literature tended to tone down God's role in the burial. Angels are depicted as burying Moses, with Michael playing a leading role.[116]

We know of the *Diathēkē/Analēpsis Mōÿseōs* through Clement,[117] Origen,[118] Didymus,[119] Photius,[120] Euodius,[121] Epiphanius,[122] Ecumenius,[123] Severus,[124] Nicephorus,[125] and a spate of medieval commentaries which exhibit extraordinary variety.[126] R. J. Bauckham[127] proposes dividing the various traditions into two basic groups. The first is a tradition reflected by three sources: (1) the Palaea Historica (a Greek narrative[128] history of the OT from Adam to Daniel which was published in the last century[129] and which dates no earlier than the ninth century),[130] (2) Ecumenius, and (3) catenae which purportedly are traceable back to the lost ending of the Assumption of Moses. The second group is said to have been composed in the second century as a response to gnostic teaching. This tradition is the one most likely known by the Alexandrian fathers.

Noting the absence of the dispute between Michael and the devil in Philo and Josephus, A. Fleischhacker[131] suggested that three streams of Moses literature—his childhood in Egypt, his flight from Egypt and stay in Midian, and his death—traditionally were in circulation. D. Flusser,[132] on the other hand, holds Jude 9 to reflect accurately the tradition of the lost part of the Assumption of Moses and doubts that there existed several distinct legends—one regarding Moses' struggle for life and one regarding Michael and the devil. While the Tg. Jon. on Deut. 34:5–6 and other rabbinic literature[133] bring us a bit closer to the background of Jude's illustration,[134] they do not inform us that Satan and Michael fought over Moses' body. K. Berger[135] examines several pseudepigrapha for traces of conflict between God and an evil angel. One such source is the Testament of Amram (4QAmr), cited by Origen[136] and translated in an Ethiopic book of angels.[137] In testament form, this work concerns both angels of light and angels of darkness. The former register all good works done by humans in a book, while the latter perform the same regarding evil. J. T. Milik[138] goes as far as to assume that both Jude 9 and the Assumption of Moses were literarily dependent on 4QAmr.

The version contained in the Palaea Historica describes Moses' death in the following manner. Samael the devil tried to bring Moses' body down to the people that they might worship him. God commands that the body be taken away, but the devil objects and enters into dispute. Using the language of Zech. 3:2, Michael rebukes the devil who then flees. The archangel subsequently brings the body away. Berger concludes that the Palaea version was probably used by Jude; there is a notable agreement between the two accounts.[139]

Although mention of Michael occurs only in 1QM 9:15 and 17:6, Jude 9 would in some respects seem to carry the stamp of Qumran, as do several other verses from the epistle. Of particular note are v 3, containing the war motif; v 18, an allusion to the "last days" *(Ep' eschatou [tou] chronou);* v 20, in which are found allusions to "building" terminology as well as the notion of praying in the spirit;[140] and v 24, where Jude's readers, after having "fought," are then made to "stand."[141] The broader contextual flow of vv 8–16 exhibits some resemblance to 1 Enoch and would thus establish further connection with the religious thought of Qumran.

An important link uniting Jude, 1 Enoch, and the Assumption of Moses is a motif shared by all three: theophany with a view of judgment. One is tempted to wonder whether works such as 1 Enoch and the Assumption circulated together in sectarian Jewish circles.[142] J. A. Goldstein,[143] as does J. Licht,[144] has dated the Assumption of Moses circa midsecond century B.C., contemporary with part of 1 Enoch. If this dating is correct, it is possible that such a collection of works indeed was in circulation. Although the theme of theophany has already been examined at some length, further discussion on Jude's borrowing of a theophany statement from 1 Enoch is yet to follow. Here, however, it is sufficient to note that a theophany statement appears as well in the Assumption. The sources being utilized by Jude show more interconnection than what might normally be observed by the reader at first glance.

> And then His kingdom will appear . . .
> And then the devil will be no more . . .
> Then the hands of the angel will be filled . . .
> And He will forthwith avenge them of their enemies.
> For the Heavenly One will arise. . . .
> And He will go forth from His holy habitation
> With indignation and wrath . . .
> For the Most High God will arise . . .
> And He will appear to punish . . .
> And He will destroy . . .
>
> (As. Mos. 10:1–7)

As with the angels in v 6, Jude is assuming audience familiarity with the tradition concerning Moses' burial. In demonstrating his knowledge and use of current popular sources, Jude draws the example of Michael into his treatment of the *houtoi*. The material in v 9 does not stand autonomous. It serves once more a didactic and paraenetic function and continues the line of thought begun earlier (note, e.g., the connectives *hōs* [v 7], *homoiōs* [v 8], and *de* [vv 8,9,10] as well as the catchword *houtoi* [vv 8,10,11]). Michael, clothed in power as a bearer of the divine *doxa*, respected the devil for his original position of authority and humbly invoked the Lord's authority. Yet in a brazen display of shame and blasphemy, Jude's opponents openly despise the heavenly powers and blaspheme the *doxai*, fully ignorant of the sober reality and consequences of their actions. Jude tailors the tradition to fit the needs of his audience.[145]

One need not assume as D. J. Rowston that Jude's use of the Assumption of Moses was to be "suppressed by 2 Pet. 2:11 owing to the disfavor with which a noncanonical book was viewed."[146] Rather, Jude and 2 Peter may be appreciated as reflecting *unique* situations which necessitated addressing particular needs—needs which more than anything contribute to the literary strategy of the author.[147]

Any attempt at reconstructing the tradition-material which stands behind Jude 9 reveals that numerous streams of tradition concerning Moses' burial are to be detected. Considering the place of Moses in Jewish history, his death was quite naturally the subject of assorted apocalyptic and midrashic accounts. In the Assumption we have a Palestinian work adapted by Jude for a specific purpose. Our present concern is not so much with the tracing or reconstruction of the background of this tradition[148] as it is to recognize the place of the use of this tradition in Jude's literary strategy. In Satan's attempt to lay claim to Moses' body and deprive him of burial by the archangel, Michael brings final vindication to the man of God by asserting divine authority over the devil. The model of Michael as one who, though vested with authority, recognizes a higher authority stands in utter contrast to the *houtoi* who flagrantly boast of their freedom from any moral authority or constraints.

Jude 14—15 and Theophany in 1 Enoch

Although in other verses of Jude traces of Enochic language and imagery can be detected, the text of Jude 14—15 is particularly significant in that it confronts the reader with an explicit citation from 1 Enoch 1:9. Our discussion as to the value of Jude's citation shall not be restricted to the Vorlage upon which Jude may have been dependent, rather it is to be viewed in light of the literary strategy at work in the polemic of the writer.[149] Jude and 1 Enoch share in common numerous touch-points: theophany, the disenfranchisement of angels, the recurring antithesis between the righteous and the ungodly, cosmic disorder linked to spiritual causes, and the certainty of final judgment. Both writings attempt to cultivate faithfulness among true believers who are surrounded by sinners and apostasy. If, as has been suggested, there are those among Jude's readers who, due to their Palestinian Jewish-Christian milieu, were familiar with or devoted to Enochic literature, Jude's exhortations would be received with even greater force.

The roles of Enoch (cf. Gen. 5:21—24) in Jewish tradition are many and diverse. He is foremost a model of righteousness (Gen. 5:22,24; Sir. 44:16; Jub. 10:17; 1 Enoch 15:1; 71:14; T.Lev. 10:5; T.Jud. 18:1; T.Dan 5:6; T.Ben. 9:1; Life of Eve 1:2; Philo, *Quaestiones et solutiones in Genesim* 1.86; cf. also Heb. 11:5 and 1 Clem. 9:2,3). Nonetheless, the brevity and mystery surrounding the biblical allusion to Enoch spawned countless traditions[150] which ascribed other functions to the patron saint of apocalyptic preachers: (1) a prototype of repentance (Sir. 44:16); (2) an intercessor (1 Enoch 10:10; 83:8; 84:2—6; 2 Enoch 7:4—5); (3) a wiseman (Jub. 4:17; 2 Enoch 35:2; T.Abr. 11:3–9 [Resc.B]; 4QMess ar 1:4; 4QTestim 1:9–12; Pis. Soph. 99); (4) a scribe in heaven (1 Enoch 81:2; 89:76; 2 Enoch 40:3; 53:1; Jub. 4:23; T.Abr. 11:3–9 [Resc.B]); (5) an end-time prophet (1 Enoch 1:3–9; 2 Enoch 42:5; 65:6,8; T.Sim. 5:4; T.Lev. 14:2; T.Jud. 18:2; T.Dan 5:6; T.Zeb. 3:4; T.Naph. 4:1; T. Benj. 9:1; Jub. 10:17; *Quaest. in Gen.* 17; Ps.–Clem. 1.52.4); (6) a sign of judgment (Jub. 4:18,23,24; 10:17; 1 Enoch 1:1; 67:12; 81:5–9; 89:63,76; 92:1; 2 Enoch 39:1); (7) the "seventh" (1 Enoch 60:8; 93:3; Lev. Reb. 29:11); (8) a seer/oracle-giver (1 Enoch 106:8–107:3; T.Sim. 5:4; T.Naph. 4:1; T.Benj. 9:1);[151] and (9) the bearer of secrets (Sir. 49:14–16; Jub. 4:19).

The biblical account of Enoch's translation (Gen. 5:24) provided much grist for the haggadist mill concerning heaven's mysteries. As a composite piece of literature, Ethiopic Enoch is known since the late fifteenth century and was translated in the early 1800s. A Semitic original is assumed by the majority of scholars to have given us our Ethiopic, Greek, and Latin versions.[152] The entire Enoch corpus includes Ethiopic (1) Enoch, the Book of Giants, Slavonic; (2) Enoch, the Coptic Enoch-Apocryphon, the Life of Enoch, Hebrew; and (3) Enoch and the Visions of Enoch. The significance of this literary corpus is that it represents a "pentateuchal collection of writings attributed to the antediluvian sage"[153] which was in use in Palestine at the advent of the Christian era. While the patriarch enjoyed unparalleled status in the Pseudepigrapha, the rabbis thought less of him.[154] The Tg.Onq. on Gen. 5:24 states that "the Lord allowed him to die." Philo's view of Enoch seems to be somewhere in between. He tends to allegorize Enoch's rapture, ascribing to it the sense of a "distancing" from home and friends.[155]

The influence of 1 Enoch in the NT, as has been noted, can hardly be disputed. In a broader sense, it is reflected in the NT's (1) christology ("Messiah," "Righteous One," "Elect One," and "Son of Man");[156] (2) frequent use of "election" terminology, (3) angelology, (4) conceptualization of future judgment, (5) flood-typology as well as (6) general phraseology.[157] It is important to understand the touch-point not merely between the NT and 1 Enoch in general terms, but between *Jude* and 1 Enoch concretely. In identifying the specific connection, we may better appreciate Jude's selection of tradition-material as the expression of a calculated literary strategy. One such touch-point is the fate of the ungodly.

Jewish literature of the second century B.C. emerged from both an Alexandrian and Palestinian milieu. That of the latter was fervently Hasidic and frequently appeared in the form of apocalypses or testaments. At the time of the Maccabean Revolt (167/66B.C.), we find the "assembly of the pious" (*ᶜadat-ḥāsîdîm* = *synagōgē Asidaiōn*), the "Hasidim," as a clearly defined Jewish sect (cf. 1 Macc. 7:13 and 2 Macc. 14:6). The Hasidim are significant for two reasons. First, they are thought to be the common root of both the Essenes and the Pharisees.[158] Second, the earliest parts of 1 Enoch are said to represent this period.[159]

The "assembly of the pious" gave expression to its values in the form of a repentance movement. In Enoch's Dream Visions, lambs which are born to deaf sheep cry out to those sheep, but to no avail (1 Enoch 90:6–7). In one of these visions, the lambs (representing the Hasidim) preach repentance to the sheep (representing Israel), who remain deaf and blind. In chapter 91ff, Enoch is depicted as a messenger of repentance and judgment.[160] Essentially, the deep crisis emerging out of the Hellenistic reform is explained by the pious conviction that this epoch was a time of *apostasy*.[161]

It is here that a state of contiguity is established between Jude, 1 Enoch, and the Assumption of Moses. All three works include in their polemic a statement of theophany:

> Then his kingdom will appear throughout his whole
>   creation.
> Then the devil will have an end.
> Yea, sorrow will be led away with him.
>
> Then will be filled the hands of the messenger,
>   Who is in the highest place appointed.
> Yea, he will at once avenge them of their enemies.
>
> For the Heavenly One will arise from his kingly throne.
> Yea, he will go forth from his holy habitation
>   With indignation and wrath on behalf of his sons.
>
> (As. Mos. 10:1–3)

Behold, he comes with myriads of his holy ones in order to execute judgment upon all, and he will destroy all the ungodly and will reprove all flesh on account of all their ungodly deeds which they have done and for the harsh things which ungodly sinners have spoken against him.[162]   (1 Enoch 1:9)[163]

Behold, the Lord comes with myriads of his holy ones to execute judgment upon all, and to reprove every person on account of all their ungodly works which they have done and for all the harsh things which ungodly sinners have spoken against him.[164]   (Jude 14–15)

The writer of the Assumption believes the time of the end to have arrived. Enoch, in similar fashion, functions as a herald of repentance and judgment. And Jude, correspondingly, reminds his audience of the sure realities of coming judgment while passionately exhorting them to "fiercely struggle" (*epagōnizesthai*, v 4)[165] against the apostate, *hoi asebeis*, who are perverting the faith "once for all delivered to the saints" (v 3).

In examining the literary relationship between the Pseudepigrapha and the NT, J. H. Charlesworth[166] distinguishes between verbatim citations, partial citations, paraphrased translations, blended and mixed quotations,[167] paraphrastic versions and allusions. Charlesworth, following C. D. Osburn,[168] notes that the alterations in Jude's quotation of 1 Enoch 1:9 are done for the purpose of clarifying that in Jesus the prediction of 1 Enoch is fulfillment. Charlesworth is further certain that Jude's introduction of the Enoch citation with the verb *proephēteusen* is proof of his belief that the book of Enoch was inspired ("If Jude had a closed canon, and Enoch was outside it, then he acknowledged inspired writings outside the canon").[169]

Charlesworth then concludes that such a view (and use) of extracanonical writings by an NT writer should necessarily influence our own definitions of canon in the present day.

> This twofold category of canon and of writings inspired by God should be commended to theologians today. If Jude had anything like a closed canon, it might have included 1 Enoch. . . . But it is improbable that Jude had a *closed* canon; perhaps he had an open canon with inspired writings like Enoch, on the fringes. . . . I take these observations to mean that we are challenged historically and theologically by the limits of "our" closed canon. How can Christians discard as insignificant, or apocryphal, a document that is . . . quoted as prophecy by an author who has been canonized?[170]

It is incumbent upon us to assess Charlesworth's statements in an attempt to answer the question that he has raised. As he himself has stated well, we are challenged to analyze the relationship between the Pseudepigrapha and the writings of the NT. In calling our attention to this and related questions, Charlesworth has done the Christian church a great service. If, building on Charlesworth's conclusion, there is (essentially) no distinction between "canon" and extracanonical ("inspired") writings on the one hand, or if there is an *inherent* distinction between "canon" and "inspiration" ("by God") on the other, is it perhaps possible that the church, in its historic interaction with the Scirptures, has erred in its view of such concepts?

Although it is not our intention to digress at this point, since the subject of canonicity has already been treated at some length[171] and thus will suffice as well for the present scrutizining of Charlesworth's statements, several observations need to be made that bear upon the questions Charlesworth raises as well as our perception of Jude. First, one must initially evaluate Charlesworth's distinction between "canonical" and "inspired" writings, and thus, Jude's view of his sources. Second, what role does prophetic continuity play in the assessment of intertestamental writings? Is it extraneous or is it integrally linked to the question of inspiration? What is the significance of the disappearance of prophecy as it relates to OT writings? And third, in this light, we must evaluate Jude's use of the verb "to prophesy."

Our earlier discussion of canonicity as it relates to the question of pseudonymity yielded several important conclusions—conclusions which warrant reiteration. Judging what may be viewed as "canonical" has theological and historical import, that is, such a notion is founded (whether consciously or unconsciously) upon particular governing theological commitments which are underscored by the scriptures themselves and, thus, is not merely a "modern" concept. Moreover, the historical veracity of statements contained in a document or tradition are inextricably connected to the integrity, and hence, inspiration of a document. Inasmuch as most scholars assume that Jude viewed 1 Enoch as "inspired," it typically follows that there is no consideration given to Jude's view of *the broad spectrum of content* in Enoch. Of the myriad of examples in 1 Enoch, several taken from Book One (predating Jude) suffice for the sake of illustration: e.g., the teaching by the fallen angels of magical medicine, incantations, cutting of roots, etc. to the women with whom they had sexual relations (chap. 7); their teaching on how to make weapons, jewelry, ornaments, and alchemy (chap. 8); Enoch's intercessory prayer on behalf of the demons (chap. 13); and the names given to heaven's angels (chap. 20). Can we, as Charlesworth apparently does, assume that Jude viewed these accounts and events as "inspired by God"[172] and therefore true? In this regard, what degree of discernment may we ascribe Jude? Are such accounts consistent with OT and NT teaching? If so or if not, does this at all have anything to do with being "inspired by God"? Even when the writers of the NT share a thought world similar to that of the authors of the OT Pseudepig-rapha, they (apart from Jude) do not quote from them. Why is this? May it have something to do with what they considered to be the "word of God" and, hence, what was viewed as absolutely authoritative?

In consideration of Charlesworth's question, "How can Chris-tians discard as insignificant, or apocryphal, a document that is . . . quoted as prophecy by an author who has been canonized?," a threefold reply is in order. First, Charlesworth equates "insignifi-cant" with "apocryphal." A distinction, however, between the two is preferable. To be considered "apocryphal" by the church his-torically is *not* to be relegated to insignificance. Without question, Jewish intertestamental literature is extremely valuable in bridg-ing the historical gap between the OT and the NT. Few would contest this. Second, Christians need *not* consider 1 Enoch insig-nificant, in the same way that books such as Jubilees, the Testa-ments of the Twelve Patriarchs, 4 Ezra, or the Testament of Job, all of which are dated as contemporary to or earlier than Jude, are recognized in their own right as having a literary relationship to the NT. Third, to be "significant" and contemporarily relevant, such as is the case with the relationship between 1 Enoch and Jude, is one thing; to be *theopneustos* is quite another. It is this seemingly blurred distinction, predicated on the witness of scrip-ture itself,[173] that cannot be eradicated. Regardless of depen-dence by the NT writer on oral *or* written tradition, the question of whether that tradition can be designated as *theopneustos* (2 Tim. 3 : 16) or issuing from *hypo pneumatos hagiou pheromenoi elalēsan apo theou anthrōpoi* (2 Pet. 1 : 21), a denotation seemingly embraced by Charlesworth ("inspired by God"), is not tangential.[174]

The discussion of tradition-material in James, four streams of which were noted to be derived from extracanonical traditions concerning Abraham, Rahab, Job, and Elijah, is relevant at this point. In his liberty with Jewish traditions which are obviously known to his audience, James demonstrates his familiarity with the Jewish haggadic tradition. This tradition-material, however, is cited for its usefulness in *addressing particular needs in the present situation*, not because James necessarily highly esteemed or viewed as "inspired" the Testament of Abraham (first century),[175] the Apocalypse of Elijah (first to fourth century),[176] or the Testament of Job (first century B.C.–first century A.D.),[177] parts of which are clearly evident in the epistle. One might argue that Jude's use of 1 Enoch 1 : 9 is an explicit citation while James's use of the Testament of Abraham, the Apocalypse of Elijah, and the Testament of Job are mere allusions.[178] Yet the point of the use of tradition-material by both James and Jude is *illustration;* both accord with conventional Jewish haggadic exegesis, while both inherited the traditional view of sacred "scripture" from their forbears. Our distinction between *exegetical approach* and any *possible inspired view of the work cited by the NT writer* is important. The former, which constitutes the heart of the present investigation, is *demonstrable;* the latter, at best inconclusive, is nevertheless broadly *assumed* by commentators, difficult to demonstrate, and therefore, in need of being seriously called into question. Furthermore, *two citations* are evidenced in Jude, not merely one. In addition to 1 Enoch 1:9 in Jude 14–15, Jude 9 contains a *partial citation,* as noted earlier. If citation itself constitutes a stronger witness for an authorial view of "inspiration" than mere allusion, the Assumption of Moses is to be placed on equally high ground as 1 Enoch. And Jude's motive for citing *both* is serious.

It has already been contended that the concept of "inspiration" has in the main, due in part to governing assumptions of modern criticism, lost its inherent sense of *theopneustos*[179] and been replaced with a sense of "canon-consciousness," whereby writers removed from the apostolic era, and thus, apostolic authority, are understood to seek to perpetuate the literary theological line of their masters. This assumption, however, was seen to negate the effectual working of the Holy Spirit in His role as custodian of the word of God.[180] It was noted that the role of the church is to *recognize,* not *establish,* canon. It is the *Spirit* who produces, guards, and affirms what is "canonical." To recognize as "canonical" is to acknowledge the "God-breathed" *(theopneustos)* character of a document. Stated otherwise, not by the will of man does prophecy have its origin, rather through men who spoke from God as they were "carried along" *(pheromenoi)* by the Holy Spirit (2 Pet. 1:21). Did the Spirit of God fail to note the *theopneustos* character of 1 Enoch (or the Testaments of Moses, Abraham, and Job, for that matter) as the canon of the Hebrew Bible was being recognized? Did the Christian church, following Judaism, fail to note this character?[181] If one takes seriously the notion of a bearly visible distinction between "canonical" and "inspired" (pseudepigraphal) writings which Charlesworth suggests, what altogether constitutes the *sacred* character of the Christian "scriptures?"[182] And, in consideration of the earlier discussion of pseudonymity, is a pseudepigraphon, no unknown commodity in the first century,[183] in fact reconcilable with the character of sacred scripture?

If inspired books came as a result of men *hypo pneumatos hagiou pheromenoi elalēsan hypo theou* (2 Pet. 1:21), the writers of the OT were the mouthpiece of God, whether in narrative or poetic, oral or written, form. The awareness that the spirit of prophecy had disappeared from Israel after Malachi, stated in 1 Macc. 9:27 and Josephus, for example, is reflected in the emergence of Jewish apocalyptic. The very convention of seeking derived authority by means of pseudonymity is an acknowledgment of the absence of the prophetic spirit. It is for this reason that John the Baptist created such a stir in Israel with his appearance. Once more the prophet was speaking. Can the writer of 1 Enoch then "prophesy" in terms we have just described? Stated simply, is *proephēteusen* in Jude 14, based on our understanding of *prophetic inspiration*, to be understood in a strict technical sense?

The verb *prophēteuein* is employed twice in the NT in attributing a citation to the OT.[184] This alone cannot sufficiently demonstrate that Jude viewed the Book of Enoch as inspired. If, however, as is generally recognized, the theological literary milieu of Jude's audience is Palestinian, by which his readers are familiar with Enoch traditions, is it not reasonable to maintain that Jude's use of *prophēteuein* is simply expressing his recognition that what was written in 1 Enoch 1:9 was true and *applicable* to the present situation?

In his application of the Enoch prediction, Jude writes *proephēteusen de kai toutois hebdomos apo Adam Henōch* (v 14a). The expression *hebdomos apo Adam* ("the seventh from Adam") occurs twice in 1 Enoch (60:8 and 93:3). Furthermore, the number seven retains great symbolic importance throughout 1 Enoch, as it did for Jews traditionally: "All sevenths are favorites in the world. . . . The seventh is a favorite among the generations."[185] Apart from the two appearances in 1 Enoch, "the seventh from Adam" occurs also in Philo[186] and Lev. Rab. 29:11, and hence, was probably conventionally understood. In Jub. 7:39 Enoch is described as "alive in his seventh generation."

Grammatically, the *kai* of v 14a could be interpreted in several ways: (1) Enoch joins *other persons*, e.g., the OT prophets, who *also* predicted the same;[187] (2) Enoch also predicted, *among other things*, concerning these men;[188] or (3) Enoch's prediction also applies to *these men, among others*.[189] One of these readings is normally assumed by commentators. If, however, Jude's literary strategy called for exploiting a work highly esteemed not by *himself*, rather by his *readers*, then the following translation of v 14a would make perfectly good sense: "For even (your own) Enoch, the seventh from Adam (i.e., of 1 Enoch), prophesied of these, saying . . . ." And if, by way of illustration, a Cretan is to the apostle Paul a "prophet" (Tit. 1:12), then Enoch, in Jude 14, can "prophesy."[190] Seen as such, vv 14–15 should not be construed as a citation of 1 Enoch due to *Jude's* elevation of the work, but rather an allusion adapted for his *theological-literary end*. The allusion bears authority most probably because *others* have a high regard for Enoch, inasmuch as we have to do here with a Palestinian literary milieu.

In addition to the fact that this interpretation is sustained grammatically by the text, it also allows for a coherence of argument throughout the epistle. Most importantly, it fits precisely into Jude's overall strategy of employing Jewish tradition-material, the understanding of which is crucial to a responsible exegesis of the epistle.

One other significant thread links Jude with 1 Enoch (and the Assumption of Moses): the boasting of the ungodly. In Jude condemnation of the boastful is part of his theophany statement, a portion of which is derived from 1 Enoch 1:9. Jude 15–16 ("all the harsh words ungodly sinners have spoken . . . their mouths speak great things") is reminiscent of 1 Enoch 5:4 ("you have . . . spoken slanderously grave and harsh words with your impure mouths") and 1 Enoch 101:3 ("you utter bold and harsh words"), as well as As. Mos. 7:9 ("their mouths will speak enormous things"). In the terror of God's might, however, the arrogant will be turned from their evil ways.[191]

Yet another noteworthy element of *asebeia* found in both Jude and 1 Enoch is that of "denial" (*arneomai*). In Jude the *asebeis* "deny our only Sovereign and Lord Jesus Christ" (*ton monon despotēn kai kyrion hēmōn Iēsoun Christon*, v 4). "Denying the name of the Lord of the Spirits" seems to be a catch-phrase for the ungodly in 1 Enoch. It occurs five times: 38:2; 41:2; 45:2; 46:6; and 48:10. The latter of these is a particularly interesting parallel to Jude 4 in that, unlike the other four, it contains *two* objects of denial: "they have denied the Lord of the Spirits *and his Anointed One*" (emphasis added).

Hence the theophany statement in Jude, a reworking of 1 Enoch 1:9, rings prophetically true with regard to Jude's opponents. As in OT antecedents and in the theophany statement found in 1 Enoch, the Lord "comes" for the purpose of dealing with the ungodly. Hereby the past is prophetically linked with the present. In sum, the theophany statement from 1 Enoch is fitting for several reasons. It agrees with the overall flavor of the epistle—a reflection of Palestinian-Jewish Christianity—and coincides with the background of the audience. More specifically, it reflects concepts rooted in distinctly Hasidic values—repentance, the faithful-ungodly antithesis, judgment, and inevitable vindication. Finally, theophany is a key feature shared by Jude, 1 Enoch, and the Assumption of Moses. Sources and audience are joined by the author through his literary strategy. The theophany statement fits Jude's theological-literary-rhetorical purpose.

PAGAN TRADITION-MATERIAL IN JUDE

Much of the strength of Jude's powerful rhetoric lies in his ability to marshall sources. Both direct and indirect referencing of the OT as well as traditions stemming from sectarian Jewish literature have been the focus of the study thus far. Although the allusion is veiled, it would appear that Jude 13 is yet another instance of popular tradition being borrowed. This reference, however, would appear to be a well-known pagan tradition.

In examining the language[192] and vivid symbolism of vv 12–13, J. P. Oleson[193] has suggested that "the wild waves of the sea, foaming up their shame" constitutes a reference to the grotesque account of Aphrodite's birth in *Theogony* 147–206, with a particular connection to vv 190–92:

> *hos pheret' am pelagos poulyn chronon,*
> *amphi de leukos aphros ap' athanatou chroos ōrnyto—*
> *tǭ d' eni koure ethrephthē.*

If this is the case, the force of Jude's rhetoric escalates as he scathes the *houtoi* in rather severe terms, identifying the apostates as sexually depraved. In this piece of literature, dated 730–700 B.C.[194] and perhaps the most ancient Greek poem available to us, Kronos, a son of Mother Earth, castrates Uranos (the Sky) using a sickle. The severed genitals are subsequently thrown into the sea where they were covered with foam *(aphros)*. Out of the foam[195] Aphrodite is nurtured, that "Lady of Cyprus" and protectress of sailors at sea. The foam then washes her ashore.

This is conceived by Oleson as a link to Jude's opponents.[196] The waves are the apostates which bring to shore the sexual organs, symbolic of the vile state into which they have returned.

> These men are *spilades*[197] ("blemishes" [?], "hidden rocks" [?]) at your love-feasts, eating with you without the slightest qualm—shepherds

who feed only themselves. They are clouds without rain, blown along by the wind; autumn trees, without fruit and uprooted—twice dead. They are wild waves of the sea, foaming up their shame; wandering stars, for whom the blackest darkness has been reserved forever. (Jude 12–13)[198]

The precise meaning of the *spilades* in v 12 is much in question.[199] We may well have here another word-play, in which Jude draws from the associations of both ideas—filth, spots, and blemishes (often *spilas*), as well as the hidden, potential danger of submerged rocks near the shore.[200] Either way, they influence the faithful. In light of the imagery being utilized, both readings would fit the context quite well. Jude uses the verb *spiloun* in his final admonition:

> *kai hous men eleate diakrinomenous,*
> *hous de sōzete ek pyros harpazontes,*
> *hous de eleate en phobō,*
> *misountes kai ton tēs sarkos espilōmenon chitōna.*

(v 23)

The point, however, is clear. These people should be avoided at all cost. Mayor[201] cites an ancient example of the verb *epaphrizein* in v 13 used to characterize the waves.[202] It is used in reference to seaweed, scum, or any refuse carried on the crest of the wave and thrown upon the beach.

The opponents of Jude are in a very real sense "foam-born," as illustrated by the Aphrodite tradition. They have an antecedent, depicted even in pagan Greek mythology.[203] Aphrodite is not merely associated in Greek mythology with love in general. There is a peculiar dark side to her as well: rape, adultery, incest, and wantonness.[204]

Jude's imagery, then, serves up a graphic picture of his opponents. They have a precedent—in Israel's past as well as that of the pagan Greeks. The accompanying symbolism serves well the literary strategy of the writer.

THE USE OF TRADITION-MATERIAL IN JUDE: A SUMMARY

An important aspect of the well-conceived literary strategy incorporated in Jude is the writer's use of extracanonical source-material. Our awareness of the role that these traditions play in addressing particular needs of the audience assists in countering the relative ignorance and misunderstanding that traditionally have been associated with the study of Jude. The writer moves freely within the world of Jewish apocalyptic thought, a reflection of the theological-literary milieu out of which his readers more than likely come.

The use of tradition-material in Jude, however, was not seen to be an isolated phenomenon in the NT. Having noted several examples in Pauline literature, we examined a significant instance of Petrine dependence on tradition-material: 1 Pet. 3:18–22. These verses, in and of themselves somewhat problematic in the history of interpretation, were noted to be essential for our understanding and interpretation of Jude, particularly in light of the line of interpretation which views 3:19 as Christ preaching to demonic spirits "in prison," thus transferring to Christ what Jewish apocalyptic literature had ascribed to Enoch. This Petrine depiction of Christ's work, though perhaps veiled or cryptic to the modern mind, demonstrates in a modified fashion inspired use of Jewish tradition-material for the purpose of illustrating the effects of Christ's redemptive activity.

Three instances of tradition-material in Jude—allusion to the rebellious angels (v 6), Michael's dispute with the devil over the body of Moses (v 9), and the Enoch citation (vv 14–15)—were analyzed in light of their relationship to the Jewish Pseudepigrapha. The notion of imprisoned spirits, veiled in the OT, was considered in light of its prominence in apocalyptic literature. The importance of the fallen angels as a paradigm in Jude was seen in its association with two other paradigms of disenfrachisement—unbelieving Israel (v 5) and Sodom and Gomorrah (v 7)—and not in the volumes of legends that undergird the Enoch tradition. Although the writer assumes the reality of evil in the *angelic* realm, his focus is *human* wickedness as it bears upon the *houtoi*. His readers are to be reminded that God judges *men* who choose to rebel from divine authority.

A study of the somewhat complex tradition that surrounds the death of Moses, ascribed to what is known to us as the Testament or Assumption of Moses, focused on what is generally agreed to be a lost, first-century writing or oral tradition of Palestinian provenance. That Jude 9 mirrors a known tradition is evidenced by Jude's use of a quotation ascribed to Michael the archangel as well as the narrative structure in which the dispute between Michael and the devil is found. Michael is used as an example in a contextual flow which unites the *houtoi* of vv 8–10 with Sodom and Gomorrah in v 7 and the woe-cry of v 11. Whereas the archangel, vested with divine authority and defending Moses' right to a burial, according to the tradition, humbly appealed to a higher authority in his contest with the devil, Jude's opponents openly and flagrantly blaspheme the heavenly powers in their boastful ignorance. Rather than focusing on attempts at a reconstruction of the tradition behind Jude 9, we have emphasized the place of the tradition as it serves in Jude's overall polemic.

Jude 14–15 confronts the reader with a citation from 1 Enoch 1:9, a statement found within the context of theophany and judgment—two prominent Enochic motifs. Numerous other touch-points between Jude and 1 Enoch were observed—among them: the disenfranchisement of angels, the antithesis between the faithful and the ungodly, cosmic disorder linked to spiritual causes, and the certainty of eschatological vindication. Having noted the Hasidic thought world reflected in 1 Enoch, traces of which can be detected in numerous parts of the NT, we recognized an underlying thematic connection between Enochic theology and that of Jude: apostasy. In assessing the literary relationship between the Pseudepigrapha and the NT, demonstrated by Jude's use of 1 Enoch and the Assumption of Moses, several conclusions were made that relate to the early Church's view of the notions of "canon," "prophetic inspiration," and character of the OT scriptures which they cited. The significance of intertestamental Jewish literature was acknowledged to be considerable, in light of its literary relationship to the NT and contemporary relevance to a first-century Jewish-Christian audience in Palestine. In that Jude is explicit in his use of extracanonical tradition-material, indeed more so than any other NT writer, we are left to conclude that either he considered "inspired" or highly esteemed the literary sources he was employing, or he was incorporating this tradition-material because of its homiletic and hortatory value for an audience to whom these traditions were very familiar, recognizing that what was written in 1 Enoch 1:9, to illustrate, was true and *applicable* to the present situation.

Acknowledging the theological and literary end which Jude's use of Jewish tradition-material serves in light of the Palestinian Jewish-Christian literary milieu reflected in the epistle, one may conclude that it is not necessary to maintain or merely assume that Jude viewed 1 Enoch as "inspired"—an assumption that remains scarcely demonstrable and thus inconclusive at best. Rather, Jude's use of 1 Enoch, as well as the Assumption of Moses, is best understood in the light of its *illustrative function*. Congruous with other instances in the NT, in which the writer borrows from extracanonical tradition-material and thereby acknowledges that which is consistent with truth and applicable in the present situation, Jude makes "inspired" use of an inspiring work without in any way offering an assessment of the character of that work. This view of 1 Enoch, most importantly, is consistent with Jude's use of tradition-material throughout the epistle—e.g., his partial citation of tradition ascribed to the Assumption of Moses—and corresponds to his readership, for which both 1 Enoch and the Assumption are strategic. The needs and make-up of the audience chiefly determine the literary strategy of the writer. Moreover, this interpretation of Jude's use of 1 Enoch allows Jude to be *representative of,* and not *at variance with,* the other writers of the NT.

One further example of tradition-material in Jude was noted to be found in v 13, belonging to a highly imaginative and metaphorical characterization of the *houtoi* (vv 12–13). Reminiscent of the account in pagan mythology of the birth of Aphrodite, Jude's third of four metaphors is a graphic depiction of the utter wantonness of his opponents who seek to influence the faithful (v 12a). Having already described the apostate in terms of licentiousness, depravity, and thorough disregard for moral restraint, Jude depicts his opponents as not only having antecedents in Jewish tradition (e.g., vv 5, 6, 7, 9, 11), but in pagan mythology as well.

6

Conclusion: In Search of a Literary Strategy

The fundamental aim of the present investigation has been to examine the use of literary device in the epistle of Jude. We have considered the writer's choice of language, imagery and resources in his attempt to forcefully persuade his audience. Literary resources are understood as they relate to a work's central purpose and theme. To determine the function of a writer's resources is to unveil a literary strategy at work. Stated in reverse, literary strategy presupposes a conscious and deliberate manipulating of literary "brick and mortar."

We have observed in Jude a rhetorical-theological polemic being waged which employs a highly stylized literary approach. The author combines a selective vocabulary with an unusual economy of speech. He utilizes word-play, repetition in varied forms, synonymous and antithetical parallelism, symmetry, contrast, alliteration and rhyme, as well as vivid imagery to affect his audience. His mode is apocalyptic, midrashic, liturgical, and rhetorical. He communicates more in a few brief stanzas than many would hope to convey in volumes.

What is Jude's chief concern? He is seeking to strengthen and exhort the *faithful* by painting in graphic terms the fate of the *unfaithful*. All of Jude's paradigms have one thing in common: they point to a place of deterioration and recession into which each has lapsed. Unbelieving Israel, the dispossessed angels, Sodom and Gomorrah, Cain, Balaam, and Korah—all *departed* in some respect; all were judged accordingly.

Yet in spite of Jude's passionate exhortations, condemnations, and woe-cry, his perception of falling away is one of calculation and willful deliberation. The believers need not be shaken by the parade of sobering paradigms. To the contrary, they may *choose* to be established in the faith, to stand without stumbling, and to be presented before the glorious presence of God. Consider again several of the tactical weapons in the literary arsenal of Jude: the word-play on *tērein-phylassein,* the frequent allusion to the love of

God (note how the readers are addressed: as *agapētoi*), the reminder to the audience in the initial greeting of their true identity
(*ēgapēmenoi, tetērēmenoi, klētoi*), and the recalling of the sure and
binding power of the apostolic teaching that undergirds them. His
exhortation is that they keep themselves *en agapē theou* (which is
suggestive of *their* responsibility). The Aorist action of "keeping" is
implemented by three participial actions: being built up in their
most holy faith, praying in the Holy Spirit, and anticipating mercy
(vv 20–21). Not only is Jude's audience thus *able* to stand, they can
also subsequently rescue others, pulling them out of the fire as
well, even the *staunchest* of adversaries (vv 22–23).

The readers are to persevere and rest in God's *keeping* power.
At work is a paradox, a mysterious balance. Some choose not to be
"kept." Hence, they are reserved for judgment, just as their antecedents in history. Yet nothing is able to uproot the faithful when
firmly grounded in the love of God. It is divine love and mercy (vv
1, 2, 3, 17, 20, 21) that will "keep" (vv 1,6,21,24) the believer. This
is one of the great, and perhaps overlooked, teachings of the
epistle of Jude.

The focus of the present study has been literary-rhetorical in
nature. What, then, of this much "overlooked" theology of Jude?
What are the implications of form for content, medium for message?

The reader, then and now, is left, having admired the style,
arrangement, and invention of a skilled writer, to ponder the
force of Jude's message which has been so marvelously framed in
poetic diction, strategic use of historical paradigms, and artful
selection of tradition-material. Although it is the explicit aim of
the writer to admonish his audience to defend the faith against
any who would distort it, it is also part of his purpose to caution
them against stumbling into the same error of deception, thereby
negating the lordship of Christ in their midst. Consider the introduction to vv 5–7: "I wish to *remind* you, though you *already know*
everything" (emphasis added). In addition to the historical paradigms, which are intended to do just that, *remind*, the reminder
terminology picks up again in v 17: "But *you*, beloved, remember
the words" (emphasis added).

As noted in earlier parts of the present study, the contrast
between "these" and "those" (i.e., the present and past examples of
ungodliness) is constant throughout the epistle. Moreover, the
contrast between "these" and the collective "you" of the community is conspicuous. Jude is writing in dead earnest: "Beloved,
being very eager to write to *you* . . ., I found it necessary to write

to *you* to wrestle" (v 3); "I wish to remind *you*, though *you* know everything." (v 5); "But *you*, beloved, remember the words of the apostles . . . for they said to *you*" (vv 17–18); "But *you*, beloved, build *yourselves*" (v 20); "Now to Him Who is able to keep *you*" (v 24).[1]

Based on a longer reading of vv 22–23, it might be argued that there are three groups of people within the writer's purview: (1) those who are wavering as a result of being influenced by the apostate, (2) those who perhaps have succumbed to disbelief and the influence of the apostate, and (3) those who are in fact perpetrating the apostasy. The first group, following this line of thinking, is to be "pitied" or "convinced" (according to the alternative reading); their doubt is "redeemable." The second group is to be "snatched from the fire," indicating that they have become sufficiently endangered as to require drastic measures for preservation. The third group is to receive mercy "in/with fear," that is, the church, in its fear of God and hatred of the immoral, should exercise utmost caution so as not to become contaminated in its dealings with those who have fallen away.[2]

Regardless of whatever textual considerations surround Jude 22–23, the epistle as a whole reflects a notable gravity with respect to the spiritual life of those being addressed. Apostasy has the character of cancer, and its consequences are deadly serious.

Yet while Jude conceives of the possibility of falling away from the faith, in no way is he intimating that apostasy constitutes a peril into which the Christian is bound or likely to fall. Jude notes initially the motivation of those who are distorting the faith: they "worm their way in through the side" (*pareisdyein*, v 4). Verses 5–16 essentially are a catalog of actions by which the faithful are to identify and isolate the apostate. Moreover, the appeal to apostolic teaching (v 17) will help in keeping the faithful rooted in the truth. Some things endure and do *not* change.

Furthermore, there are specific things that the faithful themselves can do to remain established: they are to keep themselves in the love of God, building themselves up in their most holy faith, praying in the Holy Spirit, and anticipating the mercy of the Lord (vv 20–21). These are conscious and active measures by which the Christian obediently walks out his or her faith. At work is a paradox: even though believers have been "kept by Jesus Christ" (v 2), they are nonetheless to "keep" themselves in the love of God (v 21). The Christian's walk is not static, rather it is dynamic. It appropriates by faith in the experience what God has already done as a fact. Additionally, guidance by the Holy Spirit through prayer will assure the believer that he or she is living in accord with the will of God. The presence of the Spirit in the life of the believer is the dynamic means which enables one to live the Christian life. Those who "do not have the Spirit" (v 19) are readily identifiable. Finally, perseverance is elicited as the believer looks forward to the Parousia, the fuller revelation of divine mercy in Christ.

In conclusion, and most significantly, Jude assures his readers that it is the *preserving power of God* (v 24) that safeguards their spiritual lives. God is able to "guard securely as a prison" *(phylassein)* so that they remain "free from stumbling" *(aptaistos)*. And not only are they made to stand without falling, they are made to stand "faultless in the presence of his glory with great joy" *(katenōpion tēs doxēs autou amōmous en agalliasei)*. Herewith the epistle ends. Noting the parallel between the epistle's introduction and closing, I. H. Marshall[3] writes: "Thus the end of the Epistle stresses the fact of God's activity in preserving believers from falling in the same way as the beginning where the readers are addressed as those who are called, loved, and kept by God for Jesus Christ."

This very brief letter, suffering from supreme neglect in the Christian church, is rich in its teaching on the Christian life. Written by one who was initimate with its readers (note vv 3, 17, and 20), it reminds the Christian community of the love and mercy of God, focusing on the *keeping power of God,* which has enormous implications for the faithful as well as those who have chosen to desert their glorious heritage.

The focus of the investigation, however, has not been mere theological *content.* The manner in which Jude argues, the *form* of his polemic, is equally valid for his audience. *How* truth is presented is crucial, and Jude demonstrates to what extent OT and NT literature is *rooted in culture.* Perhaps it is in this sense that modern interpretation of the epistle has been inadequate.

The epistle of Jude is highly instructive for the modern reader. Truth comes to us, the audience, *through literary form.* In Jude one discovers theological truth wrapped in literary arguments of the day. The writer's sources, it is discovered, carry significant weight with his audience. The literary form contained in the epistle reveals a literary approach on the part of Jude with specific, well-calculated rhetorical effects aimed at addressing *particular pastoral needs.*

Being cognizant of the writer's exploiting of the surrounding cultural milieu aids the reader in understanding the thought world of Jude, thereby helping to disentangle the historical situation behind the letter and assist in the task of exegesis. The epistle thus acquires profound significance for the church down through the ages while at the same time retaining a high degree of relevance for today. In truth, it is no exaggeration to suggest that there may have indeed been periods during the church's history when Jude was not far from being *the most relevant* book in all the NT.

Notes

CHAPTER 1. INTRODUCTION

1. Commentariorum in Evangelium secundum Matthaeum 17.30 (*PG* 13, 1571).

2. D. J. Rowston, "The Most Neglected Book in the New Testament," *NTS* 21 (1974/75): 554.

3. For a survey of the history of Jude study, see R. Heiligenthal, "Der Judasbrief. Aspekte der Forschung in den letzten Jahrhunderten," *TRu* 51 (1986): 117–29. It is unfortunate that most existing commentaries on Jude are highly derivative.

4. C. A. Albin, *Judasbrevet. Traditionen-Texten-Tolkningen* (Stockholm: Natur och Kultur, 1962), is a rare exception. In his recently published monograph *Invention, Arrangement, and Style: Rhetorical Criticism of Jude and 2 Peter* (SBLDS 104; Atlanta, Ga.: Scholars, 1988), D. F. Watson does a rhetorical study of both 2 Peter and Jude. Watson's copious footnoting of rhetorical guides of antiquity (e.g., Aristotle, Cicero, and Quintilian) notwithstanding, one would hope for a more thorough integration of rhetorical analysis with the theological concerns of the epistle. A key in unlocking the epistle lies in a combination of historical setting, rhetoric of argumentation, and theological content.

5. R. J. Bauckham, "The Letter of Jude: An Account of Research," *Aufstieg und Niedergang der römischen Welt. Geschichte und Kultur Roms im Spiegel der neueren Forschung.* II.25.5 (ed. W. Haase; Berlin/New York: de Gruyter, 1988), 3792. Studies in Jude in recent years include C. Daniel, "La Mention des Esséniens dans le texte grec de l'épître de Saint Jude," *Mus* 81 (1968): 503–21; W. Magass, "Semiotik einer Ketzerpolemik am Beispiel von Judas 12f," *LB* 19 (1972): 36–47; F. Wisse, "The Epistle of Jude in the History of Heresiology," *Essays on the Nag Hammadi Texts in Honour of A. Böhlig* (ed. M. Krause; Leiden: Brill, 1972), 133–43; D. J. Rowston (see n. 2); C. D. Osburn, "The Christological Use of 1 Enoch 1.9 in Jude 14,15," *NTS* 23 (1976/77): 334–41; idem, "1 Enoch 80:2–8 (67:5–7) and Jude 12–13," *CBQ* 47 (1985): 296–303; E. E. Ellis, "Prophecy and Hermeneutic in Jude," *Prophecy and Hermeneutic in Early Christianity* (Tübingen: Mohr, 1978) 221–36; I. H. Eybers, "Aspects of the Background of the Letter of Jude," *Neot* 9 (1975): 113–23; E. Szewc, " 'Les Gloires' dans les épîtres de Jude et de St. Pierre," *Collectanea Theologica* 46 (1976): 57–60; J. P. Oleson, "An Echo of Hesiod's Theogony vv. 190–2 in Jude 13," *NTS* 25 (1978/79): 492–503; F. Gryglewicz, "The Evolution of the Theology of the Letter of St. Jude," *RuBi* 33 (1980): 247–58; F. Hahn, "Randbemerkungen zum Judasbrief," *TZ* 37 (1981): 209–18; J. J. Gunther, "The Alexandrian Epistle of Jude," *NTS* 30 (1984): 549–62; R. Heiligenthal, "Der Judasbrief. Aspekte der Forschung in den letzten Jahrhunderten," *TRu* 51 (1986): 117–29; G. Sellin, "Die Häretiker des Judasbriefes," *ZNW* 77 (1986): 201–25; P.-A. Seethaler, "Kleine Bemerkungen zum Judasbrief," *BZ* 31 (1987): 261–64; J. Fossum, "Kyrios Jesus as the Angel of the

Lord in Jude 5–7," *NTS* 33 (1987): 226–43; T. R. Wolthuis, "Jude and Jewish Traditions," *CTJ* 22 (1987): 21–41; idem, "Jude and the Rhetorician," *CTJ* 24 (1989): 126–34; R. J. Bauckham, "James, 1 and 2 Peter, Jude," *It Is Written: Scirpture Citing Scripture. Essays in Honour of B. Lindars* (ed. D. A. Carson and H.G.M. Williamson; Cambridge: Cambridge University, 1988), 303–17; W. Whallon, "Should We Keep, Omit, or Alter the 'OI in Jude 12?" *NTS* 34 (1988): 156–59; J. D. Charles, " 'Those' and 'These': The Use of the Old Testament in the Epistle of Jude," *JSNT* 38 (1990): 109–24; idem, "Jude's Use of Pseudepigraphal Source-Material as Part of a Literary Strategy," *NTS* 37 (1991): 130–45; and idem, "Literary Artifice in the Epistle of Jude," *ZNW* 82/1 (1991): 106–24. Additionally, several text-critical studies, based on p72, are to be mentioned: M. Testuz, *Papyrus Bodmer VII–IX. VII: L'Épître de Jude, VIII: Les deux Épîtres de Pierre, IX: Les Psaumes 33 et 34* (Cologny-Genève: Bibliotheca Bodmeriana, 1959); R. Kasser, *Papyrus Bodmer XII. Actes de Apôtres, Épîtres de Jacques, Pierre, Jean et Jude* (Genève: Bibliotheca Bodmeriana, 1961); J. N. Birdsall, "The Text of Jude in p72," *JTS* 14 (1963): 394–99; A. Wikgren, "Some Problems in Jude 5," *Studies in the History and Text of the New Testament in Honor of K. W. Clark* (Studies and Documents 29; ed. B. L. Daniels and M. J. Suggs; Salt Lake City: University of Utah, 1967) 147–52; M. Mees, "Papyrus VII (p72) und die Zitate aus dem Judasbrief bei Clemens von Alexandria," *CDios* 181 (1968): 551–59; S. Kubo, "Text Relationships in Jude," *Studies in New Testament Language and Text* (NovTSup 44; Leiden: Brill, 1976): 276–82; idem, "Jude 22–3: Two-division Form or Three?" *New Testament Criticism. Its Significance for Exegesis. Essays in Honor of B. M. Metzger* (ed. E. J. Epp and G. D. Fee; Oxford: Clarendon, 1981), 239–53; C. D. Osburn, "The Text of Jude 22–23," *ZNW* 63 (1972): 139–44; and idem, "A Note on Jude 5," *Bib* 62 (1981): 107–15.

6. J. Muilenburg, "Form Criticism and Beyond," *JBL* 88 (1969): 6 (reproduced in *The Bible in Its Literary Milieu. Contemporary Essays* [ed. J. Maier and V. Tollers; Grand Rapids, Mich.: Eerdmans, 1979] 367–68).

7. To employ a "literary" approach is not to adopt uncritically the agenda of one of the specialized literary "schools" currently in vogue, for, as pointed out by L. Ryken ("The Bible as Literature," *BibSac* 147 [1990]: 1–15), there is something far more basic (and productive) to acquiring insights through a "literary" approach to the Bible than faddish literary-critical "models" which ride the crest of cultural winds. Because the Bible is a distinctly sacred book, literary features of the New Testament (and hence, Jude) cannot be separated from its religious meaning.

8. R. G. Moulton, *The Modern Reader's Bible* (New York: Macmillan, 1895), 1719.

9. L. Ryken, *The New Testament in Literary Criticism* (New York: Ungar, 1984), 7.

10. On the subject of literature as the reflection of human experience, see Ryken, *The New Testament*, pp. 3–4.

11. After all, it is presupposed, literary artistry is certainly not becoming of men who are considered to be *agrammatos* and *idiōtēs*, at least when compared to vocational scribes (cf. Acts 4:13).

12. Proper generic considerations will inform the reader of an appropriate reading strategy as well as of the essential structural organization of the work. The question of taxonomy then is not peripheral to the task of exegesis; it is indeed fundamental.

13. W. O. Sypherd, *The Literature of the English Bible* (New York: Oxford University, 1938), 158–59.

14. A. Augustine, *On Christian Doctrine* (vol. 4; ed. P. Schaff; Buffalo: CLC, 1887), 577.

15. Ryken, *The New Testament,* 12–13.

CHAPTER 2. LITERARY-RHETORICAL ANALYSIS OF THE EPISTLE OF JUDE

1. A. Deissmann, *Light from the Ancient East* (London: Hodder and Stoughton, 1910).

2. W. G. Doty, "The Classification of Epistolary Literature," *CBQ* 31 (1969): 193.

3. Contra N. Turner, who views Jude as a "tract" or "manifesto," but not epistolary (J. H. Moulton and N. Turner, *A Grammar of New Testament Greek—Vol. IV: Style* [Edinburgh: Clark, 1976], 139).

4. W. G. Doty (*Letters in Primitive Christianity* [Philadelphia: Fortress, 1973], 4–8) notes the variety of epistles which circulated in the first century: business, official, public, fictitious/pseudonymous, and discursive.

5. See K. Berger, "Hellenistische Gattungen im Neuen Testament," *Aufstieg und Niedergang der römischen Welt. Geschichte und Kultur Roms im Spiegel der neueren Forschung.* II.25.2 (ed. W. Haase; New York/Berlin: de Gruyter, 1984): 1039–40. By stating that pagan and Jewish-Christian forms are not always separable, we are not suggesting that the NT writings are not unique. In addition to Berger, a comprehensive examination of early Christian and secular literary genres can be found in D. E. Aune, *The New Testament in Its Literary Environment* (Philadelphia: Westminster, 1987).

6. A. Malherbe, *Ancient Epistolary Theorists* (SBLSBS 19; Atlanta, Ga.: Scholars, 1988), 1–6.

7. W. C. van Unnik, "First Century A.D. Literary Culture and Early Christian Literature," *NedTTs* 25 (1971): 29. The fifth century B.C. has been labeled "the Greek Enlightenment" for its emphasis on rationalist thinking (see F. Solmsen, *Intellectual Experiments of the Greek Enlightenment* [Princeton, N.J.: Princeton University, 1975], 3).

8. Apollos might serve as a good illustration. Luke tells us that he was an "eloquent" *(logios)* man and "powerful" *(dynatos)* in the scriptures (Acts 18:24).

9. *De rhetorica* 1.3.15 (for the Greek version with commentary in English, see E. M. Cope, *The Rhetoric of Aristotle* [Cambridge: Cambridge University, 1877]; for both Greek and English translations of the text, see Aristotle, *The "Art" of Rhetoric* [LCL; tr. J. H. Freese; Cambridge, Mass.: Harvard University 1947]). Cf. also *Rhetorica ad Herennium* 1.2 and Quintilian, *Institutio oratoria* 3.3–4.

10. I am following Doty ("Classification," 183–98) who suggests dropping the absolute distinction between "letter" and "epistle" made by A. Deissmann in his works *Bible Studies. Contributions Chiefly from Papyri and Inscriptions to the History of the Language, Literature, and the Religion of Hellenistic Judaism and Primitive Christianity* (Edinburgh: Clark, 1901), 9–10, 58, and *Light from the Ancient East,* 53, 147. One must understand Deissmann's rationale for originally making such a distinction. In reaction to certain movements within biblical scholarship, Deissmann was hoping to allow "letters" to speak with their original voice over against imposing upon them a modernistic or theological grid.

11. See H. Peter, *Der Brief in der römischen Literatur* (Leipzig: Teubner, 1901), 112.

12. On the nature of Greco-Roman education, see W. A. Smith, *Ancient Education* (New York: Philosophical Library, 1955), 147–91; H. I. Marrou, *A History of Education in Antiquity* (New York: Sheed and Ward, 1956), 95–298; M. L. Clarke, *Higher Education in the Ancient World* (Albuquerque: UNM, 1971), 11–118; and R. A. Kaster, "Notes on 'Primary' and 'Secondary' Schools in Late Antiquity," *TAPA* 113 (1983): 323–46.

13. D. L. Clark, *Rhetoric in Greco-Roman Education* (Morningside Heights, N.Y.: Columbia University, 1957), 62, 64.

14. Marrou, *A History*, 99.

15. Ibid., 273.

16. On ancient letter writing in general, see R. Hercher, *Epistolographi Graeci* (Paris: Didot, 1873); F.X.J. Exler, *The Form of the Ancient Greek Letter. A Study in Greek Epistolography* (Washington, D.C.: CUA, 1923); and more recently, J. L. White, *Light from Ancient Letters* (Philadelphia: Fortress, 1986). Hercher cites numerous samples of ancient Greek letters (26–791) and reproduces a list of twenty-one different letter types identified by Demetrius of Phalerum (1–6). These would seem to be categories for use by professional writers. Hercher also distinguishes between forty-one different letter forms, including friendly, hortatory, accusatory, consolatory, didactic, interrogatory, and postulatory (6–13). The form taken over by Christian writers, the A-to-B *charein,* was in use from the third century B.C. until the third century A.D. (Exler, 61–62).

17. M. L. Stirewalt, Jr. ("The Form and Function of the Greek Letter-Essay," *The Romans Debate* [ed. K. P. Donfried; Minneapolis, Minn.: Augsburg, 1977], 176) makes a distinction between the Greek *epistolē* and the Latin *epistulae,* observing that the latter often (1) lacked an original letter setting and (2) was intended to be published (as evidenced by the peculiar style).

18. Demetrius, *De elocutione* 223 (for an English translation, see Demetrius, *On Style* [LCL; tr. W. R. Roberts; Cambridge, Mass.: Harvard University, 1932]).

19. Cicero, *Epistulae ad Atticum* 8.14.1 (for an English translation, see Cicero, *Letters to Atticus* [LCL; tr. E. O. Winstedt; Cambridge, Mass.; Harvard University, 1913, 1918]).

20. Cicero, *Epistulae ad familiares* (for an English translation, see Cicero, *Letters to His Friends* [LCL; tr. W. G. Williams; Cambridge, Mass.: Harvard University, 1928, 1943]).

21. Demetrius, *De elocutione,* 227.

22. Ibid., 223, 226.

23. Ibid., 228.

24. Ibid., 224.

25. Ibid., 272, 276.

26. Ibid., 70, 112.

27. Ibid., 117.

28. Ibid., 139.

29. Ibid., 234. Cf. also Pseudo-Demetrius, reproduced in Malherbe, pp. 30–31.

30. See the introduction to Pseudo-Demetrius (Malherbe, 30).

31. Demetrius, *De elocutione,* 66, 197, 211.

32. Ibid., 173–76.

33. Ibid., 105.

34. Ibid., 81.

35. Ibid., 262.

36. Ibid., 232.

37. Ibid., 242. Qualities of style essential to ancient rhetoric were purity (i.e.,

correctness of language), clarity (intelligibility), decorum (appropriateness), and ornament (decorative aspects). In many respects, ancient letter writing and rhetoric attempted to affect the same goal.

38. The largest amount of rhetorical analysis being applied to NT studies has been in the Gospels and Pauline literature (for a bibliography on the application of rhetorical-criticism to the NT, see D. F. Watson, "The New Testament and Greco-Roman Rhetoric: A Bibliography," *JETS* 31 [1988]: 465–472). Since 1978, six rhetorical studies—one unpublished dissertation, four journal articles, and one monograph—have appeared relating to the general epistles: W. Wuellner, "Der Jakobusbrief im Licht der Rhetorik und Textpragmatik," *LB* 43 (1978): 5–66; L. G. Gieger, "Figures of Speech in the Epistle of James: A Rhetorical and Exegetical Analysis," unpub. dissertation: Southwestern Baptist Theological Seminary, 1981; D. F. Watson, *Invention, Arrangement, and Style: Rhetorical Criticism of Jude and 2 Peter* (SBLDS 104; Atlanta, Ga.: Scholars, 1988); idem, "A Rhetorical Analysis of 2 John according to Greco-Roman Conventions," *NTS* 35 (1989): 104–30; idem, "A Rhetorical Analysis of 3 John: A Study in Epistolary Rhetoric," *CBQ* 51 (1989): 479–501; and T. R. Wolthuis, "Jude and the Rhetorician: A Dialogue on the Rhetorical Nature of the Epistle of Jude," *CTJ* 24 (1989): 126–43 (Wolthuis's essay is an imaginary conversation that takes place between Jude and Cicero; Wolthuis's purpose is to note features in the epistle which resemble aspects of rhetoric practiced in Cicero's day, although he assumes that Jude's epistle is not consciously rhetorical in structure). On the increasing overlap between biblical studies and rhetorical analysis, see V. K. Robbins and J. H. Patton, "Rhetoric and Biblical Criticism," *QJS* 66 (1980): 327–50. Unfortunately, much "rhetorical-critical" study applied to the NT tends to interact insufficiently with the historical and theological dimensions of the texts under investigation. The reader is frequently left to wonder how it all relates to exegesis—or if in fact it should. The value of this discipline, as with any critical tool, is that it *assists* in grappling with the *meaning* of that individual text. It remains to be seen whether rhetorical criticism will be sufficiently integrated into the overall exegetical task or whether it proves to be simply one more in a line of trends fashionable in contemporary literary-critical circles, with its own set of presuppositions, which eventually moves on in search of "greener grass."

39. E. A. Judge, "Paul's Boasting in Relation to Contemporary Professional Practice," *AusBR* 17 (1968): 37–50; H. D. Betz, *Der Apostel Paulus und die sokratische Tradition* (Tübingen: Mohr, 1972); and C. Forbes, "Comparison, Self-Praise and Irony: Paul's Boasting and the Conventions of Hellenistic Rhetoric," *NTS* 32 (1986): 1–30. W. Wuellner, summing up his appeal in the essay "Paul's Rhetoric of Argumentation in Romans: An Alternative to the Donfried-Karris Debate over Romans" (*The Romans Debate,* [ed. K. P. Donfried; Minneapolis, Minn.: Augsburg, 1977], 174) makes this unabashed call for NT scholarship: "since we are surrounded by a cloud of witnesses of rhetoricians, linguistic analysts, structuralists, and others, let us lay aside every weight imposed by priorities of traditional historical and literary criticism, and by logical and dogmatic preoccupations which cling so closely, and let us run with perseverance the race that is set before us, looking to Paul, the pioneer and perfector of the spirit of faith—the rhetoric of faith argumentation."

40. Forbes, "Comparison," 22–23.

41. Judah M. Leon, a fifteenth-century Italian exegete, educator, author, and orthodox Jew, is considered by some as the earliest practitioner of rhetorical study of the Hebrew Bible. To Leon the scriptures were "inerrant in language and expression, grammatically and rhetorically perfect," full of "stylistic excellen-

cies" (J. M. Leon, *The Book of the Honeycomb's Flow (Sepher Nopheth Suphim)* [tr. I. Rabinowitz; Ithaca/London: Cornell University, 1983], lxi). As the expounders of the word of the Lord, the prophets were described by Leon as "without peer among the orators of the nations" (lxii). Book Three of his work is devoted to the effects, emotions, and norms of human behavior while Book Four deals in rich description and detail with figures of speech in the OT.

42. Muilenburg, "Form Criticism and Beyond," 16. Muilenburg is here recalling a phrase T. S. Eliot had used in his "Four Quartets" when he spoke of a poem as a "raid on the inarticulate."

43. Ibid.

44. Martin Hengel, *Judaism and Hellenism, Studies in Their Encounter in Palestine during the Early Hellenistic Period* (2 vols.: Philadelphia: Fortress, 1981), 1. 60.

45. The question of Jude's literary-rhetorical competence is taken up more fully later in this chapter.

46. Cf. also the use of *echei anagkēn* in Heb. 7 : 27.

47. For a fuller development of this thesis, see L. Wills, "The Form of the Sermon in Hellenistic Judaism and Early Christianity," *HTR* 77 (1984): 297, as well as the response of C. C. Black to Wills, in "The Rhetorical Form of the Hellenistic-Jewish and Early Christian Sermon: A Response to L. Wills," *HTR* 81 (1988): 155–79. In his survey of Hellenistic literary genres concurrent with the NT era, K. Berger ("Hellenistische Gattungen im Neuen Testament," *Aufstieg und Niedergang der römischen Welt. Geschichte und Kultur Roms im Spiegel der neueren Forschung* II.25.2 [ed. W. Haase; Berlin/New York: de Gruyter, 1984], 1049–1148) subsumes *logos parainētikos* under the heading of *symbyleutikōn*.

48. Cf. also 3 : 13 *(alla parakaleite heautous . . .);* 6 : 18 *(ischyran paraklēsin echōmen);* 10 : 25 *(mē egkataleipontes . . . alla parakalountes);* 12 : 5 *(kai eklelēsthe tēs paraklēseōs);* and 13 : 19 *(perissoterōs de parakalō touto poiēsai).* In 13 : 22 we find the author's purpose explicitly stated: *Parakalō de hymas, adelphoi, anechesthe tou logou tēs paraklēseōs.*

49. Wills ("The Rhetorical Form," 289) has applied this category to the Petrine epistles. Note, e.g., 1 Pet. 5 : 1 *(Presbyterous oun hymin parakalō),* 5 : 12 *(Dia Silouanou hymin . . . di' oligōn egrapsa parakalōn),* and the "reminding" terminology in 2 Peter (e.g., 1 : 12,19; 3 : 1,2,8,15).

50. For further discussion of the arrangement of material in Jude, see the section entitled "Arrangement" in this chapter.

51. C. C. Black ("The Rhetorical Form," 1–18) maintains that the "word of exhortation" as a classification can stand on its own even though there exists no evidence that it was formally taught in the ancient schools.

52. E.g., Rom. 11 : 25; 1 Cor. 10 : 12; 12 : 1; 2 Cor. 1 : 8.

53. Bauckham, *Jude, 2 Peter,* 111–12.

54. R. Deichgräber, *Gotteshymnus und Christushymnus in der frühen Christenheit* (SUNT 5; Göttingen: Vandenhoeck & Ruprecht, 1967), 21.

55. Ibid., 35–37.

56. Ibid., 39.

57. E. Werner, *The Sacred Bridge* (New York/London: Columbia University/ Dobson, 1963), 274.

58. Deichgräber, *Gotteshymnus,* 25.

59. Two other *tō dynamenō* doxologies occur in the NT, both employed by Paul: Rom. 16 : 25–27 and Eph. 3 : 20–21.

60. Ibid., 25.

61. P. Glaue, "Amen," *ZKG* 44 (1925): 184. Cf. also K. Berger, *Die Amen-Worte*

Jesu. Eine Untersuchung zum Problem der Legitimation in apokalyptischer Rede (BZNW 39; Berlin: de Gruyter, 1970), 15–17.

62. E.g., Neh. 8:6 and 1 Chron. 16:36.

63. E.g., Pss. 41:14; 72:19; 89:53; and 106:48.

64. E.g., Num. 5:22 and Neh. 8:6.

65. See the discussion found in Berger, *Die Amen-Worte Jesu*, 20–27.

66. Glaue, "Amen," 186.

67. Used in the NT as doxology, it appears in Rom. 1:25; 9:5; Gal. 1:5; Eph. 3:21; 1 Tim. 6:16; and 2 Tim. 4:18.

68. G. Kennedy, *The Art of Persuasion in Greece* (Princeton, N.J.: Princeton University, 1963), 23.

69. While the moral philosophy of Plato condemned rhetoric, the more "scientific" philosophy of Aristotle acknowledged it. Among the Romans, e.g., Cicero and Quintilian, rhetoric was praised as an essential feature of the Roman citizen. Cicero is generally viewed as "the great translator of Greek culture" (T. C. Burgess, "Epideictic Literature," *University of Chicago Studies in Classical Philology* 3 [1902]: 242).

70. Twentieth-century thought, particularly that of philosophers, writers, and theoretical scientists, has in the main operated out of the view that reality is unknowable. This assumption has spilled over into biblical and theological disciplines, as G. Kennedy (*New Testament Interpretation through Rhetorical Criticism* [Chapel Hill, N.C.: UNC, 1984], 159) has observed, bringing with it its fruit: less certainty concerning Christianity, biblical writers and events, and meaning in general. On this basis, the gains from any type of literary theory are limited, since the critic views the Bible in mythical categories. Disinterested in the author's intent, the critic is more interested in how the Bible "reads" by known literary "schools." The student of rhetoric, on the other hand, is concerned with the biblical text as we have it, the author's intent and the work as a unity.

71. E. Black (*Rhetorical Criticism. A Study in Method* [New York: Macmillan, 1965], 19) delineates various approaches taken to rhetoric. Some study it as a movement of discourse through history. Others concentrate on the psychology of rhetoric, focusing on the practitioner's inner life and thoughts. The vast majority, however, concern themselves with the application of classical rhetorical canons to literary texts. Most modern literary critics would belong to this group.

72. Ibid., 17. In *Greek Rhetorical Origins of the Christian Faith* (New York/ Oxford: Oxford University, 1987), J. L. Kinneavy aims to show the compatibility of the Christian faith with rhetoric. To believe *(pisteuein)* is semantically related to "persuade" *(peithein)*. Faith and rhetoric, contends Kinneavy, have a common element: persuasion (52). Seen as such, the NT is *highly* persuasive. Inasmuch as NT writers had a message to convey and sought via *persuasion* to convey it, they are "rhetorical" and thus can be examined in rhetorical categories.

73. T. R. Henn, *The Bible as Literature* (London/New York: Oxford University, 1970), 101.

74. Aristotle, *De rhetorica* 1.3.15; Cicero, *De inventione* 1.5.7 (for an English translation, see Cicero, *De inventione* [LCL; tr. H. M. Hubell; Cambridge, Mass.: Harvard University, 1949]); idem, *De oratore partitione oratoriae* 1.31.141 (for an English translation, see Cicero, *De oratore partitione oratoriae* [LCL; tr. E. W. Sutton and H. Rackham; Cambridge, Mass.: Harvard University, 1942]); Quintilian, *Institutio Oratore* 2.4.6–8 and 2.21.23 (for an English translation, see Quintilian, *Institutio oratoria* [LCL; 4 vols.; tr. H. E. Butler; Cambridge, Mass.: Harvard University, 1920–1922]). See also H. Lausberg, *Handbuch der literarischen Rhetorik* (2 vols.; München: Hüber, 1973), 1.59–65. NT examples of forensic, deliber-

ative, and epideictic rhetoric would be 2 Corinthians, the so-called "Sermon on the Mount," and John 13–17 respectively.

75. G.M.A. Grube, *How Did the Greeks Look at Life?* (Cincinnati: University of Cincinnati, 1967), 7.

76. For a thorough treatment of the role of these stylistic features in rhetoric, see R. Volkmann, *Rhetoric und Metrik der Griechen und Römer* (München: Beck, 1901), 106–244.

77. It was inevitable that what G. Kennedy (*Classical Rhetoric and Its Christian and Secular Tradition from Ancient to Modern Times* [Chapel Hill, N.C.: UNC, 1980], 4) designates "primary" rhetoric, a chiefly oral brand of persuasion as practiced in civic life by the Greeks which flourished from the fifth century B.C., would move into a "secondary" variety, which was characterized by particular techniques geared toward a literary aim. Moreover, three "strands" of rhetoric are identifiable from the fifth century B.C.: a technical art (as practiced by Aristotle and Cicero and emphasizing speech), a sophistic art (as practiced by Isocrates with its emphasis on the speaker), and philosophical art (as demonstrated by Plato with its stress on affecting the audience).

78. K. Eden, in "Hermeneutics and the Ancient Rhetorical Tradition," *Rhetorica* 5 (1987): 75–85, traces this distinction in the writings of Cicero and Quintilian.

79. 2.189–96 (see n. 74).

80. As to an ancient understanding of the purpose of the *paradeigma*, see Cicero, *De inventione* 1.49. For a more exhaustive analysis of the use of metaphor, paradigm, and parable in Aristotle through the first century A.D., see M. H. McCall, Jr., *Ancient Rhetorical Theories of Simile and Comparison* (Cambridge, Mass.: Harvard University, 1969).

81. On paradigmatic terminology in the NT in general, see E. K. Lee, "Words Denoting 'Pattern' in the New Testament," *NTS* 8 (1961/62): 166–73.

82. On Aristotle's use of paradigms, see W. L. Benoit, "Aristotle's Example: The Rhetorical Induction," *QJS* 66 (1980): 189–92. Although there exists a gap in ancient testimony between Aristotle and the first century B.C. (which would indicate that rhetorical theory had solidified in its form), a first-century A.D. rhetorical treatise, *Rhetorica ad Herennium*, is the earliest extant Latin witness available to rhetorical theory.

83. "Where is the *sophos*? Where is the *grammateus*? Where is the *syzētētēs tou aiōnos toutou*?" the apostle asks sarcastically (1 Cor. 1:20). When Paul, the archdebater for the Christian cause, tells the Corinthians "I did not come with eloquent speech" (1 Cor. 2:1), he is not saying that he did not practice good rhetorical skills. He is saying that his *boasting* is not in his powerful speech, rather in the cross of Christ.

84. Kennedy, *New Testament Interpretation*, 159–60.

85. Ibid., 160.

86. For an excellent discussion on the correlation of rational, ethical, and emotional appeals in rhetorical practice, see E.J.P. Corbett, "Introduction to Rhetorical Analysis of Literary Works," *Selected Essays of E.J.P. Corbett* (ed. R. J. Connors; Dallas, Tex.: SMU, 1989), 75–97.

87. It is unfortunate that the study of rhetoric—i.e., the art of communication which governs the relationship between speaker/writer and the audience—has waned in the nineteenth and twentieth centuries. Perhaps this is due to a lack of formal training, thus we have not recognized it as a vehicle for unfolding a literary work. It no doubt also has to do with modern "agendas," trends, and "interdisciplinary" fashions of the time. In truth, rhetorical analysis should

transcend that which is "fashionable," if indeed it concerns itself with subject matter, genre, occasion, author, purpose, and audience.

88. Kennedy, *New Testament Interpretation*, 19.

89. Watson, *Invention, Arrangement, and Style*, 32–33.

90. Watson acknowledges that the epideictic character is also at times present, though clearly secondary (32–33).

91. Vv 4 [*tines*], 8,10,11 [*autois*], 12,14,16, and 19.

92. Vv 5,6,7,9,11, and 14–15.

93. Vv 1,2,3,12,17,20,21,22, and 23.

94. *exordium.*

95. *narratio.*

96. *probatio.*

97. *peroratio.*

98. On the division of the epistle, see also Bauckham (*Jude, 2 Peter*, 5–6) and Watson (*Jude and 2 Peter*, 32–76). Further examination of the paradigmatic proofs in Jude, from a more theological standpoint, is found in chaps. 4 and 5. In comparison to the four-part arrangement customary in Greek rhetoric, the Latin rhetorical text *Rhetorica ad Herennium* arranges a speech according to six parts: *exordium, narratio, partitio, confirmatio, confutatio,* and *conclusio.* Contra Wolthuis ("Dialogue," 127), the ordering of material, use of sources and utilization of vivid imagery would indeed suggest that Jude is consciously rhetorical in structure. For a more comprehensive view of Greek as well as Roman rhetorical practice, see E. M. Cope, *The Rhetoric of Aristotle* (see ch.2, n.9); R. Volkmann, *Rhetorik und Metrik der Griechen und Römer* (München: Beck, 1901); D. L. Clark, *Rhetoric in Greco-Roman Education* (see ch. 2, n.13; G.M.A. Grube, *The Greek and Roman Critics* (Toronto: University of Toronto, 1965); G. Kennedy, *The Art of Persuasion in Greece* (see ch.2, n. 68); idem, *The Art of Rhetoric in the Roman World (300* B.C.– A.D. *300)* (Princeton, N.J.: Princeton University, 1972); E. Black, *Rhetorical Criticism* (see ch.2, n.71); M. H. McCall, Jr. *Ancient Rhetorical Theories* (see ch.2, n.80); H. Lausberg, *Handbuch* (see ch.2, n.94); and S. Schweinfurth-Walla, *Studien zu den rhetorischen Übersetzungsmitteln bei Cicero und Aristoteles* (Tübingen: Narr, 1986).

99. Cicero, *De inventione* 1.5.7; *De oratore partitione oratoriae* 1.31.141; Quintilian, *Institutio oratoria* 2.21.23.

100. The constitutive elements of rhetoric become established in the first century B.C. though they are implicit in Aristotle.

101. For a definition, see Cicero, *De inventione* 1.7.9, and *Rhetorica ad Herennium* 1.2.3.

102. Cf. Aristotle, *The "Art" of Rhetoric* (tr. J. H. Freese; LCL; Cambridge, Mass.: Harvard University, 1947), and Cicero, *De oratore partitione oratoriae* 2.27.115. For extensive treatment of both external and internal proofs, see Lausberg, *Handbuch*, 1.191–235.

103. For further discussion of ethical, logical, and pathetic modes of argumentation, see Kennedy, *New Testament Interpretation*, pp. 14–18.

104. For ancient definitions, see Cicero, *De inventione* 1.7.9, and *Rhetorica ad Herennium* 1.2.3.

105. See the basic structure given on pp. 33–36.

106. Here one would expect to find frequent occurrence of *gar, oun, kai, hoti,* and adversatives. On a comparison of the lexical style of New Testament books, see A. Kenny, *A Stylometric Study of the New Testament* (Oxford: Clarendon, 1986); for a comparative study of connectives in the New Testament books, see esp. pp. 32–35.

107. F. Blass and A. Debrunner, *A Greek Grammar of the New Testament and*

Other Early Christian Literature (tr. and rev. R. W. Funk; Chicago: University of Chicago, 1961), 225.

108. Rowston, "The Most Neglected Book," 559.

109. E.E. Ellis, "Prophecy and Hermeneutic in Jude," *Prophecy and Hermeneutic in Early Christianity* (Tübingen: Mohr, 1978), 225.

110. In the broader sense of "midrash," Jude shares this methodology. Uniting the past with the present through prophetic types, he modifies a text—1 Enoch 1:9 as an example—to suit his needs and links material together through the use of various catchwords. For further discussion, see Bauckham, "James, Peter, Jude," pp. 303–5.

111. R. J. Bauckham, *Jude, 2 Peter* (WBC 50; Waco, Tex.: Word, 1983), 3–6; also idem, "James, Peter, Jude," 303–5.

112. Bauckham, *Jude, 2 Peter,* 5.

113. "Biblical Interpretation among the Sectaries of the Dead Sea Scrolls," *BA* 14 (1951): 76.

114. On the meaning and use of the term in rabbinic literature, see A. G. Wright, "The Literary Genre Midrash," *CBQ* 28 (1966) 118–38.

115. Block, "Midrash," *DBSup* 5.1265–66.

116. J. Doeve, *Jewish Hermenutics in the Synoptic Gospels and Acts* (Assen: Van Gorcum, 1954), 52–90.

117. A. Robert, "Les Genres littéraires," *Initiation biblique* (ed. A. Robert and A. Tricot; 3d rev. ed.; Paris: Ducolot, 1954), 305–9.

118. These are designations used by Wright ("The Literary Genre Midrash," 129–30).

119. See E. Slomovic, "Toward an Understanding of the Exegesis in the Dead Sea Scrolls," *RQ* 7 (1969/70): 5–10.

120. So A. S. van der Woude, "Melchisedek als himmlische Erlösergestalt in den neugefundenen eschatologischen Midrashim aus Qumran Höhle XI," *OTS* 14 (1965): 354–73.

121. J. Cantinat (*les Épîtres de Saint Jacques et de Saint Jude* [Paris: Lib. Lecoffre, 1973], 267–69), J.R.B. Saiz ("La carte de Judas a la luz de algunos escritos judíos," *EstBib* 39 [1981]: 86), and R. J. Bauckham (*Jude, 2 Peter,* 28–29) capture the intent and coherence of the epistle in their structuring of Jude, showing the corresponding relationship between Jude's theme (vv 3–4), the illustrations (vv 5–16), and the admonitions to the faithful (vv 20–23). The focus on the various paradigms of vv 5–16 is meant to *contrast,* not supplant, the positive exhortations of vv 3,17,20–23. Jude's primary goal is not negative; it is *epagōnizesthai tȩ hapax paradotheisȩ tois hagiois pistei.*

122. This metrical arrangement of the material in Jude, though similar, deviates somewhat from the structure set forth by H. J. Cladder (see his "Strophic Structure in St. Jude's Epistle," *JHS* 5 [1904]: 600–601).

123. Cicero, *De oratore partitione oratoriae* 5.16–17; *De inventione* 1.7.9; *Rhetorica ad Herennium* 1.2.3.

124. Cicero, *De oratore partitione oratoriae* 3.52.199; 5.20; 6.21.

125. W. G. Ballantine, *Understanding the Bible* (Springfield, Mass.: Johnson, 1925), 19.

126. Thirty years ago L. Alonso-Schökel posited the thesis that biblical science had scarcely begun to develop a method of objectively investigating the subject of style ("Die stylistische Analyse bei den Propheten," *VTSup* 7 [1960]: 154–54). While the last three decades have introduced more awareness, much of this study has been concentrated in the OT. Furthermore, *genre,* more so than style, has been the primary focus of attention.

127. N. Turner, "The Literary Character of New Testament Greek," *NTS* 20 (1974): 107.

128. See J. D. Charles, "Literary Artifice in the Epistle of Jude," *ZNW* 82 (1991): 106–24.

129. Augustine, *On Christian Doctrine* (vol. 4; ed. P. Schaff; Buffalo: CLC, 1887), 579.

130. G. W. Knight, *The Christian Renaissance* (London: Methuen, 1962), 123.

131. Watson, *Jude and 2 Peter*, 79.

132. Ibid., 25.

133. The adversative *mentoi* otherwise occurs in the NT only in Jas 2:8, 2 Tim. 2:19, and five times in the Fourth Gospel.

134. As would be expected, the general epistles, when compared statistically with the rest of the NT, have a high rate of subordinating conjunctions and particles of negation. This would be due to their logical argumentation and subsequent sophisticated syntax. Jude, in this sense, is representative. See R. Morgenthaler, *Statistik des neutestamentlichen Wortschatzes* (Zürich/Frankfurt am Main: Gotthelf, 1958), and Kenny, *Stylometric Study*, pp. 26–38.

135. See Deissmann, *Light*, p. 195; also A. T. Robertson, *A Grammar of the Greek New Testament in the Light of Historical Research* (Nashville: Broadman, 1934), 124–25.

136. *La deuxième Épître de Saint Pierre. L'Épître de Saint Jude* (CNT 13b; Neuchâtel: Delachaux & Niestlé, 1980), 138.

137. The verb *goggyzein* appears eight times in the NT and sixteen times in the LXX.

138. Two phrases used in Jude—*opisō sarka* (v 7) and *pro pantos tou aiōnos* (v 25)—are not used elsewhere in the NT.

139. Not all of the *hapax legomena* in Jude warrant being designated rare. Six of these words—*ekporneuein, hypechein, spiloun, planētēs, goggystēs*, and *aptaistos*— occur in the LXX (approximately ninety percent of Jude's vocabulary is found in the nonapocryphal LXX; cf. Morgenthaler, *Statistik*, 49). Moreover, several are common to Greek usage but do not appear in the NT *(hypechein, deigma,* and *physikōs)*. Four appear in classical Greek literature; three occur in Aristotle. As a rule, the general epistles tend to have their own unique vocabulary when contrasted with the rest of the NT.

140. This is essentially the working definition proposed by E. Russell, in *Paronomasia and Kindred Phenomena in the New Testament* (Chicago: University of Chicago, 1920), 5–6.

141. Language should be viewed as the natural expression of feeling and thought.

142. On the variations of paranomasia in biblical literature, see Russell (n. 140) and G. W. Hopf, *Alliteration, Assonanz, Reim in der Bibel* (Erlangen: Deichert, 1883).

143. E. Norden, *Die antike Kunstprosa vom VI. Jahrhundert v. Christus bis in die Zeit der Renaissance* (Leipzig/Berlin: Teubner, 1923), 457, 464.

144. See chap. 4 for further discussion of Jude's use of triplets.

145. This assumes a tripartite reading of vv 22–23 as found in the Alexandrian text and not bipartite, though there are admittedly many difficulties surrounding the reconstruction of these verses. Proponents of a twofold division include J. N. Birdsall, S. Kubo (1965), and C. D. Osburn (see chap. 1, n. 5). Those favoring a threefold division include Kubo (1976), who later reassessed his earlier view (see chap. 1, n. 5), and B. M. Metzger, *A Textual Commentary on the Greek New Testament* (Stuttgart: UBS, 1971), 725–26.

146. E. W. Bullinger, *Figures of Speech Used in the Bible* (Grand Rapids, Mich.: Baker, rep. 1968) xv.

147. Stylistic literary "figures" may be classified according to their particular shade of function: figures of repetition (cf. the discussion of paronomastic figures on pp. 39–40), figures of word-order and syntax (e.g., anastrophe, prolepsis, anacoluthon, parenthese), figures of reduction (e.g., ellipse, aposiopesis), figures of accumulation or intensification (e.g., listing, hymn, aretalogy, climax), figures of substitution (e.g., antonomasia, amphibole), and tropes (while "trope" can designate figures of speech in general, we are limiting it here to instances of metaphor, simile, metonymy and synecdoche, symbol, personification, hyperbole, merism, etc). The classic text for examining the biblical use of figurative language is Bullinger's *Figures of Speech* (see n. 146). For a more recent discussion of figures of speech and their use by biblical writers, see W. Buhlmann and K. Scherer, *Stilfiguren der Bibel, Ein kleines Nachschlagewerk* (BibB 10; Bern: Schweizerisches Katholisches Bibelwerk, 1978).

148. Merism does the very opposite. In symbol, it uses A + Y in place of a complete series of facets—e.g., A + B + C . . . + X + Y.

149. However, since this is a quote, the redundancy of expression may not be attributed directly to Jude.

150. For a glossary of style, see Watson, *Invention, Arrangement, and Style,* 199–202.

151. It is not within the scope of the present investigation to enter the lively debates concerning the terms "apocalyptic" and "eschatology." The minimum that they have in common is a *future expectation.* A thorough survey of various definitions offered for "apocalyptic" as well as prominent theories on the derivation of the genre is to be found in F. Dexinger, *Henochs Zehnwochenapokalypse und offene Probleme des Apokalyptikforschung* (Leiden: Brill, 1977), 7–45. On the nature of some of the issues in the debate, see M. A. Knibb, "Prophecy and the Emergence of the Jewish Apocalypses," *Israel's Prophetic Tradition. Festschrift P.R. Ackroyd* (ed. R. Coggins, et al.; Cambridge: Cambridge University, 1982), 155–80. Specific to the present study is our interest in theophany as it appears in Jude and bears upon the above "common ground."

152. Thus, F. Dingermann, "Die Botschaft vom Vergehen dieser Welt und von den Geheimnissen der Endzeit—Beginnende Apokalyptik im Alten Testament," *Wort und Botschaft. Eine theologische und kritische Einführung in die Probleme des Alten Testaments* (ed. J. Schreiner; Würzburg: Echter, 1967), 330. Dingermann calls apocalyptic "die letzte grosse theologische Äusserung altisraelitischen Geistes" (p. 329).

153. The Hebrew view of history found in the OT was that the divine purpose was worked out through history, be it in the patriarchal wanderings, the exodus, the wilderness sojourns, conquest of Canaan, etc. History as interpreted by the prophets is dynamic, salvific, and teliological. The telos of divine history *would* come—within history. The prophets viewed divine activity as being found within current events. For an excellent discussion of history as portrayed through prophetic and apocalyptic literature, see S. B. Frost, "Apocalyptic and History," *The Bible in Modern Scholarship* (ed. J. P. Hyatt; Nashville: Abingdon, 1965), 98–113 (reproduced in *The Bible in its Literary Milieu. Contemporary Essays* [ed. J. Maier and V. Tollers; Grand Rapids, Mich.: Eerdmans, 1979], 134–47).

154. G.E. Ladd, "Apocalyptic, Apocalypse," *Baker's Dictionary of Theology* (ed. E. F. Harrison; Grand Rapids, Mich.: Baker, 1960), 50–54.

155. M. J. Cantley, "Introduction to Apocalyptic," *Contemporary New Testament Studies* (ed. M. R. Ryan; Collegeville, Minn.: Liturgical, 1965), 440.

156. Frost, "Apocalyptic and History," 137–39.

157. The Greek *apokalypsis* usually denotes a specific type of revelation, possessing a distinctive form and content. Regarding form, it is revelation mediated by an otherworldly agent (e.g., Enoch); regarding content, it is characterized by supernatural, cosmological phenomena, the activity of angels, vindication of the righteous, and punishment of the wicked (judgment being a central theme). The adjective "apocalyptic" may be applied to ideas or motifs typical of the generic apocalypse. A good bit of confusion exists due to the variety of ways in which the term is utilized. On apocalyptic form and content, see J. J. Collins, *The Apocalyptic Imagination. An Introduction to the Jewish Matrix of Christianity* (New York: Crossroad, 1984), 257–58, and idem, "The Apocalyptic Context of Christian Origins," *Backgrounds for the Bible* (ed. M. P. O'Connor and D. N. Freedman; Winona Lake, Ind.: Eisenbrauns, 1987), 257–71.

158. While the Jewish apocalypticists of the intertestamental period find antecedent material in Isaiah, Zechariah, Ezekiel, and Daniel, their basic view of history does not square with that of the OT prophets. Salvation and deliverance for the prophets are accomplished *within* and *through* historical events.

159. As is characteristic of apocalyptic literature, 1 Enoch contains no explicit historical references to the Genesis account.

160. Collins, "The Apocalyptic Context," 260.

161. Jude is not "apocalyptic" in the sense of literary genre, however it incorporates apocalyptic conventions and motifs as part of the writer's rhetorical strategy. In determining whether a work is generically an apocalypse, one must establish whether a text or writing possesses a significant group of features normally associated with apocalyptic (e.g., angelic mediation and translation of events, cosmic upheaval, cosmogony, *ex eventu* prophecy, eschatological upheaval, persecution, destruction of the wicked, vindication of the righteous, destruction of the present world, resurrection or afterlife, and, in the case of intertestamental Jewish apocalyptic, pseudonymity).

162. Thus, E. Käsemann's much debated claim that apocalyptic Judaism was the "mother of all Christian theology" (for a fuller context in which Käsemann's thesis is rooted, see his two essays "The Beginnings of Christian Theology" and "On the Subject of Primitive Christian Apocalyptic," *New Testament Questions of Today* (Philadelphia: Fortress, 1969), 82–107 and 108–37.

163. P. Minear, "Some Archetypal Origins of Apocalyptic Predictions," *Horizons in Biblical Theology—Vol. 1* (ed. U. Mauser; Pittsburgh, Pa.: Barbour, 1979), 113.

164. While the derivation of the apocalyptic genre is considered to be owing to a combination of two factors—a Jewish matrix and Hellenistic influence (see Collins, *Imagination,* p. 28)—one need not look outside of a Hebrew milieu. Representing a contrary viewpoint and attributing apocalyptic to Mesopotamian influence are W. Bousset and H. Gressmann, *Die Religion des Judentums im späthellenistischen Zeitalter* (HNT 21; Tübingen: Beck, 1926); H. L. Jansen, *Die Henochgestalt. Eine vergleichende religionsgeschichtliche Untersuchung* (Oslo: n.p., 1939); and more recently, H. S. Kvanvig, *Roots of Apocalyptic. The Mesopotamian Background of the Enoch Figure and of the Son of Man* (WMANT 61; Neukirchen-Vluyn: Neukirchener, 1988).

165. L. Morris, *Apocalyptic* (Grand Rapids, Mich.: Eerdmans, rep. 1974), 32.

166. P. Minear, *New Testament Apocalyptic* (IBT; Nashville: Abingdon, 1981), 61, 113. L. Hartman, in his two works *Asking for a Meaning: A Study of 1 Enoch 1–5* (ConB 12; Lund: Gleerup, 1979), and *Prophecy Interpreted. The Formation of Some Apocalyptic Texts and of the Eschatological Discourse Mark 13* (ConB 1; Lund:

Gleerup, 1979), is also helpful here in his examination of OT motifs which are picked up by Jewish apocalyptic writers.

167. Consider Book 3 (chaps. 72–82) of 1 Enoch, "The Book of Heavenly Luminaries" (= "The Book of Astronomical Writings" in J. T. Milik, *The Books of Enoch—Aramaic Fragments of Qumran Cave 4* [Oxford: Clarendon, 1976], 4–135), a treatise concerned with the reckoning of time and cosmic disorders of the last days.

168. Matt. 24:29–30 = Mark 13:24–26 = Luke 21:25–27. See also Matt. 27:51; Mark 15:33–39; and Luke 23:45.

169. Acts 2:16–21 (cf. Joel 2:10, 30–31).

170. Heb. 12:26–27.

171. Rev. 1:16, 20; 6:12,13; 10:1; 12:1; 21:10,23.

172. Minear, "Some Archetypal Origins," pp. 113–14.

173. Whether one views this as an absurdity or integral to one's faith, it is biblical nonetheless.

174. Minear, "Some Archetypal Origins," 117.

175. Cf. also Isaiah 60, an oracle concerning the future glory of Zion (esp. vv 2,3,19, and 20).

176. 1 Enoch 18:14–16; 21:6; 86:1–3; 90:24.

177. I am using "midrash" in the sense P.S. Alexander ("The Targumim and Early Exegesis of 'the Sons of God' in Genesis 6," *JJS* 23 [1972]: 60) has used it: an application of a text to a contemporary theological problem.

178. P.D. Hanson, "Rebellion in Heaven, Azazel, and Euhemeristic Heroes in 1 Enoch 6–11," *JBL* 96 (1977): 202–3.

179. J. T. Milik, "Escrits préesséniens de Qumrân: d'Hénoch à Amram," *Qumrân: sa piété, sa théologie et son milieu* (BETL; ed. M. Delcor; Paris: Duculot, 1978), 97–102.

180. R. Beckwith, *The Old Testament Canon of the New Testament Church and Its Background in Early Judaism* (Grand Rapids, Mich.: Eerdmans, 1985), 399–400.

181. See chap. 4.

182. W.M.L. de Wette, *Kurze Erklärung der Briefe des Petrus, Judas und Jakobus* (Leipzig: Hirzel, 1865), 101; T. Barns, "The Epistle of St. Jude: A Study in the Marcosian Heresy," *JTS* 6 (1905): 391–411; R. Knopf, *Die Briefe Petri und Judä* (MeyerK; Göttingen: Vandenhoeck & Ruprecht, 1912), 227; C. Bigg, *A Critical and Exegetical Commentary on the Epistles of St. Peter and St. Jude* (ICC; New York: Scribner, 1922), 313–15; H. Windisch, *Die katholischen Briefe* (Tübingen: Mohr, 1930), 38; E. H. Plumptre, *The General Epistles of St. Peter and St. Jude* (Cambridge; Cambridge University, 1926), 203; J. Moffatt, *The General Epistles. James, Peter, and Jude* (London: Hodder and Stoughton, 1932), 216; J.W.C. Wand, *The General Epistles of St. Peter and St. Jude* (WC; London: Methuen, 1934), 200,217; C.E.B. Cranfield, *I and II Peter and Jude* (TBC; London: SCM, 1960), 157, 158, 161; J. Schneider, *Die Briefe des Jakobus, Petrus, Judas und Johannes: Die katholischen Briefe* (NTD 10; 9th ed.; Göttingen: Vandenhoeck & Ruprecht, 1961), 123, 129, 130; W. G. Kümmel, *Introduction to the New Testament* (14th ed.; Nashville/New York: Abingdon, 1966), 299; R. H. Fuller, *A Critical Introduction to the New Testament* (London: Duckworth, 1966), 161; W. Grundmann, *Der Brief des Judas und der zweite Brief des Petrus* (THNT 15; Berlin: Evan. Verlagsanstalt, 1967), 37; J. Michl, *Die katholischen Briefe* (RNT; Regensburg; Pustet, 1968), 73–74; J.N.D. Kelly, *A Commentary on the Epistles of Peter and Jude* (London: Adam & Charles Black, 1969), 265; E. M. Sidebottom, *James, Jude, and 2 Peter* (NCB; London: Nelson, 1967), 75, 79, 87; K. H. Schelke, *Die Petrusbriefe, der Judasbrief* (3d ed.; Freiburg: Herder, 1970), 157; W. Marxsen, *Introduction to the New Testament*

(Philadelphia: Fortress, 1970), 239–40; F. Wisse, "The Epistle of Jude in the History of Heresiology," *Essays on the Nag Hammadi Texts in Honour of A. Bohlig* (ed. M. Krause; Leiden: Brill, 1972), 60; W. Schrage, "Der Judasbrief," *Die "katholischen" Briefe: Die Briefe des Jakobus, Petrus, Johannes und Judas* (NTD 10; 11th ed.; Göttingen: Vandenhoeck & Ruprecht, 1973), 218; J. Cantinat, *Les Epîtres de Saint Jacques et de Saint Jude* (Paris: Librairie Lecoffre, 1973); and G. Krodel, "Jude," *Hebrews-James-1 and 2 Peter-Jude-Revelation* (ed. G. Krodel; Philadelphia: Fortress, 1977), 93.

183. Grundmann, *Der Brief*, 31.

184. Bauckham ("The Letter of Jude," 3707–9) is one of the few to make this distinction.

185. W. Schmithals, *Gnosticism in Corinth* (Nashville, Tenn.: Abingdon, 1971).

186. Bauckham (*Jude, 2 Peter*, 11) labels them as charismatic itinerants.

187. See J. F. Keating, *The Agapé and the Eucharist in the Early Church* (London: Methuen, 1901), 52–77.

188. Jude 16c *(kai to stoma autōn lalei hyperogka)* is reminiscent of 1 Enoch 5:4: "you have transgressed and spoken slanderously grave and harsh words with your impure mouths."

189. Cf. also Col. 2:18.

190. Josh. 13:22.

191. This is the view that I. H. Marshall, in *Kept by the Power of God* (Minneapolis, Minn.: Bethany, 1969), 164–66, adopts.

192. What disqualifies Jude's adversaries from being labeled gnostic is the absence of evidence in the epistle of a spiritual-material dichotomy. Whatever their drive to depart may have been, we are not told that the opponents regarded the physical body with disdain.

193. This follows C. K. Barrett, *The Epistle to the Romans* (HNTC; Peabody, Mass.: Hendrickson, rep. 1987), 4–5.

194. Paul's language in Gal. 2:4 is much in the same order *(pareiserchomai, pareisaktoi)*.

195. Col. 2:16–23 and Eph.4:14–16. We accept the traditional view of dating for the two epistles: that of the early sixties.

196. Consider the parallels to Jude in the Corinthian correspondence: immorality, sexual license, and carnality (1 Cor. 3,5,6, and 10); eating and drinking at the love-feast (1 Cor. 11); flouting authority (5 Cor. 4 and 9); false brethren (2 Cor. 11); doctrinal error (1 Cor. 15); obligation due to knowledge (1 Cor. 8); antinomianism (1 Cor. 8,10,11); denying the Lord (1 Cor. 12); arrogance due to ecstatic experience (1 Cor. 5; 2 Cor. 12); Jesus as *Kyrios* (1 Cor. 12); allusion to angels and Satan (1 Cor. 5 and 13; 2 Cor. 2,11, and 12); divisions (1 Cor. 1); use of the OT (1 Cor. 9 and 10; 2 Cor. 3 and 11); the athletic contest as metaphor (1 Cor. 9); judgment (1 Cor. 11; 2 Cor. 5); prophesying (1 Cor. 12,13, and 14); building terminology (1 Cor. 3 and 14; 2 Cor. 5); received Gospel traditions (1 Cor. 15); use of the affirmation *amēn* (2 Cor. 1); the divine glory (2 Cor. 3); unfaithfulness (2 Cor. 6); spiritual warfare (2 Cor. 10); triple witness (2 Cor. 13); and condemnation (1 Cor. 16).

197. In this play on the verb "to keep" *(tērein)*, Jude closes the epistle in doxology by saying that God is able to "guard as securely as a prison" *(phylassein)* the faithful (v 24).

198. J. B. Mayor, *The Epistle of St. Jude and the Second Epistle of St. Peter* (Minneapolis, Minn.: Klock & Klock, rep. 1978),175.

199. Note the use of *phthora* in the LXX: Exod. 18:18 ("wasted"); Ps. 103:4

("withered"); Isa. 24:3 ("laid waste"); and Mic. 2:10 ("ruined"); also in the NT, where it carries the general sense of corruption, decomposition, or decay (Rom. 8:21; 1 Cor. 15:42,50; Gal 6:8; Col. 2:22; 2 Pet. 1:4; 2:12,19).

200. Cf. Matt. 3:10; 7:19; 15:13; John 15:6; and Rev. 21:8.

201. Marshall (*Kept,* 164) is one of the few to consider this as an alternative.

202. 1 Enoch 3.

203. 1 Enoch 5:1. Cf. also T. Naph 3: "On their [the fallen angels'] account, He ordered that the earth be fruitless *(akarpos)."*

204. Note in v 21 the combining of two catchwords/motifs: "Keep yourselves in the love of God."

205. Marshall, *Kept,* 168.

206. One notable and consistent feature of heterodoxy is the causal relationship between practice and doctrine. In a very real sense, heresy predates Christianity. It stands in a long line from Cain onward. Heretics tend to be libertine. Ignoring the many indications of moral degeneration in the epistle, G. Sellin ("Die Häretiker des Judasbriefes," *ZNW* 77 [1986]: 206–25) holds the opponents of Jude to be neither gnostics nor libertines, rather traveling pneumatics who advance ecstasy, not unlike those in Col. 2:8 which spiritualize eschatology. As argued by J. P. Oleson ("An Echo of Hesiod's Theogony vv. 190–2 in Jude 13," *NTS* 25 [1978/79], 492–503), Jude 13 is an allusion to a grotesque account of Aphrodite's birth in Hesiod's *Theogony,* and hence, a link to Jude's opponents who are sexually immoral (see also chap. 4).

207. Bauckham (*Jude, 2 Peter,* 12–13; "The Letter of Jude," 3809) as well as M. Desjardins ("The Portrayal of the Dissidents in 2 Peter and Jude: Does It Tell Us More about the 'Godly' than the 'Ungodly'?" *JSNT* 30 [1987]: 89–102) have advocated a revision of the traditional "gnostic" scenario.

208. Ernst Käsemann, "An Apologia for Primitive Christian Eschatology," in *Essays on New Testament Themes* (Philadelphia: Fortress, 1982), 169.

209. See also Käsemann's essay "Paul and Early Catholicism," in *New Testament Questions of Today* (Philadelphia: Fortress, 1969), 236–51, which was published earlier in *Distinctive Protestant and Catholic Themes Reconsidered* (JTC 3; New York: Harper and Row, 1967).

210. Ibid., 237. Paul, in Käsemann's view, is a forerunner of "early Catholicism."

211. Bauckham, "The Letter of Jude," 3804–5.

212. Ibid., 3805–6.

213. See, e.g., K. H. Schelke, "Spätapostolische Briefe als frühkatholisches Zeugnis," *Neutestamentliche Aufsätze für J. Schmid* (ed. J. Blinzer et al.; Regensburg: Pustet, 1963), 225–32; E. Käsemann, "Paul and Early Catholicism," pp. 236–51; idem, "Apologia," pp. 169–95; and A. Vögtle, "Kirche und Schriftprinzip nach dem Neuen Testament," *BuL* 12 (1971): 153–62, 260–81.

214. K. H. Schelke, "Spätapostolische Briefe," 2256–32, and idem, *Die Petrusbrief. Der Judasbrief* (HTKNT 13/2; Freiburg/Basel/Wien: Herder, 1970) 145–68.

215. Although Luther's deutero-canon of Hebrews-James-Jude-Revelation was based primarily on the criterion of content ("Christ-likeness") and not authorship, in his commentary on Jude he does express doubt that the epistle comes from the real apostle based on his understanding of v 17, which he takes to indicate a time much later than the apostolic era. See J. Pelikan and W. A. Hansen, ed., *Luther's Works—Vol. 30: The Catholic Epistles* (St. Louis: Concordia, 1967), 203.

216. Schelke, "Spätapostolische Briefe," 225.
217. E. M. Sidebottom, *James, Jude and 2 Peter* (NCB; London: Nelson, 1967), 79.
218. H. Windisch, *Die katholischen Briefe* (2d ed.; Tübingen: Mohr, 1950), 38.
219. Rowston, "The Most Neglected Book," 556.
220. Ibid., 559.
221. F. Hahn, "Randbemerkungen zum Judasbrief," *TZ* 37 (1981): 209–10.
222. Ibid.
223. D. J. Harrington, "The 'Early Catholic' Writings of the New Testament: The Church Adjusting to World-History," *The Word in the World* (ed. R. J. Clifford and G. W. MacRae; Cambridge, Mass.: Weston College, 1973), 111.
224. Bauckham, *Jude, 2 Peter*, 8.
225. See also chap. 3.
226. The expression "our only Master and Lord" *(ton monon despotēn kai kyrion hēmōn)* appears also in Philo *(De legatio ad Gaium* 286). For further discussion of the "only God" theme, see G. Delling, *"MONOS THEOS," Studien zum Neuen Testament und zum hellenistischen Judentum* (Göttingen: Vandenhoeck & Ruprecht, 1972), 391–400.
227. In the *koinē, kyrios* and *despotēs* are frequently used interchangeably, although the former carries the inflection of one who *disposes* while the latter denotes one who *possesses*. For further discussion on the usage of the terms with distinctions, see W. Bousset, *Kyrios Christos* (2d ed.; Göttingen: Vandenhoeck & Ruprecht, 1921); W. Foerster and G. Quell, *Lord* (London: A. & C. Black, 1958), 5–9; and O. Cullmann, *The Christology of the New Testament* (Philadelphia: Westminster, 1959), 195–237. Cullmann's analysis of the *kyrios*-designation is more balanced than that offered earlier this century by Bousset, who argued that the title for Jesus was adopted only due to Hellenistic influences. In a Greek, Hebrew, and Aramaic milieu, however, *kyrios, ādônai,* and *mar* seem to have been used in both an absolute sense ("the Lord," i.e., God) as well as in a general sense ("master" or "owner"). For a discussion of four possible views as to the origin of the NT usage of the *kyrios*-title, see J. A. Fitzmyer, "Der semitische Hintergrund des neutestamentlichen Kyriostitels," *Jesus Christus in Historie und Theologie: Neutestamentliche Festschrift für H. Conzelmann zum 60. Geburtstag* (ed. G. Strecker; Tübingen: Mohr, 1975), 271–72.
228. J. Fossum, "Kyrios Jesus," 226–43.
229. A *Iēsous* reading for v 5 is found in Alexandrinus, Vaticanus, a few Old Latin manuscripts, a Coptic version, and Origen.
230. No one can dispute that there has been a fair amount of textual confusion over the transmission of this verse. Of the three variants—[*ho*] *kyrios, ho theos,* and *Iēsous*—*ho theos* has the poorest support.
231. See J. Barbel's discussion of Christ as an angel in the OT in *Christos Angelos. Die Anschauung von Christus als Bote und Engel in der gelehrten und volkstümlichen Literatur des christlichen Altertums* (BRKGA 3; Bonn: Hanstein, 1941), 192–311. On the *Iēsous* reading in Jude 5, see also A. T. Hanson, *Jesus Christ in the Old Testament* (London: SPCK, 1965), 136–38, and F. F. Bruce, "Scripture and Tradition in the New Testament," *Holy Book and Holy Tradition* (Grand Rapids, Mich.: Eerdmans, 1968) 84–85.
232. To rightly understand the christology of the NT is to recognize the early church's acknowledgment that Christ was presently reigning, and that He represented the central event in the full continuum of salvation-history.
233. J. A. Fitzmyer, "New Testament Kyrios and Maranatha and Their Ara-

maic Background," *To Advance the Gospel. New Testament Studies* (New York: Crossroad, 1981), 223.

234. On christological aspects of Jude's theophany statement in vv 14–15, see C. D. Osburn, "The Christological Use of 1 Enoch 1.9 in Jude 14,15," *NTS* 23 (1976/77): 334–41.

235. Already in A.D. 55, the proof of the working of the Spirit is "Jesus is *kyrios*."

236. Note, e.g., Moffatt (*The General Epistles,* 215–17), Kelly (*A Commentary,* 247–48), Sidebottom (*James, Jude, 2 Peter,* 79), Kümmel (*Introduction,* 300), Schelke ("Spätapostolische Briefe," 225–26), and Krodel ("Jude," 95–96).

237. Käsemann, "An Apologia," 195. The assumption of a late date for Jude tends to obscure the significance of tradition in the early church (note, e.g., 1 Cor. 11:2,23; 15:3; 1 Thess. 2:13; 2 Thess. 2:15).

238. See comment by Bauckham, "The Letter of Jude," 3807.

239. In Philo (*De Abrahamo* 198) we also encounter the expression *hē hapax paradotheisē pistis.*

240. A. Schmoller, *Handkonkordanz zum Griechischen Neuen Testament* (Stuttgart: Deutsche Bibelgesellschaft, 1982), 339.

241. Cf. also 1 Pet. 3:18–22 and 1 John 4:2.

242. See the comment by G. R. Beasley-Murray in *The General Epistles. James, 1 Peter, Jude, 2 Peter* (London/New York/Nashville: Lutterworth/Abingdon, 1965), 75.

243. Epistle to the Ephesians 5 (see T. W. Crafer, ed., *The Epistles of Ignatius* [New York/London: Macmillan/SPCK, 1919], 17).

244. Epistle to the Smyrnaeans 8 (Crafer, *The Epistles of Ignatius,* 55).

245. See, e.g., Schelke, "Spätapostolische Briefe" (225–32). Writes E. Käsemann ("Paul and Early Catholicism," 237): "Early catholicism means that transition from earliest Christianity to the so-called ancient Church, which is completed with the disappearance of the imminent expectation."

246. Käsemann, "Apologia," 170.

247. H. Werdermann, *Die Irrlehre des Judas- und 2. Petrusbriefes* (Gütersloh: Bertelsmann, 1913), 54–55; W. Grundmann, *Der Brief des Judas und der 2. Brief des Petrus* (THNT 15; Berlin: Evan. Verlagsanstalt, 1967), 16–17; I. H. Eybers, "Aspects of the Background of the Letter of Jude," *NeoT* 9 (1975): 114–15; R. N. Longenecker, *Biblical Exegesis in the Apostolic Period* (Grand Rapids, Mich.: Eerdmans, 1975), 210; E. E. Ellis, "Prophecy and Hermeneutic in Jude," *Prophecy and Hermeneutic in Early Christianity* (Tübingen: Mohr, 1978), 221, 225; Bauckham, *Jude, 2 Peter,* 9–10; M. Green, *The Second Epistle General of Peter and the General Epistle of Jude. An Introduction and Commentary* (TNTC; rev. ed.; Leicester/Grand Rapids: Inter-Varsity, 1984), 177, 178.

248. Roston, "The Most Neglected Book," 561–62.

249. Ibid., 561.

250. R. M. Grant *Gnosticism and Early Christianity* (New York: Harper, 1966), 27–38.

251. Ibid., 155–62.

252. Bauckham, "The Letter of Jude," 3809.

253. This thesis is developed in more detail in chap. 5. While most commentators follow essentially the same line of thinking regarding Jude's use of sources which was advanced one hundred years ago, an adequate explanation and justification for his use of specific source-material, demonstrating how it relates to his literary strategy, has been lacking. That Jude seems to have highly es-

teemed the Book of Enoch is as far as most commentators are prepared to go in assessing his use of sources.

254. Although 2 Peter contains no explicit use of the Pseudepigrapha, the allusion to the "disobedient imprisoned spirits" in 1 Pet. 3:18–20 is germane to the present discussion for two reasons: (1) we may well have here an indirect reference to 1 Enoch, in which case (2) Peter would be utilizing the Enoch tradition based on the *needs of his audience* for the sake of *illustration*. This view is plausible if the writer is emphasizing that it was *Christ*, not Enoch, who preached to the fallen angels.

255. See chap. 5.

256. Is it perhaps likely that Jude, knowing of the prominent place in 1 Enoch the Flood plays, intentionally omitted any reference to the Deluge in order to consciously *not* endorse Enochic theology? 2 Peter, on the other hand, alludes to the Flood and Noah (2:5).

257. E. Isaac, "1 (Ethiopic Apocalypse of) Enoch," *The Old Testament Pseudepigrapha—Vol. 1: Apocalyptic Literature and Testaments* (ed. J. H. Charlesworth; Garden City, N.Y.: Doubleday, 1983), 5–7.

258. Aside from 1 Enoch, it should be noted that most of these elements are common to the Testaments of the Twelve Patriarchs, Jubilees, and the Assumption of Moses.

259. Although he does not develop this theory, E.M.B. Green (*2 Peter Reconsidered* [London: Tyndale, 1961], 32) would seem to be the only commentator who has even suggested (and this, only in passing) the possibility that Jude is writing as an *argumentum ad hominem*, whether against the readers or opponents who were devoted to such literature. This explanation for Jude's use of sources deserves more attention, particularly since the epistle stands apart from the rest of the NT in its use of pseudepigraphal source-material. One is inclined, therefore, to wonder whether the author's attitude toward the pseudepigrapha is indeed any different from that of the other NT writers.

CHAPTER 3. THE EPISTLE OF JUDE IN ITS PALESTINIAN MILIEU

1. From the beginning of Acts, the disciples of Jesus of Nazareth are consciously aware of their Jewish character and origin. Consider as examples: John the Baptist as a preparer of the way (1:5; 11:16); the expectation of a restored kingdom of Israel (1:6); a reconstituted "twelve" (1:15–26; 6:2); observance of the sabbath (1:12; 13:14,42,44; 16:13; 18:4); going to the temple (2:46; 3:1,11; 5:42); celebration of the feast of Weeks (2:1); continuity with the prophets (2:16–21,25–35; 3:18–26; 4:11,25–26; 7:52; 8:26–35; 10:43; 13:16–41; 15:15–18; 17:2–3,11; 18:28; 26:22–23); the God of Abraham, Isaac, and Jacob as the Christians' God and sender of His servant Jesus (3:13; 5:29–32; 7:2–50; 10:36; 22:14–16; 24:14; 26:6); a significant number of priests who embrace the faith (6:7); the laying on of hands (6:6; 9:12; 13:3); continuity with the Law (7:53; 10:9–13; 11:4–10; 21:20–26; 24:17–18; 26:4–5); preaching in the synagogues (9:20–22; 13:5,14; 14:1; 17:2; 18:4; 26:11); those circumcized as part of the faith (10:45; 11:2–3; 16:3); the appointing of elders (14:23; cf. also 15:22,23; 20:17; 21:18); the handling of issues related to Mosaic law (chap. 15); Paul's commitment to his Jewish brothers and Jerusalem

(20:22–24; 21:10–16; 28:17–22); and Paul's solidarity with his Jewish past (22:2–5; 23:1–8).

2. Here one might cite numerous studies over recent years which have attempted to take up this problem. Of note are J. Danielou, *The Theology of Jewish-Christianity* (London: Darton, Longman & Todd, 1964); R. N. Longenecker, *The Christology of Early Jewish Christianity* (SBT 17; London: SCM, 1970); I. H. Marshall, "Palestinian and Hellenistic Christianity: Some Critical Comments," *NTS* 19 (1972/73): 271–87; R. Murray, "Defining Judaeo-Christianity," *HeyJ* 15 (1974): 303–10; A. F. J. Klijn, "The Study of Jewish Christianity," *NTS* 20 (1974): 419–31; and S. K. Riegel, "Jewish Christianity: Definitions and Terminology," *NTS* 24 (1978): 410–15. In the discussion of what constitutes "Jewish Christianity," two general camps seem to emerge: those who focus on the study of NT sources and those who focus on extracanonical material.

3. J. Pelikan, *The Christian Tradition: A History of the Development of Doctrine— Vol. 1: The Emergence of the Catholic Tradition (100–600)* (Chicago: University of Chicago, 1971), 12.

4. Martin Hengel, *Judaism and Hellenism: Studies in Their Encounter in Palestine during the Early Hellenistic Period* (2 vols.; Philadelphia: Fortress, 1981).

5. Ibid., 1.1.

6. S. Sandmel, *The First Christian Century in Judaism and Christianity: Certainties and Uncertainties* (Oxford: Oxford University, 1969), 20–21.

7. P. Henry, *New Directions in New Testament Study* (Philadelphia: Westminster, 1979), 86. At the very least this removes the assumed *distance* in time between supposed early "Semitic originals" and later Greek transcription.

8. J. Pelikan, *The Christian Tradition*, 14.

9. Henry, *New Directions*, 92.

10. Several elements support a Palestinian origin: the strong Jewish character, use of Jewish pseudepigrapha, the audience having received apostolic teaching, and James's sphere of authority and reputation. For an opposing view, see J. J. Gunther, "The Alexandrian Epistle of Jude," *NTW* 30 (1984): 549–62. Gunther contends that Jude's associations with Palestine are "superficial" (p. 549), yet this would seem to fully ignore the letter's marked Semitic influence. Moreover, the designation *adelphos Iakōbou*, reference to *Henōch*, as well as the allusion to the Assumption of Moses would lose their force if relegated to Alexandria in the second century. Enoch might be recognized outside of Palestine, however the Assumption would be fully unknown. Gunther is reviving a hypothesis set forth in 1835 by E. Mayerhoff in his work *Historisch-kritische Einleitung in die petrinischen Schriften* (Hamburg: Perthes, 1835) and used by J. Moffatt earlier this century (*Introduction*, p. 358).

11. Forbes, "Comparison," 30. Commenting on the Greeks' proclivity toward organized education, M. Hadas (*Hellenistic Culture—Fusion and Diffusion* [Morningside Heights, N.Y.: Cambridge University, 1959], 59) writes: "The most significant characteristic of the Greeks is that no group of them settled anywhere without at once establishing a school, and organized education was the most important single factor in the process of hellenization."

12. Smith, *Ancient Education*, 189.

13. Ibid., 191.

14. V. Tcherikover, *Hellenistic Civilization and the Jews* (Philadelphia/Jerusalem: Jewish Publication Society of America/Magnes, 1959), 90.

15. Ibid.

16. Ibid.

17. Ibid., 248.

192 NOTES

18. Tcherikover, *Hellenistic Civilization*, 90–116.
19. The Greek *polis* exercised its influence in several ways—politically, culturally, linguistically, and literarily.
20. J. A. Fitzmyer, "The Languages of Palestine in the First Century A.D.," *CBQ* 32 (1970): 513.
21. The Greek language in Judea during the midthird century B.C. is reflected in the letters of Tobias, a Jew. M. Hengel (*Judaism*, 1.59) considers these letters to exhibit an excellent Greek (Tobias's letters are found in *CPJ* 1.125ff, nos. 4 and 5). For further discussion of Palestinian Jews writing in Greek, see C. Colpe, "Jüdish-hellenistische Literatur," *Der kleine Pauly: Lexikon der Antike* (Stuttgart: Drückenmüller, 1967) 1507–12, and Hengel, *Judaism*, 1.88–102.
22. He writes that he worked hard at learning Greek prose and poetry.
23. The *Hebraioi* would thus be Jews who, though able to speak Greek, knew a Semitic language as well and were most likely Palestinian-born. Those who prefer to view *Hellēnistoi* and *Hebraioi* in Acts 6:1 as a primarily *linguistic* designation include C. F. D. Moule ("Once More, Who Were the Hellenists?" *ExpTim* 70 [1958/59]: 100–102); J. N. Sevenster (*Do You Know Greek? How Much Greek Could the First Jewish Christian Have Known?* [NovTSup 19; Leiden: Brill, 1968], 28–29; J. A. Fitzmyer ("Jewish Christianity in Acts in the Light of the Qumran Scrolls," *Essays on the Semitic Background of the New Testament* [London: Chapman, 1971], 278); and I. H. Marshall, "Comments," 279.
24. See P. Lapide, "Insights into the Language of Jesus," *RQ* 8 (1975): 483–501.
25. See T. K. Abbott, *Essays on the Original Texts of the Old and New Testaments* (London: Longman, Green & Co., 1891), 129–82; also T. Nicklin, *Gospel Gleanings. Critical and Historical Notes on the Gospels* (London: Longman, Green & Co., 1950), 290ff.
26. G. A. Williamson, *The World of Josephus* (Boston: Little and Brown, 1964), 91.
27. R. Jonathan, in j. Megilla 1.8.
28. Sevenster, *Do You Know Greek?* 28–9. See also Hengel, *Judaism*, 1.58.
29. The Hellenistic era produced a new man—through *paideia*, which essentially becomes the later *humanitas* of the Romans.
30. On the ongoing work of Palestinian editing of the LXX, see E. Bickerman, "Some Notes on the Transmission of the LXX," *Alexander Marx Jubilee Volume* (New York: Jewish Theological Seminary, 1950) 149–78.
31. Stemming from zealous Jews, these books are considered to reflect a good Greek.
32. S. Lieberman, in *Hellenism in Jewish Palestine* (New York: Jewish Theological Seminary of America, 1950), seeks to demonstrate that Jews of Palestine were by no means isolated from the Mediterranean world.
33. Isocrates, *Panēgyrikos* 4.50 (for an English translation of the work, see *Isocrates* [3 vols.; tr. G. Norlin; London/New York: Heinemann/Putnam's Sons, 1928–1945]).
34. This call to combat, to fight or struggle, is particularly reflected in the War Scroll of Qumran.
35. Jewish literature, with its use of the *agōn*-motif, helps us in establishing the sense of the notion as it appears in the NT. Paul uses this metaphor on numerous occasions (e.g., Rom. 15:30; 1 Cor. 9:24–27; Phil 1:27–30; 4:3; Col. 1:29–2:1; 4:12; 1 Thess. 2:2; 1 Tim. 4:10; 6:12; 2 Tim 2:7). For the apostle *agōnizomai* is striving after the goal, struggling to receive a prize, or fighting to stand fast in the faith. In the epistle to the Hebrews, the writer uses the *agōn-*

motif in the context of running a race (12 : 1) and struggling against sin (12 : 4). Jesus' *agōn*, as expressed in Luke 22 : 44, is with death. In Jude, the basic idea conveyed by the writer is a taking part in the struggle, the *agōn*, of another *(synagōnizomai)*. Here the wrestling is a corporate, shared responsibility.

36. The *agōn* was originally the "place of assembly," then the "place of contest," and eventually came to denote "conflict" (cf. E. Stauffer, *"agōn," TDNT* 1 [1964]: 134–40.

37. The verb *agōnizomai* entails toil, labor, maximum endeavor, or intense wrestling. The term is always cast in a context of opposition. For a much wider discussion of the concept, see V. C. Pfitzner, *Paul and the Agōn Motif* (Leiden: Brill, 1967).

38. Hesiod, *Theogony,* 535ff.

39. Hengel, *Judaism,* 1.66.

40. J. Öhler, "Gymnasium," *Pauly's Real-Encyclopaedia der klassischen Alter-tumswissenschaft—Vol. 7* (ed. W. Kroll; Stuttgart: Metzler, 1912), 2004–26.

41. Note reference to the "gymnasium" in 1 Macc. 1 : 14–15 and 2 Macc. 4 : 9–14.

42. Philo, *De agricultura* 91, 113, 119; Philo, *De mutatione nominum* 81, 106; Philo, *De Abrahamo* 48; Philo, *De specialibus legibus* 2.91, 229, 246; Philo, *Legum allegoriarum* 2.108; 3.14,48,72; Philo, *De praemiis et poenis* 53; and Philo, *De somniis* 2.145. Not unlike Paul, Philo was fond of the athletic contest as a means of illustration.

43. E.g., 3 : 5; 6 : 9–11; 8 : 1–2; 9 : 8,23–26; and 11 : 20–27.

44. Here it speaks of the "agony" of martyrdom under Antiochus Epiphanes.

45. 4 Ezra 7 : 92; T. Ash. 6 : 2; and T. Jos. 2 : 2.

46. T. Job 4 : 10. The devil eventually withdraws from the contest with Job, claiming "I became like one athlete wrestling with another" who had been pinned (27 : 3).

47. Hengel, *Judaism,* 1.58–65.

48. Ibid., 1.98–99.

49. This is Hengel's term (*Judaism,* 1.99).

50. W. L. Knox, *Some Hellenistic Elements in Primitive Christianity* (London: Oxford University, 1944), 2.

51. t.soṭa 49b.

52. Matt. 10 : 2–4; Mark 3 : 16–19; and Luke 6 : 14–16.

53. W. G. Kümmel, *Introduction to the New Testament* (14th ed.; Nashville/New York: Abingdon, 1966), 84, 301.

54. See B. B. Trawick, *The Bible as Literature: The New Testament* (New York: Barnes and Noble, 1968), 139–40. Both Hebrews and James are written in an elevated Greek with a picturesque style and distinctly Jewish tone; both demonstrate great rhetorical skill.

55. M. Dibelius, *James* (Hermeneia; rev. H. Greeven; Philadelphia: Fortress, 1970). Quite striking is the manner in which James illustrates the popular moral address or Hellenistic diatribe with its use of imaginary dialogue, question and answer, raising objections, use of imperatives, irony, sharp antithesis, repetition, comparison, personification, figures of speech, and paradox.

56. As an exhorter, the paraenetic instructor assumes a doctrinal foundation on the part of his audience and seeks to underscore the ethical implications of that doctrine for daily living.

57. K. Berger, "Hellenistische Gattungen im Neuen Testament." *Aufstieg und Niedergang der römischen Welt. Geschichte und Kultur Roms im Spiegel der neueren*

Forschung II.25.2. (ed. H. Temporini and W. Haase; Berlin/New York: de Gruyter, 1984), 1076.

58. Berger, "Hellenistische Gattungen," 1076.

59. An examination of the social functions of paraenesis in James is found in L. G. Perdue, "Paraenesis in the Epistle of James," *ZNW* 72 (1981): 241–56, esp. pp. 251–56.

60. R. W. Wall, "James as Apocalyptic Paraenesis," *RestQ* 32 (1990): 11–22.

61. Ibid., 13.

62. Ibid. Cf. also K. Koch, *The Rediscovery of Apocalyptic* (SBT 22; London: SCM, 1970), 25.

63. Ibid., 21.

64. Ibid., 14–22.

65. J. A. T. Robinson, *Redating the New Testament* (Philadelphia: Westminster, 1976), 135–36.

66. Wall, "James as Apocalyptic Paraenesis," 15. On possible correlation between the *diaspora* of Acts 8:1ff and James as a sermon, see D. Bartlett, "James as a Jewish Document," *SBL Seminar Papers* (Chico: Calif.: Scholars, 1979), 116–34.

67. Wall, "James as Apocalyptic Paraenesis," 16–21.

68. E.g., 1:18; 2:12–13; 4:12–16; and 5:4–5.

69. E.g., 1:13–17,20–21,27; 2:18–19; 3:6,9–12,15:16; 4:1–10; and 5:19–20.

70. E.g., 4:11–12; and 5:4–5,7–9.

71. M. Gertner, "Midrashim in the New Testament," *JSS* 7 (1962): 267.

72. This coherence may or may not entail thematic unity.

73. In his essay, Gertner examines four instances of implicit midrash in the NT: that by Jesus in Mark 4:1–22, Luke 1:67–75, Paul in 1 Cor. 15:53,56, and the epistle of James. Gertner analyzes at some length the midrashic composition of James (pp. 283–91).

74. Gertner, "Midrashim," 284.

75. To illustrate the diversity of Jewish sources, not confined to the Pseudepigrapha, which portray Abraham according to charity and hospitality (and thus aid in elucidating James's use of the Abraham-tradition), see T. Abr. 1:1–2; Jos. *Ant.* 1.200; b. soṭa 10a–b; Midr.Teh.Ps 37:1; Tg.Ps.–Jon.Gen. 21:33; and Abot R. Nat. 7. For other examples of midrashic treatment of Abraham, cf. also 1 Macc. 2:52 and Sir 44:20. On Jewish legendary material surrounding Abraham in general, see L. Ginzberg, *The Legends of the Jews* (4 vols.; Philadelphia: Jewish Society of America, 1968), 4.183–308.

76. On Rahab in Jewish extrabiblical tradition, see Num. Rab. 3:2; Midr. Ruth; and b.Sukka 49b.

77. On Job traditions in extrabiblical literature, see the pseudepigraphal Testament of Job. Specifically on the virtue of Job's patience, see T.Job 1:5; 4:6; 5:1; and 27:4,7. Of particular interest to our study of James, the Testament of Job develops in some detail the notion of Job's generosity and clarity, a theme that intersects with James's.

78. For extracanonical Elijah-traditions, see, e.g., Sir. 48:1 –11; 4 Ezra 7:109, and the pseudepigraphal Apocalypse of Elijah, the latter being a composite work dating from the first to the fourth century A.D. The context of Elijah's mention in 4 Ezra, significantly, is a catalog of Israel's heroes who interceded for the ungodly (7:102–15). Elijah joins Abraham who prayed for Sodom, Moses who prayed for Israel in the wilderness, Joshua, Samuel, David, Solomon, and Hezekiah. The allusion to Elijah in James is parallel, occurring in the connection of drought and

rain, although James stresses Elijah's humanity, and thus, his ability to endure as an ordinary person. Rabbinic allusions to Elijah are myriad. Most of these speak of Elijah's "coming" or portray him as a man of prayer, similar to James, though these postdate James considerably. On the later Jewish conception of Elijah as a model intercessor, see, e.g., b.Sanh. 113a and j.Sanh. 10:28b. On rabbinic Elijah traditions in general, see Ginzberg, *The Legends*, 4.193–235.

79. Nearly three decades ago M. Gertner (see n. 71) noted the midrashic composition of James. Gertner's essay appeared about the same time that H. Chadwick, "Justification by Faith and Hospitality," *Studia Patrologia—Vol. 4* (TU 79; ed. F. L. Cross; Berlin: Akademie, 1961), 281, had suggested Abraham and Rahab were paradigms for hospitality in Jewish and early Christian circles. In "The Works of Abraham," *HTR* 61 (1968), 283–90, R. B. Ward developed more fully the notion that James was employing Jewish legendary material surrounding Abraham and Rahab. For more recent reworking of this thesis, see I. Jacobs, "The Midrashic Background for James ii.21–23," *NTS* 22 (1976): 457–64, and P. H. Davids, "Tradition and Citation in the Epistle of James," *Scripture, Tradition, and Interpretation* (ed. W. W. Gasque and W. S. LaSor; Grand Rapids, Mich.: Eerdmans, 1978), 113–26.

80. S. Segert, "Semitic Poetic Structures in the New Testament," *Aufstieg und Niedergang der römishen Welt. Geschicht und Kultur Roms im Spiegel der neueren Forschung*. II.25.2 (ed. W. Haase; New York/Berlin: de Gruyter, 1984), 1458.

81. "Brother of James," it should be noted, would be authoritative in the first century. No other "James" of the first century goes without explanation. Regarding the epistle of James, J. A. T. Robinson writes: "The very simplicity of the address speaks forcibly against pseudonymity" (*Redating the New Testament* [Philadelphia: Westminster, 1976], 129). If in James and Jude we indeed have pseudonymity, it is inexplicable why the writer, seeking ultimate authority, would not have said "brother of the Lord" or "Bishop of Jerusalem." In this regard, see, for example, the pseudo-Clementine letter to James (*New Testament Apocrypha* [ed. E. Hennecke et al.; 2 vols.; London: SCM, 1963, 1965], 2.111), in which James is called "bishop of bishops." A further argument for the authenticity of Jude is the writer's statement in v 3 that he had intended to write another letter. We can therefore suppose a relationship between him and his readers—an intimate one in fact—as reflected by his use of *agapētoi* three times in the brief epistle.

82. This self-designation would also reflect an earlier rather than later date.

83. One of the first to question the authenticity of James was the Renaissance scholar Erasmus. Noting that the author writes as if Greek were his mother-tongue and rhetoric were his vocation, Erasmus rejects the epistle's attribution to James, the Lord's brother. The Greek, he concludes, is simply too good to be written by a Palestinian from Nazareth. Interestingly, to Luther, James is failing on two counts. It lacks a Christ-centeredness, and hence conflicts with Pauline teaching, and it lacks a sense of order. He writes: "We should throw the Epistle of James out of this school [i.e., out of the University of Wittenberg], for it does not amount to much. It contains not a syllable about Christ. Not once does it mention Christ, except at the beginning . . . [and] there is no order or method in the epistle" (*Luther's Works—Vol. 54: Table Talk* [ed. T. G. Tappert; Philadelphia: Fortress, 1967], 424,425). On the matter of structural method, Luther continues: "he throws things together so chaotically that it seems to me he must have been some good pious man who took a few sayings from the disciples of the apostles and thus tossed them off on paper" (*Luther's Works—Vol. 35: Word and Sacrament I* [ed. E. T. Bachmann; Philadelphia: Muhlenberg, 1960], 397). And on the Greek in Jude, Luther states: "the Apostle Jude did not go to Greek-speaking lands, but

to Persia, as it is said, so that he did not write Greek" (ibid., 398). Thus, with regard to the level of language and rhetoric found in James and Jude, scholarship—Protestant and Catholic—has in the main followed the underlying assumptions of Erasmus and Luther. Nevertheless, the results of studies such as those done by Sevenster and Hengel have sufficiently demonstrated, culturally and linguistically, that James and Jude may be assigned a Palestinian provenance before A.D. 70. In this regard, see also R. P. Martin, "The Life-Setting of the Epistle of James in the Light of Jewish History," *Biblical and Near Eastern Studies* (ed. G. A. Tuttle; Grand Rapids, Mich.: Eerdmans, 1978), 97–103, and P. H. Davids, "The Epistle of James in Modern Discussion," *Aufstieg und Niedergang der römischen Welt. Geschichte und Kultur Roms im Spiegel der neueren Forschung* (ed. W. Haase; Berlin/New York: de Gruyter, 1988), 3622–25.

84. Both letters belonged to Eusebius's "disputed" classification *(ta antilegomena)*—2 Peter on authenticity; James, Jude, and 2 and 3 John on apostolicity—over against "acknowledged" writings *(ta homolegoumena)*. Interestingly, Jude fared better in the West as James did in the East. That Jude should be unknown to some churches is what one might expect. The letter's brevity as well as its Jewish character might render it less accessible to the Gentile community. Moreover, with certain spurious works in circulation, the more conservative school of Antioch, Syria would be reticent to recognize any allusions to noncanonical material. To be sure, if Jude were a pseudegraph from the second century, it would doubtless not have found the patristic recognition that it did. That both James and Jude were on Eusebius's "disputed" list is a bit misleading for several reasons. First, the *antilegomena* classification indicates that misgivings did in fact exist in some regions as to the authority of the letter. Yet at the same time it shows that it was by no oversight that the two epistles were admitted into the canon. Eusebius's *antilegomena* distinction does not mean that such books were *universally* rejected or called into question. Rather, it indicates that they were not universally *accepted,* for Eusebius himself states that they were nonetheless familiar to most: *gnōrimōn d' oun homōs tois pollois (Hist. eccl. 3.25.3).* Second, 1 Clement, written in A.D. 96 to the Corinthian Church, contains at least fourteen passages resembling the epistle of James, causing some scholars to conclude that Clement of Rome was using the letter, in which case it would have already been circulating in the first century. This reflects my basic assumption that both James and Jude are roughly contemporary with the apostolic era.

85. Although James contains only three OT citations (2:8 = Lev 19:18; 2:23 = Gen. 15:6; 4:6 = Prov. 3:34), the influence of the Psalms, Proverbs, and wisdom literature is notable. This constitutes another similarity between James and Jude: alluding to the OT without actual citation. On Jude's use of OT motifs, see chapter 4 a segment of which appears in J. D. Charles, " 'Those' and 'These': The Use of the Old Testament in the Epistle of Jude," *JSNT* 38 (1990): 109–124.

86. James and Jude reflect an early Christian piety. Their readers have received the essentials of the faith but necessitate instruction concerning ethics in a pagan world.

87. Most commentators since Martin Dibelius have been willing to acknowledge in James a minimum coherence of the paraenetic sayings found in the epistle.

88. G. H. Rendall, *The Epistle of James and Judaic Christianity* (Cambridge: Cambridge University, 1927), 39.

89. Sevenster, *Do You Know Greek?*, 190.

90. F. O. Francis, "The Form and Function of the Opening and Closing Paragraphs of James and 1 John," *ZNW* 61 (1970): 125, sees this parallel in James

and Jude as a further indication of their eschatological perspective. Francis, who views the structure of James as essentially chiastic, is followed by J. M. Reese, "The Exegete as Sage: Hearing the Message of James," BTB 12 (1982): 82–85.

91. In his work *Der Stil der Jüdisch-Hellenistischen Homilie* (Göttingen: Vandenhoeck & Ruprecht, 1955), H. Thyen analyzes the rhetorical character of the synagogue homily when compared to the diatribe. Key elements observed include synonymous parallelism, antithesis, paradox, questions, imperatives, irony, and abundant sound-play. As this relates to James, see esp. pp. 47–58. Earlier this century, H. J. Cladder attempted to trace the poetic structure of James ("Der formale Aufbau des Jakobushbriefes," *ZKT* 28 [1904]: 295–330). This was followed by the form analysis of J. H. Ropes (*A Critical and Exegetical Commentary on the Epistle of St. James* [ICC; Edinburgh: Clark, 1916]) and M. Dibelius (see n. 55; Dibelius's commentary on James, translated for the Heremeneia series in 1970, first appeared in 1929). More recently D. O. Via, Jr. ("The Right Strawy Epistle Reconsidered: A Study in Biblical Ethics and Hermeneutic," *JR* 49 [1969]: 253–67) and W. Wuellner ("Der Jakobusbrief im Licht der Rhetorik und Textpragmatik," *LB* 43 [1978]: 5–66) have sought to approach the epistle linguistically and rhetorically. While these and various other attempts to offer a satisfying explanation of the letter's structure may prove helpful, two tendencies seem to emerge: either one tries (mistakenly) to locate *the* theological center in the epistle, or one is prone to deny the book any theology.

92. Cf. A. T. Robertson, *A Grammar of the Greek New Testament in the Light of Historical Research* (Nashville, Tenn.: Broadman, 1934), 123.

93. Morgenthaler, *Statistik*, 67–157.

94. 3:6,7.

95. 1:6.

96. 1:15.

97. 3:2,6; 4:1,9; and 5:1.

98. 1:17 and 5:4.

99. 3:9.

100. 2:5,25.

101. 1:11–12; 3:6; 4:2–3; 4:11–12; and 5:2–6.

102. 2:14–16.

103. 2:13.

104. 1:2–4 and 1:14–15.

105. We distinguish here, as in chap. 2, between general figures of speech and particular word-play or paronomasia such as alliteration, assonance, homoioteleuton, word- and name-play, anaphora and epiphora, polyptoton, and heterosis.

106. We are here focusing on the breadth and frequency of verbal parallels running throughout the whole of James and Jude, unlike the literary dependence and close concurrence between 2 Pet. 2:1–18 and Jude 5–16.

107. *houtos/houtoi, agapē, agapētoi, tērein, eleos, pan, pistis, kyrios, charis, sōzein, apollymi, hoti, krisis, alla, pyr, diakrinein, planan (planē), legein, lalein, epithymia, spiloun (spilos), monos,* and *homoiōs.*

108. This excludes prepositions, pronouns, commonly used particles, and the verb *einai.*

109. While *spilos* is found in 2 Pet. 2:13 and several earlier versions of Jude 12 read "stains," the metaphor *spilades* ("hidden rocks") is best suited to the sense of the text, particularly in connection with *agapai* and *syneuōcheomai.* The notion of hidden danger or shipwreck lies behind v 12. Thus, we follow Plummer (*The General Epistles of St. James and St. Jude* [New York: Armstrong and Son, 1893],

427–30), Mayor (*Epistle*, 40–41), Kelly (*A Commentary*, 270–71), Green (*The Second Epistle General*, 173), and Bauckham (*Jude, 2 Peter*, 85–86).

110. James 1:21 and Jude 3,17.

111. On christology in the preaching of the early church, see R. N. Longenecker, *The Christology of Early Jewish Christianity* (SBT 17; London: SCM, 1970).

112. Chap. 2, pp. 55–56.

113. E. E. Kellett, "Note on Jude 5," *ExpTim* 15 (1903/4): 381.

114. Bruce, "Scripture and Tradition," 84–85.

115. A. T. Hanson, *Jesus Christ in the Old Testament* (London: SPCK, 1965), 136–38.

116. R. G. Hamerton-Kelly, *Pre-Existence, Wisdom, and the Son of Man. A Study of the Idea of Pre-Existence in the New Testament* (Cambridge: Cambridge University, 1973), 269.

117. J. Fossum, "Kyrios Jesus as the Angel of the Lord in Jude 5–7," *NTS* 33 (1987): 226–43.

118. Thus, Fossum ("Kyrios Jesus," 237). Stephen, in Act 7, is essentially doing the same thing. He states by implication (7:38) that Jesus was the angel that appeared with the assembly of Israel at Mount Sinai.

119. This distinction is treated in chapter 5. See also J. D. Charles, "Jude's Use of Pseudepigraphal Source-Material as Part of a Literary Strategy," *NTS* 37 (1991) 130–45.

120. Meade, *Pseudonymity and Canonicity*, 15.

121. Ibid., 3.

122. Ibid.

123. Ibid. On the one hand, Meade sets out to address what (in his mind) "conservative" and "liberal" scholarship has heretofore neglected—or muddled, perhaps hoping to be perceived as neutral (cf. his contrast, e.g., on pp. 2–4 and 208–15, between standard conservative and liberal approaches to the subject). On the other hand, Meade assumes from the start traditional critical conclusions (e.g., pp. 106–9 and 179–93).

124. Ibid., 3–4.

125. Ibid., 12–13.

126. Ibid., 109.

127. Ibid.

128. Ibid., 179–90.

129. Ibid., 179–80.

130. Ibid., 181. Interestingly, however, Meade later states that "our examination of the NT documents was more concerned to discover a 'theology' of authorship and revelation" (p. 194).

131. Ibid., 183.

132. Ibid., 189, 190, 194, 207.

133. Ibid., 207.

134. Ibid., 192.

135. Ibid., 193.

136. Ibid., 3, 180, 181.

137. R. B. Gaffin, Jr., "The New Testament as Canon," *Inerrancy and Hermeneutic: A Tradition, A Challenge, A Debate*, ed. H. M. Conn (Grand Rapids, Mich.: Baker, 1988), 168–69.

138. Thus, Gaffin, p. 169.

139. E.g., other "epistles" or "words" alluded to in 2 Thess. 2:2.

140. Gaffin, "The New Testament as Canon," 170.

141. Meade, *Pseudonymity and Canonicity*, 208.

142. Ibid., 211.
143. Ibid., 206.
144. Ibid.
145. Heb. 1:1–2.
146. Acts 20:28–31.
147. Gaffin, "The New Testament as Canon," 174.
148. 1 Cor. 15:5–9.
149. Cf. Luke 24:45–49; John 14:15–21, 25–26; 15:26–27; 16:12–15; Acts 1:7–8.
150. Gaffin, "The New Testament as Canon," 176.
151. Rom. 1:1; 1 Cor. 1:1; 2 Cor. 1:1; 10:8; Gal. 1:1; 2:7; Eph. 1:1; Col. 1:1; 1 Tim. 1:1; 2 Tim. 1:1; Tit. 1:1; 1 Pet. 1:1. Cf. 1 John 1:1–3.
152. Paul, in Gal. 1:8–9, could hardly state this strongly enough.
153. One might question, with good reason, whether the Spirit of God causes the church to make erroneous judgments as to the nature of Scripture. Modern scholarship, whether explicitly or implicitly, tends to assume the church has been misled regarding canon.
154. In 2 Thess. 2:2 we encounter Paul's exhortation to the Thessalonian Christians not to become unsettled in mind or alarmed over a writing that professed to originate with him. What is implied in this statement and that which follows is the element of deception. His readers should not be unsettled by a pseudepigraphon, since they will already know Paul's teaching (the subject of his teaching being the coming of the Day of the Lord). In closing his letter to the Thessalonians, the apostle writes: "I, Paul, write this greeting with my own hand, which is the distinguishing mark in all my letters. This is how I write" (3:17). The implication is that pseudonymity, evidently not a rare phenomenon, was to be distinguished from the authoritative apostolic word.
155. On the question of reconciling truth and integrity with pseudonymity, see Guthrie, New Testament Introduction, pp. 77–79, 110–13, 144–47, 151–60, 168–71; also Lea, "The Early Christian View," pp. 76–78.
156. Lea, "The Early Christian View," 75.

CHAPTER 4. THE USE OF THE OLD TESTAMENT IN JUDE

1. E.g., Wand, The General Epistles, 192; Chaine, Les Epîtres, 277; and Kelly, a Commentary, 272.
2. See chap. 2.
3. See chap. 3.
4. See the structure of Jude suggested by Bauckham (Jude, 2 Peter, 5–6). Note a similar pattern in Dan. 5:25–26; Zech. 1:10; and 4:10,14.
5. S. P. Brock, in "Translating the Old Testament," It Is Written: Scripture Citing Scripture. Essays in Honour of B. Lindars (ed. D. A. Carson and H.G.M. Williamson; Cambridge: Cambridge University, 1988) 91, distinguishes between the role of an expositor, whose task it is to bring the text to the readers, as opposed to the literal interpreter, whose goal is to bring the readers to the text.
6. Ellis, "Prophecy," 225; Bauckham, Jude, 2 Peter, 4–5; and idem, "James, 1 and 2 Peter, Jude," 303–5. The beginnings of midrash are normally traced to Ezra and his zeal for the Torah following the Exile. With his contemporaries, Ezra bridges the past with the present: "They read from the Book of the Law of God, making it clear and giving the meaning so that the people could under-

200   NOTES

stand what was being read" (Neh. 8:8). Midrash became "the queen of Jewish spiritual life" in the fourth and third centuries B.C. (Gen. Rab. 9).

7. J. A. Fitzmyer, "The Use of Explicit Old Testament Quotations in Qumran Literature and in the New Testament," *NTS* 7 (1960/61): 298.

8. Vv 4,15 [3x] and 18.

9. Most commentators have uncritically assumed that this flat rejection of authority is *proof* of a second-century gnostic scenario in Jude. However, this very attitude—the questioning of authority—along with accompanying effects in the individual's life-style, particularly sexual license, are a primary characteristic of the Corinthian church already in A.D. 55. The arrogance and sexual misconduct in 1 Corinthians, furthermore, were *flagrant* in nature.

10. This progression was suggested earlier this century by R. Knopf, *Die Briefe Petri und Judä* (MeyerK; Göttingen: Vandenhoeck & Ruprecht, 1912), 231. Cf. also G. H. Boobyer, "The Verbs in Jude 11," *NTS* (1958/59): 45.

11. Thus G. L. Lawlor, *The Epistle of Jude* (Phillipsburg, N.J.: Presbyterian and Reformed, 1972), 12.

12. J. Jeremias, *Theophanie. Die Geschichte einer alttestamentlichen Gattung* (WMANT 10; Neukirchen-Vluyn: Neukirchener, 1965), 1.

13. Ibid.

14. On the language of theophany in the OT from the standpoint of the vocabulary, see F. Schnutenhaus, "Das Kommen und Erscheinen Gottes im Alten Testament," *ZAW* 35 (1964): 1–22.

15. *Prophecy Interpreted. The Formulation of Some Apocalyptic Texts and of the Eschatological Discourse Mark 13* (ConB 1; Lund: Gleerup, 1966), and *Asking for a Meaning. A Study of 1 Enoch 1–5* (ConB 12; Lund: Gleerup, 1979). In addition, see G.W.E. Nicklesburg and M. E. Stone, *Faith and Piety in Early Judaism. Texts and Documents* (Philadelphia: Fortress, 1983), 122–30.

16. Apocalyptic writers do not quote the OT explicitly. The Hebrew prophets, in contrast, were constantly calling back to the Torah or wisdom traditions with explicit reference.

17. "Holy ones" is commonly used of angels in Judaism, especially in QL. *hoi hagioi* in Zech. 14:5 are the divine warrior's army (thus, Matt. 16:27; 25:31; Mark 8:38; and 2 Thess. 1:7). In the church, however, *hagioi* came to denote Christians. See R. J. Bauckham, "A Note on a Problem in the Greek Version of 1 Enoch 1.9," *JTS* 32 (1981): 136–38.

18. C. D. Osburn, "The Christological Use of 1 Enoch 1:9 in Jude 14,15," *NTS* 23 (1976/77): 334–41.

19. L. Hartman, *Asking for a Meaning*, 26–40.

20. For the Greek text of 1 Enoch, see M. Black, *The Book of Enoch or 1 Enoch* (Leiden: Brill, 1985).

21. Osburn, "The Christological Use," 335–36, although Osburn does not interact with the christological implications of Jesus' association with Israel based on the variant readings of v 5 (see chap. 2, pp. 55–56). For contrasting arguments on whether Jude was dependent on oral or written traditions, see J. Felton, *Die zwei Briefe des heiligen Petrus und der Judasbrief* (Regensburg: Pustet, 1929), 113, and Th. Schott, *Der zweite Brief Petri und der Brief Judä* (Erlangen: Deichert, 1863), 248. Bauckham ("James, 1 and 2 Peter, Jude," 304) assumes both oral and written are being employed.

22. W. Eichrodt, *Theology of the Old Testament* (OTL; 2 vols.; Philadelphia: Westminster, 1961), 1.464.

23. Ibid., 457. Punitive cancellation through judgment in the OT did not aim at dissolution of covenant, rather it purged the relationship.

24. See, e.g., Amos 5:2,18,20; Isa. 5:30; Ezek. 32:8; Joel 2:1; Amos 5:2; and Zeph. 1:15.

25. W. F. Moulton, A. S. Geden, and H. K. Moulton, *A Concordance to the Greek New Testament* (Edinburgh: Clark, 1978), 576.

26. J.C.H. Laughlin, *A Study of the Motif of Holy Fire in the Old Testament* (Ann Arbor, Mich.: University Microfilms, 1975), iii.

27. Deut. 4:24; 5:25; 9:3; 32:22; Heb. 12:29.

28. The peculiar association between fire and *YHWH*'s holiness, scattered throughout the OT, is well illustrated by Lev. 19:1–6 and Deut. 7:5–6,25.

29. Cf. also 2 Kings 23:15–16. After Achan was judged, Joshua was commanded to burn the city of Ai (Josh. 8:8,19).

30. 4:12,15,33,36; 5:4,22,24,26; 9:10; 10:4.

31. G. Lisowsky, *Konkordanz zum hebräischen Alten Testament* (Stuttgart: Privileg. Württ. Bibelanstalt, 1958), 162–63.

32. E.g., Isa. 1:32; 5:24–25; 31:9; Jer. 4:1–4; Lam. 2:3; Ezek. 20:47–48; Dan. 7:9–10; Hos. 8:14; Joel 2:30–31; Amos 7:4; Obad. 18; Nah. 1:6; Hab. 2:13; Zeph. 1:18; 3:8; Zech. 13:9; and Mal. 3:2.

33. Cf. also Rom. 15:4; Gal. 3:1; and Eph. 3:3.

34. For further predestination terminology in the NT, see Acts 26:5, Rom. 8:29, 11:2, and 1 Pet. 1:20 *(proginōskein);* 1 Pet. 1:2 *(prognōsis);* Acts 2:25, 2:31, 21:29 and Gal. 3:8 *(prooran);* and Acts 4:28, Rom. 8:29, 8:30, 1 Cor. 2:7, Eph. 1:5 and 1:11 *(proorizein).*

35. Cf. also Phil. 4:3.

36. Rom. 15:4; Gal. 3:1; Eph. 3:3; and Jude 4.

37. Cf. G. Schrenk, *"prographō," TDNT* 1 (1964): 770–72, and Fuchs and Reymond, *La Deuxième Épître,* 159.

38. Jewish apocalypses written prior to or shortly after the Christian advent tended to interpret the heavenly tablets solely in terms of judgment, conceiving of them as a record of good and evil deeds. The heavenly books play a quite visible role in 1 Enoch:

> You write down every excess and destruction that will be wrought. . . . Write down every destruction that each . . . shepherd causes, against their records! And read aloud before me each particular case . . . so that this may become a testimony for me against them, so that I might know all the deeds . . ., so that I may evaluate them. (89:61–64)

> I kept seeing till that man, who writes down the names of the shepherds and evaluates them before the Lord of the sheep, came; it is he who helped him and revealed everything. (90:14)

> Then I kept seeing till a throne was erected . . ., and he sat upon it . . . and took all the sealed books and opened those very books in the presence of the Lord of the sheep. (90:20)

> Now, you sinners, even if you say, "All our sins shall not be investigated or written down," nevertheless, all your sins are being written down every day. (104:7)

> As for you, wait patiently until sin passes away, for the names of the sinners shall be blotted out from the Book of Life and the books of the Holy One. (108:7)

> For some of these things were written and sealed above in heaven so that the angels may read them . . . and know that which is about to befall the sinners. (108:7)

as well in QL: e.g., 1QS 7:2; 10:6,8; 1QH 1:24; 1QM 1:13; 12:1–3; CD 3:3;

and 20:19. Although the priests from Jerusalem are specifically noted to have their evil deeds recorded, the heavenly tablets in QL are also positive. There is a book containing the names of some of Israel's past heroes, such as Isaac and Jacob, who are recorded as being "friends of God" (CD 3:3) in addition to the names of community members (1QM 12:2). Having one's name enlisted also meant fellowship with the angels (1QM 12:1–3).

39. This leads out of the normal assumption that Jude is second century.

40. This view, held by Th. Schott (*Der zweite Brief Petri und der Brief Judä* [Erlangen: Deichert, 1863], 205) and Th. Zahn (*Introduction to the New Testament* [Edinburgh: Clark, 1909], 242–43), has for the most part disappeared with the general acceptance of Jude as pre-dating 2 Peter.

41. Contra Bauckham, *Jude, 2 Peter,* 35.

42. On the correspondence of *prographein* in v 4 to *prophēteuein* in v 14 and *prolegein* in v 17, see F. Maier, "Zur Erklärung des Judasbriefes (Jud. 5)," *BZ* 2 (1904): 385–86.

43. Jude's phraseology *krisin megalēs hēmeras* is strongly reminiscent of that found in 1 Enoch: *hē hēmera tēs megalēs tēs kriseōs* (10:6; 84:4; 94:9; 98:10; 99:15; 104:5).

44. In the LXX, *doxa* occurs 445 times (E. Hatch and H. A. Redpath, *A Concordance to the Septuagint and Other Greek Versions of the Old Testament* [2 vols.; Oxford: Clarendon, 1897], 1.341–43). Although *doxa* translates roughly twenty-five Hebrew equivalent terms, *kābôd* constitutes the dominate force behind it. Following LXX usage of the term, the NT contains 154 instances of *doxa* and fifty-nine of the verb form *doxazein* (Moulton, Geden, and Maulton, *a Concordance,* 224–27).

45. See G. Kittel, *"doxa,"* TDNT 2 (1964): 237, and L. H. Brockington, "The Septuagintal Background to the New Testament Use of *DOXA,"* *Studies in the Gospels* (ed. D. E. Nineham; Oxford: Blackwell, 1955), 1–8.

46. Philo (De *specialibus legibus* 1.45) and Clement (*Adumbrationes in epistuli Judae* 1008 [*PG* 3.2080–81]) also refer to the angels as *doxai.*

47. W.M.L. de Wette, *Kurze Erklärung der Briefe des Petrus, Judas und Jakobus* (Leipzig: Hirzel, 1865), 110, used the term "Herrlichkeitsstrahlen."

48. Contra E. Szewc ("'Doxai' in den katholischen Briefen und die qumranische Literatur," *Folia Orientalia* 21 [1980]: 129–40), who cites instances in QL where satan or demonic spirits were cursed, the context in Jude calls for *contrast* (note the connective *homoiōs* which links the contrast in v 7 with v 8). Furthermore, *doxai* serves as a catchword in the epistle.

49. L. Brun, *Segen und Fluch im Urchristentum* (Oslo: Dybwad, 1932), 125. See also J. Scharbert, "'Fluchen' und 'Segnen' im Alten Testament," *Bib* 39 (1958): 1–26.

50. Kelly, *A Commentary,* 262.

51. J. Cantinat, *Les Epîtres de Saint Jacques et de Saint Jude* (Paris: Libraire Lecoffre, 1973), 281.

52. R. H. Charles, ed., *The Ascension of Isaiah* (London: SPCK, 1917), 47. Cf. also Sir. 44:3.

53. The number of occurrences of "despise" in 1 Enoch is considerable.

54. Apostolic preaching reflects the underlying premise that the OT points beyond itself, indeed finding its completion in the NT. Both eras are united by the kingdom of God.

55. B. F. Wescott, *The Epistle to the Hebrews* (London: Macmillan, 1892), 200.

56. G.W.H. Lampe and K. J. Woollcombe, *Essays on Typology* (Naperville, Ill.: Allenson, 1957), 39–40.

57. It is this factor of continuity between testaments which was largely challenged by the rise of modern critical study, predicated on the assumption that that no unity exists in the scriptures. Diversity has been customarily emphasized over unity.

58. See L. Goppelt, *Typos. The Typological Interpretation of the Old Testament in the New* (tr. D. H. Madvig; Grand Rapids, Mich.: Eerdmans, 1982), 1–20, for a helpful discussion of the nature of typology. Although allegory appears alongside typology in the early church's interpretation of the scriptures, it appears infrequently in the NT. Whereas historicity and a literal meaning of the text are inconsequential to the allegorist, who views the scriptures as a vast volume of oracles, riddles, or puzzles that are to be solved, biblical writers concern themselves with the unfolding of salvation-history. Paul, it should be noted, utilizes allegory, yet it is rooted in history.

59. See, e.g., 1 Enoch 91:16; 2 Apoc. Bar. 3:7; 17:2–4; 48:42–7; 54:15; 56:5–16; 4 Ezra 3:4–11; 7:30–1,118; and Apoc. Mos. 28. The writings of Philo contain no trace of eschatology. In his treatment of patriarchal history, for example, one encounters allegory but not typology. Philo is more concerned with a philosophy of living than with an account of redemptive history.

60. In some respects, the typological method as practiced by the Antiochian Christians might appear to be a middle ground between literalistic Jewish exegesis and the allegorizing often associated with Alexandria.

61. See E. K. Lee, "Words Denoting 'Pattern' in the New Testament," *NTS* 8 (1961/62): 166–73.

62. Two other members of this word group occur in the NT: *endeigma* (2 Thess. 1:5) and *antitypos* (Heb. 9:24 and 1 Pet. 3:21).

63. Lee, "Words Denoting " 'Pattern,' " 167.

64. Ibid., 167–68.

65. Jesus, in John 13:15, serves as a *hypodeigma* before the watchful eyes of His disciples: "I have set for you an example so that you do as I have done." The Mosaic tabernacle, according to Heb. 9:23, constituted a model *(hypodeigma)* of heavenly truth: "It was necessary, then, for the pattern of heavenly things to be purified with these sacrifices, but the heavenly things themselves with better sacrifices than these." James reminds his audience of the prophets speaking in the name of the Lord as a *hypodeigma* of patience in the face of suffering (5:10).

66. Occurring only twice in the NT, the verb *paradeigmatizein* is used of Mary in Matt. 1:19 (Joseph did not want to "suggest by example" and thereby disgrace Mary) and believers who have deserted the faith (Heb. 6:6).

67. John 20:25; Acts 7:43,44; 23:25; Rom. 5:14; 6:17; 1 Cor. 10:6,11; Phil. 3:17; 1 Thess. 1:7; 2 Thess. 3:9; 1 Tim. 4:12; Titus 2:7; Heb. 8:5; and 1 Pet. 5:3.

68. Lee, "Words Denoting 'Pattern,' " 171.

69. Two occurrences of *antitypon* are found in the NT: Heb. 9:24 (on the tabernacle's heavenly-earthly correspondence) and 1 Pet. 3:21 (baptism as the antitype which now saves). On the relationship of type to antitype, see C. T. Fritsch, *"TO ANTITYPON,"* Studia Biblica et Semitica. T. C. Vriezen (ed. W. C. Unnik and A. S. van der Woude; Wageningen: Veenman & Zonen, 1966), 100–107.

70. E.g., Christ as the Son of David, the Son of Man (the second Adam and righteous sufferer), the eschatological Prophet, the one greater than Moses, and High Priest after the order of Melchizedek; the Church as the New Israel, the Elect of God, the new Temple, the new creation, a holy priesthood, pilgrims and foreigners, and children of Abraham.

71. B. M. Metzger (*A Textual Commentary on the New Testament* [Stuttgart: UBS,

rev. 1975], 723–24) notes the substantial manuscript evidence supporting *Iēsous* over *theos* or *kyrios*. However, Metzger remarks parenthetically (p. 724) that what kept the committee from adopting this reading was the peculiar theology implied thereby: "Struck by the strange and unparalleled mention of Jesus in a statement about the redemption out of Egypt . . ., copyists would have substituted [*ho*] *kyrios* or *ho theos*." The theology of Stephen is also "strange and unparalleled" (see Acts 7:37–38), proving, in fact, to be unpopular—to ancient and modern man.

72. Sir. 16:5–15.

73. Jub. 20:2–7.

74. 3 Macc. 2:3–7.

75. T.Naph. 2:8–4:3.

76. CD 2:14–3:12.

77. m.Sanh. 10:3.

78. The generation in the wilderness belonged to a select group of paradigms in rabbinic Judaism which possessed no portion in the afterlife (m.Sanh. 10:3).

79. See Bauckham's treatment of the background to vv 5–7 in *Jude, 2 Peter*, pp. 46–47.

80. The use of *pareisdyein* ("to slip in by the side using stealth" or "to worm one's way in" [Kelly, *A Commentary*, 248]) emits a note of contempt on the part of the writer and is reminiscent of the tone in Gal. 2:4: *dia de tous pareisaktous pseudadelphous, hoitines pareisēlthen kataskopēsai tēn eleutherian*. The mode of the *houtoi* is one of undermining. Cf. also 2 Pet. 2:1.

81. Note that Israel is used in Jude while Lot is used in 2 Pet. 2:7. If 2 Peter was a copy of Jude or vice versa, or if the two letters mirror identical occasions, both of which assumptions many are quick to make, it seems strange that Israel would be found in one letter while Lot is found in the other. In truth, Lot represents the *opposite* thesis, namely that God will indeed *rescue*.

82. The *eidotas*, contra Kelly (*A Commentary*, 254), need not be construed as a gnostic counter in the form of a word-play.

83. Lisowsky, *Konkordanz*, 1640–41.

84. J. H. Thayer, *A Greek-English Lexicon of the New Testament* (New York: Harper & Brothers, 1887), 54, and *BAGD*, 80.

85. Cf. also 1 Pet. 3:18.

86. Jude's language here is somewhat reminiscent of that found in 1 Enoch: "I understood what I saw" (1:2), and "About everything I desire to learn" (25:2).

87. C. Guignebert, *The Jewish World in the Time of Jesus* (London: Routledge & Kegan Paul, 1951), 96.

88. Cf. W.O.E. Oesterley, "The Belief in Angels and Demons," *Judaism and Christianity—Vol. 1: The Age of Transition* (ed. W.O.E. Oesterley; London: Sheldon, 1937), 195–96.

89. Of interest is the LXX reading of Deut. 32:8:

> *hote diemerizen ho hypsistos ethnē,*
> *hōs diespeiren huious Adam,*
> *estēsen horia ethnōn*
> *kata arithmon aggelōn theou*

It was a belief of the Jews that each nation was ruled by an angel (cf. Dan. 10:13–21 and 12:1). Yahweh has assigned them spheres of authority and calls them to account. According to Jub. 15:31–32, God has placed over every nation spirits in authority. Ps.–Jon. 2:8, a paraphrase of Deut. 32:8, mentions both seventy angels and seventy sons of Israel. Cf. also Deut. 4:19 and Ps. 89:6.

90. The commonly depicted seven archangels of intertestamental literature, according to J. Strugnell ("The Angelic Liturgy at Qumran, 4Q *Serek Šîrôt ʿOlat Haššabāt," Congress Volume. Oxford—1959* [VTSup 7; Leiden: Brill, 1960], 329), derive from a combination of Ezekiel 9–10 or Tobit and the Semitic love for the number seven.

91. On the development of Michael's stature in postexilic Jewish thinking, see J. P. Rohland, *Der Erzengel Michael, Arzt und Feldherr: zwei Aspekte des vor- und frühbabylonishen Michaelskultes* (Leiden: Brill, 1977).

92. See L. Leuken, "Michael," *RGG*, 4.369–70. Cf. also E.A.W. Budge, *Saint Michael the Archangel: Three Encomiums* (London: Kegan Paul, Trench, Trubner & Co., 1894).

93. *Paedagogus* 3.2 (*GCS* 12.237–44).

94. The linkage itself is not mistaken, rather *how* the two verses traditionally have been linked is.

95. T. F. Glasson, *Greek Influence in Jewish Eschatology* (London: SPCK, 1961), 57–58.

96. See the discussion of v 7 in "Sodom and Gomorrah" in this chapter.

97. E.g., 1 Enoch 6–10, T.Reu. 5:5–6; T.Dan. 5:6; Jub. 5:1; 2 Apoc. Bar. 56:12–16; CD 3:4; Jos. *Ant.* 1.3.1. In Philo (*Homiliae in Ezechielem* 4.1.11–25), the fall is attributed to pride.

98. "Midrash" is here being used in the sense of application of a text to a contemporary theological problem.

99. 1 Enoch seems to be the first Jewish work identifying demons with fallen angels. These are two hundred in number (6:5), organized into groups of ten (6:7). Their leader is variously referred to as Satan, Belial, Massema, Sammael, Malkira, Beelzebub, and Azazel.

100. Cf. P. S. Alexander, "The Targumim and Early Exegesis of 'Sons of God' in Genesis 6," *JJS* 23 (1972): 60.

101. M. Green, *The Second Epistle General*, 164.

102. Noting the presence of two words from Jude 6—*desmoi and zophos*—in Hesiod's *Theogony*, T. F. Glasson (*Greek Influence*, 63–67) argues that the second-century B.C. apocalypticist may well have drawn from the Greek lore of the Titans. For further comparison of Jude 6 and 1 Enoch, see R. Rubinkiewicz, *Die Eschatologie von Henoch 9–11 und das Neue Testament* (ÖBS 6; Klosterneuburg: Österreichisches Katholisches Bibelwerk, 1984), 128–33.

103. Or, did Jude indeed accept these statements as scriptural (=inspired) and authoritative? By noting commentary on Jude from the last one hundred years, one is left with the conclusion that critical scholarship holds Jude to be remarkably undiscerning! See also n. 105.

104. Although the Enochic portrait of the Watchers is more elaborate, the Twelve and Jubilees have the core elements in common with 1 Enoch: male "watchers" beholding human females, incurred judgment, abnormal births resulting from co-habitation, and destructive giant offspring. According to Hesiod, Zeus had three thousand "guardians" *(phylakes)* who watched mortal men.

105. It is broadly assumed, indeed taken as virtually certain, that Jude's attitude toward Jewish pseudepigrapha—an attitude which might seem quite different from that of the other NT writers—was one of high esteem. Such an assumption (a supposition which eliminates any distinction between apostolic writings and other first-century literature) made of a NT writer simply does not hold up. While it is true, as B. Metzger ("Literary Forgeries and Canonical

Pseudepigrapha," *New Testament Studies—Philological, Versional, and Patristic* [Leiden: Brill, 1980], 19–20) has pointed out, that sacred writers employed any contemporary literary form as long as it was not inconsistent with truth, the latter part of Metzger's statement needs to be remembered in balancing his assertion. That Jude would have accepted all of 1 Enoch 6–36, for example, as being true is a rather low estimate of apostolic discernment. The significance of Paul's allusion in 2 Tim. 3:8 to Jannes and Jambres does not require that he viewed the underlying tradition as historical. Rather, the tradition, obviously known to Timothy, fits the occasion because it illustrates a point. It should be noted that John's Revelation, qualifying generically as an apocalypse, demonstrates the distinction between apocalyptic form and content, Jewish tradition and Christian revelation, apocalyptic language and redemptive-eschatological essence (contra J. J. Collins, "Pseudonymity, Historical Reviews and the Genre of the Apocalypse of John," *CBQ* 39 [1977]: 342, who views these differences as "superficial" and insignificant). John's vision contains no *ex eventu* prophecy, nor is it pseudonymous. The writing, furthermore, is not a secret, esoteric work. It has an epistolary framework, with the recipients named; John's visions constitute the revelation of Jesus Christ for Christian communities in Asia Minor. Most importantly, "the Lamb" is the focus of John's visions throughout—not merely the horned lamb of Jewish apocalyptic writings, rather the Lion-Lamb who mysteriously takes part in the sacrifice for the sins of God's people and who still carries the mark of slaughter at the neck, even in heaven (an image which would have been highly offensive to mainstream *or* sectarian eschatological thinking). In the NT Apocalypse we are witnesses to the heights of Christian theology.

106. Rom. 8:38.

107. The origin of Christian theology, contra E. Käsemann ("The Beginnings of Christian Theology," *New Testament Questions of Today* [Philadelphia: Fortress, 1969], 82–107), lies not with apocalyptic—be it Jewish or primitive Christian—but in the kerygma of Christ crucified and risen, as E. Lohse ("Apokalyptik und Christologie," *ZNW* 62 [1971]: 58, reproduced in *Die Einheit des Neuen Testaments. Exegetische Studien zur Theologie des Neuen Testaments* [Göttingen: Vandenhoeck & Ruprecht, 1973], 125–44) has argued. It lies in the word of the cross and is buttressed by the OT scriptures. A critique of Käsemann's view can be found in I. H. Marshall, "Is Apocalyptic the Mother of Christian Theology?" *Tradition and Interpretation in the New Testament. Essays in Honor of E. E. Ellis for His 60th Birthday* (ed. G. F. Hawthorne and O. Betz; Grand Rapids, Mich./Tübingen: Eerdmans/ Mohr, 1978), 33–42.

108. F. Dexinger, *Sturz der Gottessöhne oder Engel vor der Sinflut?* (WBT 13; Wien: Herder, 1966), 90.

109. To assume that Jude highly esteemed 1 Enoch, a position virtually taken for granted by commentators, presupposes a commitment to the view that little or no distinction exists between the NT writers and their Jewish apocalyptic contemporaries. Why are the other NT writers not quoting from intertestamental Jewish writings? Why was John the Baptist, who well may have had close contact with Jewish sectaries and whose message of "the Coming One" was filled with eschatological import, not quoting 1 Enoch as one would expect?

110. M. E. Stone, "The Book of Enoch and Judaism in the Third Century B.C.E." *CBQ* 40 (1978): 479–92.

111. The bulk of commentaries begins with the automatic assumptions that (1) the *bĕnē hāʾĕlōhîm* of Gen. 6:1–4 are angels, (2) the sin of the demons is sexual, and (3) Jude is drawing from the Genesis 6 account. These force upon Jude an acceptance of Jewish apocalyptic theology without distinguishing between apoc-

alyptic *content* and *mode*. Jude's teaching is *not* 1 Enoch's. The angels of Jude 6 are *not* necessarily the Watchers of 1 Enoch, the Testaments of the Twelve Patriarchs, and Jubilees, even though Jude is manifestly exploiting Jewish apocalyptic language and imagery. While the sin of the angels in 1 Enoch is sexual, in Jude it relates to *authority* and privilege. Bauckham (*Jude, 2 Peter*, 50–51) fails to distinguish between Jude's use of apocalyptic imagery and motifs and Jude's own theology, as does Kelly (*A Commentary*, 257), and as did J. B. Mayor (*The Epistle*, clviii–clxvi) some eighty years ago. G. E. Closen (*Die Sünde der "Sohne Gottes"* [Rom: Päpstliches Bibelinstitut, 1937], 75–216) and A.F.J. Klijn ("Jude 5 and 7," *The New Testament Age. Essays in Honor of Bo Reicke* [2 vols.; ed. W. C. Weinrich; Macon, Ga.: Mercer University, 1984], 1.238–41) are among the few who have recognized this distinction. The literature on Gen. 6:1–4 is as varied as it is voluminous. Essentially, three interpretations are held as to the identity of the *běnē hāʾělōhîm* in Gen. 6:1–4. They are (1) "sons of Seth," (2) "nobles," or (3) fallen angels. For representative views, see O. Gruppe, "War Genes. 6,1–4 ursprünglich mit der Sinflut verbunden?" *ZAW* 9 (1989): 135–60; H. Kaupel, *Die Dämonen im Alten Testament* (Augsburg: Filser, 1930), 131–39; E. G. Kraeling, "The Significance and Origin of Gen 6:1–4," *JNES* 6 (1947): 193–208; B. Childs, *Myth and Reality in the Old Testament* (Naperville, Ill.: Allenson, 1960), 48–55; F. Dexinger, *Sturz der Gottessöhne oder Engel vor der Sinflut?* (WBT 13; Wien: Herder, 1966), 45–58; U. Cassuto, "The Episode of the Sons of God and the Daughters of Men," *Biblical and Oriental Studies* (2 vols.; Jerusalem: Magnes, 1973), 1.18ff; J. W. Rogerson, *Myth in Old Testament Interpretation* (Berlin/New York: de Gruyter, 1974); and W. Van Gemeren, "The Sons of God in Genesis 6:1–4," *WTJ* 43 (1980/81): 320–48.

112. For the apocalypticist the Flood had cut off generations in terms of knowledge and understanding. Some scholars have conjectured that remains from an ancient Book of Noah (see M. E. Stone, "Books of Noah," *EncJud* 12.1198) were used in 1 Enoch 6–10,65–69,106–7 as well as Jub. 7 and 10. E. Kautzsch (*Die Apokryphen und Pseudepigrapha des Alten Testaments* [2 vols.; Tübingen: Mohr, 1900], 2.227) inspired R. H. Charles (*The Book of Enoch* [Oxford: Clarendon, 1912], xlvi) to advance this theory. Cf. also D. Barthelemy and J. T. Milik, *Discoveries in the Judean Desert, Qumran Cave 1* (Oxford: Clarendon, 1955), 84, and J. Starcky, "Cave 4 of Qumran," *BA* 19 (1956): 94–96. Opposing this view are C. C. Torrey (*The Apocryphal Literature* [New Haven, Conn.: Yale University, 1948], 112) and S. B. Frost (*Old Testament Apocalyptic* [London: Epworth, 1952], 166).

113. For a comprehensive study of Noah and the Flood motif as it appears in Jewish literature, see J. P. Lewis, *A Study of the Interpretation of Noah and the Flood in Jewish and Christian Literature* (Leiden: Brill, 1968).

114. Conversely, 2 Peter mentions Noah and the Flood but omits any reference to Enoch. This can be attributed not to 2 Peter's expurgation of material in Jude (the commonly held view), but rather to a tailoring of the material to the particular needs of the audience.

115. The Testament of Adam, dating between the second and fifth centuries A.D., depicts the Flood as the result of the sins of the daughters of Cain. In this work, the most prominent feature is its angelology. In chap. 4 a heavenly hierarchy, not unlike that depicted in 1 Enoch, of nine levels is described in ascending order:

"angels":   the lowest order; accompanying every living human being for protection

"archangels":   executing order in the created universe
"archons":   affecting the weather
"authorities":   administration of light from the solar phenomena
"powers":   containing demonic forces
"dominions":   ruling over kingdoms of the earth
"thrones":   guarding the gate to the Holy of Holies
"seraphim":   serving the inner chamber of the Lord
"cherubim":   serving the throne of God

Although the apostle Paul uses some of these terms (e.g., Eph. 1:21; 2:2; 6:12; and Col. 1:15), these levels are unimportant. His emphasis is that the principalities and powers are *all* subject to Christ.

116. These are generally dated between the second century B.C. and the seventh century A.D.

117. Or, daughter-in-law (J. J. Collins, "Sibylline Oracles," *Old Testament Pseudepigrapha—Vol. 1: Apocalyptic Literature and Testaments* [Garden City, N.Y.: Doubleday, 1983], 322).

118. For a more thorough discussion of this background, see Glasson, *Greek Influence,* 59–67.

119. This is a term used by M. Delcor, "Le Mythe de la chute des anges et de l'origine des géants comme explication du mal dans le monde dans l'apocalyptique juive. Histoire des traditions," *RHR* 190 (1976): 53. Delcor contrasts the writers of the OT, who, confronted with Canaanite mythological traditions, chose to integrate motifs into their writings without incorporating pagan pantheistic theology and Jewish apocalyptic writers, who, through syncretism, "remythologized" or fused pagan with Jewish theology.

120. In Jub. 10:8 Satan is "Prince of the spirits" (cf. Eph. 2:2: *ho archōn tēs exousias tou aeros*). In T.Dan 5:6 and T.Sim. 2:7, he is *ho archōn* and *ho archōn tēs planēs.*

121. Origen, *Paedagogus* 3.2, in Stählin, vol. 10.

122. G. Aulen, *Christus Victor* (New York: Macmillan, 1956) 111, and J. W. Boyd, *Satan and Māra* (SHR 27; Leiden: Brill, 1975), 39.

123. G. B. Caird, *Principalities and Powers* (Oxford: Clarendon, 1956), 31.

124. Note, for example, the reference in Isa. 14:13 to Mount Zaphon, the seat of the Canaanite deity. The use in 14:14 of *ʾēl ʾelyôn* would help confirm its Canaanite background. Cf. T. H. Robinson, "Hebrew Myths," *Myth and Ritual* (ed. S. H. Hooke; London: Oxford, 1933), 183; B. S. Childs, *Myth and Reality in the Old Testament* (Naperville, Ill.: Allenson, 1960), 68–69; and R. J. Clifford, *The Cosmic Mountain in Canaan and the Old Testament* (Cambridge, Mass.: Harvard University, 1972), 160.

125. The man of lawlessness in 2 Thess. 2:4 makes a similar claim: *apodeiknynta heauton hoti estin theos.*

126. Cf. T.Naph. 3:3: "The gentiles, because they wandered astray and forsook the Lord, have changed the order . . ., patterning themselves after wandering spirits *(pneumasi planēs)."*

127. See P. D. Hanson, "Rebellion in Heaven, Azazel, and Euhemeristic Heroes in 1 Enoch 6–11," *JBL* 96 (1977): 208. Some would see in Rev. 12 a parallel to the Akkadian Creation Epic, with Michael taking the place of Marduk and the dragon as a substitute for Tiamat (for the text, see J. B. Pritchard, ed., *The Ancient Near East. An Anthology of Texts and Pictures* (2 vols.; Princeton, N.J.: Princeton University, 1958), 1.31–9).

128. It is employed in vv 1, 6 (twice), 13, and 21. A strengthened form of the

tērein, phylassein, is used in the doxology (v 24).

129. Philo, *Quaestiones et solutiones in Genesim* 4.51.

130. Josephus, *J.W.* 5.566.

131. Cf. Gen. Rab. 27:3.

132. m.Sanh. 10:3.

133. Cf. 1 Enoch 67:12: "This verdict by which the angels are being punished is itself a *deigma* to the kings and rulers who control the world."

134. Philo and Josephus write that even in their day smoke was still rising from the earth (*De Abrahamo* 140–41 and *De vita Mosis* 2.56; *J.W.* 4.483).

135. The LXX uses *ekporneuein* of Tamar in Gen. 38:24 and of the Canaanites who "prostitute" themselves to their gods (Exod. 24:15).

136. I.e., a lust that gluts *(ek)* itself.

137. Most commentaries on Jude focus solely on the relationship between vv 6 and 7 and not vv 5, 6, and 7 *taken together.*

138. Rather than interpreting *ekporneusasai* alone, the participle should be taken together with *apelthousai,* thus allowing the emphasis to be on the *departure,* not merely the nature of the sin.

139. This has been rightly observed by A. Lods, "La Chute des anges," *RHPR* 7 (1927): 301.

140. On the use of *pyr aiōnion,* see 4 Macc. 12:12 and Philo, *De Abrahamo* 138–41.

141. M. Green (*The Second Epistle General,* 166–67) rightly notes this thread in vv 5–7.

142. Michael is *ho aggelos ho megas* in Dan. 10:13,21; 12:1; 1 Enoch 20:5; 40:4–9; 2 Enoch 22:6; 33:10; and As. Mos. 10:2.

143. Origen (*De principiis* 3.2 [*GCS* 5.244]) is the first to indicate that the tradition behind Jude 9 derives from the "Assumption of Moses" (*Analēpsis Mōÿseōs*).

144. A statement of interest by Paul is found in 1 Tim. 1:20. Regarding certain individuals whose faith has been shipwrecked, he says that he has "handed them over to Satan to be taught not to blaspheme."

145. The verb *diaballein* means literally "to throw across," hence, "to attack," "to accuse," or "to slander."

146. Cf., e.g., W. Eichrodt, *Theology of the Old Testament* (OTL; 2 vols.; Philadelphia: Westminster, 1967), 2.205–6. Satan's generic depiction in Job as one of the *běnē hā'ělōhîm,* who performs the work of a district attorney, is owing more to the *genre* of the book than to a precise representation of his spiritual character. The book of Job is not merely a spate of mournful reflections strung together treating the existential problem of why man must suffer. The speech throughout much of the book—between Job and the three friends, between Job and Elihu, and between Job and God—is disputational. Disputation is essentially forensic in character. Hence, the portrayal of the heavenly characters in this drama is deliberately colored by the *courtroom.*

147. Although many represent this view, it is perhaps best articulated by Boyd, *Satan,* 13–67.

148. In 2 Peter only Balaam is mentioned.

149. t.Soṭa 4.9.

150. Consider the use of the prophetic woe-cry by Jesus (11:21; 18:7; 23:13,15,16,23,25,27,29; 24:19; 26:24; Mark 14:21; Luke 6:24,25,26; 10:13; 11:42,43,44,46; 21:23; 22:22). Cf. also 1 Cor. 9:16; Rev. 8:13; 11:14; 12:12; 16:19; and 18:10.

151. N. M. Sarna, *Understanding Genesis* (New York: Schocken, 1966), 28.

152. Cf. Heb. 11:4.

153. B. K. Waltke, "Cain and His Offering," *WJT* 48 (1986): 369.

154. A. Lapple, *Key Problems of Genesis* (Glen Rock, N.J.: Paulist, 1967), 90–92.

155. Philo, *De posteritate Caini,* 35. On the tendency within Judaism to formulate stereotypes of orthodoxy and heterodoxy, see N. Brox, "Häresie," *RAC* 13 (1984): 248–97.

156. *Ant.* 1.52ff.

157. m.Sanh. 4:5.

158. M. Jastrow, *A Dictionary of the Targumim, the Talmud Babli and Yerushalmi, and the Midrashic Literature—Vol. 1* (Brooklyn, N.Y.: Traditional, 1903), 1362.

159. For examples, see J. A. Eisenmenger, *Entdecktes Judenthum* (2 vols.; Königsberg in Preussen: n.p., 1711), 1.832 and 2.428.

160. Philo, *De posteritate Caini* 38; also *De sacrificis Abelis et Caini* 1.2,3 and 13.52.

161. See, e.g., G. Vermes, *Scripture and Tradition* (Leiden: Brill, 1973), 127–77.

162. Note the connection between the announcement of judgment and the curse in Numbers 22–24 as well as the effective power acknowledged in both the curse and the blessing. The Moabite king says to Balaam: "A people has come out of Egypt; they cover the face of the land and have settled next to me. Come now and put a curse on these people. . . . Perhaps then I will be able to defeat them and drive them out of the country. For I know that those you bless are blessed, and those you curse are cursed." Cf. also Gen. 9:25 ("Cursed be Canaan. . . . May Canaan be the slave of Shem"). For a thorough examination of blessing and curse, see L. Brun, *Segen und Fluch im Urchristentum* (Oslo: Dybwad, 1932), and H. C. Brichto, *The Problem of "Curse" in the Hebrew Bible* (SBLMS 13; Philadelphia, Pa.: SBL, 1963).

163. Brichto, *The Problem of "Curse,"* 10–11.

164. *Ant.* 4.6.13.

165. m.ʾAbot 5:19.

166. Note the further word-play in v 13 *(asteres planētai).* Of interest is the frequency with which *planē* is used in the Testament of the Twelve Patriarchs; it occurs a total of twenty-five times (M. de Jonge, *The Testaments of the Twelve Patriarchs* [Leiden: Brill, 1978] 240), most of which are an allusion to a "spirit of deceit" or "spirits of deceit."

167. Kelly, *A Commentary,* 268.

168. 2 Pet. 2:15. In Rev. 2:14, Balaam is associated with defilement.

169. m.Sanh. 10:3.

170. R. J. Clifford, "The Use of *HÔY* in the Prophets," *CBQ* 28 (1966): 464.

171. Ibid., 458–64; G. Wanke, "ʾôy and hôy." *ZAW* 78 (1966): 215–18; C. Westermann, *Basic Forms of Prophetic Speech* (Philadelphia: Westminster, 1967), 190–92; J. G. Williams, "The Alas-Oracles of the Eighth-Century Prophets," *HUCA* 38 (1967): 75–91; W. Schottroff, *Der altisraelitische Fluchspruch* (WMANT 30; Neukirchen-Vluyn: Neukirchener, 1969), 112–20; W. Janzen, *Mourning Cry and Woe Oracle* (BZAW 125; Berlin/New York: de Gruyter, 1972), 64, 83–87; and H.-J. Krause, "*hôj* als prophetische Leichenklage über das eigene Volk," *ZAW* 85 (1973): 16–19.

172. Cf. also Jeremiah 9, in which we find the mourning song with the appearance of women as a significant part. On the funerary setting, see Clifford, "The Use of *HÔY,*" 459–63, and Janzen, *Mourning Cry,* 2–26. While Clifford and Janzen agree over the actual *Sitz im Leben* of *hôy*—mourning in a funerary context—they differ as to precisely when the woe-cry took on a denunciatory character. At any rate, this view, associating the woe-cry with a funerary setting,

is to be preferred over those offered by E. Gerstenberger (The Woe-Oracles," 250–51), G. Wanke, ("'oy and hôy," 215), and Westermann (Basic Forms, 190–92), who advocate that the woe-cry derives from a forecast of doom. The use of hôy, however, should not be too tightly restricted, since the prophets used and expanded it to suit their needs. 'ôy is found in historical narrative, wisdom literature, and hymnic material of the OT, while hôy, with one exception (1 Kings 13:30), is found only in the prophetic corpus.

173. Janzen, Mourning Cry, 35–39.

174. Ibid., 27. Aside from Jude, another use of the woe-cry in the NT is useful for the sake of illustration. Consider the seven woes by Jesus in Matthew 23 which are brought against Israel's leaders, viz., the "scribes and Pharisees" (vv 13,15,16,23,25,27, and 29). In the view of Jesus, these who exercised the greatest amount of influence on Israel were past the point of change. This is not mere "sorrowful pity." Although there is an element of grief inherent to the moment (e.g., 23:37–38), Jesus is foremost exhibiting wrath, similar to the OT prophets. The tenor of Matthew 23 indicates that Jesus' opponents are intractible; they will not change. Hence, they are "blind guides," "fools," "snakes," and "a generation of vipers." As hypokritai, opheis, and echidnai (vv 13,15,23,25,27,29, and 33), they are unconditionally condemned. Thus, Matthew 23 is probably imprecatory, in light of the increasing vengeance pattern of hôy already noted. Verse 32–33 would indicate that Jesus sees them running their course. There are specific reasons for the prophetic denunciation. Characteristic behavior that calls for their sentence includes:

• shutting the kingdom of heaven to others (v 13)
• going to any length to gain a proselyte, then making him "twice the son of hell" as they (v 15)
• distorting the use of oaths and vows (vv 16–22)
• ignoring "weightier matters of the law" while trifling over minute detail (vv 23–24)
• putting on an outward show of piety while being thoroughly wicked and corrupt on the inside (vv 25–28)
• demonstrating a show of reverence for the prophets of the past whom their forefathers murdered, when in fact they were a like brood of vipers (vv 29–36).

Matthew 23, then, illustrates the vengeance and reversal motifs under discussion. Israel's spiritual leaders stand guilty; their hands are tainted with blood (vv 30–31). What immediately follows the woe-oracles in 23:38–24:2 could in some respects be considered "day of the Lord" imagery. Calamity is imminent; destruction is affirmed.

It is worthy of note as well that the woe-oracle occurs frequently in 1 Enoch. The significance of this for Jude is the clear maledictory context in which the woe-cries arise. Thirty-two times in the work a woe-cry appears—a density exceeding that of any OT canonical book. In line with Jude's borrowing of (1) a theophany-statement, (2) specific theological motifs, (3) phraseology, as well as (4) abundant imagery from 1 Enoch, all of which are effective in engaging his readers, some of whom may well have been devoted to Enochic literature, the use of a woe-cry supplies further ammunition with which to condemn the houtoi.

175. H.-J. Krause, "hôj als prophetische Leichenklage über das eigene Volk," ZAW 85 (1973): 44.

176. See chap. 2.

177. See chap. 2.

CHAPTER 5. THE USE OF EXTRABIBLICAL SOURCE MATERIAL IN JUDE

1. Rowston, "Neglected," 555.

2. The subject of the Jewish matrix of Christian origins has been sufficiently treated in chapter 3.

3. An excellent study of the methods of technique in Hebrew poetry is W.G.E. Watson's *Classical Hebrew Poetry. A Guide to Its Techniques* (JSOTSS 26; Sheffield: JSOT, 1984).

4. Normally labeled "late Judaism" by most scholars, this period is designated by J. H. Charlesworth (*The Old Testament Pseudepigrapha and the New Testament. Prolegomena for the Study of Christian Origins* [SNTSMS 54; Cambridge: Cambridge University, 1985], 59) as "early Judaism" in that it represents the beginnings of synagogal Judaism, i.e., a new phase.

5. For at least one hundred years the view has enjoyed almost unquestioned status that the limits to the Hebrew canon were not established until the end of the first century A.D., i.e., well after use by Jesus, the apostles, and the NT writers. R. Beckwith, in *The Old Testament Canon of the New Testament Church and Its Background in Early Judaism* (Grand Rapids, Mich.: Eerdmans, 1985), esp. 274–337, has argued persuasively for the recognition of a canonical shape as early as the second century B.C. See also N. Geisler, "The Extent of the Old Testament Canon," *Current Issues in Biblical and Patristic Interpretation. Festschrift M. Tenney* (ed. G. F. Hawthorne; Grand Rapids, Mich.: Eerdmans, 1975), 31–46.

6. Among the many works devoted to the use of the OT in the NT are D. M. Turpie, *The New Testament View of the Old* (London: Hodder and Stoughton, 1872); C. H. Dodd, *According to the Scriptures. The Substructure of New Testament Theology* (London: Nisbet, 1952); E. E. Ellis, *Paul's Use of the Old Testament* (Edinburgh: Oliver and Boyd, 1957); idem, *Prophecy and Hermeneutic in Early Christianity* (WUNT 18; Tübingen: Mohr, 1978); R. T. France, *Jesus and the Old Testament. His Application of Old Testament Passages to Himself and His Mission* (London: Tyndale, 1971); R. Longenecker, *Biblical Exegesis in the Apostolic Period* (Grand Rapids, Mich.: Eerdmans, 1975); S. L. Johnson, *The Old Testament in the New. An Argument for Biblical Inspiration* (Grand Rapids, Mich.: Zondervan, 1980); A. T. Hanson, *The Living Utterances of God. The New Testament Exegesis of the Old* (London: Darton, Longman and Todd, 1983); and W. C. Kaiser, Jr., *The Use of the Old Testament in the New Testament* (Chicago: Moody, 1985).

7. Beckwith, *The Old Testament Canon,* 11.

8. E.g., not one of the books of the Apocrypha is cited in the NT as scripture. Not a few early fathers—including Melito, Origen, Cyril, and Athanasius—rejected these works. Interestingly, Augustine's acceptance of apocryphal books was confuted by Jerome, his contemporary. What is applied here in principle to the Apocrypha applies to the Pseudepigrapha as well.

9. Charlesworth, *The Old Testament Pseudepigrapha,* 74.

10. This is not to say, however, that the Jewish works of the intertestamental era have no historical, theological or literary value or relationship to the NT.

11. The basic threefold arrangement of the OT scriptures predates rabbinic Judaism. The prologue to the work Ecclesiasticus (ca. mid second century B.C.)

refers to "the Law and the Prophets and the Other Ancestral Books/the Rest of the Books."

12. NT formulations for an OT canon are essentially sevenfold: "the Law of Moses and the Prophets and the Psalms" (Luke 24:44); "the Law and the Prophets" (Matt. 5:17, Luke 16:16, John 1:45, Acts 24:14, 28:23, Rom. 3:21); "Moses and the Prophets" (Luke 16:29); "the Law" (1 Cor. 14:21); "the holy scriptures" (2 Tim. 3:15); "the scripture(s)" (used fifty-one times); and "the words of God" (Rom. 3:2 and Heb. 5:12). The outcome of this is that by the last two centuries B.C. the canon had become a sufficiently unified body of sacred literature so that it warranted certain comprehensive titles. The authority-formula "it is written" commonly employed in the NT is not used with reference to apocryphal works.

13. For a fuller discussion of the structure of the Hebrew canon within mainstream as well as sectarian Judaism at the advent of the Christian era, see Beckwith, *The Old Testament Canon*, 105–273.

14. See, e.g., specific evidences of Enochic phraseology which compare closely with material in the Gospels, Acts, Pauline epistles, the general epistles as well as the Revelation in R. H. Charles, ed., *The Apocrypha and Pseudepigrapha of the Old Testament* (2 vols.; Oxford: Clarendon, 1913), 1.180–81.

15. Verse 21 informs that "all the Athenians and foreigners who lived there spent their time doing nothing but speculating about and listening to the latest ideas."

16. t.Sukka 3:11. Cf. also *Bib. Ant.* 10:7 and 11:14 (late first-century) in addition to Tg. Ps.–J. Num 20:2; 22:15; b.Sabb. 351; Midr. Num. 1:2; 19:26; and m., Abot 5:6.

17. The names of these two figures are rendered in a variety of ways so that tracing them in tradition becomes exceedingly difficult. See H. Odeberg, "*Iannēs, Iambrēs*," *TDNT* 3 (1965): 192–93.

18. Gospel of Nicodemus 5.

19. Pliny, *Historia naturalis* 30.1.

20. Tg. Yer.I Exod 1:15 and 7:11; Exod. Rab. 7 and 9; b. Menaḥot 85a; and Yal. Exod 14:24.

21. Twice in his commentary on Matthew (23:37 and 27:8), Origen alludes to Jannes et Mambres liber (*PG* 17.230, 243).

22. Eusebius, *Praeparatio evangelium* 9.8 (*GCS* 8/1.494).

23. For enumeration, see M. R. James, *The Lost Apocrypha of the Old Testament* (London: SPCK, rep. 1936), 31–38.

24. R. Bloch, "Note méthodologique pour l'étude de la littérature rabbinique," *RSR* 43 (1955): 224.

25. See, for example, the discussion of the proverbial character of the Cretans in W. Barclay, *The Letters to Timothy, Titus and Philemon* (DSB; rev. ed.; Philadelphia: Westminster, 1975), 243.

26. In *The Histories* (LCL; tr. W.R. Paton; Cambridge, Mass.: Harvard University, 1960), 285, Polybius writes: "For, as a fact, this young man was not at all Cretan in character but had escaped the contagion of Cretan ill-breeding."

27. Cretism is defined as "the practice of lying or falsehood" (*Webster's New International Dictionary of the English Language* [2d ed.; Springfield, Mass.: Merriam, 1942], 624). As with the Corinthians, for whose life-style the word "corinthianize" was coined, the Cretans provided inspiration for coinage of "cretize" (*krētizein*), which meant "to lie and cheat."

28. Hymn to Jove 8 and Hymn to Zeus 1. The latter is a response to the

popular notion that Crete was perceived as being inferior. According to Cretan legend, Zeus was buried there (for both Greek and English versions of the text, see *Callimachus—Hymns and Epigrams. Lycophron* [LCL; tr. G. R. Mair; Cambridge, Mass.: Harvard University, 1969], 37ff).

29. *Theogony* 26: *poimenes agrauloi, kak' elegchea, gasteres oion*. On the role of Epimenides who lived in Crete, with whom the legend of the "Unknown God" (cf. Acts 17:23) is attached, see F. J. Foakes-Jackson and K. Lake, *The Beginnings of Christianity* (5 vols.; London: Macmillan, 1920–1933), 5.247–49.

30. Cicero, *De divinus* 1.18.

31. Luther's perplexity over these verses was thusly expressed: "Das ist ein wunderlicher Text und finsterer Spruch, als freilich einer im Neuen Testament ist, dass ich noch nicht gewiss weiss, was S. Peter meint" (*WA* 12, 367).

32. Free translation.

33. The judicious words of W. J. Dalton, a Jesuit scholar, from whose thorough investigation of these verses any student of the NT would benefit, are worth repeating: "the difficulty of the text lies not in the thought of the author, which is neither odd nor fantastic, but in our ignorance of his background and field of reference . . . studies in later Jewish apocryphal writings and in early Jewish-Christian literature reveal a whole world of ideas which was powerfully at work, all the more so because simply taken for granted, in the writers of the New Testament. The exegete . . . must try to immerse himself as deeply as possible in the mental atmosphere of the biblical writer, his pre-suppositions, his categories of thought, his literary conventions" (*Christ's Proclamation to the Spirits: A Study of 1 Peter 3:18–4:6* [Rome: Pontifical Biblical Institute, 1965], 7–9).

34. The verb *poreutheis* occurs twice—in vv 19 and 22.

35. Note the correspondence between the "spirits in prison" (v 19) and the "angels and principalities and powers" (v 22).

36. In Jewish tradition, significantly, two paradigms of righteousness stand out from the OT: Noah and Enoch.

37. For a survey of the history of the interpretation of this passage, see W. Bieder, *Die Vorstellung von der Höllenfahrt Jesu Christi* (Zürich: Zwingli, 1949), 145–97; W. J. Dalton, *Christ's Proclamation*, 15–41; also, more recently, J. S. Feinberg, "1 Peter 3:18–20, Ancient Mythology, and the Intermediate State," *WTJ* 48 (1986): 306–12. For a survey of variations of the "human" line of interpretation, see Feinberg, pp. 306–36, as well as W. Grudem, "Christ Preaching through Noah: 1 Peter 3:19–20 in the Light of Dominant Themes in Jewish Literature," *TrinJ* 7 (1986): 3–31, both of which share the same approach to these verses.

38. The view of spirits as demonic angels would probably have been taken for granted in the first century due to its prominence in Jewish apocalyptic literature and thus would appear to be the oldest interpretation. The view that Christ preached to Noah's contemporaries seems to have prevailed among the church fathers up to the time of Augustine—e.g., Clement, *Stromata* 6.6 (*PG* 9, 268–9); *Adumbrationes* (*PG* 9, 731); Origen, *De principiis* 2.5 (*GCS* 5.132–39); *Adversus Celsius* 2.42 (*PG* 11, 864); Cyril, *Lectiones* (*PG* 74, 456); John of Damascus, *De descensu ad inferos* (*PG* 94, 1101); Athanasius, *Epistula ad Epictetum* (*PG* 26, 1060); and Augustine, *Epistolae* (*PL* 33, 715ff). Irenaeus, in his commentary on 1 Peter recorded in *Adversus haeresis* (4.22.1; 4.27.2; 5.31.1), is silent on 3:19 (*PG* 7, 1046, 1058, 1208–9). One is tempted to conjecture whether this view of v 19 was owing to the same reason that Jude, in some parts of the church, encountered difficulties in being recognized, namely, an increasing wariness toward apocalyptic or pseudepigraphal works. (A fuller discussion of patristic

exegesis of 3:19–20 is found in A. Grillmeier, "Der Gottessohn im Totenreich," *ZKT* 71 [1949]: 1–53.) In the medieval and Reformation eras interpretation of these verses essentially proceeded along the same lines as that of the patristic era, not deviating substantially from an Augustinian approach. Without question the greatest divergence in interpretation of these verses has been in the post-Enlightenment era. While the Augustinian view has been perpetuated in one form or another by some, others have ascribed the background of 3:19–20 to pagan mythology or fantasy. Yet others—and they are not a few—argue that these verses teach of Christ's going to preach to demonic spirits to proclaim triumph and universal conquest over them. Among those exegetes embracing the human souls view are Th. Zahn, *Introduction to the New Testament* (3 vols.; Edinburgh; Clark, 1909), 2.289; G. Wohlenberg, *Der erste und zweite Petrusbrief und der Judasbrief* (Leipzig: Deichert, 1923), 106–15; C.E.B. Cranfield, *The First Epistle of Peter* (London: SCM, 1950), 84–85; idem, "The Interpretation of 1 Peter iii.19 and iv.6," *ExpTim* 69 (1957/58): 369–72; D. Guthrie, *New Testament Theology* (Leicester/Downers Grove, Ill.: Inter-Varsity, 1981), 842; J. S. Feinberg, "1 Peter 3:18–20, Ancient Mythology, and the Intermediate State," *WTJ* 48 (1986): 303–36 and W. Grudem, "Christ Preaching through Noah: 1 Peter 3:19–20 in the Light of Dominant Themes in Jewish Literature," *TrinJ* 7 (1986): 3–31. Those who interpret the "spirits" as demonic angels, principally adopting the view, in one form or another, articulated fully during the last century by F. Spitta, *Christi Predigt an die Geister* (Halle: Verlag der Buchhandlung des Waisenhauses, 1890), include G. Farmer, "Did Our Lord, or Enoch, 'Preach to the Spirits in Prison'?" *Expos* 6 (1902): 377–78; K. Gschwind, *Die Niederfahrt Christi in die Unterwelt* (NTAbh 2; Münster: Aschendorff, 1911); J. Dublin, "The Descent into Hades and Christian Baptism," *Expos* 11 (1916): 241–74; B. Reicke, *The Disobedient Spirits and Christian Baptism. A Study of 1 Pet. III.19 and its Context* (Kobenhavn: Munkgaard, 1946), esp. 59–92; W. Bieder, *Die Vorstellung von der Höllenfahrt Jesu Christi* (Zürich: Zwingli, 1949); E. G. Selwyn, *The First Epistle of St. Peter* (London: Macmillan, 1952), 195–99, 322–30; E. J. Goodspeed, "Enoch in 1 Peter 3:19," *JBL* 73 (1954): 91–2; M. H. Scharlemann, " 'He Descended into Hell.' An Interpretation of 1 Peter 3:18–20," *CTM* 27 (1956): 81–94; S. E. Johnson, "The Preaching to the Dead," *JBL* 79 (1960): 48–51; W. J. Dalton, *Christ's Proclamation to the Spirits. A Study of 1 Peter 3:18–4:6* (AnBib 23; Rome: Pontifical Biblical Institute, 1965); idem, "The Interpretation of 1 Peter 3, 19 and 4,6: Light from 2 Peter," *Bib* 60 (1979): 547–55; R. T. France, "Exegesis in Practice: Two Examples," *New Testament Interpretations. Essays on Principles and Methods* (ed. I. H. Marshall; Grand Rapids, Mich.: Eerdmans, 1977), 252–81, esp. 264–81; L. Goppelt, *Der Erste Petrusbrief* (MeyerK 12/1; Göttingen: Vandenhoeck & Ruprecht, 1978), 246–54; H. U. von Balthasar, "Abstieg zur Hölle," *TQ* 150 (1979): 193–201; J.N.D. Kelly, *A Commentary on the Epistles of Peter and Jude* (TC; Grand Rapids, Mich.: Baker, rep. 1981), 151–58; R. Rubinkiewicz, " 'Duchy zamkniete w wiezieniw.' Interpretacja 1 P 3,19 w swietle Hen 10,4.12," *RTK* 28 (1981): 77–86; R. Omanson, "Suffering for Righteousness' Sake," *RevExp* 79 (1982): 439–50; R. H. Mounce, *A Living Hope. A Commentary on 1 and 2 Peter* (Grand Rapids, Mich.: Eerdmans, 1982) 54–58; A. Pinto da Silva, "A Proposito del Significato Di 1 Pt 3, 18–4,6," *Salessianum* 46 (1984) 473–86; H.S. Kvanvig, "Bruken av Noahtradisjonene i 1 Pet 3,20f," *TTKi* 56 (1985): 81–98; and J. R. Michaels, *1 Peter* (WBC 49; Waco, Tex.: Word, 1988), 199–213.

39. R. T. France ("Exegesis in Practice," 265, 268), in considering the language of suffering used in 1 Peter and the general parallel between Christ's suffering and that of the readers (cf. 3:17–18; 4:1, 15, 19), considers the level of

persecution to suggest martyrdom.

40. It might well be argued that a majority of those seeking to interpret this passage fail to note the *exceeding* relevance of these verses to an audience facing *grim* persecution. The result is that one is typically forced to view 3 : 19–22 as a less-than-relevant doctrinal digression interpolated into an otherwise hortatory chain of thought.

41. J. S. Stewart, "On a Neglected Emphasis in New Testament Theology," *SJT* 4 (1951): 292–301.

42. I.e., the whole unseen world, whether *thronoi* or *kyriotētes* or *archai* or *exousiai* (Col. 1 : 16).

43. This particular interest in angels in 1 and 2 Peter is not incidental.

44. E.g., Matt. 8 : 16; 10 : 1 12 : 45; Mark 1 : 27; 3 : 11; 5 : 13; 6 : 7; Luke 4 : 36; 6 : 16; 7 : 21; 8 : 2; 10 : 20; 11 : 26; Acts 5 : 16; 8 : 7; 19 : 12, 13; 23 : 8–9; 1 Tim. 4 : 1; Heb. 1 : 7,14; 12 : 9; 1 John 4 : 1; Rev. 1 : 4; 3 : 1; 4 : 5; 5 : 6; and 16 : 13,14.

45. Evidence in the NT is not scant in its depiction of spiritual conflict in the unseen world. In the ministry of Jesus as recorded in the Gospel narratives, one is confronted almost immediately with this conflict. Jesus is at once led by the Spirit into the Judean wilderness to be tested by Satan (Matt. 4 : 1–11; Mark 1 : 12–13; Luke 4 : 1–13). A key evidence in the attestation that the kingdom of God is manifest is Jesus' casting out of demonic spirits (Matt. 12 : 22–37; Mark 3 : 23–27; Luke 11 : 17–22). Upon returning from ministry, the seventy-two disciples sent out by Jesus testify that demons submitted to them because of his name (Luke 10 : 17). In response to the seventy-two, Jesus announces the overthrow of Satan as a star falling from the heavens and affirms the spiritual power conferred upon His followers (10 : 18). At a point when the disciples seem to have been jockeying for power and position in the "kingdom" (Luke 22 : 24–38), Jesus reminds Peter of a sobering reality, doubtless not meant to be purely metaphorical if properly understood: "Simon, Simon, Satan has demanded for his own purposes to sift you as wheat. But I have prayed for you that your faith might not fail. And when you have again come to yourself, strengthen your brethren" (22 : 31–32, free translation). The fledgling church in the book of Acts is equipped by the Holy Spirit to extend the ministry of Jesus: doing good and healing all those oppressed by the devil (10 : 38). Paul's explicit testimony before Agrippa is that God had apprehended him in order "to open their [the gentiles'] eyes and turn them from darkness to light, and from the power of Satan to God, so that they may receive forgiveness and a place among those who are sanctified by faith" (26 : 18). In his writings, Paul makes frequent allusion to principalities and powers which are hostile to the purposes of God and the church (e.g., Rom. 16 : 20; 1 Cor. 5 : 5; 7 : 5; 15 : 24–28; 2 Cor. 4 : 4,11; 10 : 3–5; 11 : 14–15; Eph. 2 : 2; 6 : 10–12; Col. 2 : 15; 1 Thess. 2 : 18; 2 Thess. 2 : 9; 1 Tim. 1 : 20; 4 : 1; and 5 : 15). In each of his epistles, with the exception of Philemon, Paul alludes to Christ's rule over the hostile powers. The notion is foundational to Pauline theology (see G.H.C. MacGregor, " 'Principalities and Powers.' The Cosmic Background of Paul's Thought," *NTS* 1 [1954/55]: 17–28).

46. See, e.g., 1 Tim. 3 : 16.

47. Contra H. Holtzmann, "Höllenfahrt im Neuen Testament," *ARW* 11 (1908): 285–97, W. Bousset, "Zur Hadesfahrt Christi," *ZNW* 19 (1919/20): 50–66, J. Jeremias, "Zwischen Karfreitag und Ostern," *ZNW* 42 (1949): 201, and A. T. Hanson, "Salvation Proclaimed: I. 1 Peter 3 : 18–22," *ExpTim* 93 (1982): 100–5, all of whom in some fashion view Christ preaching to the spirits as a mythological presentation. Hanson's remarks are worth noting: "we cannot take literally Christ's descent into the realm of the dead, still less his preaching to

fallen angels." Hanson's methodology evidently is driven by theological concerns, for he cannot accept the fact that 1 Peter is teaching that those who refuse to believe await condemnation, sharing company with the rebellious angels and the contemporaries of Noah. He continues: "Thus this *apparently bizarre concept* does in fact *relieve us of the awful conclusion* accepted by so many Christians down through the ages, that *all those who have not known God in Christ are damned*" (emphasis added).

48. On the creedal formula "He descended into Hell" and its development in the thinking of the fathers up to the fifth century, see A. E. Burn, "The Descent into Hell," *ExpTim* 14 (1902/3): 554–57.

49. Cf. also 2 Pet. 2:4 *(sirois zophou tartarōsas paredōken eis krisin tēroumenous)* and Jude 6 *(eis krisin megalēs hēmeras desmois aidiois hypo zophon tetērēken)*.

50. Note also the "descending" language in Eph. 4:8–10 and Philem. 2:10.

51. See Reicke, *The Disobedient Spirits*, pp. 66–70, 96–97.

52. E.g., 1 Enoch 16–18; 21; 2 Apoc. Bar. 56:12–15; Jub. 5:6; CD 2:18–21; 1QapGen 2:1,16.

53. The OT and Judaism conceptualized the abode of the dead in terms of *šeôl (hadēs)*, never *phylakē*. In Jewish apocalyptic, *phylakē* is the place of punishment. Generally speaking, the NT, in its depiction of the realm of the demonic, would seem to conform more to the intertestamental idea of imprisonment of spirits (cf., e.g., 2 Cor. 12:2; Eph. 1:20–22; 2:2; Col. 1:16,20). In line with the rest of the NT, however, 1 Peter does not indicate geography or location. The writer's concern is kerygma (Christ's suffering, rising, and reigning) and effect (the powers being subject).

54. The literature dealing with this issue in the last two centuries is quite extensive. For representative bibliographies, see Gschwind, *Die Niederfahrt;* Bieder, *Die Vorstellung;* Reicke, *The Disobedient Spirits;* and Dalton, *Christ's Proclamation* (see n. 38).

55. On the expression *poreutheis eis ouranon,* cf. Heb. 4:14; 9:24; and Acts 1:9–11.

56. Nevertheless, as evidenced by the language in Eph. 4:8–10 and Phil. 2:10, Christ's Descent and Ascent appear as "two pillars of fact which upheld the belief of the early church in the universality of Christ's redemptive work" (Selwyn, *The First Epistle*, 322).

57. E.g., T.Levi 3:1–3; 2 Enoch 7:1–3 and 18:3.

58. Such an emphasis, in a context of fierce persecution and hostility toward the Gospel, would reflect timely encouragement and genuine pastoral concern on the part of the writer. This is one of the strengths of R. T. France's treatment of these verses (see n. 39). France attempts an interpretation which is sensitive and pastorally relevant to the context of a suffering church.

59. E.g., the fallen angels designated as *pneumata;* the notion of disobedience and imprisonment *(en phylakē, en tois desmois, en desmōtēriǭ)* of spirits; the link between the disobedient spirits and the Flood; and the commission to go preach to the disobedient spirits. The points of resemblance, however, are not enough to justify attempts in the past by some to emend 1 Pet. 3:19 to read *en hǭ kai Henōch,* based on the assumption that Enoch was omitted due to haplography (see, e.g., J. R. Harris, "A Further Note on the Use of Enoch in 1 Peter," *Expos* 6/4 [1901]: 346–49; idem, "On a Recent Emendation of the Text of St. Peter," *Expos* 6/5 [1902]: 317–20; idem, "The History of a Conjectural Emendation," *Expos* 6/6 [1902] 317–20; and Goodspeed, "Enoch," 91–92, see n. 38).

60. It is unnecessary, however, as R. H. Mounce, *A Living Hope,* 56 (see n. 38), has stressed, to link this with the common "sons of God" interpretation of

Genesis 6 traditionally associated with the discussion of Enoch, 2 Pet. 2:4, and Jude 6—an association which some, for example, J. Frings ("Zu 1 Petr 3,19 und 4,6," *BZ* 17 [1926]: 75–88), maintain to be a misunderstanding upon which Jewish apocalyptic tradition was built.

61. As far as content is concerned, *kēryssein* is neutral.

62. Dalton (*Christ's Proclamation*, 33) is correct in noting that the predominate patristic interpretation of 3:19 suffers from a misunderstanding in 3:18 of the *sarx-pneuma* contrast.

63. Accordingly, the meaning of the hapax *eperōtēma* in 3:21, often translated "appeal" or "answer," is more contractual and authoritative than most versions tend to render it. It has to do with the somber reality of renouncing the power of evil. It is declarative and juridical in nature, performed *eis theon*. See J. H. Moulton and G. Milligan, *The Vocabulary of the Greek New Testament* (London: Hodder and Stoughton, 1930), 231–32; G. C. Richards, "1 Pet. iii.21," *JTS* 32 (1931): 77; O. S. Brooks, "1 Peter 3:21—The Clue to the Literary Structure of the Epistle," *NovT* 16 (1974): 290–305; and D. H. Tripp, *"Eperōtēma* (1 Peter 3:21). A Liturgist's Note," *ExpTim* 92 (1981): 267–70.

64. 1 Pet. 3:19 is in keeping with 2 Pet. 2:5 and Jude 6 in associating the fallen angels with man's wickedness (although Jude and 2 Peter emphasize the latter, i.e., the *human* factor, while 1 Peter stresses Christ's triumph). Note, however, that in 1 Peter, just as in 2 Peter and Jude, no judgment or assessment of the tradition of the angels' sin is offered. Mystery surrounds the fall. What is explicit and prominent in intertestamental literature (e.g., 1 Enoch 10:8; 15:9,11; 19:1; 65:6) remains veiled in the OT and NT. None of the three aforementioned epistles contains one word as to the *specific nature* of the angels' sin, only that they rebelled. In 1 Peter, they "refuse to believe" *(apeithein);* in 2 Peter, they "sin" *(hamartanein);* and in Jude, they "desert" *(apoleipein).* The NT writers share a common focus: *revolt against God.* This is the element of truth, even in material considered to be legendary. The writers of 1 and 2 Peter and Jude are discreet, in line with the writers of the OT. Their purpose is illustrative.

65. Goppelt, *Der Erste Petrusbrief,* 248.

66. On the parallels between 1 Pet. 3:19–21 and 1 Enoch, see H. S. Kvanvig, "Bruken," 81–98 (see n. 38). This does not, however, presume or require widespread familiarity with the tradition among Peter's audience. Although it would seem clear that 1 Enoch was well known to many Jews, particularly Essene-types, E. Isaac ("1 [Ethiopic Apocalypse of] Enoch," *Old Testament Pseudepigrapha: Vol. 1: Apocalyptic Literature and Testaments* [Garden City: NY: Doubleday, 1983], 8) writes that information as to the usage and importance of the work in Jewish and Christian communities is sparse. Moreover, use of the tradition in 1 Peter does not require that the writer subscribed to an Enochic understanding of Genesis 6 and the "sons of God"—an association assumed by most commentators. Indeed quite a bit of Jewish literature can be cited which stresses *human,* not angelic, sin as the reason for God bringing the flood upon the earth (e.g., 3 Macc. 2:4; Philo, *Quaestiones et solutiones in Genesim* 1.99,100; 2.13; *De Abrahamo* 40–41; Jos. *Ant.* 1.74,75,98; CD 2:20–21; *Bib. Ant.* 3.2.6; Sib. Or. 1:130–31, 150–79). The expression "the generation of the flood" is frequently found in rabbinic literature as a paradigm for human wickedness (e.g., Num. Rab. 9.18; 14.6; 20.2; Eccl. Rab. 2:23; m.Sanh. 10:3).

67. E.g., 1 Enoch 10:1–4; Jub. 10:5; and T.Naph. 3:5. Cf. also 2 Pet. 2:4–5.

68. E.g., Jub. 5:19; 7:20–39 (cf. also 8:10,11; 10:1–7,12,13; 29:24); T.Benj. 10:6; 1 Enoch 67:1; 2 Enoch 35:1; Wis. 10:4; Sir. 44:17–18; 2 Esdr. 3:11; 4 Macc. 15:31; 1QapGen 6:6; Philo, *De Abrahamo,* 46; *De somniis,*

2.223,237; *De mutatione nominum,* 109; Jos. *Ant.* 1.3.2; and *Bib. Ant.* 3:9. The most extensive portrayal of Noah is found in 1 Enoch, Jubilees, and the Genesis Apocryphon. Particularly in 1 Enoch and Jubilees the literary function of the Noah story is the mirroring of the presence of an eschatological crisis, whereby the writer wishes to impress upon his readers the seriousness of judgment.

69. See J. C. VanderKam, "The Righteousness of Noah," *Ideal Figures in Ancient Judaism* (SBLSCS 12; Chico, Calif.: Scholars, 1980), 13–32, esp. pp. 16ff.

70. This does not, however, require that early Christians accepted the Enochic view of the Flood tradition. In 1 Enoch 67:2, for example, the building of the ark is ascribed to *angels,* and, according to 60:1, Enoch is forewarned of the flood in his five hundredth year of life, in contrast to Gen. 5:24, which states that he was translated at age 365.

71. The clause "when God endured in the days of Noah while the ark was being built" is normally understood to mean *contemporary* with Noah. However, it could well mean that the angels were *still* in a state of disobedience when the men of Noah's era were testing God (even though the angels fell long before Noah), as suggested by Mounce (p. 57). Grammatically, Mounce's view is sustained, since the Aorist participle *apeithēsasin* standing together with the particle *pote* yields the effect of a pluperfect, i.e., this action antedates the verb *kēryssein* in v 19. Since *pote* involves no comparison with a later event and can mean "at some time or other" (*BAGD,* 695), the translation "formerly" (RSV) is a bit misleading.

72. In "The Descent into Hades and Christian Baptism," *Expos* 11 (1916): 241–74, J. Dublin draws an interesting association between the flood typology and baptism by citing several partistic references to support the notion that, based on 1 Pet. 3:19–22, the belief existed in the early church that demonic spirits were scared away at one's baptism.

73. Thus, the "preaching" of 3:19 cannot be salvific.

74. On the transition from Noah and the flood typology to the meaning of baptism for Peter's audience, see the excellent discussion of France, "Exegesis in Practice," pp. 272–76.

75. F. C. Synge, "1 Peter 3:18–21," *ExpTim* 82 (1971/72): 311.

76. S. E. Johnson, "The Preaching to the Dead," *JBL* 79 (1960): 48–51.

77. The hymnic character of 1 Pet. 3:18–22 is fairly well acknowledged. See, e.g., O. Cullmann. "Les Origines des premières confessions de foi," *RHPR* 21 (1941): 77–110; R. Bultmann, "Bekenntnis- und Liedfragmente im ersten Petrusbrief," *Coniectanea Neotestamentica 11* (Lund/Copenhagen: Gleerup/Munksgaard, 1947), 1–14; H. Windisch, *Die Katholischen Briefe* (2d ed.; Tübingen: Mohr, 1930), 70–73; F. L. Cross, *1 Peter: A Paschal Liturgy* (London: Mowbray, 1954), 156–58; E. Lohse, "Paränese und Kerygma im ersten Petrusbrief," *ZNW* 45 (1954): 68–89; P. Boismard, *Quatres hymnes baptismales dans le première Épître de Pierre* (LD 30; Paris: du Cerf, 1961); Dalton, *Christ's Proclamation* 96–102; and C. H. Huntzinger, "Zur Struktur der Christus-Hymnen in Phil 2 und 1 Petr 3," *Der Ruf Jesu und die Antwort der Gemeinde. Festscrift J. Jeremias* (Göttingen: Vandenhoeck & Ruprecht, 1970), 142–56.

78. Pinto da Silva, "A Proposito," 480–82 (see n. 38).

79. It should be noted, however, that the contrast in 3:18–4:6 between "flesh" and "spirit" is not one of "body" versus "soul." Rather we have to do here with two modes of existence—Christ's death in the physical or natural sphere on the one hand and His risen eternal nature on the other. The expression *zōopoiētheis pneumati* in 3:18 should be interpreted as referring to the resurrected Christ.

80. In his critique of *ekēryxen* in 3:19, J. S. Feinberg ("1 Peter 3:18–20," 325–

29) rejects the view that Christ preached condemnation and doom to the spirits based on his conclusion that to "tantalize" or "taunt" them would be "out of character with Christ" (p. 328) and "improbable" (p. 329). Feinberg continues: "Were not their imprisonment and eternal damnation reprehension enough? The picture one gets of Christ is a picture of a merciless victor who has no concern for those whom he has defeated. That simply does not square with other biblical portraits of our Lord" (p. 328). Unfortunately, such sentimentality is hardly a substitute for serious exegesis. Feinberg altogether misses the contextual thread running throughout these verses and culminating in v 22: Christ's "out-of-character" subjection (*hypoteagē*) of the angels, principalities, and powers. In taking the rest of the NT seriously, one discovers that such a portrait of Christ the Triumphant One is *indeed* consistent with His ruling character. This is the language, for example, of 1 Cor. 15:24–28 and Col. 2:15 ("Having stripped the principalities and powers, he made a public spectacle of them, triumphing over them"). It is the language of conquest over *hostile* forces which are at enmity with God. What sort of "concern for those whom he has defeated" should Christ exhibit toward the demonic spirits that oppose the divine plan? Does Christ as the "Lion of Judah" not vanquish and rule His enemies as graphically portrayed in the NT Apocalypse? Evil must bow the knee, even in a hostile and unwilling state, to the Sovereign *kyrios* and *despotēs* (Jude 4).

81. Rev. 1:5 and 3:14.

82. In character, the tradition in 1 Peter 3:19–20 is similar to 1 Tim. 3:16.

83. Set within a Palestinian milieu, the "need" reflected in Jude could well have arisen from others' devotion to Enochic literature.

84. Deut. Rab. 11.10.

85. Beckwith, *The Old Testament Canon*, 403.

86. Z. H. Chajes, *The Student's Guide through the Talmud* (London: East and West Library, 1952), chaps. 26–30.

87. Beckwith, *The Old Testament Canon*, 404–5.

88. Clement of Alexandria (*Commentarium in epistula Judae* 5.1 [*PG* 9.731–4]; *Adumbrationes in epistula Judae* [*GCS* 3.2080]) viewed Jude as one of the general epistles and treated 1 Enoch as scripture. In North Africa Tertullian (*De cultu feminarum* 1.3 [*PL* 1.1421–22]) regarded the Book of Enoch as inspired, reflecting the view of Enoch in Barn. 16.5. His justification, interestingly, was founded on the view that the book literally derived from the historical patriarch, whom he viewed as the most ancient of the prophets. Noah, writes Tertullian, passed on the tradition of his great grandfather. On the other hand, Tertullian feels the tradition could just as well have been restored in Jude by the Spirit in the same way that Ezra restored the ancient scriptures to a place of reverence following the Babylonian destruction of Jerusalem. Further, Tertullian says that Enoch preached concerning the Lord and that the Book of Enoch, therefore, pertains to us in the present (see D. Guthrie, "Tertullian and Pseudonymity," *ExpTim* 67 [1956]: 341–42]). The epistle of Jude is also quoted in the second century by Polycarp (see the prologue to *The Martyrdom of Polycarp* [LCL; tr. K. Lake; London/New York: Heinemann/Macmillan, 1913]) and Athenagoras (*ANF* 2.405–6).

89. Jerome, *De viris illustribus*, 4.

90. Didymus, *Commentarius* (*PG* 39. 181ff).

91. *Epistolae heortasticae* 156 (*PG* 26. 1437–38).

92. Eusebius, *Hist. eccl.* 2.23.

93. Cyril, *Lectiones* 4 (*PG* 74.456).

94. The advice of Jerome to a young girl sums up the attitudes of many by

the late fourth century with respect to the literature of the intertestamental era: "Let her avoid all the apocryphal books, and if she ever wishes to read them, not for the truth of their doctrines but out of respect for their wondrous tales, let her realize that they are not really written by those to whom they are ascribed, that there are many faulty elements in them, and that it requires great skill to look for gold in them" (*Ad Laetam de institutione filiae*, reproduced in *Selected Letters of St. Jerome* [LCL; F. A. Wright, ed.; New York/London: Putnam's Sons/Heinemann, 1933], 365).

95. Augustine, *De civitate Dei* 15.23.4.

96. Chrysostom, *Homiliae in Genesim* 6.1 (*PG* 53.185–8).

97. See C. Kaplan, "The Pharisaic Character of the Book of Enoch," *ATR* 12 (1929/30): 531–37; also, Beckwith, *The Old Testament Canon*, 37–39.

98. This material, grouped by J. T. Milik ("Problèmes de la littérature Hénochique a la lumière des fragments araméens de Qumrân," *HTR* 64 [1971]: 333–78) as the first of five books constituting this composite work, has been traditionally dated in the second century B.C. (see, e.g., R. H. Charles, "The Book of Enoch," *APOT* 2.170, and E. Isaac, "1 [Ethiopic Apocalypse of] Enoch," *OTP* 1.7).

99. The term "watchers" is also used in Jub. 4:15,22; 8:3; 10:5; T.Reub. 5:6.; T.Naph. 3:5; and CD 2:18. Reicke (*The Disobedient Spirits*, 71) attaches the designation "watchers" to the angels' preflood identity.

100. The wording of Jude 6 is almost identical to that of Origen in his commentary on the angels' fall, suggesting perhaps a stereotyping which had become standard in Judaism: *eis krisin megalēs hēmeras desmois aidiois en zophō tēroumenoi* (*GCS* 10, 255).

101. Cf. Philo (*De sacrificiis Abelis et Caini* 81) and Josephus (*J.W.* 4.143,385; *Ant.* 2.60); also 1 Pet. 3:19 ("he also preached to the spirits in prison"); 2 Pet. 2:4 ("For if God . . . consigned them to pits of gloom and delivered them to be kept for judgment"); and Rev. 20:2 ("He seized the dragon, that ancient serpent, who is the devil, or Satan, and bound him for a thousand years").

102. Cf. also T. Naph. 3:3; Bar 3:24–38, esp. v 34 (*hoi de asteres elampsan en tais phylakais autōn kai euphranthēsan);* Philo, who writes that the celestial bodies are in prison (*De aeternitate mundi* 47 and *De somniis* 1.22); and CD 2:18, a further allusion to the "watchers" and their fall: "By walking in the stubbornness of their heart the Watchers of heaven fell. Because of it those who did not keep the commandments of God were caught" (cited in P. R. Davies, *The Damascus Document. An Interpretation of the "Damascus Document"* [JSOTSS 25; Sheffield: JSOT, 1982], 237–39).

103. Glasson (*Greek Influence*, 65–67) links the watchers to the Titans of Greek lore.

104. In "1 Enoch 80:2–8 (67:5–7) and Jude 12–13," *CBQ* 47 (1985): 296–303, C. D. Osburn recalls the resemblance noted by F. Spitta (*Die zweite Brief*, 396) between the four metaphors of Jude 12–13 and 1 Enoch. Whereas Spitta related the images of Jude to 1 Enoch 2–5, Osburn locates their background in 1 Enoch 67 and 80. 80:2–8, according to Osburn, provides the essential framework for the four metaphors—rain (v 2), fruit of the tree (v 3), and errant stars (vv 6–7)—with 67:5–7 referring to turbulent waters. There are several reasons to commend Osburn's view: (1) the cosmic symbolism that both Jude and 1 Enoch share, (2) the general construction of the metaphors (three of the four—the moon metaphor is absent—appear together in 1 Enoch), and (3) the context of impending judgment in which the three metaphors in 1 Enoch 80 appear. In terms of depicting eschatological judgment, Jude is without question at home in

the environment of apocalyptic imagery. The fourth metaphor, however, located by Osburn in 1 Enoch 67, seems far less discernible in 1 Enoch than in the pagan mythology associated with the birth of Aphrodite. In 1 Enoch 67 the "waters" being alluded to are associated with the Flood—waters in which the disobedient angels are punished. In contrast, the waters of the sea connected with the Aphrodite myth in Hesiod's *Theogony* produce foam from which Aphrodite is born and nurtured. The conceptual and verbal parallels between *Theogony* 190–92 and Jude 13a are too close to deny, whereas the purported allusion by Jude to 1 Enoch 67:2–5 suggested by Osburn is indiscernible. More importantly, the Aphrodite tradition epitomizes the immorality of the *houtoi* (see n. 204).

105. While the events in heaven *do* effect those on earth, this emphasis is secondary in Jude 6 and 9, where the heavenly-earthly correlation is mentioned in passing. For a similar context in which this distinction is made, see D. Suter, "Fallen Angel, Fallen Priest: The Problem of Family Purity in 1 Enoch 6–16," *HUCA* 50 (1979): 116–17.

106. See chap. 4.

107. The argument that Sodom and Gomorrah in Jude 7 are linked to the angels of Jude 6 via sexual sin rests chiefly upon the assumption that the angels' sin was sexual, based, again, on an assumed interpretation of Gen. 6:1–4. This, however, is not the statement, nor the intent, of the writer. What is explicit in Jude 6 from the text is that the angels *rebelled from God's authority*.

108. NIV.

109. While this view of Genesis 6 in no way negates the notion that demonic spirits of the unseen world contribute to human evil perpetrated in the visible world (cf., e.g., 2 Cor. 4:4; 11:14; Eph. 2:2; 6:12), it is not the intention of the writer to highlight angels. Human wickedness is the cause of the flood.

110. Although this rabbinic material postdates the NT and relevant Jewish apocalyptic works, these references reflect within mainstream Judaism a line of tradition which did not interpret the *běnē hā̆ʾĕlōhîm* as angelic beings.

111. On the range of views as to the dating of this work, see J. Priest, "The Testament of Moses," *OTP* 1.920–1.

112. Bauckham (*Jude, 2 Peter*, 67) argues that inasmuch as the literary genre of testament normally concludes with an account of the subject's death and burial, and the next-to-last chapter of the Testament of Moses alludes to Moses' burial ("What place will receive you, or where will be the marker of your sepulcher? Or who as a man will dare to move your body from place to place? For all who die, there are appropriately their sepulchers in the earth, but your sepulcher is from the rising to the setting of the sun," [As. Mos. 11:6–8]), it is most probable that this work ended with an account of Moses' death. J. H. Charlesworth (*Pseudepigrapha and the NT*, 76) considers it unwise to argue that testaments normally conclude with such an account of burial and death, citing the Testament of the Twelve Patriarchs as an example. He remains unconvinced that Jude is quoting from a lost ending of the Testament of Moses (p. 77). Charlesworth further reiterates that both *Diathēkē Mōÿseōs* and *Analēpsis Mōÿseōs* are to be found in patristic lists of apocryphal works.

113. In distinguishing between the "Assumption of Moses" and the "Testament of Moses," both of which are found in ancient lists of apocryphal books, *Bauckham* (*Jude, 2 Peter*, 75–6) posits that either the text represented by the extant Latin MS was concluded by an anti-gnostic version of the dispute over Moses' body, and known as the "Assumption of Moses," or the "Assumption" was a revised version of an earlier "Testament of Moses," in which some material remained unchanged.

114. Charlesworth, *Pseudepigrapha and the NT,* 139. For an extensive discussion of an attempted reconstruction of the tradition behind Jude 9, see Bauckham's excursus "The Background and Source of Jude 9," in *Jude, 2 Peter,* pp. 67–76.

115. On the role of Moses in Israel's history, see D. L. Tiede, *The Charismatic Figure as Miracle Worker* (SBLDS 1; Missoula, Mont.: SBL, 1972), 178–206.

116. On the developing tendencies in the interpretation of Moses' death in Jewish literature, see K. Haacker and P. Schafer, "Nachbiblische Traditionen vom Tod des Mose," *Josephus-Studien* (ed. O. Betz et al.; "Göttingen: Vandenhoeck & Ruprecht, 1974), 147–74; and S. E. Loewenstamm, "The Death of Moses," *Studies on the Testament of Abraham* (SBLSCS 6; ed. G.W.E. Nicklesburg; Missoula, Mont.: Scholars, 1976), 184–203.

117. Clement, *Stromata* 6.15 (*PG* 9.355–8).

118. Origen, *De principiis* 3.2.1 (*GCS* 5.244).

119. Didymus, *In epistola Juda enarratio* 6.307 (*PG* 39.1811–18).

120. Photius, *Ad amphilochium* 151 (*PG* 101.813a).

121. Cited in M. R. James, *The Lost Apocrypha of the Old Testament—Their Titles and Fragments* (London/New York: SPCK/Macmillan, 1920), 45.

122. Epiphanius, *Haeresis* 1 (cited in James, *Lost Apocrypha,* 48).

123. Ecumenius, *In epistola Judae* (*PG* 119.713bc). See also J. A. Cramer, ed., *Catena in Epistolas Catholicas Accesserunt Oecumenii et Arethae Commentarii in Apocalypsin. Ad Fidem Codd. MSS.* (Hildesheim: Olms, 1967), 153–70.

124. See his commentary on Deut. 34:6 in Catena Nicetas 1.1672–3, reproduced in M. R. James, *The Testament of Abraham* (Texts and Studies; Cambridge: Cambridge University, 1892), 17.

125. Necephorus, Stichometria Sacrorum Librorum (cited in James, *Testament,* 17).

126. Moses' death in Ethiopic, Slavonic, and Armenian traditions is dealt with more extensively in J. H. Charlesworth, *The Pseudepigrapha in Modern Research* (Missoula, Mont.: Scholars, 1976), 160–63. For a survey of rabbinic, patristic, and medieval elaboration of Moses' ascension, as well as related literature in the last two hundred years, see A.-M. Denis, *Introduction aux Pseudepigraphes Grecs D'Ancien Testament* (Leiden: Brill, 1970), 128–41.

127. Bauckham, *Jude, 2 Peter,* 65–76.

128. The PH is narrative in form with theological interpretations blended in. It is considered to be *sēfer hayyāšār,* a Byzantine "book of wisdom."

129. This collection of codices was published by A. Vassiliev, in *Anecdota Graeco-Byzantina* (Mosquae: Univeritatis Caesareae, 1893). Reference to the body of Moses is found on p. 258. For further appraisal of the Palae Historica, see also M. R. James, *Apocrypha Anecdota II* (Cambridge: Cambridge University, 1897), 156–57, in whose opinion the PH account is based on the Assumption of Moses (p. 156); D. Flusser (see n. 130); and K. Berger (see n. 135).

130. D. Flusser, "Palaea Historica—An Unknown Source of Biblical Legends," *Scripta Hierosolymitana—Vol. 22: Studies in Aggadah and Folk-Literature* (Jerusalem: Hebrew University, 1971), 50.

131. A. Fleischhacker, *Der Tode Mose's nach der Sage* (Halle: Universität Halle, 1888), 5–6, 11–12.

132. Flusser, "Palaea Historica," 74.

133. A fascinating work published in the early 1700s is J. A. Eisenmenger's *Entdecktes Judenthum* (2 vols.; Königsberg in Preussen: n.p., 1700, 1711). These two volumes are essentially a compendium of rabbinic teachings on the unseen world. E.g., volume 2, chap. 5 (pp. 295–322): "Was die Juden von dem Paradies schreiben und lehren" ("What the Jews Write and Teach concerning Paradise");

chap. 6 (pp. 322–70): "Was die Juden von der Hölle lehren" ("What the Jews Teach concerning Hell"); chap. 7 (pp. 370–407): "Was die Juden von den guten Engeln lehren" ("What the Jews Teach concerning the Good Angels"); and chap. 8 (pp. 408–68): "Was die Juden von den Teufeln lehren" ("What the Jews Teach concerning the Demons"). Of particular interest to the present investigation are chaps. 7 and 8. Volume 2 also contains rabbinic legends pertaining to Korah (pp. 208ff).

134. See D. H. Wallace, "The Semitic Origin of the Assumption of Moses," *TZ* 11 (1955): 321–28.

135. K. Berger, "Der Streit des guten und des bösen Engels um die Seele. Beobachtungen zu 4QAmrb und Judas 9," *JSJ* 4 (1973): 1–18.

136. Origen, *Scholia in Lucam* (*PG* 17.367).

137. This has been published in W. Leslau, ed., *Falasha Anthology* (Yale Judaica Series 6; New Haven, Conn.: Yale University, 1963), 52–56.

138. J. T. Milik, "4Q Visions de 'Amram et une citation d'Origine,'" *RB* 79 (1972): 90–97.

139. Berger, "Streit," 14.

140. See H. Braun, "Qumran und das Neue Testament. Ein Bericht über zehn Jahre Forschung (1950–1959)," *TRu* 30 (1964): 118.

141. On the standing-falling motif in QL, see W. Grundmann, "Stehen und Fallen im qumranischen und neutestamentlichen Schrifttum," *Qumran-Probleme* (ed. H. Bardtke; Berlin: Akademie, 1963), 147–66.

142. Earlier this century, M. R. James (*The Lost Apocrypha*, 50) contended that Jubilees and the Assumption of Moses circulated together in a volume containing several works.

143. J. A. Goldstein, "The Testament of Moses: Its Content, Its Origin, and Its Attestation in Josephus," *Studies on the Testament of Moses* (SBLSCS 4; ed. G.W.E. Nicklesburg; Cambridge, Mass.: SBL 1973), 45, 47.

144. J. Licht, "Taxo, or the Apocalyptic Doctrine of Divine Vengeance," *JJS* 12 (1961): 95–103. Cf. also J. J. Collins, "The Testament (Assumption) of Moses," *Outside the Old Testament* (Cambridge: Cambridge University, 1985), 145–58.

145. C. Bigg, *A Critical and Exegetical Commentary on the Epistles of St. Peter and St. Jude* (ICC; New York: Scribner's, 1922), 331, thinks he sees in Gal. 3:19 another use of the Assumption of Moses.

146. Rowston, "The Most Neglected Book," 557.

147. What Jude and 2 Peter have in common, apart from the obvious literary dependence, is the pressing need for a forceful polemic against heretical types. We may grant that both letters specifically reflect adversaries who despise the prophetic word (2 Pet 1:19–2:1), operate by stealth (2:1 = v 4), deny the Lord (2:1 = v 4), manifest licentiousness (2:2 = v 4), stand condemned (2:3 = vv 6,15,23), are antitypes of the fallen angels and Sodom and Gomorrah (2:4, 6 = vv 6,7), are ungodly (2:6 = vv 4,15,18), await the day of judgment (2:9; 3:12 = vv 6,14,15), follow corrupt desires of the flesh (2:10 = vv 7,16,18), despise and blaspheme angelic powers (2:10 = v 8), are arrogant (2:10 = vv 15,16), are as ignorant, unreasoning beasts (2:12 = v 10), are blemishes in the community (2:13 = v 12), share in the love-feast (2:13 = v 12), are cursed (2:14 = v 11), are addicted to sin (2:14 = v 15), are apostate (2:15,20 = vv 5,6,7,11), live in error (2:15, 18; 3:17 = vv 11, 13), influence others (2:2 = vv 17–21), compare to clouds or springs without water (2:17 = v 12), are as if driven by the wind (2:17 = v 12), have darkness reserved for them (2:17 = vv 6,13), and utter boastful words (2:18 = v 16). What distinguishes the opponents in 2 Peter from those in Jude nonetheless is several-fold. First, although both epistles manifest a

strongly Jewish character, 2 Peter exhibits strong Hellenistic traits as well. 1 Enoch and the Assumption of Moses, particularly the latter work, would mean less to pagan Gentiles outside of Palestine (hence, the difference in the two epistles with respect to the use of source-material). Second, the OT is alluded to less frequently in 2 Peter (what one would expect in accord with a Hellenistic milieu). Third, the emphasis in 2 Peter on "prophecy" and "prophets" (1:19,20,21; 2:15, 16; 3:2) leads one to conclude that the adversaries are self-styled prophets (*pseudoprophētai* and *pseudodidaskaloi*, 2:1) and that they interpret themselves (*idias epilyseōs*, 1:20; *thelēmati anthrōpou*, 1:21). They are introducing new *haireseis* (2:1); their doctrinal reformulation, resulting from their advanced stage of apostasy, has become set. The text of Jude, in contrast, reads in more general terms: "certain persons" (*tines anthrōpoi*, v 4) have come to the fore. Fourth, the particular stress on doctrine in 2 Peter gives way in Jude to a decidedly *ethical* tone. Fifth, a key element in the opponents' doctrinal reformulation in 2 Peter is the denial of the Parousia (3:4ff). Hence, the apostate in 2 Peter require a different literary strategy than the one employed in Jude. Note the point of denial in 2 Pet. 3—the Lord's *coming*—as well as the point of the writer's attack—the *certainty* of His coming and the *manner* of that coming. Thus, differences in the opponents reflect differences in the historical situation behind Jude and 2 Peter. Ultimately, it is these differences, in spite of the striking parallels found in the two letters, which shape the literary strategy of each writer.

148. Due to the diversity and lateness of possible sources, this task remains hypothetical at best.

149. See chap. 2.

150. For a survey of diverse theories as to the development of Enoch in the apocalyptic tradition particularly, see J. C. VanderKam, *Enoch and the Growth of an Apocalyptic Tradition* (CBQMS 16; Washington, D.C.: CBA, 1984).

151. The various roles filled by Enoch in Jewish literature are discussed at some length in K. Berger, "Henoch," *RAC* 107/8 (1987/88): 483–505.

152. On the Ethiopic, Aramaic, Greek, and Latin texts of 1 Enoch, see B. Dehandschütter, "Pseudo-Cyprian, Jude and Enoch. Some Notes on 1 Enoch 1:9," *Tradition and Re-Interpretation in Jewish and Early Christian Literature. Essays in Honour of J.C.H. Lebram* (Leiden: Brill, 1986), 114–20. See also n. 163.

153. J. A. Fitzmyer, "Implications of the New Enoch Literature from Qumran," *TS* 38 (1977): 339.

154. It is interesting to note, however, that rabbinical Judaism of the third century A.D. adopts certain of the Enoch traditions which flourished within earlier apocalyptic circles. 3 (the Hebrew Book of) Enoch is a mixture of rabbinic and apocalyptic, almost gnostic, notions (see H. Odeberg, *3 Enoch or the Hebrew Book of Enoch* [Cambridge: Cambridge University, 1928]).

155. Philo, *De praemiis et poenis*, 17.

156. "Son of Man" is not used in a titular sense before the Christian advent.

157. The Book of Enoch is cited with some frequency in patristic literature, giving the impression of apparent authority in the early church. The prevailing context, however, of the majority of the patristic allusions seems to be over the issue of *Jude's* authenticity, in light of his use of material from 1 Enoch, not *1 Enoch's* authority. H. J. Lawlor, "Early Citations from the Book of Enoch," *JP* 25 (1897): 188–225, prefers to examine this phenomenon according to geographical factors, not mere chronology. He notes that Alexandria (Barnabas, Clement, Origen, Didymus) and North Africa (Tertullian, J. Africanus, Cyprian, Lactantius) for example, exhibit a higher view of 1 Enoch than Italy or Syria (Jerome, Hilary, J. Chrysostom).

158. Hengel, *Judaism*, 1.175. See also J. Morgenstern, "The HASIDIM—Who are They?" *HUCA* 38 (1967): 59–73.

159. Hengel, *Judaism*, 1.176.

160. Cf. Sir 44 : 16: "Enoch pleased the Lord and was taken up as a warning to generations."

161. Significantly, two catchwords in the Testaments of the Twelve Patriarchs (roughly contemporary with 1 Enoch) are *asebeia* and *planē*, occurring seventeen and twenty-five times respectively.

162. Cited from *Apocalypsi Henochi Graece. Fragmenta Pseudepigraphorum Quae Supersunt Graeca* (ed. M. Black and A.-M. Denis; Leiden: Brill, 1970), 19.

163. See J. VanderKam, "The Theophany of Enoch 1.3b–7.9," *VT* 23 (1973): 129–50. In light of the impressive comparison between Jude's Greek, the Ethiopic version of 1 Enoch and the Aramaic version of the same, it is well possible that Jude was dependent on an Aramaic Vorlage of 1 Enoch. The alterations in the text can be attributed to the writer's christology (C. D. Osburn, "The Christological use," 334–41). For a comparison of the text in Jude with the Aramaic, Ethiopic, Greek, and Latin (Pseudo-Cyprian) versions of Enoch, with accompanying discussion, see Bauckham, *Jude, 2 Peter*, pp. 94–6; Charlesworth, *Pseudepigrapha and the NT*, 72–74; and Dehandschütter, "Pseudo-Cyprian," 114–20. Osburn, Bauckham, and Charlesworth favor a Semitic original with which Jude supposedly was working; Dehandschütter favors a Greek, though influenced by the Semitic language (see also the relevant discussion in "SNTS Pseudepigrapha Papers" in Charlesworth, *Pseudepigrapha and the NT*, 137–38).

164. In a precise sense, Jude 14–15 is not a citation of 1 Enoch, rather it can be considered a revision of the text of Greek Enoch with a common vocabulary. This view would coincide with that of M. Black, *The Book of Enoch or 1 Enoch* (Leiden; Brill, 1985), 109.

165. Jude's language here resembles the cry developed in the Qumran War Scroll. It is a call to combat. Finally, after Jude's readers have "fought" (v 3), they are able to "stand" (*histēmi*, v 24), "not stumbling" (*aptaistos*), a motif also frequently appearing in QL. To "stand" is a gift from God; standing implies conflict and an adversary. Statements in QL concerning "standing" and "falling" predominate in thanksgiving songs, two examples of which follow:

> Those who greatly desire you will stand forever
> > Those who wander in the way of your heart stand
> > eternally
> And I, while I hold fast on to you,
> > Pull myself up and stand up against my despisers.

(1QH 4:21)

> I praise you, Lord!
> > For you support me through your strength.
> And you have poured upon me your Holy Spirit
> > So that I do not stumble.

(1QH 7:6)

For a fuller discussion of this theme, see Grundmann, "Stehen und Fallen," 147–66.

166. Charlesworth, *Pseudepigrapha and the NT*, 70–80.

167. The former would relate to more than one quotation from the same document; the latter, from different sources.

168. Osburn, "The Christological Use," 334–41.

169. Charlesworth, *Pseudepigrapha and the NT,* 74.

170. Ibid.

171. See the appendix in chap. 3.

172. In that the word "inspired" is a relatively flexible term in the hands of many who use it, Charlesworth's qualification of the term is important: 1 Enoch is "inspired *by God.*" Thus, we propose to interact with Charlesworth (who is representative of many), based on the use of *his* terms.

173. Note, e.g., the prophetic introductory formulas of the OT, their adaption in the NT, as well as Jesus' and apostolic citing of the OT. In this connection, cf. also 2 Thess. 2:2.

174. This question is a wholly different issue than the question of *literary strategy,* yet is crucial *because of assumptions* imported wholesale into normal discussions of Jude's use of the Pseudepigrapha.

175. E. P. Sanders, "Testament of Abraham," *OTP* 1.874–5.

176. O. S. Wintermute, "The Apocalypse of Elijah," *OTP* 1.729–30.

177. R. P. Spittler, "Testament of Job," *OTP* 1.833–4.

178. See Charlesworth, *Pseudepigrapha and the NT,* 70–8, for distinctions.

179. 2 Tim. 3:16 (cf. also 2 Pet. 1:21).

180. Charlesworth's designation "inspired by God" for a pseudepigraphal work such as 1 Enoch further clouds this distinction.

181. Note that Charlesworth assumes that the canon of the Hebrew Bible was not yet "closed" in the first century A.D. (*Pseudepigrapha and the NT,* 74).

182. In this regard, Paul's view of Christian "tradition" *(paradosis)* is both oral and literary (cf., e.g., 1 Cor. 11:23; 15:3; 1 Thess. 2:13; 2 Thess. 2:15).

183. 2 Thess. 2:2.

184. Matt. 15:7 and Mark 7:6.

185. A rabbinic midrash cited in J. M. Sasson, "A Genealogical 'Convention' in Biblical Chronology," *JBL* 90 (1978): 171. It was customary in Hebrew genealogies to make minor alterations by placing individuals worthy of attention in the seventh position of a tree. Note, for example, that Nimrod is the seventh from Enoch (Gen. 5:21–32; 10:1–11) and Abraham is the seventh from Eber (Gen. 11:10–29). The OT does not call Enoch "the seventh from Adam," although it can be inferred from a reading of Genesis 5.

186. Philo, *De posteritate Caini,* 173.

187. So Fuchs and Reymond, *La Deuxième Épître,* 175.

188. So J. Huther, *Kritisch-exegetisches Handbuch über den 1. Brief des Petrus, den Brief Judas und den 2. Brief des Petrus* (MeyerK; Göttingen: Vandenhoeck & Ruprecht, 1887), 305.

189. So C. F. Keil, *Commentar über die Briefe des Petrus und Judas* (Leipzig: Dorffling und Franke, 1883), 320.

190. In response to the possible objection that Paul, in Titus 1, is sarcastic while Jude is engaged in serious exhortation, several remarks are in order. First, it should be noted that our primary thesis concerns the place of tradition-material in the writer's *literary strategy.* As to the psychology of the NT writers as it relates to their selection of sources, we are only left to speculate. Nevertheless, the subject of Paul's admonitions in Titus can hardly be considered lighthearted; the issue of character among leaders in the church is deadly serious. *Paul's own editorial* on the pagan tradition is noteworthy: *hē martyria hautē estin alēthēs* (Tit. 1:13a)! Paul is affirming the content of the tradition, regardless of its origin. Its truth is reason enough to "rebuke sharply" (1:13b) the rebellious (1:10ff). In truth, Jude is not isolated in his use of extrabiblical traditions. If even a pagan saying is consistent with truth, then it communicates to an audience to which it is

familiar. Second, Jude is justified in utilizing the Enoch "prophecy" on the introductory statement of the writer concerning his heavenly vision (1 Enoch 1:2): "I look not for this generation but for the distant one that is coming."

191. Cf. G. Zuntz, "Enoch on the Last Judgment," *JTS* 45 (1944): 161–70.

192. Four *hapax legomena* occur in these two verses (*spilas, phthinopōrina, epaphrizonta,* and *planētai*).

193. J. P. Oleson, "An Echo of Hesiod's Theogony vv. 190–2 in Jude 13," *NTS* (1978/79): 492–503.

194. Hesiod, *Theogony* (M. L. West, ed.; Oxford: Clarendon, rep. 1982), 45.

195. Oleson suggests that "Aphrodite" means "foam-born" (p. 495).

196. Oleson, "An Echo," 496.

197. 2 Pet 2:13 employs *spiloi.*

198. This depiction of Jude's opponents would seem to have a parallel in 2 Peter as well, where apostasy as it relates to the present situation is described in similar terms:

> It would have been better for them not to have known the way of righteousness, than to have known it and then to turn their backs on the sacred command that was passed on to them. Of them, the proverbs are true: "A dog returns to its vomit," and "a sow that is washed goes back to her wallowing in the mud" (2 Pet. 2:21–22).

199. See, e.g., A. D. Knox, "*SPILADES,*" *JTS* 14 (1913): 547–49, and H. S. Jones, "*SPILAS—APARCHĒ PNEUMATOS,*" *JTS* 23 (1922): 282–83, who give several examples from antiquity.

200. Bauckham prefers the interpretation "dangerous reefs" (*Jude, 2 Peter,* 85).

201. Mayor, *The Epistle of St. Jude,* 43.

202. Similar imagery can be found in Jer. 49:23, Wisd. of Sol. 14:1, and James 1:6.

203. Oleson considers it not unthinkable that a well-educated Palestinian would be familiar with and utilize Greek mythological traditions. Contra Oleson, C. D. Osburn ("1 Enoch 80:2–8," pp. 299 and 302), considers it a "perplexing dilemma" to account for the presence of such a "disgusting" and "grotesque" pagan legend in a portion of Jude which is influenced so strongly by Jewish apocalyptic. In favor of Oleson's view, we should note the language and imagery used in Jude to describe the *houtoi: aselgeia* (v 4), *Sodoma kai Gomorra* (v 7), *ekporneuein* (v 7), *aperchomai opisō sarkos heteras* (v 7), *zōa* (v 10), *phtheirein* (v 10), *dis apothanonta* (v 12), *aischynē* (v 13), *kata tas epithymias heautōn poreuomai* (vv 16 and 18), and *misountes kai ton apo tēs sarkos espilōmenon chitōna* (v 23). In truth, Jude could not have picked a better ancient tradition with which to depict and denounce his adversaries!

204. In Homer's *Iliad* she is foremost the goddess of seduction and rape. In Corinth she is bisexual and found in bearded form (representing a unity of the sexes in fertility), surrounded and served by ministers of the cult.

CHAPTER 6. CONCLUSION: IN SEARCH OF A LITERARY STRATEGY

1. Emphasis added.

2. See I. H. Marshall, *Kept by the Power of God. A Study of Perseverance and Falling Away* (Minneapolis, Minn.: Bethany Fellowship, Inc., 1969), 164–66.

3. Marshall, *Kept,* 167.

Bibliography

Abbott, T. K. *Essays on the Original Texts of the Old and New Testaments*. London: Longman, Green & Co., 1891.

Ackroyd, P. R., and C. F. Evans, ed. *The Cambridge History of the Bible—Vol. 1: From the Beginnings to Jerome*. Cambridge: Cambridge University, 1970.

Aland, K. "The Problem of Anonymity and Pseudepigraphy in Christian Literature of the First Two Centuries." In *The Authorship and Integrity of the New Testament*, edited by K. Aland, 1–13. London: SPCK, 1965.

Albin, C. A. *Judasbrevet. Traditionen-Texten-Tolkningen*. Stockholm: Natur och Kultur, 1962.

Alexander, P. S. "The Targumim and Early Exegesis of 'Sons of God' in Genesis 6." *JJS* 23 (1972): 58–69.

Alonso-Schökel, L. "Die stylistische Analyse bei den Propheten." *VTSup* 7 (1960): 154–64.

Anderson, B. W. "Tradition and Scripture in the Community of Faith." *JBL* 100 (1981): 5–21.

Anderson, F. I. "2 (Slavonic Apocalypse of) Enoch." In *The Old Testament Pseudepigrapha—Vol. 1: Apocalyptic Literature and Testaments,* edited by J. H. Charlesworth, 91–221. Garden City, N.Y.: Doubleday, 1983.

Aptowitzer, V. *Kain und Abel in der Aggada, den Apokryphen, der hellenistischen, christlichen und muhammedanischen Literatur*. Wien/Leipzig: Lowit, 1922.

Aristotle. *The "Art" of Rhetoric*. LCL. Translated by J. H. Freese. Cambridge, Mass.: Harvard University, 1947.

Augustine, A. *The City of God*. 2 vols. Translated by J. Healey. London: Dent and Sons, Reprint 1957.

———. *On Christian Doctrine*. NPNF 4. Edited by P. Schaff. Buffalo: CLC, 1887.

Aulen, G. *Christus Victor*. New York: Macmillan, 1956.

Aune, D. E. *The New Testament in Its Literary Environment*. Philadelphia: Westminster, 1987.

Austin, B. R. *Clouds without Water*. Nashville, Tenn.: Broadman, 1968.

Baasland, E. "Literarische Form, Thematik und geschichtliche Einordnung des Jakobusbriefes." In *Aufstieg und Niedergang der römischen Welt. Geschichte und Kultur Roms im Spiegel der neueren Forschung*. II.25.5 Edited by W. Haase, 3646–84. Berlin/New York: de Gruyter, 1988.

Bachmann, E. T. *Luther's Works—Vol. 35: Word and Sacrament 1*. Philadelphia: Muhlenberg, 1960.

Ballantine, W. G. *Understanding the Bible*. Springfield, Mass.: Johnson, 1925.

Barbel, J. *Christos Angelos. Die Anschauung von Christus als Bote und Engel in der gelehrten und volkstümlichen Literatur des christlichen Altertums*. BRKGA 3. Bonn: Hanstein, 1941.

Barclay, W. *The Letters of James and Peter*. DBS. Rev. ed. Philadelphia: Westminster, 1976.

———. *The Letters to Timothy, Titus and Philemon*. DBS. Philadelphia: Westminster, 1975.

Barns, T. "The Epistle of St. Jude. A Study in Marcosian Heresy." *JTS* 6 (1905): 391–411.

Barthelemy, D., and J. T. Milik. *Discoveries in the Judean Desert, Qumran Cave 1*. Oxford: Clarendon, 1955.

Bartlett, D. "James as a Jewish Document." In *SBL Seminar Papers*, 116–34. Chico, Calif.: Scholars, 1979.

Barton, G. A. "The Origin of the Names of Angels and Demons in the Extra-canonical Apocalyptic Literature to 100 A.D." *JBL* 31 (1912): 156–67.

Bauckham, R. J. "James, 1 and 2 Peter, Jude." In *It Is Written: Scripture Citing Scripture. Essays in Honour of B. Lindars*, edited by D. A. Carson and H.G.M. Williamson, 303–17. Cambridge: Cambridge University, 1988.

———. *Jude, 2 Peter*. WBC 50. Waco, Texas: Word, 1983.

———. "The Letter of Jude: An Account of Research." In *Aufstieg und Niedergang der römishen Welt. Geschichte und Kultur Roms im Spiegel der neueren Forshung*. II.25.5. Edited by W. Haase, 3791–3826. Berlin/New York: de Gruyter, 1988.

———. "A Note on a Problem in the Greek Version of 1 Enoch 1.9." *JTS* 32 (1981): 136–38.

Bauer, W. *A Greek-English Lexicon of the New Testament and other Early Christian Literature*. 2d ed. Edited by F. W. Gingrich and F. W. Danker. Chicago: University of Chicago, 1958.

———. *Orthodoxy and Heresy in Earliest Christianity*. Philadelphia: Fortress, 1946.

Beasley-Murray, G. R. *The General Epistles. James, 1 Peter, Jude, 2 Peter*. London/New York/Nashville: Lutterworth/Abingdon, 1965.

Beckwith, R. *The Old Testament Canon of the New Testament Church and Its Background in Early Judaism*. Grand Rapids, Mich.: Eerdmans, 1985.

Benoit, W. L. "Aristotle's Example: The Rhetorical Induction." *QJS* 66 (1980): 189–92.

Berger, K. *Die Amen-Worte Jesu. Eine Untersuchung zum Probleme der Legitimation in apokalyptischer Rede*. BZNW 39. Berlin: de Gruyter, 1970.

———. "Hartherzigkeit und Gottes Gesetz. Die Vorgeschichte des antijüdischen Vorwurfs in Mc10.5." *ZNW* 61 (1970): 1–47.

———. "Hellenistische Gattungen im Neuen Testament." In *Aufstieg und Niedergang der römischen Welt. Geschichte und Kultur Roms im Spiegel der neueren Forschung*. II.25.2 Edited by H. Temporini and W. Haase, 1034–1432. Berlin/New York: de Gruyter, 1984.

———. "Henoch." *RAC* 107/8 (1987/88): 473–545.

———. *Jüdische Schriften aus hellenistischer-römischer Zeit—II: Das Buch der Jubiläen*. Gütersloh: Mohn, 1981.

———. "Der Streit des guten und des bösen Engels um die Seele: Beobachtungen zu 4QAmr3 und Judas 9." *JSJ* 4 (1973): 1–18.

Betz, H. D. *Der Apostel Paulus und die sokratische Tradition*. Tübingen: Mohr, 1972.

———. "The Problem of Rhetoric and Theology according to the Apostle Paul."

In *L'Apôtre Paul*. EBETL 73. Edited by A. Vanhoye, 16–48. Leuven: Peteers-Leuven University, 1986.

Bickerman, E. "Some Notes on the Transmission of the LXX." In *Alexander Marx Jubilee Volume*, 149–78. New York: Jewish Theological Seminary, 1950.

Bieder, W. "Judas 22f." *TZ* 6 (1950): 75–77.

———. *Die Vorstellung von der Höllenfahrt Jesu Christi*. Zürich: Zwingli, 1949.

Bigg, C. *A Critical and Exegetical Commentary on the Epistles of St. Peter and St. Jude*. ICC. New York: Scribner, 1922.

Birdsall, J. N. "The Text of Jude in p72." *JTS* 14 (1963) 394–99.

Birt, T. *Kritik und Hermeneutik nebst Abriss des antiken Buchwesens*. München: Beck, 1913.

Black, C. C. "The Rhetorical Form of the Hellenistic Jewish and Early Christian Sermon: A Response to L. Wills." *HTR* 81 (1988) 155–79.

Black, E. *Rhetorical Criticism. A Study in Method*. New York: Macmillan, 1965.

Black, M., and A.-M. Denis. *Apocalypsis Henochi Graece. Fragmenta Pseudepigraphorum Quae Supersunt Graeca*. Leiden: Brill, 1970.

Black, M. *The Book of Enoch or 1 Enoch*. Leiden: Brill, 1985.

———. "Critical and Exegetical Notes on Three New Testament Texts: Hebrews xi.11, Jude 5, James i.27." In *Apophoreta. Festschrift E. Haenchen*. BZNW 30. Edited by W. Eltester and F. H. Kettler, 39–45. Berlin: Töpelmann, 1964.

———. "The Maranatha Invocation and Jude 14,15 (1 Enoch 1:9)." In *Christ and Spirit in the New Testament. Studies in Honour of C.F.D. Moule*, edited by B. Lindars and S. Smalley, 189–96. Cambridge University, 1973.

Blackman, P., ed. *Mishnayoth—Vol. IV: Order Nezekim*. Gateshead: Judaica, 1977.

Blass, F., and A. Debrunner, *A Greek Grammar of the New Testament and Other Early Christian Literature*. Translated and revised by R. W. Funk. Chicago: University of Chicago, 1961.

Bloch, J. *On the Apocalyptic in Judaism*. Philadelphia: Dropsie, 1952.

Bloch, R. "Midrash." In *Dictionnaire de la Bible, Supplément*. Vol. 5, edited by L. Pirot et al., 1263–81. Paris: Librairie Letouzey, 1957.

———. "Note méthodologique pour l'étude de la Littérature rabbinique." *RSR* 43 (1955): 194–225.

Blinzler, J. "Judasbrief." *LThK* 5 (1960): 1155–56.

Boismard, P. *Quatre Hymnes Baptismales dans le Première Epître de Pierre*. LD 30. Paris: du Cerf, 1961.

Boobyer, G. H. "The Verbs in Jude 11." *NTS* 5 (1958/59): 45–47.

Bousset, W. *Die Religion des Judentums im neutestamentlichen Zeitalter*. Berlin: von Reuther & Reichard, 1903.

———. "Zur Hadesfahrt Christi." *ZNW* 19 (1919/20): 50–66.

Bousset, W., and H. Gressmann. *Die Religion des Judentums im späthellenistischen Zeitalter*. HNT 21. Tübingen: Beck, 1926.

Boyd, J.W. *Satan and Māra*. SHR 27. Leiden: Brill, 1975.

Braun, H. "Qumran und das Neue Testament. Ein Bericht über 10 Jahre Forschung (1950–1959)." *TRu* 30 (1964) 1–38, 89–137.

Brichto, H. C. *The Problem of "Curse" in the Hebrew Bible*. SBLMS 13. Philadelphia: SBL, 1963.

Brock, S. P. "Translating the Old Testament." In *It Is Written: Scripture Citing Scripture. Essays in Honour of B. Lindars,* edited by D. A. Carson and H.G.M. Williamson, 87–98. Cambridge: Cambridge University, 1988.

Brockington, L. H. "The Septuagintal Background of the New Testament Use of *DOXA.*" In *Studies in the Gospels,* edited by D. E. Nineham, 1–18. Oxford: Blackwell, 1955.

Brooks, O. S. "1 Peter 3:21—The Clue to the Literary Structure of the Epistle." *NovT* 16 (1974): 290–305.

Brownlee. W. H. "The Background of Biblical Interpretation at Qumran." In *Qumrân: sa piéte, sa théologie et son milieu,* edited by M. Delcor, 183–93. Paris: Duculot, 1978.

―――. "Biblical Interpretation among the Sectaries of the Dead Sea Scrolls." *BA* 145 (1951): 54–76.

Brox, N. *Falsche Verfasserangaben. Zur Erklärung der frühchristlichen Pseudepigraphie.* Stuttgart: KBW, 1975.

―――. "Häresie." *RAC* 13 (1984): 248–97.

Bruce, F. F. "Scripture and Tradition in the New Testament." In *Holy Book and Holy Tradition,* edited by F. F. Bruce and E. G. Rupp, 68–93. Manchester: University of Manchester, 1968.

―――. "Some Thoughts on the Beginning of the New Testament Canon." *BJRL* 65 (1983): 37–65.

Brun, L. *Segen und Fluch im Urchristentum.* Oslo: Dybwad, 1932.

Budge, E.A.W. *Saint Michael the Archangel: Three Encomiums.* London: Kegan Paul, Trench, Trubner & Co., 1894.

Buhlmann, W., and K. Scherer. *Stilfiguren der Bibel. Ein kleines Nachschlagewerk.* BibB 10. Bern: Schweizerisches Katholisches Bibelwerk, 1978.

Bullinger, E. W. *Figures of Speech in the Bible.* Grand Rapids, Mich.: Baker, rep. 1968.

Bultmann, R. "Bekenntnis- und Liedfragmente im ersten Petrusbrief." In *Coniectanea Neotestamentica.* Vol. 11, 1–14. Lund/Copenhagen: Gleerup/Munksgaard, 1947.

Burgess, T. C. "Epideictic Literature." *University of Chicago Studies in Classical Philology* 3 (1902): 89–261.

Burn, A. E. "The Descent into Hell." *ExpTim* 14 (1902/3): 554–57.

Caird, G. B. *Principalities and Powers.* Oxford: Clarendon, 1965.

Calvin, J. *Commentaries on the Catholic Epistles.* Translated by Owen. Edinburgh: Calvin Translation Society, 1855.

Candlish, J. S. "On the Moral Character of Pseudonymous Books." *Expos* 4/4 (1891): 91–107, 262–79.

Cantinat, J. *Les Épîtres de Saint Jacques et de Saint Jude.* Paris: Libraire Lecoffre, 1973.

Cantley, M. J. "Introduction to Apocalyptic." In *Contemporary New Testament Studies,* edited by M. R. Ryan, 439–43. Collegeville, Minn.: Liturgical, 1965.

Cassuto, U. "The Episode of the Sons of God and the Daughters of Men." In *Biblical and Oriental Studies.* Vol. 1, 18–45. Jerusalem: Magnes, 1973.

Cavallin, H.C.C. "The False Teachers of 2 Peter as Pseudo-Prophets." *NovT* 21 (1979): 263–70.

Chadwick, H. "Justification by Faith and Hospitality." In *Studia Patrologia*. Vol. 4. T.U. 79. Edited by F. L. Cross, 281–85. Berlin: Akademie, 1961.

Chaine, J. *Les Épîtres Catholiques*. Paris: Études Bibliques, 1939.

Chajes, Z. H. *The Student's Guide through the Talmud*. London: East and West Library, 1952.

Charles, J. D. "Jude's Use of Pseudepigraphal Source-Material as Part of a Literary Strategy." *NTS* 37 (1991): 130–45.

———. "Literary Artifice in the Epistle of Jude." *ZNW* 82/1 (1991): 106–24.

———. "'Those' and 'These': The Use of the Old Testament in the Epistle of Jude." *JSNT* 38 (1990): 109–24.

Charles, R. H. *The Apocrypha and Pseudepigrapha of the Old Testament*. 2 vols. Oxford: Clarendon, 1913.

———. *The Ascension of Isaiah*. London: SPCK, 1917.

———. *The Assumption of Moses*. London: Adam & Charles Black, 1897.

———. *The Book of Enoch*. Oxford: Clarendon, 1912.

Charlesworth, J. H., ed. *The Old Testament Pseudepigrapha*. 2 vols. Garden City, N.Y.: Doubleday, 1983, 1985.

———. *The Old Testament Pseudepigrapha and the New Testament. Prolegomena for the Study of Christian Origins*. SNTSMS 54. Cambridge: Cambridge University, 1985.

———. *The Pseudepigrapha in Modern Research*. Missoula, Mont.: Scholars, 1976.

Cherwitz, R. A. "The Contributory Effect of Rhetorical Discourse: A Study of Language-in-Use." *QJS* 66 (1980): 33–50.

Childs, B. S. *Myth and Reality in the Old Testament*. Naperville, Ill.: Allenson, 1960.

Cicero, *De Inventione*. LCL. Translated by H. M. Hubell. Cambridge, Mass.: Harvard University, 1949.

———. *Letters to Atticus*. LCL. 2 vols. Translated by E. O. Winstedt. Cambridge, Mass.: Harvard University, 1913, 1918.

———. *Letters to His Friends*. LCL. 2 vols. Edited and translated by W. G. Williams. Cambridge, Mass.: Harvard University, 1928, 1943.

———. *De Oratore Partitione Oratoriae*. LCL. Translated by E. W. Sutton and H. Rackham. Cambridge, Mass.: Harvard University, 1942.

Cladder, H. J. "Der formale Aufbau des Jakobusbriefes." *ZKT* 28 (1904): 295–330.

———. "Strophic Structure in St. Jude's Epistle." *JHS* 5 (1904): 589–601.

Clark, D. L. *Rhetoric in Greco-Roman Education*. Morningside Heights, N.Y.: Columbia University, 1957.

Clarke, M. L. *Higher Education in the Ancient World*. London: Routledge & Kegan Paul, 1971.

Clarke, W.K.L. *The First Epistle of Clement to the Corinthians*. London/New York: SPCK/Macmillan, 1937.

Clifford, R. J. *The Cosmic Mountain in Canaan and the Old Testament*. Cambridge, Mass.: Harvard University, 1972.

———. "The Use of HÔY in the Prophets." *CBQ* 28 (1966): 458–64.

Clines, D.J.A., et al., ed. *Art and Meaning: Rhetoric in Biblical Literature*. JSOTSS 19. Sheffield: University of Sheffield, 1982.

Closen, G. E. *Die Sünde der "Söhne Gottes."* Rom: Päpstliches Bibelinstitut, 1937.

Collins, J. J. "The Apocalyptic Context of Christian Origins." In *Backgrounds for the Bible,* edited by M. P. O'Connor and D. N. Freedman, 257–71. Winona Lake, Ind.: Eisenbrauns, 1987.

———. *The Apocalyptic Imagination: An Introduction to the Jewish Matrix of Christianity.* New York: Crossroad, 1984.

———. "Pseudonymity, Historical Reviews and the Genre of the Apocalypse of John." *CBQ* 39 (1977): 124–40.

———. "Sibylline Oracles." In *The Old Testament Pseudepigrapha—Vol. 1: Apocalyptic Literature and Testaments,* edited by J. H. Charlesworth, 317–472. Garden City, N.Y.: Doubleday, 1983.

———. "The Testament (Assumption) of Moses." In *Outside the Old Testament,* edited by M. de Jonge, 145–58. Cambridge: Cambridge University, 1985.

Colpe, C. "Jüdisch-hellenistische Literatur." In *Der kleine Pauly: Lexikon der Antike,* edited by K. Ziegler and W. Sontheimer, 1507–12. Stuttgart: Drückenmüller, 1967.

Conzelmann, H. *The Theology of St. Luke.* London: Hodder and Stoughton, 1960.

Corbett, E. J. P. "Introduction to Rhetorical Analyses of Literary Works." In *Selected Essays of E. J. P. Corbett,* edited by R. J. Connors, 75–97. Dallas, Tex: SMU, 1989.

———. "The Usefulness of Classical Rhetoric." In *Selected Essays of E.J.P. Corbett,* edited by R. J. Connors, 14–21. Dallas, TX: SMU, 1989.

Cope, E. M. *The Rhetoric of Aristotle.* Cambridge: Cambridge University, 1877.

Cothenet, E. "Les Prophètes chrétiens comme exégètes charismatiques de l'écriture." In *Prophetic Vocation in the New Testament and Today.* NovTSup 45. Edited by J. Panagopoulos, 77–107. Leiden: Brill, 1977.

———. "La Tradition selon Jude et 2 Pierre." *NTS* 35 (1989): 407–20.

Coughenour, R. A. "The Woe-Oracles in Ethiopic Enoch." *JSJ* 9 (1978): 192–97.

Crafer, T. W., ed. *The Epistles of Ignatius.* New York/London: Macmillan/SPCK, 1919.

Cramer, J. A., ed. *Catena in Epistolas Catholicas Accesserunt Oecumenii et Arethae Commentarii in Apocalypsin.* Hildesheim: Olms, 1967.

Cranfield, C.E.B. *The First Epistle of Peter.* London: SCM, 1950.

———. "The Interpretation of 1 Peter iii.19 and iv.6." *ExpTim* 69 (1957/58): 369–72.

Cross, F. L. *1 Peter: A Paschal Liturgy.* London: Mowbray, 1954.

Cullmann, O. *Christology of the New Testament.* London: SCM, 1963.

———. "Les Origines des premières confessions de foi." *RHPR* 21 (1941): 77–110.

Dalton, W. J. *Christ's Proclamation to the Spirits. A Study of 1 Peter 3 : 18–4 : 6.* AnBib 23. Rome: Pontifical Bible Institute, 1965.

———. "The Interpretation of 1 Peter 3,19 and 4,6: Light from 2 Peter." *Bib* 60 (1979): 547–55.

Daniel, C. "La Mention des Esséniens dans le texte grec de l'épître de Saint Jude." *Museon* 81 (1968): 503–21.

Danielou, J. *The Theology of Jewish-Christianity.* London: Darton, Longman & Todd, 1964.

Danker, F. W. "Epistle of Jude." In *International Standard Bible Encyclopedia*. Vol. 2, edited by G. W. Bromiley, 1153–55. Grand Rapids, Mich.: Eerdmans, 1982.

Daube, D. "Rabbinic Methods of Interpretation and Hellenistic Rhetoric." *HUCA* 22 (1949): 239–64.

Davids, P. H. "The Epistle of James in Modern Discussion." In *Aufstieg und Niedergang der römischen Welt. Geschichte und Kultur Roms im Spiegel der neueren Forschung*. II.25.5. Edited by W. Haase, 3621–45. Berlin/New York: de Gruyter, 1988.

———. "Tradition and Citation in the Epistle of James." *Scripture, Tradition, and Interpretation*, edited by W. W. Gasque and W. S. LaSor, 113–26. Grand Rapids, Mich.: Eerdmans, 1978.

Davies, P. R. *The Damascus Document. An Introduction to the "Damascus Document."* JSOTSS 25. Sheffield: JSOT, 1982.

Dehandschütter, B. "Pseudo-Cyprian, Jude and Enoch. Some Notes on 1 Enoch 1 : 9." In *Tradition and Re-Interpretation in Jewish and Early Christian Literature. Essays in Honour of J.C.H. Lebram*. Leiden: Brill, 1986. Pp. 114–20.

Deichgräber, R. *Gotteshymnus und Christushymnus in der frühen Christenheit*. SUNT 5. Göttingen: Vandenhoeck & Ruprecht, 1967.

Deissmann, A. *Bible Studies. Contributions Chiefly from Papyri and Inscriptions to the History of the Language, Literature and the Religion of Hellenistic Judaism and Primitive Christianity*. Edinburgh: Clark, 1901.

———. *Light from the Ancient East*. London: Hodder and Stoughton, 1910.

de Jonge, M. *The Testaments of the Twelve Patriarchs*. Leiden: Brill, 1978.

Delcor, M. "Le Mythe de la chute des anges et l'origine des géants comme explication du mal dans l'apocalyptique juive. Histoire des traditions." *RHR* 190 (1976): 3–53.

Delling, G. *"MONOS THEOS."* In *Studien zum Neuen Testament und zum hellenistischen Judentum*, 391–400. Göttingen: Vandenhoeck & Ruprecht, 1972.

Demetrius. *On Style*. LCL. Translated by W. R. Roberts. Cambridge, Mass.: Harvard University, 1932.

Denis, A.-M. "Fragmenta Pseudepigraphorum Graeca." In *Pseudepigrapha Veteris Testyamenti Graeca III*, edited by A.-M. Denis and M. de Jonge, 63–67. Leiden: Brill, 1970.

———. *Introduction aux Pseudepigraphes Grecs D'Ancien Testament*. Leiden: Brill, 1970.

Desjardins, M. "The Portrayal of the Dissidents in 2 Peter and Jude: Does It Tell Us More about the 'Ungodly' than the 'Godly'?" *JSNT* 30 (1987): 89–102.

de Wette, W. M. L. *Kurze Erklärung der Briefe des Petrus, Judas und Jakobus*. Leipzig: Hirzel, 1865.

Dexinger, F. *Henochs Zehnwochenapokalypse und offene Probleme der Apokalyptikforschung*. Leiden: Brill, 1977.

———. *Sturz der Gottessöhne oder Engel vor der Sinflut?* WBT 13. Wien: Herder, 1966.

Dibelius, M. *James*. Hermeneia. Rev. H. Greeven. Philadelphia: Fortress, 1970.

Dingermann, F. "Die Botschaft vom Vergehen dieser Welt und von der Geheimnissen der Endzeit—Beginnende Apokalyptik im Alten Testament." In *Wort und Botschaft. Eine theologische und kritische Einführung in die Probleme des Alten Testaments*, edited by J. Schreiner, 329–42. Wurzburg: Echter, 1967.

Dixon, P. *Rhetoric*. London: Methuen, 1971.

Doeve, J. *Jewish Hermeneutics in the Synoptic Gospels and Acts*. Assen: Van Gorcum, 1954.

Doty, W. G. "The Classification of Epistolary Literature." *CBQ* 31 (1969): 183–98.

———. *Letters in Primitive Christianity*. GBS 7. Philadelphia: Fortress, 1973.

Dodd, C. H. *According to The Scriptures. The Substructure of New Testament Theology*. London: Nisbet, 1952.

Drazin, N. *History of Jewish Education from 515 B.C.E. to 22 C.E.* Baltimore, Md.: Johns Hopkins, 1940.

Dubarle, A.-M. "Le Péché des anges dans l'épître de Jude." In *Memorial J. Chaine*, 145–49. Paris/Lyon: Facultes Catholiques, 1950. Pp. 145–49.

Dublin, J. "The Descent into Hades and Christian Baptism." *Expos* 11 (1916): 241–74.

Duhm, H. *Die bösen Geister im Alten Testament*. Tübingen/Leipzig: Mohr/Siebeck, 1904.

du Plessis, P. J. "The Authorship of the Epistle of Jude." In *Biblical Essays: Proceedings of the Ninth Meeting of die Ou-Testamentiese Wekgemeenskap in Suid-Afrika*, 191–99. Potchefstroom: Potchefstroom Herald Beperk, 1966.

Eden, K. "Hermeneutics and the Ancient Rhetorical Tradition." *Rhetorica* 5 (1987): 59–86.

Eichrodt, W. *A Theology of the Old Testament*. OTL. 2 vols. Philadelphia: Westminster, 1961.

———. *Ezekiel. A Commentary*. OTL. Philadelphia: Westminster, 1970.

Eisenmenger, J. A. *Entdecktes Judenthum*. 2 vols. Königsberg in Preussen: n.p., 1700.

Ellis, E. E. "A Note on First Corinthians 10:4." *JBL* 76 (1957): 53–56.

———. *Paul's Use of the Old Testament*. Edinburgh: Oliver and Boyd, 1957.

———. "Prophecy and Hermeneutic in Jude." In *Prophecy and Hermeneutic in Early Christianity*, 221–36. Tübingen: Mohr, 1978.

Eusebius. *The History of the Church—from Christ to Constantine*. Translated by G. A. Williamson. Minneapolis: Augsburg, 1975. Reprint.

Exler, F.X.J. *The Form of the Ancient Greek Letter. A Study in Greek Epistolography*. Washington, D.C.: CUA, 1923.

Eybers, I. H. "Aspects of the Background of the Letter of Jude." *Neot* 9 (1975): 113–23.

Fantham, E. "Imitation and Decline: Rhetorical Theory and Practice in the First Century after Christ." *CP* 73 (1978): 1–16.

Farmer, G. "Did Our Lord, or Enoch, 'Preach to the Spirits in Prison'?" *Expos* 6 (1902) 377–78.

Farrar, F. W. *The Early Days of Christianity*. New York: Alden, 1883.

Feinberg, J. S. "1 Peter 3 : 18–20, Ancient Mythology, and the Intermediate State." *WTJ* 48 (1986): 303–36.

Felton, J. *Die zwei Briefe des heiligen Petrus und der Judasbrief*. Regensburg: Reimer, 1929.

Fischer, K. M. "Anmerkungen zur Pseudepigraphie im Neuen Testament." *NTS* 23 (1976): 76–81.

Fitzmyer, J. A. "Implications of the New Enoch Literature from Qumran." *TS* 38 (1977): 332–45.

———. "Jewish Christianity in Acts in Light of the Qumran Scrolls." In *Essays on the Semitic Background of the New Testament,* 271–303. London: Chapman, 1971.

———. "The Language of Palestine in the First Century A.D." *CBQ* 32 (1970): 501–31.

———. "Der semitische Hintergrund des neutestamentlichen Kyriostitels." In *Jesus Christus in Historie in Theologie: Neutestamentliche Festschrift H. Conzelmann zum 60. Geburgstag,* edited by G. Strecker, 270–97. Tübingen: Mohr, 1975.

———. *To Advance the Gospel. New Testament Studies.* New York: Crossroad, 1981.

———. "The Use of Explicit Old Testament Quotations in Qumran Literature and in the New Testament." *NTS* 7 (1960/61): 297–333.

Fleischhacker, A. *Der Tod Mose's nach der Sage.* Halle: Universität Halle, 1888.

Flusser, D. "Apocalypse." In *Encyclopaedia Judaica.* Vol. 3, 179–80. Jerusalem/ New York: Macmillan, 1971.

———. "Palaea Historica: An Unknown Source of Biblical Legends." In *Scripta Hierosolymitana—Vol. 22: Studies in Aggadah and Folk-Literature,* 48–79. Jerusalem: Hebrew University, 1971.

Foakes-Jackson, F. J., and K. Lake. *The Beginnings of Christianity.* Vol. 5. London: Macmillan, 1933.

Foerster, W., and G. Quell. *Lord.* London: Adam & Charles Black, 1958.

Forbes, C. "Comparison, Self-Praise and Irony: Paul's Boasting and the Conventions of Hellenistic Rhetoric." *NTS* 32 (1986): 1–31.

Fornberg, T. *An Early Church in a Pluralistic Society: A Study of 2 Peter.* ConBNT 9. Lund: CWK Gleerup, 1977.

Fossum, J. "Kyrios Jesus as the Angel of the Lord in Jude 5–7." *NTS* 33 (1987): 226–43.

France, R. T. "Exegesis in Practice: Two Examples." In *New Testament Interpretation. Essays on Principles and Methods,* edited by I. H. Marshall, 252–81. Grand Rapids, Mich.: Eerdmans, 1977.

———. *Jesus and the Old Testament. His Application of Old Testament Passages to Himself and His Mission.* London: Tyndale, 1971.

Francis, F. O. "The Form and Function of the Opening and Closing Paragraphs of James and 1 John." *ZNW* 61 (1970): 110–26.

Frings, J. "Zu 1 Petr 3,19 und 4,6." *BZ* 17 (1926): 75–88.

Fritsch, C. T. "*TO ANTITYPON.*" In *Studia Biblica et Semitica. T. C. Vriezen,* edited by W. C. van Unnik and A. S. van der Woude, 100–107. Wageningen: Veenman & Zonen, 1966.

Frost, S. B. "Apocalyptic and History." In *The Bible in Its Literary Milieu,* edited by J. Maier and V. Tollers, 134–47. Grand Rapids, Mich.: Eerdmans, 1979.

———. *Old Testament Apocalyptic.* London: Epworth, 1952.

Fuchs, E., and P. Reymond. *La Deuxième Épître de Saint Pierre. L'Épître de Saint Jude.* CNT 13b. Neuchâtel: Delachaux & Niestlé, 1980.

Gaffin, R. B., Jr. "The New Testament as Canon." In *Inerrancy and Hermeneutic: A Tradition, A Challenge, A Debate,* edited by H. Conn., 165–83. Grand Rapids, Mich.: Baker, 1988.

Garland, D. E. *The Intention of Matthew 23.* NovTSup 52. Leiden: Brill, 1979.

Geisler, N. "The Extent of the Old Testament Canon." In *Current Issues in Biblical and Patristic Interpretation. Festschrift M. Tenney*, edited by G. F. Hawthorne, 31–46. Grand Rapids, Mich.: Eerdmans, 1975.

Gerstenberger, E. "The Woe-Oracles of the Prophets." *JBL* 81 (1962): 249–63.

Gertner, M. "Midrashim in the New Testament." *JSS* 7 (1962): 267–92.

Ginzberg, L. *The Legends of the Jews*. vols. 3, 4, and 6. Philadelphia: Jewish Publication Society of America, 1911, 1968.

Glasson, T. F. *Greek Influence in Jewish Eschatology*. London: SPCK, 1961.

Glaue, P. "Amen." *ZKG* 44 (1925): 184–98.

Goldstein, J. A. "The Testament of Moses: Its Content, Its Origin and Its Attestation in Josephus." In *Studies on the Testament of Moses*, edited by G.W.E. Nicklesburg, 44–52. SBLSCS 4. Cambridge, Mass.: SBL, 1973.

Goppelt, L. *Der Erste Petrusbrief*. MeyerK 12/1. Göttingen: Vandenhoeck & Ruprecht, 1978.

———. *Typos. The Typological Interpretation of the Old Testament in the New*. Translated by D. H. Madvig. Grand Rapids, Mich.: Eerdmans, 1982.

Goodspeed, E. J. "Enoch in 1 Peter 3:19." *JBL* 73 (1954): 91–92.

Green, E.M.B. *2 Peter Reconsidered*. London: Tyndale, 1961.

Green, M. *The Second Epistle General of Peter and the General Epistle of Jude. An Introduction and Commentary*. TNTC. Rev. ed. Leicester/Grand Rapids, Mich.: Inter Varsity/Eerdmans, 1987.

Greenwood, D. "Rhetorical Criticism and Formgeschichte: Some Methodological Considerations." *JBL* 89 (1970): 418–26.

Grelot, P. "Hénoch et les écritures." *RB* 82 (1975): 481–55.

———. "La Légende d'Hénoch dans les apocryphes et dans la Bible: Origine et signification." *RSR* 46 (1958): 5–26, 181–210.

Grillmeier, A. "Der Gottessohn im Totenreich." *ZKT* 71 (1949): 1–53.

Grintz, J. M. "Apocrypha and Pseudepigrapha." In *Encyclopaedia Judaica*. Vol. 3, 181–86. New York/Jerusalem: Macmillan, 1971.

Grotius, H. *Annotationes in libros Evangeliorum*. Amsterdam: Apud Ioh e Cornelium Blaev, 1641.

Grube, G.M.A. *The Greek and Roman Critics*. Toronto: University of Toronto, 1965.

———. *How Did the Greeks Look at Literature?* Cincinnati: U. of Cincinnati, 1967.

Grudem, W. "Christ Preaching Through Noah: 1 Peter 3:19–20 in the Light of Dominant Themes in Jewish Literature." *TrinJ* 7 (1986): 3–31.

Grundmann, W. *Der Brief des Judas und der zweite Brief des Petrus*. THNT 15. Berlin: Evan. Verlagsanstalt, 1967.

———. "Stehen und Fallen im qumranischen und neutestamentlichen Schrifttum." In *Qumran-Probleme*. SSA 42, edited by H. Bardtke, 147–66. Berlin: Akademie, 1963.

Gruppe, O. "War Gen. 6,1–4 ursprünglich mit der Sinflut verbunden?" *ZAW* 9 (1889): 135–60.

Gryglewicz, F. "The Evolution of the Theology of the Letter of St. Jude." *RuBi* 33 (1980): 247–58.

Gschwind, K. *Die Niederfahrt Christi in die Unterwelt*. NTAbh 2. Münster: Aschendorff, 1911.

Guignebert, C. "Angels and Demons." In *The Jewish World in the Time of Jesus*, 96–105. London: Routledge & Kegan Paul, 1951.

Gundry, R. H. "The Language Milieu of First-Century Palestine." *JBL* 83 (1964): 404–8.

Gunther, J. J. "The Alexandrian Epistle of Jude." *NTW* 30 (1984): 549–62.

Guthrie, D. "The Development of the Idea of Canonical Pseudepigrapha in New Testament Criticism." In Vox *Evangelica 1*, edited by R. P. Martin, 43–59. London: Tyndale, 1962.

———. *Early Christian Pseudepigraphy and Its Antecedents*. Dissertation: University of London, 1961.

———. *New Testament Introduction—Vol. 3: Hebrews to Revelation*. London: Tyndale, 1964.

———. "Tertullian and Pseudonymity." *ExpTim* 67 (1956): 341–42.

Haacker, K. and Schäfer, P. "Nachbiblische Traditionen vom Tod Mose." In *Josephus-Studien: Untersuchungen zu Josephus, dem antiken Judentum und dem Neuen Testament. O. Michel zum 70. Geburtstag Gewidmet*, edited by O. Betz et al., 147–74. Göttingen: Vandenhoeck & Ruprecht, 1974.

Hadas, M. *Hellenistic Culture—Fusion and Diffusion*. Morningside Heights, N.Y.: Columbia University, 1959.

Haenchen, E. "Matthäus 23." *ZTK* 48 (1951): 46–63.

Hahn, F. "Randbemerkungen zum Judasbrief." *TZ* 37 (1981): 209–18.

Hall, R. G. "The Rhetorical Outline for Galatians: A Reconsideration." *JBL* 106 (1987): 277–87.

Hamerton-Kelly, R. G. *Pre-Existence, Wisdom, and the Son of Man. A Study of the Idea of Pre-Existence in the New Testament*. Cambridge: Cambridge University, 1973.

Hanson, A. T. *Jesus Christ in the Old Testament*. London: SPCK, 1965.

———. *The Living Utterances of God. The New Testament Exegesis of the Old*. London: Darton, Longman & Todd, 1983.

———. "Salvation Proclaimed: I. 1 Peter 3 : 18–22." *ExpTim* 93 (1982): 100–105.

Hanson, P. D. *The Dawn of Apocalyptic*. Philadelphia: Fortress, 1975.

———. "Rebellion in Heaven, Azazel, and Euhemeristic Heroes in 1 Enoch 6–11." *JBL* 96 (1977): 195–233.

Harris, J. R. "A Further Note on the Use of Enoch in 1 Peter." *Expos* 6/4 (1901): 346–49.

Hartman, L. *Asking for a Meaning. A Study of 1 Enoch 1–5*. ConB 12. Lund: Gleerup, 1979.

———. *Prophecy Interpreted. The Formation of Some Apocalyptic Texts and of the Eschatological Discourse Mark 13*. ConB 1. Lund: Gleerup, 1966.

Hatch, E., and H. A. Redpath. *A Concordance to the Septuagint and Other Greek Versions of the Old Testament*. 2 vols. Oxford: Clarendon, 1947.

Heiligenthal, R. "Der Judasbrief. Aspekte der Forschung in den letzten Jahrhunderten." *TRu* 51 (1986): 117–29.

Hempel, J. "Die israelitischen Anchauungen von Segen und Fluch im Lichte altorientalischer Parallelen." *ZDMG* 79 (1925): 20–110.

Hengel, M. "Anonymität, Pseudepigraphie und literarische Fälschung in der jüdisch-hellenistischen Literatur." In *Pseudepigrapha I: Pseudopythagorica, Let-*

240   BIBLIOGRAPHY

tres de Platon, Littérature pseudepigrapha juive. EAC 18, edited by K. von Fritz, 231–308. Genève: Fondation Hardt, 1972.

———. *Judaism and Hellenism. Studies in Their Encounter during the Early Hellenistic Period.* 2 vols. Philadelphia: Fortress, 1980.

Henn, T. R. *The Bible as Literature.* London/New York: Oxford University, 1970.

Hennecke, E., et al., ed. *New Testament Apocrypha.* vol. 2. Philadelphia: Westminster, 1965.

Henry, P. *New Directions in New Testament Study.* Philadelphia: Westminster, 1979.

Hercher, R. *Epistolographi Graeci.* Paris: Didot, 1873.

Hesiod. *Theogony.* Edited by M. L. West. Oxford: Clarendon, 1982. Reprint.

Hester, J. D. "The Rhetorical Structure of Gal. 1:11–2:14." *JBL* 103 (1984): 223–33.

Hill, D. "Christian Prophets as Teachers or Instructors in the Church." In *Prophetic Vocation in the New Testament and Today,* edited J. Panagopoulos, 108–30. NovTSup 45. Leiden: Brill, 1977.

———. *New Testament Prophecy.* London: Marshall, Morgan and Scott, 1979.

Holtz, B. W. *Back to the Sources.* New York: Summit, 1984.

Holtzmann, H. "Höllenfahrt im Neuen Testament." *ARW* 11 (1908): 285–97.

Hopf, G. W. *Alliteration, Assonanz, Reim in der Bibel.* Erlangen: Deichert, 1883.

Hulley, K. K. "Principles of Textual Criticism Known to St. Jerome." *HSCP* 55 (1944): 104–9.

Huntzinger, C. H. "Zur Struktur der Christus-Hymnen in Phil 2 und 1 Petr 3." In *Der Ruf Jesu und die Antwort der Gemeinde. Festschrift J. Jeremias,* 142–45. Göttingen: Vandenhoeck & Ruprecht, 1970.

Huther, J. *Kritisch-exegetisches Handbuch über den 1. Brief des Petrus, den Brief Judas und den 2. Brief des Petrus.* MeyerK. Göttingen: Vandenhoeck & Ruprecht, 1887.

Isaac, E. "1 (Ethiopic Apocalypse of) Enoch." In *The Old Testament Pseudepigrapha—Vol. 1: Apocalyptic Literature and Testaments,* edited J. H. Charlesworth, 5–89. Garden City, N.Y.: Doubleday, 1983.

———. "New Light upon the Book of Enroch from Newly-Found Ethiopic Manuscripts." *JAOS* 103 (1983): 399–411.

Jaeger, W. *Early Christianity and Greek Paideia.* Cambridge, Mass.: Harvard University, 1961.

James, M. R. *Apocrypha Anecdota II.* Cambridge: Cambridge University, 1897.

———. *The Lost Apocrypha of the Old Testament—Their Titles and Fragments.* London/New York: SPCK/Macmillan, 1920.

———. *2 Peter and Jude.* Cambridge: Cambridge University, 1912.

———. *The Testament of Abraham.* Texts and Studies. Cambridge: Cambridge University, 1892.

Jansen, H. L. *Die Henochgestalt: Eine vergleichende religionsgeschichtliche Untersuchung.* Oslo: n.p., 1939.

Janssen, E. "Die Himmelfahrt Moses." In *Das Gottesvolk und seine Geschichte und Selbstverständnis im palästinensischen Schrifttum von Jesus ben Sirach bis Jehuda ha-Nasi.* Neukirchen-Vluyn: Neukirchener, 1971, 101–39.

Janzen, W. *Mourning Cry and Woe Oracle.* BZAW 125. Berlin/New York: de Gruyter, 1972.

Jastrow, M. *A Dictionary of the Targummim, the Talmud Babli and Yerushalmi, and the Midrashic Literature*. Vol. 1. Brooklyn, N.Y.: Traditional, 1903.

Jeremias, Joa. "Zwischen Karfreitag und Ostern." *ZNW* 42 (1949): 129–45.

Jeremias, Jor. *Theophanie. Die Geschichte einer alttestamentlichen Gattung*. WMANT 10. Neukirchen-Vluyn: Neukirchener, 1965.

Johnson, S. E. "The Preaching to the Dead." *JBL* 79 (1960): 48–51.

Johnson, S. J., Jr. *The Old Testament in the New. An Argument for Biblical Inspiration*. Grand Rapids, Mich.: Zondervan, 1980.

Jones, H. S. *"SPILAS—APARCHĒ PNEUMATOS." JTS* 23 (1922): 282–83.

Judge, E. A. "Paul's Boasting in Relation to Contemporary Professional Practice." *AusBR* 16 (1978): 37–50.

Junker, H. "Zur Erklärung von Gen. 6,1–4." *Bib* 16 (1935): 205–12.

Kaiser, W. C., Jr. *The Use of the Old Testament in the New Testament*. Chicago: Moody, 1985.

Kaplan, C. "The Pharisaical Character of the Book of Enoch." *ATR* 12 (1929/30): 531–38.

Käsemann, E. "An Apologia for Primitive Christian Eschatology." In *Essays on New Testament Themes*, 169–95. Philadelphia: Fortress, 1982.

———. "The Beginnings of Christian Theology." In *New Testament Questions of Today*, 82–107. Philadelphia: Fortress, 1969.

———. "On the Subject of Primitive Christian Apocalyptic." In *New Testament Questions of Today*, 108–37. Philadelphia: Fortress, 1969.

Kasser, R. *Papyrus B. XII. Actes de Apôtres, Épîtres de Jacques, Pierre, Jean et Jude*. Genève: Bibliotheca Bodmeriana, 1961.

Kaster, E. "Notes on 'Primary' and 'Secondary' Schools in Late Antiquity." *TAPA* 113 (1983): 323–46.

Kaupel, H. *Die Dämonen im Alten Testament*. Augsburg: Filser, 1930.

Kautzsch, E. *Die Apokryphen und Pseudepigrapha des Alten Testaments*. 2 vols. Tübingen: Mohr, 1900.

Keating, J. F. *The Agapé and the Eucharist in the Early Church*. London: Methuen, 1901.

Kee, H. C. "The Testaments of the Twelve Patriarchs." In *The Old Testament Pseudepigrapha—Vol. 1: Apocalyptic Literature and Testaments,* edited J. H. Charlesworth, 775–828. Garden City, N.Y.: Doubleday, 1983.

Keil, C. F. *Commentar über die Briefe des Petrus und Judas*. Leipzig: Dörffling und Franke, 1883.

Kellett, E. E. "Note on Jude 5." *ExpTim* 15 (1903/4): 381.

Kelly, J.N.D. *A Commentary on the Epistles of Peter and Jude*. London: Adam & Charles Black, 1969.

Kennedy, G. *The Art of Persuasion in Greece*. Princeton, N.J.: Princeton U., 1963.

———. *Classical Rhetoric and Its Christian and Secular Tradition from Ancient to Modern Times*. Chapel Hill, N.C.: University of North Carolina, 1980.

———. *New Testament Interpretation through Rhetorical Criticism*. Chapel Hill/New York: UNC, 1984.

Kenny, A. *A Stylometric Study of the New Testament*. Oxford: Clarendon, 1986.

Kinneavy, J. L. *Greek Rhetorical Origins of Christian Faith: An Inquiry*. New York/Oxford: Oxford University, 1987.

Kistemaker, S. *Peter and Jude*. NTC. Grand Rapids, Mich.: Baker, 1987.

Kittel, G., and G. von Rad. *"doxa."* In *Theological Dictionary of the New Testament.* Vol. 2, edited by G. Kittel, 233–55. Grand Rapids, Mich.: Eerdmans, 1964.

Klijn, A.F.J. "Jude 5 to 7." In *The New Testament Age. Essays in Honor of B. Reicke,* edited by W. C. Reinrich, 237–44. 2 vols. Macon, Ga.: Mercer University, 1984.

———. "The Study of Jewish Christianity." *NTS* 20 (1974): 419–31.

Knaake, J.K.F., et al. *D. Martin Luthers Werke.* Kritische Gesammtausgabe 12. Weimar: Bohlau, 1891.

Knibb, M. A. "Prophecy and the Emergence of the Jewish Apocalypses." In *Israel's Prophetic Tradition. Festschrift P.R. Ackroyd,* edited R. Coggins, et al., 155–80. Cambridge: Cambridge University, 1982.

Knight, G. W. *The Christian Renaissance.* London: Methuen, 1962.

Knoch, O. *Der 2. Petrusbrief, Der Judasbrief.* WB 8. Dusseldorf: Reimer, 1967.

Knopf, R. *Die Briefe Petri und Judä.* Göttingen: Vandenhoeck & Ruprecht, 1912.

Knox. A. D. *"SPILADES."* *JTS* 14 (1913): 547–49.

Knox, W. L. *Some Hellenistic Elements in Primitive Christianity.* London: Oxford University, 1944.

Koch, K. *The Rediscovery of Apocalyptic.* SBT 22. London: SCM, 1970.

König, E. *Stilistik, Rhetorik, Poetik in Bezug auf biblische Literatur.* Leipzig: Dieterich, 1900.

Kornfield, W. *Religion und Offenbarung in der Geschichte Israels.* Wien: Tyrolia, 1970.

Kraeling, E. G. "The Significance and Origin of Gen. 6:1–4." *JNES* 6 (1947): 193–208.

Krause, H.-J. *"hôj* als profetische Leichenklage über das eigene Volk." *ZAW* 85 (1973): 15–46.

Krodel, G. "Jude." In *Hebrews-James-1 and 2 Peter-Jude-Revelation,* edited by G. Krodel, 92–98. Philadelphia: Fortress, 1977.

Kubo, S. "Jude 22–3: Two-division Form or Three?" In *New Testament Textual Criticism. Its Significance for Exegesis. Essays in Honor of B. M. Metzger,* edited by E. J. Epp and G. D. Fee, 239–53. Oxford: Clarendon, 1981.

———. "Text Relationships in Jude." In *Studies in New Testament Language and Text,* 276–82. NovTSup 44. Leiden: Brill, 1976.

Kugelman, R. *James and Jude.* NTM 19. Wilmington, Del.: Glazier, 1980.

Kuhl, E. *Die Briefe Petri und Judae.* MeyerK 12. 6th ed. Göttingen: Vandenhoeck & Ruprecht, 1897.

Kümmel, W. G. *Introduction to the New Testament.* 14th ed. Nashville/New York: Abingdon, 1966.

Kurz, W. S. "Hellenistic Rhetoric in the Christological Proof of Luke-Acts." *CBQ* 42 (1980): 171–95.

Kvanvig, H. S. "Bruken av Noahtradisjonene i 1 Pet 3,20f." *TTKi* 56 (1985): 81–98.

———. *Roots of Apocalyptic. The Mesopotamian Background of the Enoch Figure and of the Son of Man.* Neukirchen-Vluyn: Neukirchener, 1988.

Ladd, G. E. "Apocalyptic, Apocalypse." In *Baker's Dictionary of Theology,* edited by E. F. Harrison, 50–54. Grand Rapids, Mich.: Baker, 1960.

Lampe, G.W.H., and K. J. Woollcombe. *Essays on Typology*. Naperville, Ill.: Allenson, 1957.

Lapide, P. "Insights into the Language of Jesus." *RQ* 8 (1975): 483–501.

Lapperrousaz, E. M. "Le Testament de Moise: Traduction avec introduction et notes." *Sem* 19 (1970): 1–140.

Lapple, A. *Key Problems of Genesis*. Glen Rock, N.J.: Paulist, 1967.

Laughlin, J.C.H. *A Study of the Motif of Holy Fire in the Old Testament*. Ann Arbor, Mich.: Xerox Microfilms, 1975.

Lausberg, H. *Handbuch der literarischen Rhetorik*. 2d ed. 2 vols. München: Huber, 1973.

Lawlor, G. L. *The Epistle of Jude*. Phillipsburg, N.J.: Presbyterian and Reformer, 1972.

Lawlor, H. J. "Early Citations from Enoch." *JP* 25 (1897): 164–225.

Lea, T. D. "The Early Christian View of Pseudepigraphic Writings." *JETS* 27 (1984): 65–75.

Lee, E. K. "Words Denoting 'Pattern' in the New Testament." *NTS* 8 (1961/62): 166–73.

Leivestad, R. *Christ the Conqueror*. London: SPCK, 1954.

Leon, J. M. *The Book of the Honeycomb's Flow (Sepher Nopheth Suphim)*. Translated by I. Rabinowitz. Ithaca/London: Cornell University, 1983.

Leslau, W., ed. *Falasha Anthology*. Yale Judaica Series 6. New Haven: Yale University, 1963.

Leuken, L. "Michael." In *Die Religion in Geschichte und Gegenwart*, edited by vol. 4. Edited by F. M. Schiele and L. Harnack. Vol. 4. Tübingen: Mohr, 1913.

Lewis, J. P. *A Study of the Interpretation of Noah and the Flood in Jewish and Christian Literazture*. Leiden: Brill, 1968.

Licht, J. "Taxo, or the Apocalyptic Doctrine of Divine Vengeance." *JJS* 12 (1961): 95–103.

Lieberman, S. *Greek in Jewish Palestine*. New York: Jewish Theological Seminary of America, 1942.

———. *Hellenism in Jewish Palestine*. Texts and Studies 18. New York: Jewish Theological Seminary, 1950.

Lietzmann, H. *Mass and Lord's Supper*. Leiden: Brill, 1979.

Lisowsky, G. *Kondordanz zum hebräischen Alten Testament*. Stuttgart: Priv. Württ. Bibelanstalt, 1958.

Lods, A. "Le Chute des anges." *RHPR* 7 (1927): 295–315.

Loewenstamm, S. E. "The Death of Moses." In *Studies on the Testament of Abraham*, edited by G.W.E. Nickelsburg, 184–203. SBLSC 56. Missoula, Mont.: Scholars, 1976.

Lohse, E. "Apokalyptik und Christologie." *ZNW* 62 (1971): 48–67.

Longenecker, R. N. *Biblical Exegesis in the Apostolic Period*. Grand Rapids, Mich.: Eerdmans, 1975.

———. *The Christology of Early Jewish Christianity*. SBT 17. London: SCM, 1970.

Lovestam, E. "Eschatologie und Tradition im 2. Petrusbreif." In *The New Testament Age. Essays in Honor of B. Reicke*, edited by W. C. Weinrich, Vol. 2. Macon, Ga.: Mercer, 1984.

Lührmann, D. "Henoch und die Metanoia.' *ZNW* 66 (1975): 103–16.

MacGregor, G.H.C. " 'Principalities and Powers.' The Cosmic Background of Paul's Thought." *NTS* 1 (1954/55): 17–28.

Magass, W. "Semiotik einer Ketzerpolemik am Beispiel von Jude 12f." *LB* 19 (1972): 36–48.

Maier, F. "Zur Erklärung des Judasbriefes (Jud. 5)." *BZ* 2 (1904): 377–97.

Mair, G. R. *Callimachus—Hymns and Epigrams. Lycophron.* LCL. Cambridge, Mass.: Harvard University, 1969.

Malherbe, A. J. *Ancient Epistolary Theorists.* SBLSBS 19. Atlanta, Ga.: Scholars, 1988.

Marcus, R., ed. *Questions and Answers on Genesis.* Cambridge, Mass./London: Harvard University/Heinemann, 1961.

Marrou, H. I. *A History of Education in Antiquity.* New York: Sheed and Ward, 1956.

Marrow, S. B. "Apocalyptic Genre and Eschatology." In *The Word in the World. Essays in Honor of F. L. Moriarity,* 71–81. Cambridge, Mass.: Harvard University, 1973.

Marshall, I. H. "Is Apocalyptic the Mother of Christian Theology?" In *Tradition and Interpretation. Essays in Honor of E. E. Ellis for His 60th Birthday,* edited by G. F. Hawthorne and O. Betz, 33–42. Grand Rapids, Mich./ Tübingen: Eerdmans/Mohr, 1978.

———. *Kept by the Power of God.* Minneapolis, Minn.: Bethany Fellowship, 1969.

———. "Palestinian and Hellenistic Christianity: Some Critical Comments." *NTS* 19 (1972/73): 271–87.

Marshall, J. T. "The Contest for the Body of Moses." *ExpTim* 11 (1899/1900): 390–91.

Martin, J. *Antike Rhetoric. Technik und Methode.* HAW 2/3. München: Beck, 1974.

Martin, R. P. "The Life-Setting of the Epistle of James in the Light of Jewish History." In *Biblical and Near Eastern Studies,* edited by G. A. Tuttle, 97–103. Grand Rapids, Mich.: Eerdmans, 1978.

Marxsen, W. *Der "Frühkatholizimus" im Neuen Testament.* BibS 21. Neukirchen: Neukirchener, 1958.

———. *Introduction to the New Testament.* Philadelphia: Fortress, 1970.

Mayerhoff, E. *Historisch-kritische Einleitung in die petrinischen Schriften.* Hamburg: Perthes, 1835.

Mayor, J. B. *The Epistle of St. Jude and the Second Epistle of St. Peter.* Minneapolis, Minn.: Klock & Klock, 1978. Reprint.

———. *"PHTHINOPŌRINOS." Expos* 9 (1904): 98–104.

McDonald, J.I.H. *Kerygma and Didache. The Articulation and Structure of the Earliest Christian Message.* SNTSMS 37. Cambridge: Cambridge University, 1980.

Meade, D. G. *Pseudonymity and Canonicity. An Investigation into the Relationship of Authorship and Authority in Jewish and Earliest Christian Tradition.* WUNT 39. Tübingen: Mohr, 1986.

Mees, M. "Papyrus VII (p72) und die Zitate aus dem Judasbrief bei Clemens von Alexandria." *CDios* 181 (1968): 551–59.

Metzger, B. M. "Literary Forgeries and Canonical Pseudepigrapha." In *New Testament Studies—Philological, Versional and Patristic,* 1–22. Leiden: Brill, 1980.

———. *A Textual Commentary on the Greek New Testament*. London/New York: UBS, 1971.

Michaels, J. R. *1 Peter*. WBC 49. Waco, Tex.: Word, 1988.

Michel, O. *Paulus und Seine Bibel*. Gütersloh: Bertelsmann, 1929.

Michl, J. *Die katholischen Briefe*. RNT 8. 2d ed. Regensburg: Pustet, 1968.

Midrash Rabbah. Vol. 1. Translated by H. Freedman and M. Simon. London: Soncino, 1939.

Migne, J. P., ed. *Patrologiae Cursus Completus*. Series Graeca. Vols. 7, 9, 11, 13, 17, 26, 39, 53, 74, 94, 101, and 119. Paris: Migne, 1842–1890.

———. *Patrologiae Cursus Completus*. Series Latina. Vols. 1, 23, and 33. Paris: Migne, 1872–1890.

Milik, J. T. *The Books of Enoch: Aramaic Fragments of Qumran Cave 4*. Oxford: Clarendon, 1976.

———. "Problèmes de la littérature Hénochique à la lumière des fragments araméens de Qumrân." *HTR* 64 (1971): 333–78.

———. "4Q Visions d'Amram et une Citation d'Origene." *RB* 79 (1972): 77–97.

Minear, P. S. *New Testament Apocalyptic*. IBT. Nashville, Tenn.: Abingdon, 1981.

———. "Some Archetypal Origins of Apocalyptic Predictions." In *Horizons in Biblical Theology*. Vol. 1, edited by U. Mauser, 103–35. Pittsburgh, Pa.: Barbour, 1979.

Moffatt, J. *The General Epistles. James, Peter, and Jude*. London: Hodder and Stoughton, 1932.

———. *An Introduction to the Literature of the New Testament*. New York: Scribner's Sons, 1915.

Morgenthaler, R. *Statistik des neutestamentlichen Wortschatzes*. Zürich/Frankfurt am Main: Gotthelf, 1958.

Morgenstern, J. "The HASIDIM—Who are They?" *HUCA* 38 (1967): 59–73.

Morris, L. *Apocalyptic*. Grand Rapids, Mich.: Eerdmans, Reprint. 1974.

Moule, C.F.D. *An Idiom Book of New Testament Greek*. Cambridge: Cambridge University, 1953.

———. "Once More, Who Were the Hellenists?" *ExpTim* 70 (1958/59): 100–102.

Moulton, J. H., and G. Milligan, *The Vocabulary of the Greek New Testament*. London: Hodder and Stoughton, 1930.

Moulton, J. H., and N. Turner, *A Grammar of New Testament Greek—Vol. 4: Style*. Edinburgh: Clark, 1976.

Moulton, R. G. *The Modern Reader's Bible*. New York: Macmillan, 1895.

Moulton, W. F., A. S. Geden, and H. K. Moulton, *A Concordance to the Greek New Testament*. Edinburgh: Clark, 1978.

Mounce, R. H. *A Living Hope. A Commentary on 1 and 2 Peter*. Grand Rapids: Eerdmans, 1982.

Muilenburg, J. "A Study in Hebrew Rhetoric: Repetition and Style." In *International Congress for the Study of the Old Testament*, 97–111. VTSup 1. Leiden: Brill, 1959.

———. "From Criticism and Beyond." In *The Bible in Its Literary Milieu. Contemporary Essays*, edited by J. Maier and V. Tollers, 362–80. Grand Rapids: Eerdmans, 1979.

Murray, R. "Defining Judaeo-Christianity." *HeyJ* 15 (1974) 303–10.

Neyrey, J. N. "The Form and Background of the Polemic in 2 Peter." *JBL* 99 (1980): 407–31.

Nickelsburg, G.W.E. "An Antiochan Date for the Testament of Moses." In *Studies on the Testament of Moses*, 33–37. SBLSCS 4. Missoula, Mont.: Scholars, 1973.

———. "Apocalyptic and Myth in 1 Enoch 6–11." *JBL* 96 (1977): 383–405.

Nickelsburg, G.W.E., and M. E. Stone. *Faith and Piety in Early Judaism—Texts and Documents*. Philadelphia: Fortress, 1983.

Norden E. *Die antike Kunstprosa vom VI Jahrhundert v. Chr. bis in die Zeit der Renaissance*. Leipzig/Berlin: Teubner, 1923.

Nork, F. *Rabbinische Quellen und Parallelen zu neutestamentlichen Schriftstellen*. Leipzig: Schumann, 1839.

Nötscher, F. "Himmlische Bücher und Schicksalsglaube in Qumran." *RQ* 1 (1959): 405–11.

———. *Zur theologischen Terminologie der Qumrantexte*. BBB 10. Bonn: Hanstein, 1956.

Odeberg, H. "Henoch." *TWNT*. Vol. 11. Stuttgart: Kohlhammer, 1935.

———. "*Iannēs, Iambrēs*." In *Theological Dictionary of the New Testament*. Vol. 3, edited by G. Kittel and G. W. Bromiley, 192–93. Grand Rapids: Eerdmans, 1965.

———. *3 Enoch or the Hebrew Book of Enoch*. Cambridge: Cambridge University, 1928.

Oesterley, W.O.E. "The Belief in Angels and Demons." In *Judaism and Christianity—Vol. I: The Age of Transition*, edited by W.O.E. Oesterley, 193–209. London: Sheldon, 1937.

Öhler, J. "Gymnasium." In *Paulys Real-Encyclopädia der klassischen Altertumswissenschaft*. Vol. 7, edited by W. Kroll, 2004–26. Stuttgart: Metzler, 1912.

Oleson, J. P. "An Echo of Hesiod's Theogony vv 190–2 in Jude 13." *NTS* 25 (1978/79): 492–503.

Omanson, R. "Suffering for Righteousness' Sake." *RevExp* 79 (1982): 432–50.

Osburn, C. D. "The Christological Use of 1 Enoch 1.9 in Jude 14,15." *NTS* 23 (1976/787): 334–41.

———. "1 Enoch 80:2–8 (67:5–7) and Jude 12–13.: *CBQ* 47 (1985): 296–303.

———. "The Text of Jude 22–23." *ZNW* 63 (1972): 139–44.

———. "A Note on Jude 5." *Bib* 62 (1981): 107–15.

Packer, J. I. *"Fundamentalism" and the Word of God*. London: Inter-Varsity, 1958.

Parks, E. P. *The Roman Rhetorical Schools as a Preparation for the Courts under the Early Roman Empire*. Baltimore, Md.: Johns Hopkins, 1945.

Pelikan, J. *The Christian Tradition. A History of the Development of Doctrine—Vol. 1: The Emergence of the Catholic Tradition (100–600)*. Chicago: University of Chicago, 1971.

Pelikan, J., and W. A. Hansen, ed. "Sermons on the Epistle of Jude." In *Luther's Works—Vol. 30: the Catholic Epistles*, 205–15. Translated by M. H. Bertram. St. Louis: Concordia, 1967.

Perdue, L. G. "Paraenesis in the Epistle of James." *ZNW* 72 (1981): 241–56.

Peter, H. *Der Brief in der römischen Literatur*. Leipzig: Teubner, 1901.

Pfitzner, V. C. *Paul and the Agōn Motif*. Leiden: Brill, 1967.

Philo-III. Translated by F. H. Colson and G. H. Whitaker. London/New York: Heinemann/ G. P. Putnam's Sons, 1930.

Pinnock, C. *Biblical Revelation—The Foundation of Christian Theology.* Chicago: Moody, 1971.

Pinto da Silva, A. "A Proposito del Significato Di 1 Pt 3,18–4,6." *Salesianum* 46 (1984): 473–86.

Plummer, A. *The General Epistles of St. James and St. Jude.* New York: Armstrong and Son, 1893.

Plumptre, E. H. *The General Epistles of St. Peter and St. Jude.* Cambridge: Cambridge University, 1926.

Polybius. *The Histories.* LCL. Translated by W. R. Paton. Cambridge, Mass.: Harvard University, 1960.

Priest, J. "Testament of Moses." In *The Old Testament Pseudepigrapha—Vol. 1: Apocalyptic Literature and Testaments,* edited by J. H. Charlesworth, 919–34. Garden City, N.Y.: Doubleday, 1983.

Pritchard, J. B., ed. *The Ancient Near East. An Anthology of Texts and Pictures.* Vol. 1. Princeton, N.J.: Princeton University, 1958.

Quintilian. *Institutio Oratoria.* LCL. 4 vols. Translated by H. E. Butler. Cambridge, Mass.: Harvard University, 1920–1922.

Rampf, R. *Der Brief Judä.* Sulzbach: Reimer, 1854.

Reese, J. M. "The Exegete as Sage: Hearing the Message of James." *BTB* 12 (1982): 82–85.

Reicke, B. *Diakonie, Festfreude und Zelos in Verbindung mit der altchristlichen Agapenfeier.* UUA 1951/5. Uppsala/Wiesbaden: Lundequistska/Harrassowitz, 1951.

———. *The Disobedient Spirits and Christian Baptism. A Study of 1 Peter III.19 and Its Context.* Kobenhavn: Munksgaard, 1946.

———. *The Epistles of James, Peter, and Jude.* Anchor Bible. New York: Doubleday, 1964.

Reider, J. *The Book of Wisdom. An English Translation with Introduction and Commentary.* New York: Harper and Brothers, 1957.

Rendall, G. H. *The Epistle of James and Judaic Christianity.* Cambridge: Cambridge University, 1927.

Rhetorica ad Herennium. LCL. Translated by H. Caplan. Cambridge, Mass.: Harvard University, 1981.

Richards, G. C. "1 Pet. iii.21." *JTS* 32 (1931): 77.

Riegel, S. K. "Jewish Christianity: Definitions and Terminology." *NTS* 24 (1978): 410–15.

Rist, M. "Pseudepigraphy and the Early Christians." In *Studies in the New Testament and Early Christian Literature. Festschrift A. P. Wikgren, edited by D. E. Aune,* 75–91. Leiden: Brill, 1972.

Robbins, C. J. "Rhetorical Structure in Phil. 2:6–11." *CBQ* 42 (1980): 73–82.

Robbins, V. K., and J. H. Patton. "Rhetoric and Biblical Criticism." *QJS* 66 (1980): 327–50.

Robert, A. "Les Genres littéraires." In *Initiation Biblique,* edited by A. Robert and A. Tricot, 305–9. 3d ed. Paris: Duculot, 1954.

Roberts, A., and J. Donaldson, ed. *The Ante-Nicene Fathers.* Vols. 1, 2, 3, and 4. Grand Rapids, Mich.: Eerdmans, 1979.

Robertson, A. T. *A Grammar of the Greek New Testament in Light of Historical Research.* Nashville, Tenn.: Broadman, 1934.

Robinson, J.A.T. *Redating the New Testament.* London: SCM, 1976.

Robinson, T. H. "Hebrew Myths." In *Myth and Ritual,* edited by S. H. Hooke, 172–96. London: Oxford U., 1933.

Rogerson, J. W. *Myth in Old Testament Interpretation.* Berlin/New York: de Gruyter, 1974.

Rohland, J. P. *Der Erzengel Michael, Arzt und Feldherr: zwei Aspekte des vor- und frühbabylonischen Michaelskultes.* Leiden: Brill, 1977.

Ropes, J. H. *A Critical and Exegetical Commentary on the Epistle of St. James.* ICC. Edinburgh: Clark, 1916.

Rowley, H. H. *The Relevance of Apocalyptic. A Study of Jewish and Christian Apocalypses.* London: SPCK, 1963.

Rowston, D. J. "The Most Neglected Book in the New Testament." *NTS* 21 (1974/75): 554–63.

———. *The Setting of the Letter of Jude.* Dissertation. Southern Baptist Theological Seminary, 1971.

Rubinkiewicz, R. "'Duchy zamkniete w wiezieniw.' Interpretacja 1 P 3,19 w swietle Hen 10,4.12." *RTK* 28 (1981): 77–86.

———. *Die Eschatologie von Enoch 9–11 und das Neue Testament.* ÖBS 6. Klosterneuburg: ÖKB, 1984.

Russell, D. S. *The Method and Message of Jewish Apocalyptic 200* B.C.–A.D. *100.* London: SCM, 1964.

Russell, E. *Paronomasia and Kindred Phenomena in the New Testament.* Chicago: University of Chicago, 1920.

Ryken, L. "The Bible as Literature." *BibSac* 147 (1990): 1–15.

———. *The New Testament in Literary Criticism.* New York: Ungar, 1984.

Saiz, J.R.B. "La carta de Judas a la luz de algunos escritos judiós." *EstBib* 39 (1981): 83–105.

Sale, W. M. "Aphrodite." *Encyclopaedia Britannica.* Vol. 2, 110–12. Chicago: University of Chicago, 1973.

Sandmel, S. *The First Christian Century in Judaism and Christianity: Certainties and Uncertainties.* Oxford: Oxford University, 1969.

Sarna, M. N. *Understanding Genesis.* New York: Schocken, 1966.

Sasson, J. M. "A Genealogical 'Convention' in Biblical Chronology?" *JBL* 90 (1978): 171–85.

———. "Generation, Seventh." In *Supplement to Interpreter's Dictionary of the Bible,* edited by G. A. Buttrick, 354–56. Nashville/New York: Abingdon, 1976.

Scharbert, J. "'Fluchen' und 'Segnen' im Alten Testament." *Bib* 39 (1958): 1–26.

Scharlemann, M. H. "'He Descended into Hell.' An Interpretation of 1 Peter 3:18–20." *CTM* 27 (1956): 81–94.

Schelke, K. H. "Der Judasbrief bei den Kirchenvätern." In *Abraham Unser Vater. Festschrift O. Michel,* edited by O. Betz, et al., 405–16. Leiden/Köln: Brill, 1963.

———. *Die Petrusbriefe—Der Judasbrief.* HTKNT 13/2. 3d edited by Freiburg/Basel/Wien: Herder, 1970.

———. "Spätapostolische Briefe also frühkatholisches Zeugnis." In *Neutestamen-*

taliche Aufsätze für J. Schmid, edited by J. Blinzler, et al., 225–32. Regensburg: Pustet, 1963.

Schlatter, A. *Der Evangelist Matthäus. Seine Sprache, Sein Ziel, Seine Selbständigkeit.* Stuttgart: Calwer, 1929.

Schlosser, J. "Les Jours de Noé et de Lot: À propos de Luc XVII,26–30." *RB* 80 (1973): 13–36.

Schmithals, W. *The Apocalyptic Movement—Introduction and Interpretation.* Nashville, Tenn.: Abingdon, 1975.

Schmoller, A. *Handkonkordanz zum Greichischen Neuen Testament.* Stuttgart: Deutsche Bibelgesellschaft 1982.

Schneider, J. *Die Briefe des Jakobus, Petrus, Judas und Johannes: Die katholischen Briefe.* NDT 10. 9th ed. Göttingen: Vandenhoeck & Ruprecht, 1961.

Schnutenhaus, F. "Das Kommen und Erscheinen Gottes im Alten Testament." *ZAW* 35 (1964): 1–22.

Schott, Th. *Der zweite Brief Petri und der Brief Judä.* Erlangen: Deichert. 1863.

Schottroff, W. *Der altisraelitische Fluchspruch.* WMANT 30. Neurkirchen-Vluyn: Neukirchener, 1969.

Schrage, W., and H. Balz. *Die "katholischen" Briefe: Die Briefe des Jakobus, Petrus, Johannes und Judas.* NTD 10. Göttingen: Vandenhoeck & Ruprecht, 1973.

Schrank, G. "*prographō.*" In *Theological Dictionary of the New Testament.* Vol. 1, edited by G. Kittel, 770–72. Grand Rapids, Mich.: Eerdmans, 1964.

Schultz, J. P. "Angelic Opposition to the Ascension of Moses and the Revelation of the Law." *JQR* 61 (1971): 282–307.

Schulz, S. "Maranatha und Kyrios Jesus." *ZNW* 53 (1962): 125–44.

Schweinfurth-Walla, S. *Studien zu den rhetorischen Überzeugungsmitteil bei Cicero und Aristoteles.* Tübingen: Narr, 1986.

Seethaler, P.-A. "Kleine Bemerkungen zum Judasbrief." *BZ* 31 (1987): 261–64.

Segert, S. "Semitic Poetic Structures in the New Testament." in *Aufstieg und Niedergang der römischen Welt. Geschichte und Kultur Roms im Spiegel der neueren Forschung.* II.25.2. Edited by H. Temporini and W. Haase, 1433–62. Berlin/New York: de Gruyer, 1984.

Seitz, O.J.F. "Two Spirits in Man: An Essay in Biblical Exegesis." *NTW* 6 (1959/60): 82–95.

Sellin, G. "Die Häretiker des Judasbriefes." *ZNW* 77 (1986): 201–25.

Selwyn, E. G. *The First Epistle of St. Peter.* London: Macmillan, 1952.

Sevenster, J. N. *Do You Know Greek? How Much Greek Could the First Jewish Christian Have Known?* NovTSup 19. Leiden: Brill, 1968.

Shaw, R. D. "Pseudonymity and Interpretation." In *The Pauline Epistles*, 477–86. Edinburgh: Clark, 1903.

Sickenberger, J. "Engels- oder Teufelslästerer im Judasbriefe (8–10) und im 2. Petrusbriefe (2,10–12)?" *MSGVK* 13–14 (1911/12): 621–39.

Sidebottom, E. M. *James, Jude, and 2 Peter.* NCB. London: Nelson, 1967.

Sint, J. A. *Pseudonymität im Altertum, ihre Formen und ihre Gründe.* Innsbruck: Universitätsverlag, 1960.

Sloan, T. O. "Rhetoric: Rhetoric in Literature." In *The New Encyclopaedia Britannica.* Vol. 15, 798–99. 15th ed. Chicago: University of Chicago, 1975.

Slomovic, E. "Toward an Understanding of the Exegesis in the Dead Sea Scrolls." *RQ* 7 (1969/70): 3–16.

Smith, W. A. *Ancient Education*. New York: Philosophical Library, 1955.

Soards, M. L. "1 Peter, 2 Peter, and Jude as Evidence for a Petrine School." In *Aufstieg und Niedergang der römischen Welt. Geschichte und Kulture Roms im Spiegel der neueren Forschung*. II.25.5. Edited by W. Hasse, 3826–49. Berlin/New York: de Gruyter, 1988.

Solmsen, F. *Intellectual Experiments of the Greek Enlightenment*. Princeton, N.J.: Princeton University, 1975.

Sonne, I. "A Hymn Against Heretics in the Newly Discovered Scrolls." *HUCA* 23 (1950): 275–313.

Speyer, W. "Religiose Pseudonymität und literarische Fälschung im Altertum." *JAC* 8/9 (1965/66): 88–125.

Spicq, C. *Agapé in the New Testament*. Vol. 2. St. Louis/London: Herder, 1965.

Spitta, F. *Christi Predigt an die Geister*. Halle: Verlag der Buchhandlung des Waisenhauses, 1890.

———. *Die zweite Brief des Petrus und der Brief des Judas*. Halle: Verlag der Buchhandlung des Waisenhauses, 1885.

Spittler, R. P. "The Testament of Job." In *The Old Testament Pseudepigrapha—Vol. 1: Apocalyptic Literature and Testaments,* edited by J. H. Charlesworth, 829–68. Garden City, NY: Doubleday, 1983.

Stählin, O., et al., ed. *Die Griechischen Christlichen Schriftsteller der ersten drei Jahrhunderte*. Vols. 5, 8, and 10. Leipzig: Hinrich, 1909–1935.

Starcky, J. "Cave 4 of Qumran." *BA* 19 (11956): 94–96.

Stauffer, E. *"agōn."* In *Theological Dictionary of the New Testament*. Vol. 1, edited by G. Kittel, 134–40. Grand Rapids, Mich.: Eerdmans, 1964.

Stendahl, K. *The School of St. Matthew and Its Use of the Old Testament*. Philadelphia: Fortress, 1968.

Stewart, J. S. "On a Neglected Emphasis in New Theology." *SLT* 4 (1951): 292–301.

Stirewalt, M. L., Jr. "The Form and Function of the Greek Letter-Essay." In *The Romans Debate,* edited by K. P. Donfried, 175–206. Minneapolis, Minn.: Augsburg, 1977.

Stone, M. E. "The Book of Enoch and Judaism in the Third Century B.C." *CBQ* 40 (1978): 479–92.

———. "Books of Noah." In *Encyclopaedia Judaica*. Vol. 12. Jerusalem/New York: Macmillan, 1971. P. 1198.

Stowers, S. K. *Letter Writing in Greco-Roman Antiquity*. Philadelphia: Westminster, 1986.

Strack, H., and P. Billerbeck. *Kommentar zum Neuen Testament aus Talmud und Midrash*. Vol. 3. München: Beck, 1924.

Stugnell, J. "The Angelic Liturgy at Qumran, 4Q Serek Sîrôt ʿOlat Haššabāt." In *Congress Volume. Oxford—1959,* 318–45. VTSup. Leiden: Brill, 1960.

Suter, D. "Fallen Angel, Fallen Priest: The Problem of Family Purity in 1 Enoch 6–16." *HUCA* 50 (1979): 113–36.

Synge, F. C. "1 Peter 3:18–21." *ExpTim* 82 (1971/72): 311.

Sypherd, W. O. *The Literature of the English Bible*. New York: Oxford University, 1938.

Szewc, E. "'Doxai' in den katholischen Briefen und die qumranische Literatur." *Folia Orientalia* 21 (1980): 129–40.

———. "'Les Gloires' dans les épîtres de Jude et de St. Pierre." *Collectanea Theologica* 46 (1976): 57–60.

Tappert, T. G. *Luther's Works—Vol. 54: Table Talk*. Philadelphia: Fortress, 1967.

Tcherikover, V. *Hellenistic Civilization and the Jews*. Philadelphia/Jerusalem: Jewish Publication Society of America/Magnes, 1959.

Testuz, M. *Papyrus Bodmer VII–IX. VII: L'Épître de Jude, VIII: Les deux Épîtres de Pierre, IX: Les Psaumes 33 et 34*. Cologny/Genève: Bibliotheca Bodmeriana, 1959.

Thayer, J. H. *A Greek-English Lexicon of the New Testament*. New York: Harper and Brothers, 1887.

Thyen, H. *Der Stil der Jüdisch-Hellenistischen Homilie*. Göttingen: Vandenhoeck & Ruprecht, 1955.

Torm, F. *Die Psychologie der Pseudonymität im Hinblick auf die Literatur des Urchristentums*. Gütersloh: Bertelsmann, 1932.

Tiede, D.'L. "The Figure of Moses in Palestine from 157 B.C. to 70 A.D." In *The Charistmatic Figure as Miracle Worker*, 178–206. SBLDS 1. Missoula, Mont.: SBL, 1972.

Torrey, C. C. *The Apocryphal Literature*. New Haven, Conn.: Yale University, 1948.

Trawick, B. B. *The Bible as Literature: The New Testament*. New York: Barnes and Noble, 1968.

Tripp, D. H. "*Eperōtēma* (1 Peter 3:21). A Liturgist's Note." *ExpTim* 92 (1981): 267–70.

Turner, N. "The Literary Character of New Testament Greek." *NTS* 20 (1974): 107–14.

Turpie, D. M. *The New Testament View of the Old*. London: Hodden and Stoughton, 1872.

VanderKam, J. *Enoch and the Growth of an Apocalyptic Tradition*. CBQMS 16. Washington, D.C.: CBA, 1984.

———. "The Righteousness of Noah." In *Ideal Figures in Ancient Judaism*, 13–22. SBLSCS 12. Chico, Calif.: Scholars, 1980.

———. "The Theophany of Enoch 1.3b–7.9." *VT* 23 (1973): 129–50.

van der Woude, A. S. "Melchisedek als himmlische Erlösergestalt in den neugefundenen eschatologischen Midrashim aus Qumran Höhle XI." *OTS* 14 (1965): 354–73.

Van Gemeren, W. A. "The Sons of God in Genesis 6:1–4." *WTJ* 43 (1980/81): 320–48.

van Unnik, W. C. "First Century A.D. Literary Culture and Early Christian Literature." *NedTT* 25 (1971): 28–43.

Vassiliev, A. *Anecodta Graeco-Byzantina*. Mosquae: Universitatis Caesareae, 1893.

Vermes, G. "The Story of Balaam." In *Scripture and Tradition in Judaism*, 127–77. Leiden: Brill, 1973.

Via, D. O., Jr. "The Right Strawy Epistle Reconsidered: A Study in Biblical Ethics and Hermeneutic." *JR* 49 (1969): 253–67.

Vögtle, A. "Kirche und Schriftprinzip nach dem Neuen Testament." *BuL* 12 (1971): 153–62, 260–81.

Volkmann, R. *Rhetorik und Metrik der Griechen und Römer.* München: Beck, 1901.

Volkmar, G. "Über die katholischen Briefe und Henoch." *ZWTh* 3 (1860): 427–54.

von Balthasar, H. U. "Abstieg zur Hölle." *TQ* 150 (1979) 193–201.

von Dobschütz, E. "Zwei- und dreigliedrige Formeln." *JBL* 50 (1931): 117–47.

Vos, G. *The Pauline Eschatology.* Grand Rapids, Mich.: Eerdmans, 1961.

Vrede, W. *Judas-, Petrus- und Johannesbriefe.* BNT 9. Bonn: Hanstein, 1932.

Wall, R. W. "James as Apocalyptic Paraenesis." *RestQ* 32 (1990): 11–22.

Wallace, D. H. "The Semitic Origin of the Assumption of Moses." *TZ* 11 (1955): 321–28.

Waltke, B. "Cain and His Offering." *WTJ* 48 (1985/86): 363–72.

Wand, J.W.C. *The General Epistles of St. Peter and St. Jude.* WC. London: Methuen, 1934.

Wanke, G. " *'ôy* and *hôy.*" *ZAW* 78 (1966): 215–18.

Ward, R. B. "The Works of Abraham." *HTR* 78 (1966): 215–18.

Watson, D. F. *Invention, Arrangement, and Style: Rhetorical Criticism of Jude and 2 Peter.* SBLDS 104. Atlanta, Ga.: Scholars, 1988.

———. "The New Testament and Greco-Roman Rhetoric: A Bibliography." *JETS* 31 (1988): 465–72.

Watson, W. G. E. *Classical Hebrew Poetry. A Guide to Its Techniques.* JSOTSS 26. Sheffield: JSOT, 1984.

Watts, J.D.W. *Isaiah 1–33.* WBC 24. Waco, Tex.: Word, 1985.

Webster's New International Dictionary of the English Language. 2d ed. Springfield, Mass.: Merriam, 1942.

Weiss, B. *Die katholischen Briefe. Textkritische Untersuchungen und Textherstellung.* TUGAL 8/3. Leipzig: Hinrich, 1892.

Werdermann, H. *Die Irrlehrer des Judas- und 2 Petrusbriefes.* Gütersloh: Bertelsmann, 1913.

Wernberg-Møller, P. *The Manual of Discipline.* Leiden: Brill, 1957.

Werner, E. *The Sacred Bridge.* New York/London: Columbia University/Dobson, 1963.

Westcott, B. F. *The Epistle to the Hebrews.* London: Macmillan, 1892.

Westermann, C. *Basic Forms of Prophetic Speech.* Philadelphia: Westminster, 1967.

Whallon, W. "Should We Keep, Omit, or Alter the 'OI in Jude 12?" *NTS* 34 (1988): 156–59.

White, J. L. "Ancient Greek Letters." In *Greco-Roman Literature and the New Testament,* edited by D. E. Aune, 85–105. SBLSBS 21. Atlanta, Ga.: Scholars, 1988.

———. *The Body of the Greek Letter.* SBLDS 2. Missoula, Mont.: Scholars, 1972.

———. *Light from Ancient Letters.* Philadelphia: Fortress, 1986.

Wikgren, A. "Problems in Jude 5." In *Studies in the History and Text of the New Testament,* edited by B. L. Daniels and J. M. Suggs, 147–52. Texts and Documents 9. Salt Lake City: University of Utah, 1967.

Williams, J. G. "The Alas-Oracles of the Eighth-Century Prophets." *HUCA* 38 (1967): 75–91.

Williams, P. H., Jr. "The Watchers in the Twelve and at Qumran." In *Texts and Testaments,* edited by W. E. March, 71–99. San Antonio, Tex.: Trinity University, 1980.

Williamson, G. A. *The World of Josephus.* Boston: Little and Brown, 1964.

Wills, L. "The Form of the Sermon in Hellenistic Judaism and Early Christianity." *HTR* 77 (1984): 277–99.

Windisch, H. *Die katholischen Briefe.* 2d ed. Tübingen: Mohr, 1930.

Wintermute, O. S. "The Apocalypse of Elijah." In *The Old Testament Pseudepigrapha—Vol. 1: Apocalyptic Literature and Testaments,* edited by J. H. Charlesworth, 721–53. Garden City, N.Y.: Doubleday, 1983.

Wisse, F. "The Epistle of Jude in the History of Heresiology." In *Essays on the Nag Hammadi Texts in Honour of A. Böhlig,* edited by M. Krause, 133–43. Leiden: Brill, 1972.

Wohlenberger, G. *Der erste und zweite Petrusbrief und der Judasbrief.* KNT 15. Leipzig: Deichert, 1915.

Wolthuis, T. R. "Jude and Jewish Traditions." *CTJ* 22 (1987): 21–41.

———. "Jude and the Rhetorician." *CTJ* 24 (1989): 126–34.

Wright, A. G. "The Literary Genre Midrash." *CBQ* 28 (1966): 105–38, 417–57.

Wright, F. A., ed. *Select Letters of St. Jerome.* LCL. New York/London: Putnam's Sons/Heinemann, 1933.

Wuellner, W. "Where Is Rhetorical Criticism Taking Us?" *CBQ* 49 (1987): 448–63.

———. "Der Jakobusbrief im Licht der Rhetorik und Textpragmatik." *LB* 43 (1978): 5–66.

Zahn, Th. *Introduction to the New Testament.* New York: Scribner's Sons, 1909.

Zuntz, G. "Enoch and the Last Judgment." *JTS* 45 (1944): 161–70.

Index of Subjects

Index of Authors